NEW YORK
HISTORICAL MANUSCRIPTS:
DUTCH

NEW YORK
HISTORICAL MANUSCRIPTS:
DUTCH

Old First Dutch Reformed Church of Brooklyn, New York

First Book of Records, 1660-1752

Translated and Edited by
A. P. G. Jos van der Linde

With an Introduction by Dr. Howard G. Hageman

Published Under the Direction of the Scholarship Committee
of The Holland Society of New York

Baltimore
GENEALOGICAL PUBLISHING CO., INC.
1983

To the memory of

RICHARD HENRY AMERMAN

whose years of faithful devotion to
The Holland Society of New York
and its objectives were exemplified
in his roles as President, Trustee,
Captain of the Burgher Guard,
editor and ardent scholar of the
colonial Dutch period in America.

CONTENTS

ACKNOWLEDGEMENTS

This edition of the earliest Breuckelen Church Records would not have appeared in print without the assistance and never failing support of the following people. I am very grateful to the members of the Scholarship Committee of The Holland Society of New York, who appropriated the funds that made this project possible: Mr. Hubert T. Mandeville, the Rev. Louis O. Springsteen, Mr. John W. Van Siclen, and especially Mr. John H. Vander Veer, Chairman, and the Rev. Dr. Howard G. Hageman, whose introductory chapter on Henricus Selijns greatly adds to the value of this book. I regret that another member of the Scholarship Committee, Mr. J. Cornell Schenck, did not live to see the completion of the project to which he lent his wholehearted support. The members of the Historical Publications Committee of The Holland Society were equally helpful and supportive: Mr. Ralph L. DeGroff, Jr., Chairman, Mr. Frederick W. Bogert, Mr. James M. Van Buren, II, again Dr. Hageman, and above all, Mr. Ralph L. DeGroff, Sr., whose friendship and stimulating enthusiasm proved invaluable.

Mr. DeGroff, Sr., is also the Director of the Editorial Board supervising the New York Historical Manuscripts Project, and I want to thank him and the other members of the Board for considering this book worthy of inclusion among the select volumes published under their direction. Mr. DeGroff's co-editors are Dr. Kenneth Scott, Dr. Kenn Stryker-Rodda, Mr. Peter R. Christoph, and Dr. Charles T. Gehring, to whom I am especially indebted for information provided from the New York State Library in Albany. A considerable part of this book was prepared in the library of The Holland Society of New York in Manhattan and I would like to thank Mrs. Patricia Bereday, librarian, and especially Mrs. Barbara W. Stankowski, Executive Secretary of the Society, for their invaluable aid. Many thanks are also due to Mr. Michael Tepper of the Genealogical Publishing Company in Baltimore, Mr. Russell Gasero of the Gardner A. Sage Library in New Brunswick, N.J., and the Rev. Stephen Th. Giordano of the Old First Reformed Church of Brooklyn. Finally, I am deeply grateful to my wife, Jane, for the meticulous way she reviewed my translations, her assistance in the preparation of the index, and above all, her indispensable love and support.

J.v.d.L.

INTRODUCTION

By the Rev. Dr. Howard G. Hageman*

In 1654, the search of the congregations in the three Long Island towns of Midwout (Flatbush), Nieuw-Amersfoort (Flatlands), and Breuckelen (Brooklyn) for a domine came to an unexpected end. In September of that year, Johannes Theodorus Polhemius, a refugee from the aborted Dutch colony in Brazil, landed with others in Nieuw-Amsterdam instead of in the Netherlands where his wife and family were expecting him. He indicated his willingness to remain in the new world and serve the new congregations in Long Island.

Since Midwout was the most centrally located of the three towns, a simple church building and parsonage were erected there. Sunday morning services were held regularly in Midwout with Sunday afternoon visits by the domine alternately in Nieuw-Amersfoort and Breuckelen. As early as 1656, however, the Breuckelen congregation began to object to this arrangement. When the magistrates of the other two towns asked Director-General Stuijvesant that the people of Breuckelen should contribute to the domine's support either by tax or voluntary subscription, that village replied that it would be glad to do so if Domine Polhemius "might be allowed to preach alternately in Breuckelen and Midwout."[1] Because of the geography involved, Stuijvesant denied the request.

That did not stop Breuckelen's dissatisfaction, however. When in December of the same year, the inhabitants were assessed 300 guilders toward Polhemius' salary, they stated that they were not willing to

> . . . contribute anything for such a poor and meagre service as that with which they [the Breuckelen people] thus far have been regaled. Every fortnight on Sundays, he [Polhemius] comes here only in the afternoon for a quarter of an hour, when he only gives us a prayer in lieu of a sermon, by which we can receive very little instruction; while often, when one supposes the prayer or sermon (whichever name might be preferred for it) is beginning, then it is actually at an end, by which he contributes very little to the edification of his congregation.

The statement concluded with the following language:

> However, permit us to say in conclusion, and be it said in reverence, that as those of Midwout have engaged said Polhemius alone, without our knowledge, and without any previous consultation (with us), we have no objection whatever.

---

*Notes to Dr. Hageman's Introduction are found on p. 243.

Nay, we are rather satisfied that the people of Midwout shall enjoy exclusively the whole service of the aforesaid Rev. Polhemius. And in case the aforesaid Polhemius should again desire to say his prayers here, in lieu of giving a sermon, as he did before, although we are unwilling to put ourselves under any obligation, still we are disposed to make him, from time to time, as opportunity shall offer, some allowance, as proof of our good will.[2]

Matters continued to deteriorate until on 6 July 1658, Stuijvesant issued an order forbidding the inhabitants of Breuckelen to harvest their crops until they had paid their tithes to the government, which were appropriated for the minister's salary.

In 1659, Breuckelen petitioned the government for a minister of its own. Probably to get rid of a bad situation (for it was by no means clear that the village was able to support its own domine), Stuijvesant forwarded the request to the Classis of Amsterdam through the West India Company. At that time the Classis had six possible candidates for service in New Netherland, a surprising number considering the usual complaint that volunteers for such service could not be found. Through careful examination the number was reduced to three and a second set of examinations finally resulted in the choice of Henricus Selijns on 16 February 1660.

Selijns, a Leiden graduate, was twenty-three at the time. The son of a family prominent in Amsterdam church affairs (his father served as an elder from 1639 to 1663), he is said by Eekhof to have been the best educated and most influential domine to come to New Netherland during its entire history.[3] Together with Domine Hermanus Blom, who had been designated for service in Esopus (Kingston), Selijns set sail for his new post on the ship *The Golden Beaver* ("de Vergulde Bever"), probably on 29 March 1660, or shortly thereafter. With the two domines the West India Company sent a supply of "little psalm books, prayer books, and books with verses for the instruction of the congregation, to be distributed and used in their respective parishes."[4] These books had been edited to make Reformed usages more acceptable to the Lutherans in the colony.

The Golden Beaver reached Nieuw-Amsterdam on 11 June. Director-General Stuijvesant was then in the midst of negotiating a peace treaty with the Esopus Indians and as a consequence, Blom and Selijns were not instituted in their respective ministries until almost three months later.[5] As for Selijns, the Director-General himself apparently recognized the unusual quality of the new domine for on 3 September he arranged a kind of installation service for him, the only one of its kind on record. (Perhaps Stuijvesant was anxious that the difficult people of Breuckelen should know exactly what they were getting into!)

In any event, on that September morning both Nicasius de Sille, the Nieuw-Amsterdam fiscal, and Marten Kregier, mayor of the town, accompanied the young domine to Breuckelen, presenting him to the Magistrates and Consistory. Selijns then presented his credentials and testimonials and preached his first sermon. Domine Polhemius was thanked for his services and turned over to Selijns a list of twenty-five members living in the jurisdiction of Breuckelen.[6]

Writing to the Classis of Amsterdam on 4 October 1660 to tell of his safe arrival and installation, Selijns said that there was no church building, but that services were held in a barn. He had found one elder and two deacons in Breuckelen, twenty-four members (one fewer than on Polhemius' list), thirty-one families, and one hundred thirty-four persons. Selijns noted that his colleague Blom's church in Esopus needed more people, but his church in Breuckelen needed more money.[7] That was a reference to the fact that in spite of their strong desire to have their own domine, the people of Breuckelen were simply not able to come up with the 1200 guilders which they had promised in salary. Once again Director-General Stuijvesant came to their rescue by paying Selijns 250 guilders annually in return for conducting a Sunday afternoon service each week at his "Bouwerije" just north of the town of Nieuw-Amsterdam.

The young domine had contracted with the West India Company for just four years. Early in 1664, therefore, he began to indicate his desire to return home. Things had gone well in his ministry, both in Breuckelen and at the Director-General's Bowery. Though no church building had as yet been constructed, a parsonage had been built in which Selijns lived with his young wife, Mechtelina Specht, a lady from the village of Nieuw-Utrecht whom he had married on 25 July 1662.[8]

Nobody wanted him to leave, but Selijns persisted in his desire to go. He cited the needs of his aging parents in Amsterdam as his reason for wishing to return,[9] but one suspects that continued dissatisfaction with his salary, together with a growing conviction that the days of New Netherland were numbered, were strong reasons also. However that may be, in either July or August 1664, he set sail for the Netherlands on the same *Golden Beaver* that had brought him four years earlier. On 29 September of that year he attended a meeting of the Classis of Amsterdam seeking a call to a church somewhere in the home country. His suspicion about the future of New Netherland proved to be correct; on 4 September, perhaps while Selijns was still on his way home, an English fleet appeared outside Nieuw-Amsterdam and that chapter came to an end.

Selijns had a second career in the new world. When the Church in New York was looking for a minister in 1681, they could think of no one better suited for them than the young domine who had served in Brooklyn 17 years earlier. As they wrote to the Classis of Amsterdam,

We remember Domine Henricus Selyns. His faithful services, his pious life, his peculiar zeal, his amiable conversation, his pleasing and ready speech, left a deep impression upon many hearts. If his reverence were inclined to come over again, this would be very agreeable to our congregation.[10]

Selijns did come over again and became the respected leader of the New York congregation from 1682 till his death in 1701. But that chapter in his career belongs to another story.

Quite possibly among the books which came over on *The Golden Beaver* in 1660 through the courtesy of the West India Company, was a handsome volume of blank pages for record keeping. In any event, soon after his arrival in Breuckelen, the young domine began keeping his *Prothocol,* a minute book of the baptisms and marriages which he performed as well as notes on events in the life of his congregation. The fine penmanship is undoubtedly his through 1664 after which the entries were continued by other people.

No complete translation of Selijns' *Prothocol* has ever been made. The baptismal and marriage records which it contains have been translated and published, not without errors and omissions. But much of the other material contained in this ancient volume has never been available in English. The Holland Society of New York is therefore pleased to make Selijns' *Prothocol,* one of the oldest record books in New York State, available to the American scholar. It is also grateful to the Consistory of the Old First Reformed Church in Brooklyn for sharing its treasure with us. The *Prothocol* still belongs to the Old First Church, although it is presently kept in the archives of Gardner Sage Library in New Brunswick, N.J.

Howard G. Hageman
New Brunswick Theological Seminary

EDITOR'S INTRODUCTION

The church records published in this book are among the finest in the United States. It is not so much the age of the entries (1660-1752) that makes this collection unique, but the diversity of subjects dealt with in a single volume: a protocol consisting of minutes of the consistory; registers of baptisms, marriages, and members of the congregation; accounts of the deaconry and other financial records; cows leased for the benefit of the poor; and orphan records. Tribute for the arrangement of this volume should be paid to Domine Henricus Selijns (1636-1701), who in 1660 was installed as minister of Breuckelen in New Netherland and immediately began keeping a record of all noteworthy events taking place in his congregation.

The volume with blank pages that Selijns had taken with him from Amsterdam or acquired in New Amsterdam for his record keeping in Breuckelen was well-manufactured. Selijns and his successors used it for almost a hundred years. Even two and a quarter centuries after the final entry, dated 1752, the wear and tear of time had hardly affected the excellent physical condition of the record book, then still preserved in the Old First Reformed Church in Brooklyn, New York, at Seventh Avenue and Carroll Street. In 1978, however, the church was burglarized. The intruder(s) ransacked the office of the Rev. Stephen Th. Giordano and cracked the old safe, probably in the hopes of finding money. Although the safe held no money, it did contain several fine artifacts as well as the invaluable records of the church. The contents of the safe were strewn all over the office and in the process the oldest book of records sustained considerable damage, especially to its binding.

A year later, in 1979, the 325th anniversary of the founding of the congregation was commemorated. Historians and the media alike paid attention to the unique history of the church. There was also a growing awareness of the need to preserve the original documents recording that history. With the recent burglary in mind, the Rev. Giordano of Brooklyn and the Rev. Dr. Howard G. Hageman of the Theological Seminary in New Brunswick, New Jersey, discussed the possibility of moving the records to a safer and more suitable environment: the Gardner A. Sage Library in New Brunswick, one of the largest archival depositories of documents relating to the history of the Dutch Reformed Church in North America. Early in 1980, the Brooklyn Church Records were transferred to the Sage Library, on the understanding that the Old First Reformed Church would retain ownership.

It was at Dr. Hageman's invitation that I first saw the oldest Brooklyn volume in the Sage Library later that year. Dr. Hageman asked me (1) to make a detailed inventory of the record book; (2) to investigate what parts of it had been published in the past and whether these translations were accurate; and (3) to write a report on my findings and file that with the Scholarship and Publication Committees of The Holland Society of New York. In the fall of 1980, the Scholarship Committee of the Society decided to appropriate funds for the translation and publication of the entire volume.

Earlier Publications

A complete translation of the oldest volume of the Brooklyn Church Records—henceforth simply referred to as Breuckelen Church Records—has never been published before. Parts of the contents, however, have appeared in print in the past. Some of these publications are mentioned below; I wish to emphasize that the following titles probably do not represent an exhaustive list.

As early as 1828-1829, General Jeremiah Johnson translated and published a fragment of the Protocol in the *Magazine of the Reformed Dutch Church* [vol. III (1828-1829), 52, 54], namely Domine Henricus Selijns' letter-of-call, dated February 16, 1660 (entered in the Protocol on September 7, 1660). Twenty years later, the famous list of the first twenty-five members of the Breuckelen congregation, registered in the September 12, 1660 entry of the Protocol, was included by E. B. O'Callaghan in his *History of New Netherland; or, New Netherland under the Dutch* [2 vols. (New York, 1846 and 1848), II, 437]. The registers of baptisms, marriages, and members were all edited by Teunis G. Bergen in the second half of the 1860s: the members in Henry R. Stiles' *A History of the City of Brooklyn* [3 vols. (Brooklyn, 1867-1870), I, 425-426]; the marriages in the *Manual of the Common Council of the City of Brooklyn for 1867* [(Brooklyn, 1867), 407-412]; and the baptisms in the *Manual, etc. for 1869* [(Brooklyn, 1869), 448-504]. Bergen's transcriptions of the baptisms and marriages were later reprinted, unrevised, in the *Kings County Genealogical Club Collections* [vol. I, nos. 4, 5, and 6 (1888 and 1894), 53-96].

Besides Bergen's list of the members, Stiles also published some of the Protocol entries [*op. cit.*, 140-141, 166, 428-430]. A. J. Beekman relied on information provided by General Jeremiah Johnson, Teunis G. Bergen, and "Dr. P. H. Vander Weyde, organist of the Church," for his *History of the Corporation of the Reformed Dutch Church of the Town of Brooklyn (Known as the First Reformed Dutch Church)* (Brooklyn, 1886), which includes a couple of entries from the Protocol [*op. cit.*, 7-9, 14]. Beekman also referred to Stiles' book mentioned above. Henry Whittemore should have done the same, as virtually every page of Chapters I and II in his *History of the First Reformed Protestant Dutch Church of Breuckelen, now known as The First Reformed Church of Brooklyn, 1654 to 1896*

(Brooklyn, 1896) was copied verbatim from Stiles [*op. cit.*, I, Chs. IV and VI: "Ecclesiastical History of Breuckelen, 1628-1664" and *"ibid.*, 1664-1803"]. Whittemore failed to give a source reference, however. As for the handful of passages from the Breuckelen Church Records that Stiles had included in his book, Whittemore copied some of them (with alterations), omitted the others, and added a couple of "new" entries from the Protocol. It is only because of the inclusion of this new material from the Breuckelen Church Records that Whittemore's book is mentioned here.

To summarize the list so far, only parts of the Breuckelen Church Records had been published by the end of the 19th century. None of the Accounts, Orphan Records, and Cow Records had appeared in print. With the exception of some entries, most of the Protocol had never been published either. Moreover, the quality of the publications listed above varies from mediocre to very poor. Translators are never satisfied with the work of their predecessors, of course, and I, too, should be careful in my criticism. However, my strong reservations about the translations published by the pioneering editors of the 19th century are shared by practically all of today's New Netherland experts. As for the publications mentioned above, inaccuracies, grave errors, and outright misreadings abound. In addition, the translations are often incomplete without any indication of omissions on the part of the editor.

Most of these deficiencies can be explained by the fact that the original documents recording New York's earliest colonial history often posed great problems to American scholars. Anyone publishing New Netherland records should have a perfect reading ability of 17th-century Dutch handwritings as well as a thorough knowledge of the Dutch language of that period. The problems that 19th-century editors had with the unusual handwritings in the Dutch manuscripts are especially evident in the publications that did not require the translation of complicated texts but simply the transcription of names. In E. B. O'Callaghan's list of the first twenty-five members of the Breuckelen congregation (see above), twelve names are misspelled. The transcriptions made by Teunis G. Bergen in the 1860s are extremely poor: not only did he misread hundreds of names, but he also omitted the third list of baptisms (cf. pp. 159-163 of this volume). None of these errors was corrected in the *Kings County Genealogical Club* reprints of 1888 and 1894.

Perhaps it was for these reasons that in 1897, Dingman Versteeg made an entirely new transcription of the baptisms, marriages, and members registered in the Breuckelen Church Records. His lists were published under the title "First Book of Records of the Dutch Reformed Church of Brooklyn, New York," in *Yearbook Of The Holland Society Of New York, 1897* (New York, 1897), 133-194. Versteeg's work was a great improvement upon the editorial projects undertaken by Bergen three decades earlier. Yet, the number of names misspelled in the Holland Society *Year-book* is great, although it should be pointed out that most of Versteeg's transcription errors are minor and—unlike many of Bergen's—cannot be labeled outright misreadings. One flaw in Versteeg's publication is inexcusable, though. Three of the baptisms registered in the first list of the Breuckelen Church Records cannot be accounted for in the *Yearbook*. (They do appear in Bergen's transcriptions.) Omissions due to carelessness are bad enough, of course, but Versteeg was too good an editor to "forget" three baptisms. I am convinced that he omitted these entries on purpose. Each of the three cases was exceptional in that the baptism was attended only by the mother of the child and one or two witnesses. It is obvious that Versteeg allowed moral judgments to compromise his integrity as a historian. How selective these judgments were is illustrated by the fact that he did include the baptism at which only the father of the child and a (female) witness were present. [Cf. the baptisms of Aeltje, Khatarijnje, Johannes, and Marijtje on pp. 116, 117, 136, and 130 respectively of this volume, as well as the *Yearbook* mentioned above, 150, 151, 169, and 163.]

Translations of some of the Protocol entries were included in the *Ecclesiastical Records, State of New York,* 7 vols. (Albany, 1901-1916), edited by the Rev. Edward T. Corwin under the supervision of Hugh Hastings, State Historian. Professor Eekhof praised Corwin for this monumental editorial project but at the same time he voiced concern about "incorrect interpretations." He also lamented the fact that, once again, records relating to the history of New Netherland had been translated and published in English while the original Dutch text of the manuscripts had remained behind in the archives [A. Eekhof, *De Hervormde Kerk in Noord-Amerika (1624-1664),* 2 vols. ('s-Gravenhage/The Hague, 1913), I, 16-17]. I agree with Eekhof; it is to be hoped that the inclusion of the original entries of the Breuckelen Church Records in this volume will set a precedent for future publications. Eekhof's reservations about the quality of the translations in the *Ecclesiastical Records* are equally justified: see, for instance, the comments I made in footnotes on pp. 244, 245, 256, and 257, as well as my introductory remarks on Appendix A below. On the whole, however, in spite of his errors, Corwin's work is so much better than that of the 19th-century editors mentioned above that, whenever possible, his *Ecclesiastical Records* are referred to or discussed in the footnotes of this volume.

Unpublished Translations

More than a century before the publication of this book, William Henry Stillwell set himself to the arduous task of translating the entire Protocol of the Breuckelen Church Records. His manuscript translation, dated 1880, is preserved in the library of the Long Island Historical Society in Brooklyn, New York. It seems that Stillwell started out with great enthusiasm but became frustrated along the way. As one leafs through his notebook, comparing the translation with the original Protocol, the quality of his work declines considerably: complicated passages are summarized; omissions increase in frequency and vary in length from a couple of lines to several pages; names and even amounts of money are misread.

Stillwell's translation was never published. Some time after its "completion," Stillwell lent his notebook to Morris Patterson Ferris. The latter made a typescript copy of it, which was indexed by Edna Huntington. Ferris' copy, too, is in the Long Island Historical Society Library and never appeared in print. Publication would have been unwarranted anyway in view of its many deficiencies. For inexplicable reasons, large portions of Stillwell's (incomplete) translation were ignored by Ferris. One of the omissions equals no less than sixteen pages in Stillwell's notebook.

Two more items in the fine collections of the Long Island Historical Society Library should be mentioned here. A typescript index of the lists of baptisms, marriages, and members registered in the Breuckelen Church Records was compiled by Wilson Van Doren Ledley in 1957 under the auspices of The Holland Society of New York. The index is based upon Dingman Versteeg's transcription, published sixty years earlier in the *Yearbook* of that Society, and it includes, therefore, the errors committed by Versteeg (see above under "Earlier Publications"). Another copy of Ledley's index is preserved in the library of The Holland Society in Manhattan.

At the initiative of Mrs. Harriet Mott Stryker-Rodda, a microfilm dealing exclusively with the records of the Old First Reformed Church of Brooklyn was made for the Long Island Historical Society in 1961. It contains not only the above-mentioned works by Stillwell, Ferris, and Ledley, but also the transcriptions of the baptisms and marriages made in the 1860s by Teunis G. Bergen (see "Earlier Publications"), as well as an index by Mrs. Stryker-Rodda, and finally, all the original manuscript records of the church including the First Book of Records published in this volume.

I would like to conclude this review of published and unpublished translations with a reference to the Sterling Potter Collection preserved in the New York State Library in Albany, New York. The Potter Collection includes "Records of the Reformed Dutch Church of Brooklyn, N.Y." This is a typescript translation of the Protocol, Accounts, Orphan Records, and Cow Records, attributed to Henry Pennington Toler, who revised James Riker's *History of Harlem* (New York, 1904). Sterling Potter copied Toler's translation and added it to his collection of early records in 1903. Since Dingman Versteeg had edited the baptisms, marriages, and members in the *Yearbook Of The Holland Society Of New York* six years earlier (see above), Potter must have been the only researcher prior to the publication of this book who owned a more or less complete translation of the First Book of Records. Toler's work shows serious deficiencies, however. His translation is poor and above all chaotic. Many words are crossed out and insertions crowd the margins of the typescript pages. Frequently, alternative translations are given without any indication of the translator's preference. Some passages proved so problematic to Toler that he simply reproduced the Dutch text without giving a translation. Furthermore, he omitted the Protocol entries dating from the 1750s. The Orphan Records and Cow Records are incomplete and abridged.

When we make up the balance of the transcriptions and translations listed on the preceding pages, we should be grateful to the scholars who in the last one and a half centuries have contributed greatly to our knowledge of people and society in 17th and early-18th-century Breuckelen, in spite of such major obstacles as the handwritings and language contained in the original manuscript records dating from that period. Yet, the quality of their work falls short of the high standards we apply today to scholarly translating and editing. I have made every effort to meet those standards in this book.

The Breuckelen Church Records—Some General Remarks

At the beginning of my introduction I made some comments on the present physical condition of the Breuckelen Church Records. Unopened, the volume measures 32.5 by 21 cm. It numbers 146 leaves altogether (292 pages), including several loose sheets inserted between the original pages of the record book. Eight of the leaves are completely blank.

Although the majority of the pages are numbered, there is no consistent numbering system running from the beginning to the end of the original record book. To avoid confusion, and in order to make it possible to refer to any particular page in the record book, I introduced a new numbering system. To that end I applied the classic method of numbering the leaves (not the pages) 1 through 146. In accordance with this method, distinction between the front side and the back side of an individual leaf is made by supplementing the leaf number with a letter "r" (= recto) or a "v" (= verso) respectively. For instance, 125^r indicates the front side of the 125th leaf in the manuscript volume. Throughout this book, the reader will find references to the corresponding pages in the original Breuckelen Church Records, usually in the upper right corner of the page, between brackets. In those sections of the book where both the original text and an English translation are printed, only the Dutch pages show these references. In many cases, the reference to the corresponding page in the manuscript volume includes a second number, printed between quotation marks, e.g. [91^v: "179"]. The second number is the one actually given on the corresponding page in the Breuckelen Church Records. Whenever possible, that number is included in the reference, so that researchers looking for a certain passage in the handwritten pages of the record book can locate it without having to count leaves. However, as I mentioned above, not all of the pages in the original volume are numbered. If, for example, someone would like to have a look at Jan Martyn's signature under the custody contract registered on page 120^r of the Breuckelen Church Records (see pp. 198-199 of this book), he would have to count 120 leaves to find it since none of the pages in that section (Orphan Records) is numbered. (Needless to say, I did not write my numbering system on the leaves of the original Breuckelen Church Records. The new numbers do appear, however, in the complete xerox copy of the record book, preserved in the library of The Holland Society of New York in Manhattan.)

The arrangement of this book in seven major sections—Protocol of the Consistory, Baptisms, Accounts of the Deaconry, Orphan Records, Cow Records, Marriages, and Members of the Congregation respectively—is not mine. I simply followed the example set by Domine Henricus Selijns, who in 1660 brought the record book with him to Breuckelen and filled more than half of its pages. It is highly unfortunate that after Selijns' return to Holland in 1664, his exemplary record keeping could not be matched by any of the registrars who succeeded him in the course of almost a century. As a consequence, the years of Selijns' brief ministry (1660-1664) are the best documented in the early church history of Brooklyn.

No less than seventeen different handwritings are distinguishable in the Breuckelen Church Records. Their quality varies from Henricus Selijns' fine hand to the almost illegible scribbles of the mid-18th-century entries. The identities of six of the registrars can be ascertained. All entries through July 1664 were written by Selijns, with the exception of two items inserted between the pages of his record book: the account signed by Hendrick Jansen van de Vin in 1662 and Frederick Philipsen's note of 1663 (see pp. 188-190 and 191 respectively of this book). Hendrick Slecht, who in March 1677 was appointed precentor of the Breuckelen congregation (see pp. 100-101), authored numerous entries: all baptisms recorded in the First List from August 1674 through October 1697, with the exception of the December 9, 1694 entry; all marriages from 1677 through 1696, except the entry dated January 26, 1695; all members registered in the Second List from 1677 through 1696; and finally, the Protocol entry dated May 28, 1693, in which Slecht recorded his confirmation as elder of the congregation (see pp. 116-138, 215-219, 223-224, and 100-101 respectively, especially the November 9, 1695 entry on p. 219). Comparison with autographed letters preserved in the Sage Library in New Brunswick, New Jersey, proved my supposition that it was Domine Johannes Theodorus Polhemius who listed the contents of the treasury in the Midwout church as of May 15, 1676 (see p. 191). The Third List of Baptisms, 1688-1696, was written by Domine Wilhelmus Lupardus (see pp. 159-163 and my remarks on the Third List under "The Baptismal Register," fourth paragraph). The final events recorded in the Protocol, in the years 1750-1752, were probably entered by Domine Ulpianus van Sinderen, although I had no opportunity to compare these pages with van Sinderen's autographed letters in the Sage Library (see pp. 102-107).

The case of Hendrick Slecht proves that it was not always the Domine who did the record keeping. Yet, before making some comments on each of the individual sections of this book, it is appropriate, I think, to list all the ministers who have worked in Breuckelen and the other Dutch communities on western Long Island during the period chronicled in the Breuckelen Church Records, 1660-1752. This is not the place to describe their lives; only the years they were active on western Long Island will be given: Johannes Theodorus Polhemius (1654-1676), whose ministerial duties in Breuckelen were temporarily taken over by Henricus Selijns (1660-1664); Wilhelmus van Nieuwenhuijsen (1676-1677), minister of the New York congregation from 1671 until 1681, who on June 9, 1676, one day after Polhemius' death, came to an agreement with the Dutch congregations on Long Island to officiate four times a year among them at an annual salary of up to 200 guilders (see pp. 98-99 and 156 of this volume); Casparus van Zuuren (1677-1685); Rudolphus Varick (1686-1694); Wilhelmus Lupardus (1695-1702); Bernardus Freeman (1705-1741) and Vincentius Antonides (1705-1744) simultaneously; Johannes Arundeus (1742-1750, see footnotes 67, 68, 71, and 72 on p. 248); and finally, Ulpianus van Sinderen (1746-1784), whose successive colleagues on western Long Island, after Arundeus' departure, were Antonius Curtenius (1755-1756) and Johannes Casparus Rubel (1759-1783).

The record book mentions four other ministers who officiated at least once in Breuckelen or in Midwout. For the sake of completeness, I will include them in this listing. On July 25, 1662 Domine Johannes Megapolensis came from New Amsterdam to Breuckelen to marry his colleague Henricus Selijns to Mechtelina Specht (see p. 212). Gideon Schaats, minister in Rensselaerswijck, baptized five children in Midwout at Whitsuntide, 1677 (p. 156). Both in October 1695 and March 1696, Domine Giliam (Guillaume) Bertholf of New Jersey attended the confirmation of new members in Breuckelen (p. 224). Two other Breuckelen members were confirmed in June 1702 by Gualtherus du Bois, minister of the New York congregation (ibid.).

The Protocol, 1660-1752 (pp. 1-107 of this book)

The Protocol is a chronicle of noteworthy events in the congregation, recorded by the Domine or other member of the consistory. Although it covers a period of 93 years, most of the entries date from the brief ministry of Henricus Selijns in Breuckelen, 1660-1664. Unfortunately, the Protocol was practically discontinued after Selijns' return to Holland. With the exception of the years 1750-1752, the century following Selijns' departure is ill-documented and marked by enormous gaps.

Selijns wrote all entries through 1664. As for the other registrars, I could identify only one of them beyond doubt: comparison has shown that Hendrick Slecht, an elder, was the author of the entry dated May 28, 1693. The turbulent events of 1750-1752 were probably recorded by Domine Ulpianus van Sinderen. (See my discussion of the handwritings under "The Breuckelen Church Records—Some General Remarks," fourth paragraph.)

The Baptismal Register, 1660-1719 (pp. 109-164 of this book)

There are four lists of baptisms in the Breuckelen Church Records. The First List (pp. 109-155 of this volume) covers half a century, 1660-1710, and is virtually uninterrupted. It was initiated by Domine Henricus Selijns. After his return to Holland in 1664, six successive registrars continued the list. The identity of only one of them is known: Hendrick Slecht recorded all baptisms from August 1674 through October 1697, with the exception of the December 9, 1694 entry. (Cf. my discussion of the handwritings under "The Breuckelen Church Records—Some General Remarks," fourth paragraph.)

The First List of Baptisms covers almost one hundred pages in the original manuscript volume. In the margins of many of these pages, an anonymous researcher has written brief comments (most of them in ink!) on the genealogies of some of the pioneering families living in 17th-century Breuckelen and the other Dutch communities on western Long Island. Similar marginal notes appear in the Marriage Register. I had no opportunity to confirm or disprove my suspicion that most of these comments were written by Teunis G. Bergen, the 19th-century genealogist with a special interest in Kings County's earliest settlers. Whoever the author was, his notes are unreliable and I decided, therefore, to ignore them completely.

The Second List of Baptisms (pp. 156-158) consists of three loose leaves, the edges of which have sustained considerable damage. Originally, these leaves were not part of the Breuckelen record book. The baptisms and other events documented in the Second List took place in Midwout, in the two and a half years following the death of Domine Johannes Theodorus Polhemius in June 1676. As the list shows, his successor in the Dutch communities on Long Island, Casparus van Zuuren, did not arrive until September 1677. In the meantime, the spiritual needs of the Long Island settlers were attended to by Domine Wilhelmus van Nieuwenhuijsen of New York. On one occasion, Whitsuntide 1677, Domine Gideon Schaats from Rensselaerswijck officiated in Midwout. (Cf. my discussion of the ministers under "The Breuckelen Church Records—Some General Remarks," fifth and sixth paragraphs.)

The three leaves from Midwout do not only contain baptisms and ministers. On the front side of the first leaf, which I numbered 143^r, a shaky hand made notes on the receipts of the deaconry from the end of May, 1675, until the beginning of June, 1676. Most of the entries mention merely a date and the amount of money received. However, the right edge of the paper is so worn that practically every amount is mutilated. The only entry containing valuable information is a listing of the contents of the treasury as of May 15, 1676; it is included in this volume at the conclusion of the Financial Records (p. 191). When I compared the handwriting on this page with autographed letters preserved in the Sage Library in New Brunswick, New Jersey, my supposition was confirmed that these are actually the final notes made by Domine Polhemius before his death on June 8, 1676. The last amount of money he recorded on this page is dated June 4. The next entry, on the reverse side of the page, mentions his death (see p. 156).

The Third List of Baptisms (pp. 159-163) consists of two leaves. Although the edges are worn, most of the damaged dates and words could be reconstructed. The list is incomplete: the first leaf contains baptisms in the years 1688-1690, the second leaf dates from 1694-1696. Since both periods are well-documented in the First List of Baptisms which was kept in Breuckelen, the Third List probably originates from Midwout. The handwriting and ink color are so consistent throughout the list, that all entries were written, I think, on one occasion, not on the dates of the individual baptisms. Proof of this hypothesis can be found in the May 8, 1696 entry which establishes Domine Wilhelmus Lupardus as the author of the list. Lupardus was not ordained by the Classis of Amsterdam until October 24, 1695, and cannot have arrived in Long Island before the end of that year at the earliest. Therefore, he must have copied at least part of the list, possibly all of the entries, from other records. [For Lupardus' ordination, see Rev. E. T. Corwin, editor, and Hugh Hastings, supervisor, *Ecclesiastical Records, State of New York,* 7 vols. (Albany, 1901-1916), II, 1131.]

The Fourth List of Baptisms (p. 164) is hardly worthy of its name. It consists of a small, more or less triangular fragment of paper, covered with all sorts of scribbles. The only valuable notes are six baptisms dated "17019," which probably means 1719.

All names recorded in the four lists of the Baptismal Register, as well as those appearing in the other sections of the Breuckelen Church Records, were transcribed and proofed with the greatest possible care. The spelling in 17th-century Dutch manuscripts will be discussed at some length in my introductory remarks on the Index (p. 259). The only thing I would like to emphasize here is the complete lack of consistency in the way people spelled in those days. Even within a single entry, a family name is often spelled in various ways. What occasionally might be construed as a typographical error by the reader, is in fact the accurate transcription of an inconsistent spelling in the original entry. To give just three examples: in the entry dated August 10, 1684, third baptism (p. 123), we find the name "Strijker" three times, but "Strijkers" and even "Stijker" also occur. On October 20, 1695, second baptism (p. 135), the name "Seberingh" was written consistently three times, but the mother's name was spelled "Seuberingh." In the October 18, 1696 entry (p. 137), the name "Rappalje" appears three times, "Rappaljee" once. Since, in my view, the people using this book should know exactly what the original registrars recorded, even obvious slips of their pens were left in place in this volume. For instance, in the entry dated May 25, 1690, second baptism (p. 129), the registrar probably meant to write "Strijcker"; instead, he wrote "Strcker." In the August 1, 1708 entry (p. 153), "Ctrina" should have been spelled "Catrina," of course. "Stoffel Gerritje" in the April 26, 1696 entry, fourth baptism (p. 163), should have been "Stoffel Gerritse." It is not the task of an editor, I believe, to modernize, simplify, or otherwise alter the spelling of the names recorded in the documents he is publishing. That option should be left to the historians and genealogists consulting his book.

The original spelling of geographical names, too, has been preserved throughout this volume. See my introductory remarks on Appendix B below.

The Financial Records, 1657-1676 (pp. 165-191 of this book)

The detailed account of the Receipts and Expenditures of the Deaconry (pp. 165-187) was kept by Domine Henricus Selijns and covers, therefore, only the years of his brief ministry in Breuckelen, 1660-1664. Selijns' meticulous, well-arranged bookkeeping has been reproduced as accurately as possible in this volume with the receipts appearing on the left pages and the expenditures on the right.

The Breuckelen record book also includes other financial documents pertaining to members of the congregation. The account signed by Hendrick Jansen van de Vin in New Amsterdam on October 23, 1662 covers five and a half years of transactions between himself and Teuntie Straetsmans (pp. 188-190). Straetsmans had died on October 19 and van de Vin filed his account with the trustees of her estate, Domine Henricus Selijns and deacon Teunis Jansen Coevors. His claims on Straetsmans' children were eventually settled on August 6, 1663 (see pp. 50-53 and 72-75). Originally, the account consisted of one large sheet of paper, folded twice. Through wear and tear, however, the document fell apart in two pieces along one of the fold lines.

Frederick Philipsen's transaction, too, was a direct consequence of Teuntie Straetsmans' death (p. 191). On May 18 and 25, 1663 he bought the tobacco she had left behind. He did not pay his bill, however, until November 1 of that year (see p. 253, footnote 49). As one of the two trustees of Straetsmans' estate, Henricus Selijns must have carefully kept both van de Vin's account and Philipsen's note in his record book. The autographed slip of paper documenting the tobacco transaction is so small, that someone, possibly Selijns himself, attached it to the bottom of a page in the Protocol with a pin (cf. p. 245, footnote 14; the page in the Protocol is 5^r "Pag. 9").

At the end of the Financial Records (p. 191), I have edited a fragment of text appearing on the front side of the first leaf of the Second List of Baptisms. It lists the contents of the treasury of the Midwout church as of May 15, 1676. The registrar was Domine Johannes Theodorus Polhemius, who died 24 days later. (See my discussion of this entry under "The Baptismal Register," fourth paragraph.)

The Orphan Records, 1662-1664 (pp. 193-201 of this book)

All entries in the Orphan Records are written in Domine Henricus Selijns' fine hand. He recorded four custody contracts involving three Breuckelen orphans. One of the orphans, Laurens Haf (or Haff), stayed with Selijns for more than one and a half years until the minister returned to Holland in the summer of 1664.

The Cow Records, 1662-1669 (pp. 203-209 of this book)

The deaconry of Breuckelen owned four cows which were leased for the benefit of the poor. In addition to the original contracts, the newborn calves of each of the cows were also registered in the Breuckelen Church Records since one of the conditions in the lease provided for the division of the offspring among lessor and lessee. The Cow Records were initiated by Domine Henricus Selijns, who authored all entries through 1664. A second registrar continued his work for five more years.

The Marriage Register, 1660-1696 (pp. 211-219 of this book)

The Marriage Register covers eight leaves in the Breuckelen Church Records, three of which are heavily damaged at the bottom, leaving a number of entries incomplete. With the exception of just one marriage, the registrars of the list are known. Domine Henricus Selijns wrote the entries through July 1664. Hendrick Slecht listed all other marriages except the one on January 26, 1695. (Cf. my discussion of the handwritings under "The Breuckelen Church Records—Some General Remarks," fourth paragraph.) In spite of Slecht's longevity as a registrar, the list shows considerable gaps throughout the three decades following Selijns' departure in 1664.

In the margins of the original manuscript pages listing the marriages, an anonymous researcher has written brief comments on the genealogies of some of the pioneering families living in 17th-century Breuckelen and the other Dutch communities on western Long Island. He did the same in the First List of the Baptismal Register. As in the case of the baptisms, I decided to ignore the notes because they are not reliable. (Cf. my theory as to the possible identity of the annotator under "The Baptismal Register," second paragraph.)

All names recorded in the Marriage Register, as well as those appearing in the other sections of the Breuckelen Church Records, were carefully transcribed and checked. The original spelling of geographical names, too, has been preserved throughout this volume. (Cf. my comments on the spelling of names in 17th-century Dutch documents under "The Baptismal Register," seventh paragraph, and my introductory remarks on Appendix B below.)

The Register of Members, 1663-1702 (pp. 221-224 of this book)

Each of the two Lists of Members in the Breuckelen Church Records consists of a single loose leaf. The edges of the leaves, especially the top of the Second List, are badly worn, but the damage to the entries is minimal. The First List (pp. 221-222) was kept by Domine Henricus Selijns during the last two years of his ministry in Breuckelen, in 1663 and 1664. It is probably incomplete since he confirmed members during the first half of his tenure as well, 1660-1662. Fortunately, Selijns considered the confirmation of new members such an important event that he made entries on each of them in the Protocol. The names of all the members recorded in the First List can be found back in the Protocol, and so can the members whose confirmation took place prior to 1663.

The Second List of Members (pp. 223-224), beginning in 1677, was entirely written by Hendrick Slecht, with the exception of the final entry in 1702. (Cf. my discussion of the handwritings under "The Breuckelen Church Records—Some General Remarks," fourth paragraph.)

All names recorded in the Register of Members, as well as those appearing in the other sections of the Breuckelen Church Records, were carefully copied and proofed. The original spelling of geographical names, too, has been preserved throughout this volume. (Cf. my comments on the spelling of names in 17th-century Dutch documents under "The Baptismal Register," seventh paragraph, and my introductory remarks on Appendix B below.)

APPENDIX A: Two Letters by Domine Henricus Selijns, 1660 and 1664 (pp. 225-233 of this book)

The invaluable archival collections preserved in the Gardner A. Sage Library in New Brunswick, New Jersey include two letters written by Domine Henricus Selijns to the Classis of Amsterdam during his ministry in Breuckelen. The first letter is dated October 4, 1660, shortly after Selijns' arrival in New Netherland; the second is from June 9, 1664, about two months before he sailed back to Holland. A passage in the second letter suggests that Selijns did not write any other letters to the Classis during his tenure in Breuckelen (see p. 231, second paragraph).

Both in 1660 and in 1664, Selijns gave his superiors in Amsterdam an informative evaluation of the situation not only in Breuckelen, but in other parts of New Netherland as well. In the second letter he included an assessment of his four-year ministry in Breuckelen. Selijns' letters to the Amsterdam Classis represent such a fine supplement to the records he kept in Breuckelen that I decided to append them to this volume, both in the Domine's own words and in an English translation.

This is not the first time the letters have appeared in print. Edmund B. O'Callaghan published a translation of the 1660 letter in the *Documentary History of the State of New York* [4 vols. (Albany, 1849-1851), III, 108]. Henry R. Stiles, in *A History of the City of Brooklyn* [3 vols. (Brooklyn, 1867-1870), I, 142], copied O'Callaghan's translation and was in his turn copied by Henry Whittemore who printed parts of the letter in the *History of the First Reformed Protestant Dutch Church of Breuckelen, now known as The First Reformed Church of Brooklyn, 1654-1896* [(Brooklyn, 1896), 12-13]. A fragment of some ten lines from the 1664 letter was included by Berthold Fernow in the *Documents Relative to the Colonial History of the State of New York* [15 vols. (Albany, 1856-1887), XIII, 384]. The Rev. Edward T. Corwin translated and published both letters in his *Ecclesiastical Records, State of New York* [7 vols. (Albany, 1901-1916), I, 487-489 and 547-550 respectively—henceforth: *Ecclesiastical Records*]. When J. Franklin Jameson edited his *Narratives of New Netherland, 1609-1664* [(New York, 1909), 406-411], he included Corwin's translation of the two letters. As for the original Dutch text, the major part of the 1660 letter and some brief passages from the 1664 letter were quoted—not without minor transcription errors—by A. Eekhof in *De Hervormde Kerk in Noord-Amerika (1624-1664)* [2 vols. ('s-Gravenhage/ The Hague, 1913), I, 215-217 and 219-221 respectively].

Although this list is not exhaustive, it is unlikely that the original 17th-century text of Selijns' letters from Breuckelen has ever appeared in print completely, without omissions. For this reason, I transcribed the manuscripts in the Sage Library. Originally, I intended to publish my own transcriptions with the translations by Corwin, which are generally known for their scholarliness and for being more reliable than O'Callaghan and Fernow's work in the 19th century. However, when Corwin's translations were compared with Selijns' original words, they turned out to contain numerous inaccuracies and errors. Moreover, in his translation of the second letter, Corwin omitted a brief passage. I preferred, therefore, to make an English translation of my own. [Just three of Corwin's errors are discussed in footnotes 1, 3, and 6 on pp. 255-257. As for his omission in the 1664 letter, the second half of the third paragraph and the beginning of the fourth paragraph cannot be accounted for in the *Ecclesiastical Records*, I, 548.]

Selijns' letters from Breuckelen crossed the Atlantic twice. Upon their arrival in Amsterdam, they were read and dealt with by the Classis and eventually stored in its archives. They remained there for almost two centuries. In the early 1840s, a large collection of manuscripts, including Selijns' letters, was given by the Classis to John Romeyn Brodhead, who in the archives of several Dutch cities, as well as in London and Paris, was collecting the material that O'Callaghan later published in the first ten volumes of the monumental *Documents Relative to the Colonial History of the State of New York* (see above). Brodhead was authorized by the Classis of Amsterdam to take the manuscripts to the United States as a loan to the General Synod of the Reformed Dutch Church in North America. In 1846, however, the Classis yielded ownership of the collection to the American General Synod. The letters have been preserved in New Brunswick, N.J., ever since [cf. Corwin, *Ecclesiastical Records*, I, 13].

APPENDIX B: Explanatory List of Geographical Names
(pp. 235-241 of this book)

As I pointed out before, the names of all people appearing in the Breuckelen Church Records have been transcribed and proofed with the greatest possible care. I considered it desirable to preserve the original spelling of geographical names as well. That intention posed no problems, of course, in those sections of the book where not only an English translation but also a complete transcription of the original Dutch text is printed. In the Registers of Baptisms, Marriages, and Members of the Congregation, however, the original spelling of the geographical names has been reproduced between quotation marks. Many of the geographical terms applied in 17th and 18th-century Dutch manuscripts are now obsolete or hard to recognize because of a distorted spelling. For this reason, all geographical names mentioned in the Breuckelen Church Records were included in an explanatory list appended to this book.

Jos van der Linde
Leiden, April 1983

NEW YORK
HISTORICAL MANUSCRIPTS:
DUTCH

OLD FIRST DUTCH REFORMED CHURCH
OF BROOKLYN, NEW YORK

First Book of Records,
1660-1752

<u>PROTOCOL OF THE CONSISTORY</u>

of

<u>BREUCKELEN IN NEW NETHERLAND</u>

Original

[1^r]

PROTHOCOL

DES KERCKENRAETS VAN BREUCKELEN

Den 5 Septemb̃. 1660

De Gemeijnte van Breuckelen per Request versocht hebbende van den
E: H. Direct͞r Generael en Raden, omme (met de moeijelijckheijt
van de Weg van Breuckelen naer Middelwout, en hooge ouderdom van
den Eerwaerdigen d⁰ Johannes Polemijus, die sulcks oock swaer
valt) selve een Predicant te mogen hebben tot bevorderinge van de
ware Godsdienst, en t'harer stichtinge, 't Welck geappoincteert
was, dat 't Versoeck in billicheijt bestaende, daer van kennisse
aen de H. H. Bewinthebbers soude gedaen worden met verwachtinge
van Rescriptie.
Ende ten Voorgemelte Versoeck verkregen hebbende den Persoon van
Henricus Selyns, om 't Euangelium daer te verkondigen, en Sacramenten te bedienen, heeft den Hooggemelte H. Generael, nare verscheyden Conferentie en behoorlyck Contract van de Gedeputeerde
van Breuckelen, derwaerts den voor͞n Predicant gesonden, vergesel-
schapt van de H. H. Gedeputeerde, de H͞r Nicasius de Silla, Raet
en Fiscael van N. Nederl͞t, en de H͞r Marten Kregier, Burger͞m. van
Amsterdam in N. Nederl͞t, om den gemeynte voorgestelt, ende als
Predicant bevestigt te worden: met den navolgende Missive,

     Eersaeme, lieve, besondere,

Dese weijnige en oopene letteren dienen alleen tot geleijde van
den Vertoonder, den Eerwaerdigen D⁰ Henricus Selijns, bij de Ed:^{le}
grootachtbaare Heeren bewinthebberen ter Camere Amsterdam op UL.
Versoeck en onse voorschrijven aengenoomen om het Predickampt, en
wat daer aen dependeert, in de durpe Breuckelen waer te neemen:
Wij willen UL: ernstelyck gerecommandeert hebben de Opgemelte, so
als dat behoort, met alle toegeneegentheyt te ontfangen, in
respect, eere, en liefde te houden, den dienst bij hem te doen
met naerstigheijt bij te woonen, en volgens gedaene belofte van
een eerlijcke en bequame Wooninge te versorgen, ten eijnde in syn
dienst, Gode ter eeren, en UL. ter Salicheyt, meer en meer geencou-
rageert mag worden, Waer toe den alleen Goede Godt sijn seegen wil
verleenen, waermede eyndigende sullen na groetenisse UL. gesament-
lijck in Godes schut en scherm beveelen, en blyven

Actum, For͞t Amsterd͞m   V L. Goetgunstigen Vrunt en
in N. Nederl͞t a⁰ 1660   Gouverneur
den 3. Septemb͞r   (Onderteeckent)

                               P: Stuijvesant

Translation

PROTOCOL

OF THE CONSISTORY OF BREUCKELEN

September 5, 1660

After the congregation of Breuckelen had petitioned the Hon. Lord Director-General and Councillors for permission to have a minister of their own for the furtherance of the true religion and for their edification (in view of the difficulty of the road from Breuckelen to Midwout and the very old age of the Reverend Domine Johannes Polemijus, for whom [the trip] is hard), it had been resolved that, since the request was fair, the Lords Directors[1] would be informed thereof, in anticipation of a rescript.

And having received, upon the request mentioned above, the person of Henricus Selyns, in order to preach the Gospel there and administer the Sacraments, the afore-mentioned Lord General, after several conferences and a proper contract with the delegates from Breuckelen, sent the aforesaid minister thither, accompanied by the Gentlemen Delegates, Mr. Nicasius de Silla, Councillor and Fiscal of New Netherland, and Mr. Marten Kregier, Burgomaster of Amsterdam in New Netherland, to be introduced to the congregation and instituted as minister - with the following missive:

Respectable, dear, [and] special [people],

This brief and open letter merely serves as an introduction to the bearer, the Reverend Domine Henricus Selijns, engaged by the Hon. Highly Esteemed Lords Directors of the Chamber of Amsterdam, at your request and through our intercession, to hold the office of minister in the village of Breuckelen and to perform all duties that pertain to that office. We want to recommend strongly that you receive the afore-mentioned with complete affection, as it is proper; that you respect, honor, and love him; that you diligently attend the services he will hold; and that you provide him with a true and decent house in accordance with your promise; so that [he] may be encouraged more and more in his ministry, to the glory of God and your salvation. May the only good God give His blessing to this. Concluding herewith, [we] send you our greetings and will commend all of you to God's shelter and protection; and [we] remain,

Your Obliging Friend and
Done in Fort Amsterdam   Governor,
in New Netherland,   (was signed)
September 3, 1660.

P. Stuijvesant

3

Original

[1^{v}: "Pag. 2"]

Desen Brief dan voorgeleesen sijnde, door den meergenoemde H^{r}
Fiscael voor den E: kerckenraedt en Scheepenen van Breuckelen,
heeft de kerckenraedt en scheepenen den E: Heer Generael ende
sijner Gedeputeerde bedanckt, ende den Voorgemelte Henricus Selyns
voor haren Wettige Predicant aengenoomen, die daer op met den
meergemelte gedeputeerde gegaen is om syn Predicatie te doen tot
aenvanck van syn dienst, en verclaringe van syn geneegentheyt tot
syn toevertrouwde Gemeynte.

Den 7. Dicto

Naer behoorlijck gebruijck der kerckelijcke Ordonantien ben ick
verscheenen in de kerckenraet, ende hebbe haer overgeleevert, so
mijn Beroep-brief van 't Eerwaerdige Classis van Amsterdam, met
approbatie van de H. H. Bewinthebbers ter Camere Amsterdam, als
Classicale en kerckelycke Attestatien, myn Beroep tot deser Gemeijnte belangende; welcke sijn dese,

    Beroep-Brief

Alsoo het nootsaeckelijck is, dat na alle vermogen gevordert werden de Eere Godts, ende de salicheijt der menschen, ende ten dien
eynde de Godtsdienstige vergaderinge dienen aengestelt en onderhouden te worden door de suijvere Predicatien van Godts Woort,
Wettige bedienige der Sacramenten, openbare aenroepinge van de
naam des Heeren, ende wat voorts tot den regtmatigen Godtsdienst
gehoort; ende de gelegentheyt van Breuckelen in Nieuw-Nederlant
vereijst, dat een Gequalificeerd Persoon als een wettelijck beroepen Predicant derwaerts gesonden werde, die het Predickampt in
alle sijne deele aldaer bediene, forme van kercke en kerckelycke
Regeringe na de Woorde Godts, en conform de loffelijcke gewoonte
van de Gereformeerde kercke hier te lande, oock aldaer instelle,
ende voort onderhouden; So ist, dat wij, dienaren des Goddelijcken
woorts, ende Ouderlingen der Gemeente Christi resorteerende onder
de E: Classis van Amsterdam, onder de aenroeping van de name Godts
in syne Vrese, met Approbatie van den E: E: H. H. Bewinthebberen,
na voorgaende behoorlijck ondersoeck in de Hooftstucken der Christelijcke leere, en na genoegsaem bewijs van Godtsaligheyt des leevens, oock bevindinge van nodige en bequame gaven tot den H. kerckendienst, op voorgaende onderteeckinge van de Nederlantsche belijdenisse, Christelycke Catechismus, ende Canones Sijnodi Nation.
Dordrac̃., met oplegginge der Handen solemnelyck hebben ingestelt,
ende instellen mits desen, den Eerwaerdige, Godtsalige, Voorsienige,
Welgeleerden D. Henricum Selyns, omme te water ende te lande,
onderwegen, ende insonderheijt daer ter plaetse gekoomen synde,
Godes H. en alleensaligmaeckende Woort suyverlyck te predicken, de
Sacramenten na Christi instellinge recht te bedienen, de Gemeente
Christi met openbare gebeeden voor te gaen, de selve nevens de
Gewoonlycke mederegeerders in goede discipline ende ordre te houden, alles na Godts-woort, ende in Conformiteyt van de Nederlant-
sche kercke, Confessie, ende Christelycke Catechismus. Versoecken
aen alle de geenen, tot de welcke onse Eer̃w. Medebroeder sal

Translation

After this letter had been read to the Hon. Consistory and schepens of Breuckelen by the Lord Fiscal mentioned above, the consistory and schepens thanked the Hon. Lord General and his delegates and accepted the afore-mentioned Henricus Selyns as their lawful minister, who then joined the afore-mentioned delegates to deliver the sermon with which he began his ministry, and in which he expressed his affection for the congregation entrusted to him.[2]

[September] 7 [1660]

As it is prescribed in the Ordinances of the Church, I appeared in the consistory and handed them both my letter-of-call from the Reverend Classis of Amsterdam, with the approval of the Lords Directors of the Chamber of Amsterdam, and attestations from the Classis and the Church relating to my calling to this congregation, namely the following:

Letter-of-call

Since it is necessary to promote the glory of God and the salvation of men to the best of our abilities, and religious assemblies must be instituted and maintained for that purpose by the pure preaching of the Word of God, lawful administration of the Sacraments, public invocation of the Name of the Lord, and whatever else belongs to the rightful divine worship; and [since] the occasion of Breuckelen in New Netherland requires that a qualified person be sent there as a lawfully called minister, to hold the ministry there in all its duties, and to institute, and subsequently also maintain, church forms and church governments there in accordance with the Word of God and in conformity with the laudable customs of the Reformed Church here in this country; - Therefore, we, ministers of the Word of God and elders of the congregation of Christ under the jurisdiction of the Rev. Classis of Amsterdam, calling in fear upon the Name of God, with the approbation of the Hon. Lords Directors, after having examined [him] properly on the principal parts of Christian doctrine and having obtained sufficient evidence of godliness of life, and also having found able talents needed for the divine service, upon subscription [by him] to the Dutch Confession of Faith, the Christian Catechism, and the Canons of the National Synod of Dordrecht, have solemnly instituted and institute hereby, with the laying on of hands, the Reverend, godly, prudent, [and] learned Domine Henricus Selyns, to preach the pure, holy, and only saving Word of God, on water and on land, on his way, and especially after having arrived there[3], to administer the Sacraments properly as they were instituted by Christ, to lead the congregation of Christ in public prayers, [and] to preserve good discipline and order among them and [among] the ordinary[4] co-administrators, everything in accordance with God's Word and in conformity with the Dutch Church, Confession of Faith, and Christian Catechism. [We] ask all to whom our Rev. colleague will come,

5

Original

[2^V: "Pag. 4"]

koomen, datse de selve gelieven als een wettelijck beroepen dienaer J. Christi te erkennen, hem in eere te houden om syns Wercks
wille, mede hem na vermogen behulpelijck te wesen, ten eijnde syn
waerde syn ampt onverhindert en met vreugde mag bedienen tot
grootmaeckinge van Godes H. Name, bekeeringe en Zalicheyt van
veele Zielen.
De almachtige Godt, die syn E: tot dese H. Dienst heeft beroepen,
verrijcke hem so langs, so meer, met alle nodige gaven synes H.
Geests, segene synen arbeyd overvloediglyck tot syns naems eere
en bekeeringe van veele menschen, en beschencke hem, wanneer de
overste Herder der Schapen verschynen sal, met de onverwelke-
lycke Croone der eeuwiger Heerlyckheyt. Aldus gedaen in onse
Classicale Vergaderinge binnen Amstelredam, den 16 februarij,
1660.

                    Uijt aller name en last
        (onderteeckent)

                Petrus Proëlius, Eccls. Amstelodam.
                    et deputatorum ad Causas Indicas p.t. Scriba

                Samuel Coop à Groen, Ecclesiastes Amstelodamensis,
                    & Classis p.t. deputatus

                Lucas van Noort, Ecclests. in Diemen,
                    et p.t. ad causas Indicas deputatus

Op de Rugge van den Voorgemelte Beroep-brief stont den navolgende
acte van Approbatie;

De ommestaende Acte van de Classis van Amsterdam is bij de Bewinthebberen der geoctroijeerde Westindische Comp^e ter Camere alhier
geapprobeert, desen xxvi Martij, 1660.

                (Onderstont)

                    David van Baerle

                    Eduard Man

Ende belangende den Voorn Attestatien, met de welcke wij gesonden
sijn van't Eerwaerdigste Classis ende kerckenraedt van Amsterdam
tot de gemeynte van Breuckelen, en dien wij den kerckenraet des
laestgenoemde gemeynte vertoont hebben, syn als Volgt;

        Classicale Attestatie

D^o Henricus Selijns, Amstelodam. S. Theol. Candidatus, is per-
emtorie geexamineert in de Classis van Amsterdam ende heeft so
in syn Propositie, als in het Examen self, uijter maten contente-
ment gegeeven aen de gantsche vergaderinge: dat sijn E: daer op
met eenpariger stemme, ja toejuijchinge van alle, met toewenschinge
van des Heeren rijcken seegen, geadmitteert is tot het hoogweerdige

Translation

to acknowledge him as a lawfully called minister of Jesus
Christ, to honor him for the sake of his work, and also, to
assist him as well as one can, so that the Reverend may practice his profession unhindered and with joy, to the glory of
God's Holy Name [and] the conversion and salvation of many
souls.
May Almighty God, who has called him to this holy service,
enrich him ever more with all necessary gifts of His Holy Spir-
it, abundantly bless his labor in honor of His Name and for the
conversion of many people, and grant him, when the Supreme
Shepherd of the Sheep will appear, the unwithering crown of
eternal glory. Done in our meeting of the Classis in Amsterdam, February 16, 1660.

On behalf and by order of all,
(was signed)

Petrus Proëlius, Minister in Amsterdam, and for
the time being[5], Scribe of the Deputies for
Indian Affairs[6]

Samuel Coop à Groen, Minister in Amsterdam, and
for the time being, Deputy of the Classis

Lucas van Noort, Minister in Diemen, and for the
time being, Deputy for Indian Affairs

On the reverse side of the afore-mentioned letter-of-call was
the following certificate of approbation:

The Act of the Classis of Amsterdam on the other side of this
page was approved by the Directors of the Chartered West-India
Company in the Chamber here[7], this [day,] March 26, 1660.

(underneath stood)

David van Baerle

Eduard Man[8]

And as for the aforesaid attestations with which we were sent
by the Most Reverend Classis and consistory of Amsterdam to the
congregation of Breuckelen, and which we showed to the consistory
of the latter congregation, [they] are as follows:

Attestation by the Classis

Domine Henricus Selijns, Candidate in the Study of Theology in
Amsterdam, was peremptorily examined in the Classis of Amsterdam and gave both in his proposition and in the examination itself extraordinary satisfaction to the entire assembly, so that
he was thereupon admitted unanimously to the worthy ministry,
indeed with cheers by everyone wishing him the Lord's rich

Original

[3^r: "5"]

Predickampt: dewijle sij[n]* E: dan wettelyck beroepen is tot
Predicant in Nieuw-Nederlant, in de plaetse genaemt Breuckelen:
wert sijn E: mits desen met approbatie van 't selve beroep, gesonden voor Wettelyck predicant na de selve plaetse: niet twyffelende, oft hij sa[l]* bevonden worden een gesegent jnstrument
van de kercke Godts [:]* de groote Herder, en Heere des oogsts,
gelieve na syn grondeloos[e]* Barmhertigheyt, vele sodanige getrouwe Arbeijders uyt te senden. Hier mede wenschen wy onse
waerde medebroeder de overvloedige genade onses Salichmaeckers
Jesu Christi.

In onse Clasicale Vergaderinge   Uijt aller naem
Tot Amsterdam, 16 februarij
         1660   (Onderstont)

                         Johannes de Mourcourt, Classis pro t.
                            Praeses et Examinator

                         Cornelius Cossius, Classis p.t.
                            Scriba

        Kerckelijcke Attestatie

Wij, Dienaren des Goddelijcke Woorts, ende ouderlingen der gemeijnte Jesu Christi binnen Amsterdam, getuijgen bij desen, dat
d'Eerwaerdige, Godtsalige, ende Welgeleerde d^O Henricus Selyns,
Verkoorene Predicant tot de kercke Jesu Christi tot Breuckelen
in Nieuw-Nederlant, een litmaet is van de ware Gereformeerde
Christelijcke kercke, ende dat hij dien tijdt, de welcke hy onder
ons gewoont heeft, niet alleen de H. Ordinantien Godts neerstig-
lijck tot bevorderinge van syn eijgene salicheijt gebruijckt,
maer oock dickmaels door sijn aengenaeme Predicatien onse gemeente
gesticht, ende voorts in syn Wandel sig Godtsaliglyck ende vroom
(immers so veel ons bekent is) gedragen heeft. Versoecken oversulcks alle de E: Broeders ende opsienders der Gemeente Jesu
Christi, den welcke dit ons getuygenisse sal worden vertoont,
desen onsen waerde Medebroeder voor sodanig t'erkennen, ende in
alle Christelycke liefde, op ende aen te neemen. Wenschen voorts
syn E: een spoedige ende gelucksalige Reyse, ende den rycken segen
des Heeren in syne Bedieninge, tot grootmaeckinge van de name des
Heeren, ende uytbreydinge van het Coninckrycke Jesu Christi.
Actum in onse kerckelycke vergaderinge desen 11. martij, 1660.

               Uyt aller naem ende by laste

       (Onderstont)   Johannes Rulicius, Ecclesiastes
                           Amstelodamensis, et p.t.
                           Sijnedrij Scriba

[* Brackets [] followed or preceded by an asterisk * mark
     passages which are illegible because of damage to the
     original manuscript.]

Translation

blessing. Since he was then lawfully called to be minister in New Netherland, in the place called Breuckelen, he was sent there as a lawful minister with his call approved. [We] do not doubt that he will be found a blessed instrument of the Church of God. May the Great Shepherd and Lord of the Harvest send out many such loyal workers, in accordance with His unfathomable mercy. Herewith, we wish our Reverend colleague the abundant grace of our Savior, Jesus Christ.

In our meeting of the Classis   On behalf of all,
in Amsterdam, February 16,
          1660.   (underneath stood)

                    Johannes de Mourcourt, for the time being,
                         President and Examiner of the Classis

                    Cornelius Cossius, for the time being,
                         Scribe of the Classis[9]

          Attestation by the Church

We, ministers of the Word of God and elders of the congregation of Jesus Christ in Amsterdam, hereby testify that the Reverend, godly, and learned Domine Henricus Selyns, chosen to be minister in the Church of Jesus Christ in Breuckelen in New Netherland, is a member of the true Reformed Christian Church, and that during the time he lived among us he not only diligently observed the Holy Ordinances of God for the furtherance of his own salvation, but also often edified our congregation by his pleasant sermons, and moreover, as to his conduct, behaved in a devout and godly way (that is, as far as we know). For this reason, [we] ask all Rev. Brethren and supervisors of the Church of Jesus Christ to whom this our testimony will be shown, to acknowledge our dear colleague as such and to receive and accept him in all Christian love. In addition, [we] wish him a speedy and blessed voyage and the rich blessing of the Lord in his ministry, to the glory of the Name of the Lord and the expansion of the Kingdom of Jesus Christ. Done in our church meeting, this [day,] March 11, 1660.

                    On behalf and by order of all,

     (underneath stood)   Johannes Rulicius, Minister
                           in Amsterdam, and for the
                           time being, Scribe of the
                           Synod[10]

Original

[4^r: "7"]

Vorders, wiert omgevraegt, oft 't niet nootsaeckelyck ende behoorlijck soude wesen, den Eerw^e, Godtzaligen, en Hooggeleerde d^o
Johanni Polhemio voor sijn getrouwe die[nst]* en sonderlinge
moeyte, die sijn E: (niet tegenstaende sijn Hooge ouderdom) met
groote vlijt getoont heeft, met den Tegenwoordige geleegentheijt
te bedancken, ende syn E: een letter van danckbaerheyt door de
E: kerckenraet van de gemeijnte van Breuckelen toetesenden;
't Welcke volkomentlijck geoordeelt wiert Haer Plicht te wesen,
tot een teecken van behoorlijcke danckseginge: ende hebben syn
Eerw^e dese Missive toegesonden,

Eerwaerde en Waerde Broeder in Christo Jesu,

Alsoo de Salicheijt der menschen vereijst de uytlegging en Gehoor
des Salichmaeckende Euangeliums, en gebruijck der Hoogweerdige
Sacramenten, So begeeren wij in geen deele oock ondanckbaer te
wesen; Wij dancken de Godt des Heme[ls]* en Aerdbodems, die so
vaderlijck en getrouwelijck syn g[...]* en kennisse Syns Woorts
uytgedeelt heeft in onse gemeente, en wij bedancken UE: voor uw
seer getrouwe dienst en gedienstige onderricht. Bij onse Zijde
is de schu[ld]* so wy geen Vruchten van Heijligheijt en Boetveerdigheijt voortbrengen. Maer insiende uw Hooge ouderdom en seer
moeyelycke bedieninge, so hebben wij omtrent de E: Dr Generael en
Grootachtb^e H. H. Bewinthebberen uwe ontlastinge met alle ootmoe-
digheyt versocht, en 't selvige door Godts Genade geobtineert,
waer door sij gesonden hebben D. Henricum Selijns, die op Breuckelen door de H. H. Fiscael Nicasius de Sille en Burgermeester
Marten Kregiers met voorgaende last en bij-Schryvens des E. D^{rs}
Generaels gebracht, en bij de Gemeente in liefde aengenoomen is.
Erkent dan, Eerwaerde en waerde Broeder, onse danckbaerheyt,
ondertusschen U.E. en Uw Waerde gemeenten in de beschierminge des
Alderhoogsten van Herten beveelende.
Vale, Uyt Breuckelen
den 7 Sept. 1660.   Uyt name des kerckenraets,

              (onderstont)   Joris Dirckzen

                               Willem Bredenbent

Ten regarde van de kerckenraet, die neffens den aengenoomen d.
Henricus Selyns bestont in Joris Dirckzen tot ouderling, ende
Wilhelmus Bredenbent en Pieter Montfoort tot diaconen, wiert van
de Broeders voorgestelt en gevraegt, oft 't best sout wesen, met
den Voorgem ouderling en diaconen te vergenoegen, ofte een Twede
ouderling met de Eerste Geleegentheijt te verkiesen. Maer om
redenen is 't goet gevonden 't getal, als 't tegenwoordig is, te
laten, tot nader kennisse en meerder Tal der ledematen.
Ende ten besten van de Gemeente, die seer verspreyt woont met de
geleegentheyt van de Gujanes, Walebocht, en 't Veer, ende nauwe-
lijcks soude kunnen ten behoorelycke tydt verschijnen tot het
Gehoor des Salichmaeckende Euangeliums, oft niet billick was, dat
de Predicatien ten Half tienen voortaen begonnen, om soo met

[* Brackets [] followed or preceded by an asterisk * mark
     passages which are illegible because of damage to the
     original manuscript.]

Translation

Furthermore, the question was put to the assembly whether it would not be necessary and proper to thank the Rev., godly, and very learned Domine Johannes Polhemius on this occasion for his loyal service and the exceptional pains taken by him with great diligence (in spite of his old age), and to let the Hon. Consistory of the congregation of Breuckelen send him a letter of thanks. This was judged to be their rightful duty, an appropriate token of gratitude. And [they] sent the Rev. this missive:

Reverend and dear brother in Jesus Christ,

Since the salvation of men requires the explaining and hearing of the sanctifying Gospel and the receiving of the venerable Sacraments, we do not want to be ungrateful by any means. We thank the God of Heaven and Earth who so fatherly and loyally bestowed His grace[11] and knowledge of His Word upon our congregation, and we thank you for your very loyal service and attentive instruction. It is we who are to blame if we do not produce fruits of sanctity and penitence. Realizing, however, your old age and very difficult ministry, we humbly asked the Hon. Director-General and Highly Esteemed Lords Directors for your release which we obtained through the grace of God. For that reason, they sent Domine Henricus Selijns who was taken to Breuckelen by the Gentlemen the Fiscal, Nicasius de Sille, and Burgomaster Marten Kregiers, by order of, and with an accompanying letter from, the Hon. Director-General, and he was accepted in love by the congregation. Acknowledge our gratitude, Reverend and dear brother, while we heartily commend you and your dear congregation to the protection of the Most High. Farewell from Breuckelen,
September 7, 1660.   On behalf of the consistory,

          (underneath stood)   Joris Dirckzen

                    Willem Bredenbent[12]

With regard to the consistory, which besides Henricus Selyns, the newly accepted Domine, consisted of Joris Dirckzen, elder, and Wilhelmus Bredenbent and Pieter Montfoort, deacons, a proposition was made and a question asked by the brethren whether it would be best to be content with the elder and deacons mentioned above, or to elect a second elder at the first opportunity. For [certain] reasons, however, it was agreed to leave the number as it is today, until the members are better known and have increased in number.
And for the benefit of the congregation which is very scattered on account of the locations of the Gowanus, Wallabout, and the Ferry, and [which] would hardly be able to appear at the appropriate time to hear the sanctifying Gospel, [the question was asked] whether it would not be reasonable to begin the sermon henceforth at 9.30 so that the Gospel could be preached more fruitfully and

Original

[4^v]

meerder gehoor en Vruchten 't Euangelium te verkondigen: 't Welck
toegestaen is.
Maer terwijle de Gemeijnte van Breuckelen sig verbonden hadde, met
beloften, om te maecken een Eerlycke en bequame wooninge voor haer
Voorgem. Predicant, en 't welcke wiert boven aengeroert met de
Missive van de E: H^r Dr Generael Petrus Stuijvesant tot meerder
verplichtinge en nader opweckinge, Wiert voorgeslagen, oft niet
billick was, 't Voornoemde Huijs, ende so 't mogelijck was, een
kleijn kerckie of separate Plaetse tot de Godsdiensten te timmeren,
en Wie tot opsichters, oft bij forme van kerckmeesters best bequaem soude wesen tot bevorderinge van dit werck.   't Welck in
Consideratien genoomen sijnde, wiert best geoordeelt sig voor den
Presente tijdt te vergenoegen, met den tegenwoordige ongeleegent-
heijt der Huijslieden, om haer beloften te voldoen, en behoorlijck
Predicants huys te timmeren: Ende dat tot opsichters van dien
genoomen soude worden Joris Dirckzen, ouderling, die oock tot
Breuckelen wonachtig is, met Versoeck, dat Albert Cornelissen,
Scheepen ende jnwoonder te Breuckelen, Hem daer toe met eene soude
laten gebruycken;   opdat Moses en Aäron mochten t'samen gaen, ende
met Eene te neemen van de kerckenraedt, en Eene te versoecken van
de Magistratuur, mochte 't Voorschreven Huys beter gevordert en
voltoyt worden: En 't welcke van beijde voornoemt aengenoomen is.

           Den 12 dicto

Heeft Joris Dirckzen gerapporteert, den Brief van de E: kerckenraet aen den Eerw^e, Godtzaligen, en Hoog-geleerde D^o Johannes
Polhemius behandigt te hebben met behoorlijcke Dancksegginge voor
syn E: gedane bedieninge, die sulcks seer aengenaem was, ende Hem
gegeeven hadde de navolgende Lyste van de Ledematen, tot de Jurisdictie van Breuckelen behoorende,

      Joris Dirckzen, Susanna Dubbels, Albert Cornelissen,
      Trijntie Hadders, Willem Gerritsen van Couwenhooven,
      Aelte Joris, Pieter Montfoort, Sara de Plancke,
      Jan Evertsen, Tryntie Sijmons, Willem Bredenbent,
      Aeltie Brachunee, Jan Pieterszen, Grietie Jans,
      Teunis Nijssen, Femmetie Jans, Adam Brouwer,
      Magdalena Jacobs, Johannes Marcus, Elsie Hendricks,
      Teunis Jansen, Barber Lucas, Jan Jorissen,
      Jan Hibon, onder Censure, Getruyt Barents.

Belangende 't Avontmael des Heeren, wiert voorgestelt, wat Tijdt
't bequaemste soude wesen, om 't Heijlige en Hoog-gemelte Avontmael te houden in de gemeynte van Breuckelen.   Ende wiert goetgevonden, dat 't Avontmael gehouden soude worden voor de Eerste
mael in de toekoomende maent van October;   maer terwijle Henricus
Selijns niet alleene bedient de gemeynte van Breuckelen met voor
de middag te predicken, maer daer en boven de gemeijnte van 's
Generaels-Bouwerije door een Avont predicatie, ende so doende
qualijck soude koomen 't Avontmael te houden sonder behoorlycke
dancksegginge, wiert voorgestelt, oft 't niet alderbequaemste
soude wesen 't Meergemelte Avontmael te houden (na de Exempelen

12

Translation

with a larger audience. This was granted.
     Since the congregation of Breuckelen had bound itself with
promises to make a true and decent house for its afore-mentioned
minister - which was touched upon above, in the missive from
the Hon. Lord Director-General Petrus Stuijvesant, as an extra
obligation and further incentive - it was suggested that it
would be proper to build the aforesaid house and, if possible,
a small church or separate place for the divine worship, and [to
consider] who would be the most competent people to promote this
work as supervisors or in the capacity of church-wardens. Upon
further consideration it was judged best, in view of the present
inability of the villagers to make good their promises, to be
content for the time being with the construction of a proper
house for the minister. And as supervisor would be designated
Joris Dirckzen, elder, who is also living in Breuckelen, with the
request that Albert Cornelissen, schepen and a native of Breuckelen, make himself at once available for that purpose, so that
Moses and Aaron would stand together.[13] And by taking one person
from the consistory and asking another from among the magistrates,
[it was hoped that] the aforesaid house would make better progr-
ess and be finished earlier. This was accepted by both people
mentioned above.[14]

            [September] 12 [1660]

     Joris Dirckzen reported that he had handed the letter of the
Hon. Consistory to the Rev., godly, and very learned Domine Johannes Polhemius with appropriate expressions of gratitude for his
ministry. He was very pleased by it and had given him the following list of members belonging to the jurisdiction of Breuckelen:

        Joris Dirckzen, Susanna Dubbels, Albert Cornelissen,
        Trijntie Hadders, Willem Gerritsen van Couwenhooven,
        Aelte Joris, Pieter Montfoort, Sara de Plancke,
        Jan Evertsen, Tryntie Sijmons, Willem Bredenbent,
        Aeltie Brachunee, Jan Pieterszen, Grietie Jans,
        Teunis Nijssen, Femmetie Jans, Adam Brouwer,
        Magdalena Jacobs, Johannes Marcus, Elsie Hendricks,
        Teunis Jansen, Barber Lucas, Jan Jorissen,
        Jan Hibon (under censure), Getruyt Barents.[15]

     With regard to the Lord's Supper, a proposal was made [to
consider] what would be the most suitable time to administer the
afore-mentioned Lord's Supper in the congregation of Breuckelen.
And it was decided that the Lord's Supper would be administered
for the first time in the coming month of October. However,
since Henricus Selijns is serving not only the congregation of
Breuckelen by preaching in the morning but, in addition to that,
the General's Bowery [= farm] with sermons in the evening, and
[since], therefore, the Lord's Supper would unfortunately have to
be administered without proper prayers of thanks, it was suggested that it would be most convenient to administer the afore-
mentioned Supper during the Christmas days, Easter, and

Original

[6^r: "Pag. 11"]

van verscheijden gereformeerde kercken in 't Vaderlant) met de
Kersdagen, Paesschen, en Pinxsteren, om de Twede dag te houden tot
bequame geleegentheyt van dancksegginge, ende bovendien in 't
laeste van September, of begin van October, 'T geene volkomentlyck
gearresteert en vastgestelt is.

Den 17 Octob.

Na de aenroepinge des Alderhoogsten, wiert geproponeert, oft de
geene die begeerig waren om toe gelaten te worden tot den Tafel
des Heeren en aengenoomen te worden tot de Christelycke gemeijn-
schap, soude Confessie en belijdenisse doen in 't particulier en
besonder, oft ter Presentie van de Volkomen kerckenraedt en tegen-
woordigheyt der Getuygen. Maer diesaengaende wiert geoordeelt,
dat de geene die sig begeeven, oft t'eeniger tydt begeeven sullen,
den kerckenraedt en getuygen present sijnde, haer Belijdenisse
sullen geeven van 't Ware en Salichmaeckende geloove. Ende ter
voorschreven Resolutie syn toegelaten den navolgende,

    Maria Fredericks, van den Haeg,
        Getuijgen,
           Jan Joriszen, Pieter Montfoort.
    Pieter Janssen, van de Manhatans, ende
    Annetie Jans, van Amsterdam,
        getuygen van Beijde,
           Jan Pieterszen, Grietie Jans.

Op 't Versoeck van 't gerechte tot Breuckelen, om vijftig guldens
Seewant Haer E: te verschieten tot betalinge van de timmerlieden,
Aucke Jans en Frans Bloetgoet van der Goude, om 's Predicants Huys
te maecken, wiert toegestaen, dat de diaconen Haer E: verschieten
soude de voorgemelte Somme van 't Armgelt by conditie van gewoonelycke Intresse.

Den 19 Decem͠b.

Voor 't houden van 't Heylige en Hoogweerdige Avontmael met den
aenstaende Kerstydt, syn tot Ledematen aengenoomen, so door kerckelijcke Attestatien en getuygenissen, als met behoorlijcke belydenisse, dese navolgende Persoonen,

    Wiggert Reijnierszen, uyt Oostvrieslant,
        Met Attestatie van de Manhatans.
    Swaentie Jans, wed. van Cornelis Potter,
        Met Attestatie van de Manhatans.
        Ende
    Jan Martijn, van Campen,
        Getuijgen,
           Albert Cornelissen, Willem Bredenbent.

Translation

Whitsuntide (after the example of several reformed churches in the fatherland) [and] to reserve the day following [each feast-day], as well as [some day] at the end of September or the beginning of October, as suitable occasions for prayers of thanks. This was entirely approved and confirmed.

October 17 [1660]

Upon the invocation of the Most High, the question was posed whether those who wanted to be admitted to the Lord's Table and accepted in the Christian community should be confirmed in private or in the presence of the entire consistory with witnesses. In this matter it was decided that those who are applying or will apply at any one time, will confess their true and sanctifying faith in the presence of the consistory and witnesses. And upon the aforesaid resolution the following people were admitted:

Maria Fredericks, from The Hague;
        witnesses:
        Jan Joriszen, Pieter Montfoort.
Pieter Janssen, from Manhattan, and
Annetie Jans, from Amsterdam;
        witnesses for both:
        Jan Pieterszen, Grietie Jans.

Upon the request of the Court of Breuckelen for an advance of fifty guilders in sewan, in order to pay the carpenters, Aucke Jans and Frans Bloetgoet van der Goude, for building the house for the minister, permission was given to the deacons to advance the afore-mentioned sum out of the poor relief fund on the usual interest conditions.

December 19

In order to partake of the Lord's Holy and Consecrated Supper during the imminent Christmas season, the following persons were confirmed as members, both on the basis of church attestations and testimonies and upon proper confessions of faith:

Wiggert Reijnierszen, from East Friesland,
        with an attestation from Manhattan.
Swaentie Jans, widow of Cornelis Potter,
        with an attestation from Manhattan.
        And
Jan Martijn, from Kampen;
        witnesses:
        Albert Cornelissen, Willem Bredenbent.

Original

[7^v: "Pag. 14"]

Anno 1661

Den 9 Februar.

Nademael met 't overlijden van Joris Dirckzen, ouderling, die Verleeden 16 Januar̃. gestorven, en Pieter Montfoort, die den 4 der
selfder maent overleeden syn, seer nootsaeckelijck was, omme Haer
plaetsen te vervullen, ende den kerckenraedt te brengen tot 't
Voorgaende getal van ouderling en diaconen, ten eijnde de Gemeynte
J. Christi met behoorlycke ordre geregeert, de bedroefde en arme
Huysgenooten des Geloof bequamelyck versorgt, ende ongerelge te
beter gebracht werden door de kerckelycke Ban, oft tot berouw en
leetwesen, ofte tot afsonderinge van den Voorgemelte gemeijnte.
Wiert goetgevonden, na de aenroepinge van de name des Heeren, tot
diacon te verkiesen Teunis Janssen Coevors, ende tot een Twede
diacon 't lot te trecken over Willem Gerritsen van Couwenhooven,
schoonsoon van den voorñ. Joris Dirckzen Sạl, ende Jan Joriszen,
't welcke Jan Jorissen toegevallen is, die sulcks met den Voor-
schr̃. Teunis Jansen aengeseyt sijnde, beyde aengenoomen hebben,
gelyckerwys Willem Bredenbent 't ouderlingschap voor diacon te
wesen aen genoomen heeft. Welcke Verkiesinge naer kerckelycke
gewoonte den Gemeynte voorgestelt soude worden, oft iemant tegens
de Verkoosene iets wettelijcks mochte inbrengen tot verhinderinge
der Bevestinge, 't geen wij niet verhoopen sullen.

Den 2. Martij

Om de Broeders, die den 27ste february bevestigt sijn, te geeven,
't welck betamelyck was, een suijvere Reeckening van 's Diaconies
middelen en overwinste, Heeft den oude Kerckenraedt den Reeckening
van ontfang en uytgift der diaconen opgenoomen, ende na de volgende
Balance aldus bevonden,

       Ontfangen

Met het jaer 1660	Gld.	255- 5
met het jaer 1661, van p.^{r}		
jan. tot Pri. maert	Gld.	61-18
Somma	Gld.	317- 3

       Uijtgegeeven

met het jaer 1660 van		
den 20 oct. tot ult. dec.	Gld.	66-15
met het jaer 1661 van		
p.^{r} jan. tot Prim. mart.	Gld.	50- 0
Somma	Gld.	116-15

[continued on p. 18]

Translation

A.D. 1661

February 9

Because of the deaths of Joris Dirckzen, elder, who died
January 16 last, and Pieter Montfoort, who died on the 4th of the
same month, it was very urgent to fill their places and bring the
consistory to the previous number of elder and deacons, so that
the congregation of Jesus Christ would be ruled in proper order,
the distressed and poor companions in the faith efficiently taken
care of, and the unruly[16] better induced - by means of excommun-
ication - either to penitence and regret or to separation from
the afore-mentioned congregation. After invoking the Name of the
Lord, it was decided to elect Teunis Janssen Coevors deacon, and
to draw lots for the second position as deacon among Willem
Gerritsen van Couwenhooven, son-in-law of the late Joris Dirckzen
mentioned above, and Joris Joriszen. The lot fell upon Jan Jorissen who, when notified, accepted [his appointment], as did the
aforesaid Teunis Jansen. Similarly, Willem Bredenbent assented
to being elder instead of deacon. In accordance with church
customs, the appointments would be presented to the congregation
[to see] whether anyone might raise rightful objections against
the elected preventing their confirmation, which we do not hope.

March 2

In order to give the brethren who were confirmed on February
27, an accurate account of the deaconry's means and surplus,
which is proper, the old consistory made up the account of the
deacons' receipts and expenditures and found it to be in accordance with the following balance:

Received,

in the year 1660:	Gld.	255- 5
in the year 1661, from the first of January till the first of March:	Gld.	61-18
Total:	Gld.	317- 3

Spent,

in the year 1660, from October 20 till the last of December:	Gld.	66-15
in the year 1661, from the first of January till the first of March:	Gld.	50- 0
Total:	Gld.	116-15

[continued on p. 19]

17

Original

[8^r: "Pag. 15"]

Overgeschooten

Bij cassa in gereede specie	Gld. 151-0
Bij Testament van Barent	
Balde aen de armen van	
Breuckelen	Gld. 50-0
Somma	Gld. 101-0

Dit dan alsoo bevonden, ende by Henricus Selyns en Willem Bredenbent onderteeckent, wiert den nieuwe Diacons, Teunis Jansen en Jan
Joris, overgegeeven, met Verwellekoominge, en toewenschinge van de
seegen des Heeren.

Den 10 April

Na de Visite, en gewoonelycke noodinge tot den Tafel des Heeren,
in de welcke 't geen ons voorgekoomen was, naer ons Vermogen afgemaeckt en parthijen bevreedigt hebben, syn de navolgende Persoonen,
so door belydenisse als kerckelycke Attestatien, tot onser Gemeijn-
schap, ende gebruyck van 't Heylige en Hoogwaerdige Avontmael aengenoomen en ingeschreeven,

 Sara Joris Rapalie, van Nieuw-Nederlant,
   met Attestatie van de Manhatans.
 Dirck Janssen, van Amsterdam, ende
 Marritien Teunis, van Nieuw-Nederlant,
   getuijgen van Beyde,
    Teunis Nijssen, en Swaentie Potters.
 Thomas Janssen, van Nieuw-Uytrecht,
   getuijgen,
    Jan Thomassen, en Trijntie Agens.
 Fijtie Dircks, van Amsterdam,
   getuijgen,
    Jan Martijn, en Saertie de Plancke.
 Pieter Prae, van Diepe, ende
 Catharina Lethie,
   met Attestatie van Middelwout.
 Marcus Soisson, ende
 Lijsbeth Rossillon, van Leijden,
   met Attestatie van de Manhatans.

Den 29 Maij

Door Versterf van Joris Dirckzen, ouderling, die door sijn sonderlinge ijver tot de Godsdiensten vrijwillig in onser gemeete voor-
gesongen heeft, ende Henricus Selyns seer moejelyck en niet wel
mogelijck was beijde sijn Dienst te doen van predicken ende voor
en na te singen, 't Welck voornamentlijck hem nadeelig was, ten
dele om de Schuur, daer gepreeckt wort, en geen of weynig galms is:
en ten deele om sijn Dienst van hem naer de middag oft na den avont
gaende te doen op de Bouwerije van de E: H^r Petrus Stuijvesant,

Translation

Remaining,

in the treasury in cash:	Gld. 151-0
Barent Balde's bequest to the poor of Breuckelen:	Gld. 50-0
Total:	Gld. 101-0[17]

This [account], found accurate and signed by Henricus Selyns and Willem Bredenbent, was handed over to the new deacons, Teunis Jansen and Jan Joris, with words of welcome and wishes for the Lord's blessing.

April 10 [1661]

After [we] had visited [the congregation] and had customarily invited [the people] to the Lord's Table, while settling whatever had occurred to the best of our ability and making peace between [quarreling] parties, the following persons were confirmed and registered in our congregation and admitted to the Lord's Holy and Consecrated Supper, both through confessions of faith and on the basis of church attestations:

Sara Joris Rapalie, from New Netherland,
        with an attestation from Manhattan.
Dirck Janssen, from Amsterdam, and
Marritien Teunis, from New Netherland;
        witnesses for both:
                Teunis Nijssen, and Swaentie Potters.
Thomas Janssen, from New Utrecht;
        witnesses:
                Jan Thomassen, and Trijntie Agens.
Fijtie Dircks, from Amsterdam;
        witnesses:
                Jan Martijn, and Saertie de Plancke.
Pieter Prae, from Dieppe, and
Catharina Lethie,
        with an attestation from Midwout.
Marcus Soisson, and
Lijsbeth Rossillon, from Leiden,
        with an attestation from Manhattan.

May 29

Because of the death of Joris Dirckzen, elder, who out of his extraordinary devotion to the faith had voluntarily led the sing- ing in our congregation; and because it was very difficult and hardly possible for Henricus Selyns, both to carry out his preach- ing duty and to lead the singing, [a situation] which was partic- ularly unfavorable to him partly on account of the fact that the barn in which the sermons are held has very poor acoustic qualit- ies, and partly because of the service to be conducted by him in the afternoon or towards evening at the Bowery [= farm] of the Hon. Lord Petrus Stuijvesant, Director-General of New Netherland;

Original

[9^r: "Pag. 16"]

d^r Generael van Nieuw-Nederlant, wiert voorgeslagen, omme behoorlyck devoir te doen, ende omtehooren naer een bequaem persoon, om
de dienst van Voorleeser, Voorsanger, en Schoolmeester te becleden,
en die van der Gerechte wegen mochte tot gerechtsbode sijn.
't Welcke van jegelyck van de Broeders wiert aengenoomen, met Versoeck, dat de voorgemelte Henricus Selijns soude diesaengaende na
't Fort Orangien ende Esopus Schrijven, 't geen hy belooft heeft
voor sijn particulier te doen.

Ende tot Ledematen syn wederom aengenoomen dese navolgende Persoonen,

> Sijmon Joosten, van Marrelbeeck,
>> getuijgen,
>>> Willem Gerritsen, Dirck Janssen.
> Anneken Barents, van Amsterdam,
>> getuijgen,
>>> Swaentie Potters, Getruij Barents.
> Teunis Gijsbertsen, van Heijkoop,
>> getuijgen,
>>> Sara Joris, Jan Martijn.
> Arie Willemszen, van Nieuw-Nederlant,
>> getuygen,
>>> Willem Bredenbent, Aeltie Brackunee.
> Gerrit Dirckzen Crousen, van Wijnschoot,
>> getuygen,
>>> Teunis Nyssen, Jan Martijn.
> Janneken Pieters, Huysv. van Jan Corñ. de Zeeu:
>> met Attestatie van Middelwout.

Middelerwijle, wiert swaricheyt gemaeckt ten regarde van de laest
genoemde, Janneken Pieters, die tot ons gekoomen is, en hebbende
den navolgende seer slechte Attestatie, belangende van weynig tot
Middelwout gekomen te syn tot het gehoor des salichmaeckende
woorts, 't welck aldus was,

Janneken Pieters, Huysvr. van Jan Cornelissen de Seeuw, wert
by ons gekent, datse bij ons heeft gecommuniceert, doch alsoo sij
weijnig ten gehoor gekoomen is, konnen van haer comportement niet
seggen, &c.

(onderteeckent)

Joh. Th. Polhemius

Den Voorschreeven Janneken Pieters hier over gesproocken, en na
behooren gestraft sijnde, gaf tot Antwoort en Verontschuldinge,
dat sij tot Boschwijck woonende door de ongeleegentheyt van de
Durpe Middelwout weijnig occasie hadde, om daer te koomen ter
gewoonelijcke Verkondinge des Euangeliums, en daerom versocht
hadde, om Attestatie te hebben, en tot Breuckelen, dat nader was,
te communiceeren, met beloften, om naerstiger te verschijnen tot
't Salichmaeckende gehoor van Godes Woort.
Dit dan overweegende na den aert der liefde, ende beloften van
beterschap aenneemende ter goeder trouwe, wiert den meergemelte

Translation

it was proposed to do one's proper duty and to inquire for a competent person for the function of reader, precentor, and schoolmaster, who would also be permitted to serve as court-messenger
on behalf of the Court. This was accepted by everyone among the
brethren, with the request that the aforesaid Henricus Selijns
write to Fort Orange and Esopus for that purpose, which he promised to do privately.

And the following persons were confirmed as members:
Sijmon Joosten, from Merelbeke;
      witnesses:
         Willem Gerritsen, Dirck Janssen.
Anneken Barents, from Amsterdam;
      witnesses:
         Swaentie Potters, Getruij Barents.
Teunis Gijsbertsen, from Heikop;
      witnesses:
         Sara Joris, Jan Martijn.
Arie Willemszen, from New Netherland;
      witnesses:
         Willem Bredenbent, Aeltie Brackunee.
Gerrit Dirckzen Crousen, from Winschoten;
      witnesses:
         Teunis Nyssen, Jan Martijn.
Janneken Pieters, wife of Jan Corn[elissen] de Zeeu,
      with an attestation from Midwout.

Meanwhile, objections were raised against the last, Janneken
Pieters, who came to us with the following very bad attestation,
to the effect that she had seldom come to Midwout to hear the
sanctifying Word [of God]; it read as follows:

Janneken Pieters, wife of Jan Cornelissen de Seeuw, was
known among us as she received Holy Communion with us, but
since she seldom came to hear [the Word of God], [we] cannot
say anything about her conduct, etc.

(was signed)

Joh. Th. Polhemius

When the aforesaid Janneken Pieters was questioned about this
and duly sanctioned, [she] apologized and replied that she, a
resident of Boswijck, had little opportunity to go to the village
of Midwout to attend the ordinary preaching of the Gospel there
because of its unfavorable location. For that reason, she had
asked for an attestation and [for permission] to receive Holy
Communion in Breuckelen which was closer, while promising to come
and hear the sanctifying Word of God more diligently.
After [we] had taken this into consideration in the name of
love and had accepted the sincerity of [her] promises to behave
better in the future, the afore-mentioned [Janneken] was admitted

21

Original

[10^r: "Pag. 18"]

tot den Tafel des Heeren toegelaten, ende, als boven, voor ledemaet aengenoomen van de kercke van Breuckelen.

Den 6 Julij

Naer behoorlyck ondersoeck om te koomen tot een Voorsanger, en
Schoolmeester, is ons te vooren gekomen den Persoon van Mr Carel
d'Beauvois, Schoolmeester tot Amsterdam in Nieuw-Nederlant, dien
wij syn bequaemheyt ondersocht hebbende, met Approbatie en Subsidie van Dr Generael en Raden van Nieuw-Nederlant, hebben tot
Schoolmeester, Voorleser en Voorsanger aengenoomen, van der kerckenraet wegen tot den Voorgemelte contribuerende Vry Huys Huur
en 25 guld. seewant, Ende van der Gerechte-wegen, om te zijn tot
gerechts-bode, zyn Tractement, buyten den voornoemde Subsidie van
den E: Compagnie, vervullende. Zijn order, Reglement, ende jnstructie sal den navolgende sijn, naer de gewoonte van ons Vaderlant.
Eerstelijck sal de Voorgeschreven Voorleeser respectivelijck sorge
dragen, dat de Psalm, die voor de Predicatien gesongen wort, tydelyck op 't Psalm-bort aengeteeckent sal worden.
Ten tweeden, sal hy na behooren 't eerste geluyt beginnen, hem
selfs met het Twede in de kerck of preeckplaets laten vinden,
stoelen oft bancken setten, en volgens gewoonelycke ordre by den
kerckenraedt gestelt oft te stellen eenige Capittelen uyt de H.
Schrifture, oock de Wet des Heeren, en Twalef Articulen des Christelycke geloofs voor de Predicatie leesen.
Ten derden, men sal insonderheijt voorleesen de boecken des Nieuwe
Testaments, en onder de Boecken des Oude Testaments, voornament-
lijck de Psalmen en Propheten: ofte achtneemen geduerende de Be-
dieninge des H. Avontmaels des Heeren op de 22. 23. 31. 40. 42.
51. 69. 110. 111. 112. en 132ste Psalmen, Op 't 53ste Capittel
Jesaia, ende 6ste capittel Johannis, ende van 't 13ste capittel
Johannis tot 't Eijnde des Selfde Euangeliums, op 't 26 en 27ste
Capittelen Matthaei. Item 1. Cor. 10. en 11. Capittelen. Uyt den
Senbrief tot den Hebreen cap. 7. 8. 9. 10. ofte Apoc. 2 ende 3ste
Capittelen.
Ten Vierden, hij sal terstont met het derde geluyt den opgestelde
Psalm beginnen te singen.
Ten Vijfden, bij Sieckte oft nodige Absentie sal den Voornoemde
Voorleeser oock niemant laten voorleesen oft voorsingen, ten zij
Persoonen van een goet leeven en getuijgenisse, met waerschouwinge
en bekentmaeckinge omtrent den kerckenraedt.
Ten Sesten, Hij sal oock in sijn School behoorlijcke Vlyt en
naerstigheyt aenwenden, jnsonderheyt de vrese des Heeren van
jongsaf den Schoolkinderen inscherpen, met een goet Exempel voor
te gaen, met de gebeeden het School te beginnen, en Psalmen te
eijndigen, ende de jeugt met eene te oeffenen uyt de Vragen en
Grontregulen van den Eerw^e, godtsalige, en seer geleerde Vader
d^o Johannes Megapolensis, bedienaer des Euangeliums tot Amsterdam
in Nieuw-Nederlant.
Ten laesten, dat den Voorgemelte Voorleeser, behalven 't Tractement by den E: H. Dr Generael en Raden van N. Nederl^t en Rechtbanck en kerckenraet van Breuckelen te betalen, van de voorschr.

22

Translation

to the Lord's Table and confirmed as above as a member of the
Church of Breuckelen.

July 6 [1661]

After a careful search for a precentor and schoolmaster, the
person of Mr. Carel d'Beauvois came to the fore, schoolmaster in
Amsterdam in New Netherland, whom we engaged as schoolmaster,
reader, and precentor, after having checked his competence, with
the approval of, and subsidy from, the Director-General and
Councillors of New Netherland. The consistory will provide the
afore-mentioned with rent-free housing and 25 guilders in sewan,
while the Court will pay his salary by supplementing the aforesaid subsidy from the Hon. Company, so that he will [also] be a
court-messenger. His orders, regulations, and instructions will
be the following, as is customary in our fatherland:
First, the aforesaid reader shall see to it that the hymn to
be sung before the sermon is written in time on the hymn-board.
Second, he shall duly carry out the first ringing of the bell.
By the time of the second ringing, he shall make sure to be in
the church or [other] place of preaching, set chairs or pews,
and, before the sermon, read some chapters from the Holy Scriptures as well as the Law of the Lord and [the] Twelve Articles of
the Christian Faith, in accordance with the customary order prescribed by, or to be prescribed by, the consistory.
Third, he shall read in particular the Books of the New Testament, and of the Books of the Old Testament especially the
Psalms and the Prophets. During Holy Communion services, [he
shall] pay attention to the 22nd, 23rd, 31st, 40th, 42nd, 51st,
69th, 110th, 111th, 112th, and 132nd Psalms, the 53rd chapter of
Isaiah, the 6th chapter of John, the 13th chapter of John until
the end of the same Gospel, [and] the 26th and 27th chapters of
Matthew; similarly, [from] I Corinthians: the 10th and 11th
chapters; from the Epistle to the Hebrews: chapters 7, 8, 9,
[and] 10, or [from] Apocalypse: the 2nd and 3rd chapters.
Fourth, as soon as the bell rings for the third time, he shall
begin to sing the prescribed psalm.
Fifth, in case of illness, or absence necessitated by [other]
causes, the aforesaid reader shall allow only persons of good
conduct and repute to do the reading or lead the singing, while
alerting and notifying the consistory.
Sixth, in his school, too, he shall show proper diligence and
assiduity; in particular, [he shall] impress upon the school-
children from their earliest childhood the fear of the Lord, set
a good example, begin classes with the prayers and end with
psalms, and rehearse the youth at once in the questions and
principles by the Rev., godly, and very learned father Domine
Johannes Megapolensis, Minister of the Gospel in Amsterdam in New
Netherland.
Finally, besides [receiving] the salary to be paid by the Hon.
Lord Director-General and Councillors of New Netherland and by
the Court and consistory of Breuckelen, the afore-mentioned

Original

kerckenraet daerenboven van Huyshuur bevryt, en met bequaeme Huys-
vestinge versorgt sal worden.

Den 7 August.

Verstaen hebbende tot ons leetwesen, dat Teunis Jansen, laest verkosen diacon van onser gemeente, soude beschuldigt syn, van Een
oft Twee Verckens opgehouden te hebben, out omtrent drie jaren,
ende behoorende aen Michiel Tades, wonachtig tot Amsterdam in
N. Nederlant: Ende daer van soude d'Eene verkocht hebben aen
Mr Evert Duycking, glasemaecker ter Voorgemelte Plaetse. Ja alrede tot accoort getreden was ten Huysen van Albert Co$\widetilde{rn}$. Wantenaers, out schepen, en wonachtig tot Breuckelen, ende ter Presentie van Verscheijden: 't Welcke groot suspicie en Ergernisse
gaf. Wiert hij diesaengaende gevraegt, en serieuselyck opgestre-
den, oft de Voornoemde Verckens syn Eygen waren, ofte tot den
Voorsch$\widetilde{r}$. Tades behoorende. Maer verclaerde met een goede conscientie de sijne te wesen, en beloofde ten vollen te bewijsen met
geloofwaerdige getuijgen, die se t'allen tijden gekent hebben, en
bekennen sullen.
Ende als wij seijden, wat hem dan bewoogen hadde, om 't Voorgemelte contract te maecken, 't welck niemant, die ontschuldig is,
gehouden is te doen, gaf tot Antwoort, en seyde, dat 't hem om de
minste moeijte, van 't meeste geselschap geraden was, en bevon tot
syn nadeel bedroogen te wesen. Hebben hem, die hoog en leeg syn
selven ontschuldig verclaerde van aengehouden te hebben 't geen
eens anders was, geraden, so hy syn name lief hadde, en ter werelt
geen oorsaecke socht te geeven van onstichtinge, dat hij syn
devoir sout doen, omme attestatie te beleggen t'sijner ontschul-
dinge, 't Accoort te wederroepen voor de Gerechte van Breuckelen,
oft 't welck geraetsaem was, voor de H. Dr Generael en Raden van
N. Nederl^t, Ende de Suspicien so doende weg te neemen, welcke door
't schriftelyck accoort gegeeven waren, oft dat wy ter contrarie
genootsaeckt soude wesen om te doen, 't geen wy sagen seer on-
gaerne.

Den 21 Septemb.

Jan Thomaszen en Soon voor de kerckenraedt van Breuckelen, over
seecker ongeluck van syn mes getrocken en Jan Cleeft in de Durpe
Nieuw-Uijtrecht gequest te hebben, gedachvaert, Bekende, dat hij,
n$\widetilde{am}$. den voorgemelte Jan Thomassen (bij geleegentheijt van een
Half-Vat bier, op het Vertrecken van Sr Johannes Verveelen, burger
en Brouwer van Amsterdam in Nieuw-Nederlant), in woorden geraeckt
is met eenen Claertie de Mof, selfs tot slaens toe, en dat sijn
Hemb van de voornoemde soude opgescheurt wesen. Maer dat de
voorsch$\widetilde{r}$. Kleeft daer op gekoomen is, ende trock den opgemelte Jan
Thomassen bij het Haijr, die syn mes getrocken, en daer mede vier
sneden gegeeven heeft in 't Wambaijs van den meergemelte Cleeft,
ja de selfde eijndelijck gewont heeft.
Sijn Soon Thomas Janssen bekende, dat hij uijt kinderlijcke

Translation

reader shall also be exempted from houserent and provided with
comfortable housing by the aforesaid consistory.

August 7 [1661]

We were sorry to hear that Teunis Jansen, the latest deacon
elected in our congregation, reportedly was accused of having
detained one or two pigs, about three years of age and belonging
to Michiel Tades, living in Amsterdam in New Netherland. And
[he] was reported to have sold one of them to Mr. Evert Duycking,
glazier in the place mentioned above; indeed, reportedly [he] had
already made an arrangement [to that end] at the home of Albert
Corn[elissen] Wantenaers, a former schepen living in Breuckelen,
in the presence of several people, which caused great suspicion
and annoyance. He was questioned about this and seriously
challenged [in his contention] that the aforesaid pigs were his
and did not belong to the aforesaid Tades. However, [he] declared in good conscience that they were his and promised to prove it
fully with reliable witnesses who have known them all the time
and will acknowledge it.
When we asked what, then, had motivated him to make up the
afore-mentioned contract, which no innocent person would ever
consider necessary, [he] replied and said that he had been advised to do so by most of his acquaintances in order to prevent any
kind of trouble and that he had found himself deceived [in this
respect] to his own disadvantage. Upon his insistence that he
was innocent of detaining someone else's property, we advised him
that, if he loved his own name and did not seek to cause any
offense to the world, he should do his duty in order to secure
an attestation as to his innocence: [he should] revoke the
arrangement in the Court of Breuckelen or, [even more] expedient,
in the presence of the Lord Director-General and Councillors of
New Netherland, and in so doing, remove the suspicions caused by
the written agreement, or [else] we would be compelled to take
action against him which we would dislike very much.

September 21

Jan Thomaszen, summoned by the consistory of Breuckelen together with his son on account of a certain unfortunate incident
whereby he had drawn his knife and wounded Jan Cleeft in the village of New Utrecht, acknowledged that he, namely the afore-
mentioned Jan Thomassen (while enjoying half a barrel of beer on
the occasion of the departure of Sir Johannes Verveelen, burgher
and brewer of Amsterdam in New Netherland), had gotten into an
argument with a certain Claertie de Mof[18]; that they even had
come to blows; and that his shirt had been torn by the aforesaid
[Claertie]. Thereupon, however, the aforesaid Kleeft had come
and had pulled the afore-mentioned Jan Thomassen's hair, who
[then] drew his knife and made four cuts in the afore-mentioned
Cleeft's jerkin - indeed, wounding him eventually.
His son, Thomas Janssen, declared that because of filial

Original

Affectie niet en konde verdragen, dat sijn Vader Jan Thomassen van
de voorgenoemde Jan van Cleeft by 't Haijr gevat en qualyck mis-
handelt wiert, so heeft den meergemelte Thomas syn Vader te hulpe
gekoomen, en Jan van Cleeft bij de Schouders afgeruckt. Hier mede
vat oock van Cleeft den voorschreven Thomas bij het Haijr, ende
Hendrick Matthijssen vat hem by de voeten, en smyten hem ter
aerden. Maer Thomas Janssen verclaert mitsdesen geen van beijde
wederom geslagen te hebben; maer alleenlyck om los gelaten te worden, Jan van Cleeft bij 't haijr gevat te hebben.
Daervan met malkanderen gesproocken hebbende, oordeelen dat (alsoo
Jan Thomaszen eijgentlijck geen ledemaet van de kercke J. Christi
tot Breuckelen is, maer daer, tot noch, op sijn Versoeck 't Avontmael des Heeren genooten heeft, behoorende tot de gemeynte van
Middelwout, en wonachtig in de durpe Nieuw-Uytrecht) Voor dese
wyse hem selven sal moeten van de Tafel des Heeren in de durpe van
Breuckelen onthouden, omdat syn saecke tegenwoordig is berustende
bij de E: H^r Dr Generael en Raden, nochte versoent is met den opgemelte Cleeft, die seer gewont is, nochte met dese gemeente, die
daer van geergert soude wesen. Maer dat syn Soon, te deser
Plaetse tot Ledemaet aengenoomen, en meer berouw en leetwesen be-
toonende, soude toegelaten worden, ende met eene gewaerschouwt, om
sig voortaen te wachten, en voorsichtig te wesen omme onse gemeente in sulcke oft andere Voorvallen geen occasie van Ergernisse
te geeven. 't Welcke beijde aengeseyt en voorgestelt is.

Alsoo Theunis Jansen, tegenwoordig diacon van de gemeynte tot
Breuckelen, daer te vooren van gesproocken is, beschuldigt was van
Twee driejarige Beerverckens, toebehoorende (so men seijde) aen
eene Michiel Tades, opgehouden, ende Een van beijde aen Mr Evert
Duijcking verkocht te hebben, en daer op tot geen geringe naden-
ckinge met den Voornoemde Michiel Tades geaccoordeert was op Vijf
en sestig guldens in de maent februario eerstkoomende te betalen,
so hebben wy wederom met den opgemelte Theunis Janssen daer van
gesproocken, sijn beschuldinge voorgeleijt, Ende Ergernisse, den
Swacken gegeeven, met droeffenisse te vooren gedragen.
Waer op de geseijde Teunis verklaert heeft, gelijck hij verclaert
bij desen voor syn medebroederen, van geenderlye ophoudinge bewust
te wesen, maer blijckelijck bij Attestatie van Mr Evert Duijcking,
en gantsche Huysgesin, bij Attestatie van Sara de Plancke, ledemaet, en weduwe van Pieter Montfoort, by wijlen Diacon van onse
gemeente, als oock van Jan Martijn, jnwoonder en ledemaet der
Durpe en kercke van Breuckelen, bij Attestatien van Willem Gerritsen van Couwenhooven, ledemaet en Scheepen, Ende ten laesten by
Attestatie van Jacob Leendertsen van der Grift, jnwoonder van
Bergen, bewesen te hebben, dat hij geen andere, maer syn Eygen
Beerverckens verkocht ofte opgehouden heeft. Vertoonende oock
seeckere Citatie van de E: H. Directeur Generael door de Gerechts-
bode op Albert Cornelissen Wantenaer, out Schepen en ledemaet, en
Salomon la Chair, notaris der Stede Amsterdam in N. Nederl^t, Haer
selfs offereerende Arbiters van de Voorgemelte Saecke, om wederom
Haer gegeeven uytspraecke te sien, oft te hooren voor de E: H. D^r
Generael en H. H. Raden van Nieuw-Nederlant, annihileeren, ten
minsten corrigeeren, oft beteren. Mitsgaders 't Extract uyt het
Register der Sententien, daer de Hooggemelte H. Dr Generael en
H. H. Raden annihileeren, ende annulleeren ten vollen, den

Translation

affection he could not bear the fact that his father, Jan Thomassen, was grabbed by the hair and badly maltreated by the aforesaid Jan van Cleeft, so the afore-mentioned Thomas came to the
help of his father and pulled Jan van Cleeft off by the shoulders.
Thereupon, Van Cleeft grabbed the aforesaid Thomas, too, by the
hair and Hendrick Matthijssen grabbed him by his feet; and [they]
threw him on the floor. Thomas Janssen hereby contends, however,
that he struck neither of the two again but merely grabbed Jan
van Cleeft by the hair in order to be let go.
     After discussing the matter among ourselves, it is [our] judge-
ment, (as Jan Thomaszen strictly speaking is not a member of the
Church of Jesus Christ in Breuckelen but so far has partaken of
the Lord's Supper there at his own request, while belonging to
the congregation of Midwout and living in the village of New
Utrecht) that because of his conduct, [he] will have to stay
away from the Lord's Table in the village of Breuckelen since his
case is currently in the hands of the Hon. Lord Director-General
and Councillors and since [he] has reconciled himself neither
with the afore-mentioned Cleeft, who is seriously injured, nor
with this congregation, which would be offended by it. His son,
however, who was confirmed as a member in this place and showed
more penitence and regret, would be admitted and at the same time
warned to be on guard and careful in the future in order not to
cause any offense to our congregation with such or other incid-
ents. Both were notified and informed of this.
     Since, as we mentioned before, Theunis Jansen, currently
deacon of the congregation in Breuckelen, had been accused of
detaining two three-year-old boars belonging (reportedly) to a
certain Michiel Tades, selling one of the two to Mr. Evert Duijcking and thereupon making an arrangement with the aforesaid Michiel Tades[19] for the payment of sixty-five guilders in the month
of February next, which caused no small suspicion, we talked
again about this to the afore-mentioned Theunis Janssen, confront-
ed him with the accusations against him, and expressed our
sorrow about the offense caused to the poor man.
     Whereupon the said Teunis declared, as he declares hereby to
his brethren, that he was unaware of any detention but had
proved - as it appears from an attestation by Mr. Evert Duijcking and [his] entire family; from an attestation by Sara de
Plancke, a member and widow of Pieter Montfoort, the late deacon
of our congregation; as well as [from one] by Jan Martijn, a resident and member of the village and Church of Breuckelen; from
an attestation by Willem Gerritsen van Couwenhooven, a member and
schepen; and finally, from an attestation by Jacob Leendertsen
van der Grift, a resident of Bergen - that he had not sold or
detained any boars but his own. He also showed a certain.citat-
ion by the Hon. Lord Director-General, [taken] by the court-
messenger to Albert Cornelissen Wantenaer, former schepen and
member, and to Salomon la Chair, notary of the town of Amsterdam
in New Netherland, who had offered themselves as arbitrators in
the afore-mentioned case, [a citation] to the effect that they
should revise their sentence or hear [the case] in the presence
of the Hon. Lord Director-General and the Lords Councillors of
New Netherland, [and that they should] annul, [or] at least
correct or improve, [the sentence]. Furthermore, [he showed] the
abstract from the register of sentences in which the afore-
mentioned Lord Director-General and Lords Councillors annul and

Original

[13^r: "Pag. 24"]

voorgenoemde abusive uytspraecke, met eenen verclaerende, dat
Michiel Tades t'onrechte eenige Actie ten lasten van Teunis Jansen
heeft gevonteert ter saecke van de meergemelte Verckens.
Met de Broederen des kerckenraets daer van spreeckende, ende alles
pro en Contra overweegende, wort geoordeelt naer serieuse en rijpe
deliberatien, uyt de veelvoudige Attestatien en documenten, die
ten meestendeele van de ledematen van Breuckelen; voornamentlijck
uyt de Sententie des Hooge Raets van Nieuw-Nederlant, syn onschult
t'eenemael vertoonende, ende contrarie annulleerende, Ende daerenboven uyt syn geloofwaerdige Verclaringe, die hy op syn conscientie
gedaen heeft, den voorgemelte onschult belangende, dat wy ter weerelt geen redenen soude hebben, als Syn Eerw^e te continueeren in
syn seer loffelycke bedieninge, gelyck wy Syn Eerw^e continueeren
mits desen, ende, als vooren, met broederlijcke Affectie en toege-
neegentheeden omhelsen, Hem ex officio bestraffende van dit voorgenoemde accoort, ende seer beclagende over de jnjurie en opgeviste
beschuldinge. Actum, ut supra.

Den 2. octob.

Naer behoorlycke belijdenisse des Geloofs, ende gewoonelycke beloften van Christelycke Subjectie des kerckelycke Ban, dien wij
onderworpen syn, niet ongesont te wesen van leer oft leeven, wiert
tot een litmaet der Christelycke kercke aengenoomen,

        Jan Clerck, van Braziel,
            Wiens getuygen syn,
                Jan Jorissen, Gerrit Dirckzen Crousen.

Vorders heeft Jan Hibon, die bij de kercke van Amsterdam in Nieuw-
Nederlant gecensureert was, versocht om toegelaten te worden tot
het gebruyck des Avontmaels, ende hebbende aen Henricus Selyns,
Predicant van de gemeynte J. Christi tot Breuckelen, daegs te
vooren gebracht syn Attestatie van den Eerw^e Vader d^o Johannes
Megapolensis, dienaer des Goddelijcke Woorts tot Amsterdam in
N. Nederlant, dien syn Eerw^e, als 't blyckt, in de latijnsche Tale
om seer gewichtige Reedenen geschreeven hadde;

Lator hujus, Jan Hibon dictus, ante hac, hic habitans, nec bene
vivens, ei Caena fuit interdicta. Aliquoties petyt, ut sibi ad
Caenam Domini accedere liceret, ut nost[r]i. Quod si resipuerit
ab illâ malâ Vitâ, et bene modo vivat (quod Vestri Pagi Incolis
melius notum erit, quam nobis) per nos licebit, ut eum ad usum
Caenae recipiatis.
Amsmi. i. 8br. 1661
                (onderstont)

                J. Megapolensis

Ende na den Voornoemde Jan Hibon ten dien eijnde verneemende, so
bij de leedematen die met hem op het Veer sijn woonende, als bij
ieder lit van de kerckenraedt, seyde t'samen, dat hij, so veel

Translation

fully nullify the aforesaid erroneous sentence, stating at the same time that Michiel Tades had unjustly taken action against Teunis Jansen in the case of the pigs mentioned above.

After discussing this with the brethren of the consistory and weighing all pros and cons, it is judged, upon serious and careful deliberations, that - based upon the manifold attestations and documents, most of which [written] by members of Breuckelen, [and] especially, the sentence of the High Council of New Netherland, which shows his innocence altogether and completely annuls the unfavorable [verdict], and moreover, the credible statement that he made in good conscience with regard to the aforesaid innocence - there is no other consideration in the world for us than to continue him in his very laudable service, as we continue him herewith, and to embrace him as before with brotherly affection and love, reprimanding him "ex officio" [20] for this aforesaid arrangement, and pitying him strongly about the harm [done to him] and the trumped-up charge. Done, as above.

October 2 [1661]

Upon a proper confession of faith and customary pledges of Christian subjection to the ban of the Church, which we are [all] subject to [and which commands us] not to be unsound in doctrine or conduct, the following person was confirmed as a member of the Christian Church:

Jan Clerck, from Brazil,
whose witnesses are:
Jan Jorissen, Gerrit Dirckzen Crousen.

Furthermore, Jan Hibon, who had been placed under censure by the Church of Amsterdam in New Netherland, requested to be admitted to the Lord's Supper. The day before, he had taken to Henricus Selyns, minister of the congregation of Jesus Christ in Breuckelen, his attestation from the Rev. father Domine Johannes Megapolensis, minister of the Word of God in Amsterdam in New Netherland, which, it turned out, the Rev. had written in Latin for very important reasons:

The bearer of this, Jan Hibon, who lived here in the past and whose conduct was improper, was barred from taking the Lord's Supper. Several times he requested permission to partake of the Lord's Supper with us. And if he comes to his senses, abandons his sinful life, and shows good conduct (which will be better known to the people living in your area than to us), you will have our permission to re-admit him to the Lord's Supper.
Amsterdam, October 1, 1661.

(underneath stood)

J. Megapolensis

And after we had made inquiries to that end about the aforesaid Jan Hibon, both among the members who are living with him

29

Original

[14^r: "Pag. 26"]

haer bekent was, tegenwoordig geen onstichtelijck leeven was leij-
dende, Ende ter contrarie seer naerstig tot 't gehoor van Godts
woort koomende. 't Welcke jnsiende, mitsgaders syn onuytspreecke-
lycke geneegentheijt om wederom ten Avontmael te verschynen, hebben
(met 't voorgem. consent van den Hoog-gemelte d? Megapolensis,
welcke hem belast hadde om geen Ergernisse te geven, voor een tydt
te blijven Van de Tafel des Heeren) den meergenoemde Jan Hibon in
genade aengenoomen, ende serieuselijck vermaent om Christelijck te
leeven, en sig te wachten van Schandale en ergernisse, 't geen hy
den Broeders belooft heeft met syn Rechterhant, den Vergaderinge
voor den Tegenwoordige toelatinge bedanckende.

Den 27 Novemb.

Geeft Henricus Selijns te kennen, dat hij heeden met den Aenstaende Wintertijdt sijn Predicatiens wederom sal opschorten op
de Bouwerije van de E: H. Generael Petrus Stuijvesant, en daer
door ten besten van de gemeente tot Breuckelen bequame geleegentheyt heeft, omme 's Sondags na de middag, oft tot Breuckelen te
predicken, ofte als voorgaende Winter geschiet is, te Catechisee-
ren. Maer bevindende dat de Broeders meest geneegen waren om verscheyden redenen tot de catechetische onderwijsinge ten regarde
van de gronden en fundamenten der Christelycke Religie, wiert van
den Voornoemde Henricus Selijns voorgestelt, Oft, gelyckerwijs 't
geschiet in de Schoole tot Breuckelen, en doorgaens in de kercke
en Schoolen van Amsterdam in Nieuw-Nederlant, niet 't alderprofy-
telyckste soude wesen, om 't alderbondigste Vrageboecsken van den
Eerw? Vader D^O Johannes Megapolensis te gebruycken, en na te volgen; geintituleert, Een Korte maniere om de Jeugt te onderwijsen
in de beginselen der Christelycke Religie, ende begrypende Boven
de middelen totter Godsalicheyt en saligheijt dienende, so de verclaringe van de Twaelf Articulen des Christelycke geloofd, als
daer en boven van 't gebedt des Heeren, die beijde seer geleert en
beknoptelyck van syn Eerw? uytgeleyt, ende met Vragen en Antwoort
voorgestelt worden. 'T welcke na 't gebruyck der Amsterdamsche
kercke in N. Nederlant oock vastgestelt en beslooten is.

Den 25 Decemb.

Tot ledematen sijn heden aengenoomen, met behoorlycke Attestatien
van de kercke van Amsterdam in Nieuw-Nederlant, dese navolgende
Persoonen,

    Willem Willemsen,

    Getruyd van Mullem,

    Thomas Verdon,

    Janneken Claes.

Translation

at the Ferry, and from each member of the consistory, [they] all
said that, as far as they knew, he was not leading an offensive
life nowadays, and that, on the contrary, he very diligently came
to hear the Word of God. Acknowledging this, as well as his
ineffable determination to appear at the Lord's Supper again,
[we] (with the afore-mentioned consent of Domine Megapolensis
mentioned above, who had ordered him to stay away from the Lord's
Table for a while in order not to cause any offense) received the
aforesaid Jan Hibon back into favor and admonished him seriously
to live in a Christian way and to refrain from scandal and
offense, which he promised the brethren with his right hand,
whereupon he thanked the meeting for his admission today.

November 27 [1661]

Henricus Selijns notifies us that as per today, in view of the
imminent winter season, he will suspend his preaching at the Hon.
Lord General Petrus Stuijvesant's Bowery [= farm] again, and that
as a consequence, for the benefit of the congregation of Breuckelen, he will have a fine opportunity either to preach or, as in
the previous winter, to give confirmation classes in Breuckelen
on Sundays in the afternoon. However, upon finding that for
several reasons, the brethren were mostly inclined towards cat-
echetic instruction in the principles and foundations of the
Christian religion, it was suggested by the aforesaid Henricus
Selijns [to consider] whether it would not be most rewarding, as
it is done in the school in Breuckelen and usually in the Church
and schools of Amsterdam in New Netherland, to use and follow the
very concise little catechism by the Rev. father Domine Johannes
Megapolensis, entitled: A Brief Method Of Instructing The Youth
In The Principles Of The Christian Religion, comprising not only
the means to attain godliness and salvation, but also the explan-
ation of the Apostles' Creed and, moreover, of the Lord's Prayer,
both of which are explained by the Rev. in a very learned and
concise way and are presented in the form of questions and
answers. This was confirmed and approved in accordance with the
practice in the Amsterdam Church in New Netherland.

December 25

Today, the following persons were confirmed as members, with
proper attestations from the Church of Amsterdam in New Netherland:

Willem Willemsen,

Getruyd van Mullem,

Thomas Verdon,

Janneken Claes.

31

Original

[15^V: "29"]

Anno 1662

Den 22 Januar.

Belangende van Tjerck Thomassen, een Persoon van geen Godtsalig-
heijt, die ons vreemt was, als alleenig dat hij sig qualyck gevoe-
lende, en daer toe een seer been hebbende, sig tot Breuckelen begeeven hadde, ten huyse van Lange Barent, Twee Vogels van eender
Veeren, omme van onse diaconie onderhouden te worden. 't Welcke
(den Voornoemde Tjerck om syn wont en Sieckte na de Stadt gebracht
hebbende) gedaen heeft den Voorschr̄ Diaconie ten halven met de diaconie van Amsterdam in Nieuw-Nederl̄t Maer de Sieckte, met luyich-
eyt vermengt, al te lang duurende, ende voornamentlyck vreesende,
dat schier of morgen onse Armen, die ons nader syn, mochte nadeelig wesen, wiert goet gevonden den Reeckening van de diaconen van
Amsterdam in N. Nederlant, t'onser lasten en t'syner halven uytgeschreeven, ende ver beloopende over de Hondert guldens, te voldoen,
met Versoeck, dat den meergemelte Tjerck mochte volkomentlyck wesen ten lasten van den voorgemelte Diaconie van Amsterdam. Ten
minsten, dat wy ter weerelt niet geneegen waren hem, die 't onwaer-
dig was, meerder te geeven, ende d'Onse te onthouden. 't Geene
Henricus Selyns ende Jan Jorissen aengenoomen Hebben den voornoemde diaconen van Amsterdam aentedienen, en t'geen wy schuldig waren
te betalen.

Den 12 Martij

Met de seegeninge des Alderhoogsten, ten besten van Nieuw-Nederlant, wiert ons door de Gerechte van Breuckelen ter hande gestelt,
dese Navolgende Uijtschryvinge van de E: H. D̄r Generael en Raden,
omme metten aenstaende Woensdag te houden eene algemeene Danck,
Vast en Bededag, ende in diervoegen luijdende,

Eersame, Lieve, Besondere,

Niet tegenstaende den Grooten God, als een Rechtvaerdige Richter,
dese Provintie in 't gemeen, en Veele jngeseetenen in 't besonder,
't Verleeden jaer om onser veelvoudiger Sonden wille (onder de
welcke de minste niet en sijn, onse ondanckbaerheeden wegens voor
genooten Weldaden, Segeningen en Bescherminge tegens buijten en
binnen lantsche Vijanden) merckelyck besocht heeft, Elders met
heete Pestilentiale en voor desen noyt gehoorde koortsen, Sieckte,
en quellingen, Elders met onverwachte Regen en watervloeden in de
Somer, waer door de apparente oogst de inwoonderen t'eenemael onvruchtbaer is gemaeckt, Elders met al te groote en heete Sonne-
schijn, de verwachten Vruchten des Velts bevangen Schaers en by-
cans onvruchtbaer syn geworden, neffens meer andere besoeckinge,
so geen Straffen. Efter heeft Hy oock als een barmhertigen
goedertieren Vader in 't midden syner Rechtvaerdige oordeelen des
ontfermens gedacht, segenende dese Provintie in 't gemeen, en
veele ingeseetenen in 't besonder, met aenmerckelycke en

Translation

A.D. 1662

January 22

This concerns Tjerck Thomassen, a person without piety who was
a stranger to us except for the fact that, feeling poorly and
having a sore leg for that purpose, he had come to Breuckelen, to
the house of Lange [= Tall] Barent, two birds of a feather, in
order to be supported by our deaconry. The aforesaid deaconry
did so [indeed], (after it had taken the aforesaid Tjerck to the
town[21] because of his wound and illness), together with the
deaconry of Amsterdam in New Netherland on a fifty-fifty basis.
However, because the ailment, mixed with laziness, lasted too
long and especially because [we] feared that, sooner or later, it
might be disadvantageous to our poor who are dearer to us, it was
decided to pay the bill of the deacons of Amsterdam in New Netherland, made out to us on his behalf and amounting to far more than
a hundred guilders, with the request that the afore-mentioned
Tjerck become entirely chargeable to the afore-mentioned deaconry
of Amsterdam, [and informing them] that at any rate, we had no
intention in the world to give any more to him, who was unworthy
of it, and to withhold it from our people.
Henricus Selyns and Jan Jorissen took it upon themselves to
notify the aforesaid deacons of Amsterdam hereof and to pay what
we owed.

March 12

With the blessing of the Most High for the best of New Netherland, we were handed by the Court of Breuckelen the following
ordinance from the Hon. Lord Director-General and Councillors,
calling for a general day of thanksgiving, fasting, and prayers
to be held this Wednesday; it read as follows:

Respectable, Dear, [and] Special [People],

The Great God, as a righteous judge, considerably afflicted
this province in general, and many of its inhabitants in particular last year, on account of our manifold sins (not the least
of which is our ingratitude for benefits, blessings, and protection received against foreign and domestic enemies). In some
places, [He struck] with the hot plague and unheard-of fevers,
illnesses, and torments; in other places, with unexpected rains
and summer floodings, rendering the apparent crops entirely
worthless to the inhabitants; elsewhere, with too much and too
hot sunshine, scourging the expected produce of the fields so
that it became scarce and almost worthless; as well as with
other visitations if not punishments. On the other hand, however, as a merciful and clement father, in the middle of His
righteous judgements, He also remembered to take pity, blessing
this province in general, and many inhabitants in particular,

Original

[16^r: "Pag. 30"]

danckbaerheyts-waerdige gunsten en weldaden, onder de welcke de
geringste niet en sijn, De genadige afwendinge en geneesinge van
Bovengemelte ongemeene Sieckte en koortsen, de continuatie van ge-
wenste Ruste en Vrede in 't midden van so veele Vyanden, en tegen
v̄scheyden geruchte van nieuwe onlusten en benaderingen, Elders
wederom met een goede en Vruchtbaren ooghst.   En het welcke noch
boven alle desen te Estimeeren is, de onderhoudinge van synen
Suyvere Godtsdienst, en Vreedsame genietinge van het heldere en
onbevleckte licht Synes Euangeliums op onse kandelaer.   't welck
(hoewel beclaegelyck) op veele plaetsen, oft door vervolginge ver-
druckt, oft door menschelycke jnsettinge bevleckt en verdonckert
wert, welcke en veele meer andere gonsten, segeningen en weldaden,
ons dan niet alleen aen de Zyde behooren te verplichten tot alle
danckbaerheyt, nemaer oock de Vermengelinge van syne Vaderlycke
Castydinge, soo geen straffen, onder de selve ons dan oock behooren te bewegen tot opmerckinge om d'eene door danckschuldige gebeeden over ons te behouden, de andere door ware demoet en Boet-
veerdigheyt des leevens van ons te weeren, 't welck dan om in de
eerste plaetse neffens den alleen goeden Godt te betoonen, ende in
de tweede plaetse van hem als Autheur en geever van alle geeste-
lycke en lichaemelycke Weldaden te verwerven.   Het heeft den
Direct:^{r} Generl en Raeden nodig gedacht, tot dien eijnde te bera-
men en uytteschryven een algemeene Danck, Vast en Bededach, die
alomme binnen desen Provintie gehouden sal worden op Woensdag
synde den 15 meert.   oversulcks worden alle ingeseetenen Deser
Provintie, so wel officieren als onderdaenen bij desen gelast, ten
Voorschr. daege in de kercke, ofte daer men gewoon is Godts woort
te predicken oft voor te leesen, te verschijnen, omme na aenhooringe des Selfs, met nedrige en verslagen Herte, de Name des Heeren vieriglyck aenteroepen, Hem te bidden, en te smeecken, dattet
syn Goddelijcke Majesteijt gelieve sijne Rechtvaerdige Plaegen en
wel verdiende Straffen van ons af te wenden en te doen cesseren,
de Vrede en goede Correspondentie onder ons en onse nabueren te
continueeren, en ons in dese eerst opluyckende provintie in sijn
Vaderlycke bescherminge aen te neemen, en tegens alle quade prac-
ticquen te mainteneeren, de Vruchten der aerden met Vroegen en
Spaeden Regen te Seegenen, en voor al onder ons te laten wassen en
toeneemen synes naems Vreese en kennisse, en onser eygener sonden
haet, 't welck opdat te beter gepractiseert en naergekomen mag
worden, Direct^r Generl. en Raeden verbieden ten Voorsc Danck, Vast
en Bededag alle Exercitie en oeffeninge, van kaetsen, Balslaen,
Visschen, Vaeren, ploegen en Saeijen, mitsgaders alle ongeoorlofde Speelen, als dobbelen en droncken drincken, op d'amende voormaels daer op gestelt, en worden de dienaren van Godes H. Woort
binnen dese Provintie versocht, haere Predicatien en gebeeden ten
voorsch. eijnde te willen formeeren.   Aldus gedaen ter Vergaederinge van den E: Heere Direct^r Generael en Raden gehouden in 't
fort Amsterdam in N. Nederl^t den 26 januarij, A^o 1662.
                    (onderstont)

                              P. Stuijvesant

Ter ordonnantie van den E: H^{re} Dr Generael en Raden van
N. Nederl^t,
                    (leger stont)

                              C V Ruijven, Secrets.

Translation

with remarkable favors and benefits worthy of gratitude, not the
least of which are the merciful warding off and cure of the afore-
mentioned unusual illnesses and fevers, the continuation of the
desired calm and peace amidst so many enemies and in spite of
rumors about new disturbances and approaches, and in other places,
a good and rich harvest; also, and deserving even more appreciat-
ion than all of this, the preservation of the purity of the
divine worship and the peaceful enjoyment of the clear and un-
blemished light of His Gospel on our candlestick, which in many
places (no matter how regrettable it is), either was repressed
by persecution or blemished and darkened through human doing.
Not only should these and many other favors, blessings, and
benefits oblige us to be very grateful, the fact that they were
mixed with His paternal castigations, if not punishments, should
also induce us to do what we can to preserve the former for us
through the prayers of thanks that we owe Him, and to turn the
latter away from us through genuine humbleness and penitent
behavior, so that first of all we show the only good God [our
gratitude], and second, we honor Him as the author and giver of
all spiritual and material benefits. The Director-General and
Councillors have deemed it necessary to plan and prescribe a general day of thanksgiving, fasting, and prayers for that purpose,
which will be held everywhere in this province on Wednesday,
March 15. For this reason, all inhabitants of this province,
both administrators and subjects, are hereby ordered to appear in
church on the aforesaid day, or wherever one is accustomed to
preach or read the Word of God, in order to hear the Word of God,
to invoke ardently the Name of the Lord with a humble and submissive heart, and to beg and beseech Him, if His Divine Majesty
pleases, to turn His righteous plagues and well-deserved punishments away from us and to put an end to them; to continue the
peace and good harmony between us and our neighbors; to take us
and this nascent province under His paternal protection and to
preserve us from all evil practices; to bless the fruits of the
earth with early and late rains; and especially, to make the fear
and knowledge of His Name, and the hatred of our own sins, grow
and increase among us. For the sake of optimum compliance [with
our orders], the Director-General and Councillors prohibit all
exertion and exercise on the aforesaid day of thanksgiving,
fasting, and prayers, namely handball and other ball games [22],
fishing, sailing, plowing, and sowing, as well as all illegal
pastimes such as playing dice and getting drunk, on the penalties
laid down in the past; and the ministers of the Holy Word of God
within this province are requested to word their sermons and
prayers to the aforesaid end. Done in the meeting of the Hon.
Lord Director-General and Councillors, held in Fort Amsterdam in
New Netherland on January 26, 1662.
          (underneath stood)

P. Stuijvesant

By order of the Hon. Lord Director-General and Councillors of
New Netherland,
          (underneath stood)

C. V. Ruijven, Secretary[23]

35

Original

[17^V: "Pag. 33"]

Den 2 April

Na de gewoonelycke Aenroepinge des Alderhoogsten en belydenisse
des ware Gereformeerde gelooft is tot lidtmaet geworden,

Brechtie Hans, van N. Nederl^t,
wiens getuygen sijn,
Teunis Gijsbertsen, en Jan Jorissen.

En daer na wiert voorgestelt de Saecke van Rem Jansen en Janneken
Joris, voor dese beijde ledemaeten van de kercke J. Christi tot
Beverwijck hier te lande. Sij brachten, tot ons koomende, geen
Attestatie door absentie van de Eerw^e D^o Gideon Schaets, bedienaer
des H. Euangeliums van de voorgemelte plaetse, maer Acte van getuijgenisse van wijle d^o Bogardus. Hebben ten dien eijnde afgevordert, gelijck dit allenthalven behoorlyck is, nieuwe Attestatie,
aengaende Hun leeven en geloove, van den Tegenwoordige Predicant
en Opsiender des Gemeynte. Sulcks geschreeven synde, door Rem
Jansen oft door de syne, kreeg eijgentlyck geen Attestatie, maer
eerder Reprehensie van ordinarische versuyminge der Publycke Godsdiensten, met nader Vermaninge om naerstiger sigh na desen te begeeven tot de Predicatien en gehoor des Goddelycke Woorts. En dit
wiert behalven hem geschreeven aen de leeraren des Gemeynte van
Amsterdam in N. Nederl^t Wy dan volgens plicht, becommert over de
saecke, verwondert van de getuygenisse, konde nochte Rem Janssen
tot ledemaet, nochte syn Attestatie accepteeren voor genoegsaem,
dat meerder streckte tot detestatie.
Maer geschreeven hebbende na voorgaende Communicatie van den E:
kerckenraet belangende 't Voorverhaelde comportement van Rem
Janssen met warachtige Declaratie aengaende syn tegenwoordige
comportement en yver tot de publycke Predicatien, t'samen gevoegt
met Godtsalicheyt des leevens, wiert ons van den Eerw^e D^o Gideon
Schaets metten eersten gerepliceert en geschreeven: dat men hem
soude aenneemen beneffens syn Huysvrouw naer onse tegenwoordige
Getuijgenisse, en dat sijn Voorgemelt Schrijvens eer streckte tot
Vermaninge, en opweckinge in de Practijcke der Godtsalicheyt, als
tot gewoonelycke getuygenisse. So is't, dat wij de saecke in de
kerckenraedt voorgestelt, Advijsen ten dien eynde afgevordert,
ende tot dese Resolutien gebracht hebben, dat beijde Rem Janssen
en Janneken Joris van Couverden, alrede bij 't jaer onder ons gewoont, geen Ergernisse tot noch toe gegeeven, sorvuldiglyck tot
het gehoor des Salichmaeckende Woorts gekoomen, na desen niet Pro-
visioneel, maer na voorgaende Afkondinge voor de Gemeente, neffens
onse ledematen sullen tot 't bovengemelte gebruijck des Avontmaels
toegelaten werden, en daer wy toe wenschen de Segen des Heeren, en
volstandigheyt des geloofs en Godtsalicheyt tot salicheyt hunner
beijde, en afweeringe van Ergernisse uyt de gemeente des Heeren.

Boven dit wiert den Eerw^e Kerckenraedt voorgedragen, tot leetwesen
en cleijnachtinge der Selfde, dat Gerrit Dirckzen Croesen van
Wynschooten, ledemaet onser gemeente, met seer groote Stouticheijt
en onbeschaemtheijt heeft sig derven onderwinden, Omme (buyten
alle Kerckelijcke Ordonnantien, gewoonelycke Proceduuren, recht en
reden, en buijten tijdts, Selfs den Sabbathdag, ten Godtsdienst
verordineert en streckende tot Voorbereijdinge en Beproevinge ten

Translation

April 2 [1662]

Upon the customary invocation of the Most High and a confession of the true Reformed faith, the following person became a member:

Brechtie Hans, from New Netherland,
whose witnesses are:
Teunis Gijsbertsen, and Jan Jorissen.

Thereupon, the case of Rem Jansen and Janneken Prins was brought to the fore, both of them previously members of the Church of Jesus Christ in Beverwijck in this country. Because of the absence of the Rev. Domine Gideon Schaets, minister of the Holy Gospel in the afore-mentioned place, they did not bring along an attestation when they came to us, but a certificate of good character by the late Domine Bogardus. [We] demanded, therefore, as is perfectly proper, a new attestation with regard to their conduct and faith from the present minister and supervisor of the congregation. After Rem Jansen or his people had sent a letter for that purpose, [he] in fact did not receive an attestation but, rather, a reprehension for frequently missing the public worship, with a further exhortation to attend the sermons and hear the Word of God more diligently in the future. And this was written on his behalf to the ministers of the congregation of Amsterdam in New Netherland. We, worried about the case and surprised by the certificate, did our duty and could neither confirm Rem Janssen as a member, nor be content with his attestation, which in fact was a detestation.

However, after the preceding communication, the Hon. Consistory wrote a letter concerning the aforesaid Rem Janssen's conduct, including a true statement as to his current behavior and devotion to the public worship, combined with his pious way of life. The Rev. Domine Gideon Schaets replied at once and wrote us that, based upon our present attestations, we should confirm him as well as his wife [as members], and that his afore-mentioned letter had served as an exhortation and urge to live piously, rather than as an ordinary attestation. For that reason, we raised the matter in the consistory, took advice, and came to the following resolution: that both Rem Janssen and Janneken Joris van Couverden [= of Coevorden] - who have already been living among us for almost a year, causing no offense so far and taking care to attend the preaching of the sanctifying Word - will be permitted to partake of the afore-mentioned Lord's Supper, henceforth no longer on a provisional basis but, upon a proclamation to the congregation, together with our members. And we wish [them] the Lord's blessing to that end and firmness in faith and piety, for the sake of their salvation and for the preservation of the Lord's congregation from any offense.

Furthermore, it was brought to the attention of the Hon. Consistory, to their regret and disdain, that Gerrit Dirckzen Croesen van Wynschooten [= of Winschoten], a member of our congregation, has dared, with extreme wickedness and impudence (in violation of all Ordinances of the Church and customary procedures, without any right or justification, and at an inappropriate time, abusing even the Sabbath for this impudent scheme, a day reserved for the

Original

[18^V: "Pag. 35"]

Aenstaende Avontmale, tot dit onbeschaemt Voorneemen misbruyckende)
den Persoon Henricus Selyns, in qualite syn wettige Predicant en
Leeraer, ende gekoomen in Commissie van den Kerckenraet om sijn
Visite te doen en ledematen te nodigen tot den Tafel des Heeren,
te citeeren, en te doen citeeren door den Gerechtsbode, omme
metten eerste Sitdag te verschijnen voor den Subalterne banck van
Breuckelen, uyt oorsaecken van seeckere onbehoorlycke, en t'eenemael on Christelycke Geruchten, die wy hem Ex Officio, Conscienties
wegen, en volgens kerckelycke Resolutien bekentgemaeckt hebben, met
onse seer waerde Medebroeder Wilhelmus Bredebend, Ouderling en Gedeputeerde tot de Visite, niet binnen's huys, om voor syn huysvrouw
niet beschaemt te worden, maer buytens huys met den voorgemelte
Crousen tredende, om ten bequaemste maniere en na behooren onderricht te worden aengaende de Geruchten, die alomme notoir en bekent
waren, van seeck're Bomen verleeden Beedag uytgegraven en meê genoomen te hebben, die hem niet toe en quamen.
Desen Geruchten dan Loopende en serieuselyck geconfirmeert worden-
de, seyde den Voorgemelte Henricus Selyns en Willem Bredenbend,
dat sij ('t welcke te vooren bij de kerckenraet goetgevonden was)
den Voornoemde Croesen niet konden noodigen tot den Tafel des Heeren, dan met Christelijcke en schuldige openbaringe van 't geene
dat alreede achter syn rugge verspreyt wiert, beyde tot sijner en
onser Gemeentes Schantvlecke. Ende spraecken tot den meergemelte
Crousen ten dien eynde, so 't waer was, dat dit Streckte en behoorde te dienen tot berouw en ware Bekeeringe, So 't logen was,
tot Waerschouwinge, om allenthalven sig te mijden van dese en diergelycke Ergernisse, ende in alle gevallen wiert hij ten dien eynde
aengesproocken van den Voornoemde Selyns, als syn Predicant, die
't toekomt plichtshalven syn Ledematen tydelyck en̄ ontydelyck te
vermanen, ende in sulcke voorvallen na de aerdt der liefde te waerschouwen.
Den Eerw? kerckenraedt, seer misnoegt metten voorgemelte onbehoorlycke Proceduuren en noytgehoorde Citatie, ende approbeerende 't
geene Henricus Selyns, Predicant, ende Wilhelmus Bredenbend, ouderling, beyde onse seer waerde medebroeders ende gedeputeerde ter
Visite en gewoonelijcke noodinge onser ledematen, volgens plicht
en voorgaende toestemminge gesproocken hebben tot den Persoon van
Gerrit Dircksen Croesen van Wynschoten, daer de geruchten voornoemt van waren, Oordeelen, dat den meergemelte Henricus Selijns
onwettiglyck, ontdiglyck en onbehoorlyck geciteert is voor den
Politicen Rechtbanck, daer geen kerckelycke Geschillen oft kunnen
oft meugen na de jnstellinge Christi afgedaen worden, Van ledematen tusschen ledematen, Veel min dan van ledematen tegens de kerckenraet ofte gecommitteerde der Selfde, ten Eynde der kerckelycke
discipline, die Christus ten dien regarde ingestelt, en den Voorn.
Croesen selfs belooft heeft na gewoonelycke maniere der Aenneeminge
sig t'allen tyden te onderwerpen.
Ende wat daer op behoorde te volgen, wiert Goet gevonden, den meergemelte Selyns te versoecken, om daer van te spreecken met den
Eerw?, Godtsalige, en Hooggeleerde Vader d^O Johannes Megapolensis,
bedienaer des Goddelycke Woorts tot Amsterdam in Nieuw-Nederlant.
Of wy soude den Voornoemde Gerrit Dircksen Crousen voor den kerckenraet metten eersten ontbieden, oft niet, Of wy tegens hem
handelen soude met kerckelycke Censure, oft niet, ende of wy
voor den Gerechte geciteert verschijnen soude, ofte niet.

Translation

divine worship and for abstinence in preparation of the imminent Lord's Supper), to cite, and to have cited by the court-messenger, the person of Henricus Selyns, his lawful minister and teacher who under commission of the consistory had come [to him] for a pastoral visit inviting the members to the Lord's Table. [The citation read] to the effect that he[24] will have to appear in the Lower Court of Breuckelen during the next day of session in connection with certain improper and utterly unchristian rumors that we [25] informed him [26] of "ex officio"[27], conscientiously, and in accordance with Church resolutions, accompanied by our very dear colleague, Wilhelmus Bredebend, elder and deputy present during the pastoral visit - not inside the house, but after we had gone outside with the afore-mentioned Crousen lest he be embarrassed in front of his wife, so that he was told in the most suitable and proper way about the rumors which were notorious and known everywhere [and which implied] that on the latest day of prayers he had dug out and taken with him certain trees that did not belong to him.

As these rumors were circulating and were confirmed beyond doubt, the afore-mentioned Henricus Selyns and Willem Bredenbend said (with the congregation's approval) that they could not invite the aforesaid Croesen to the Lord's Table unless there would be a Christian and penitent disclosure of what was already being said behind his back, to the disgrace of both himself and our congregation. And [we] talked to the afore-mentioned Crousen for that purpose [telling him] that, if it were true, this would and should induce him to [show] remorse and true repentance, and if it were a lie, this would serve as a warning to avoid these and similar offenses by all means. Anyway, he was addressed for that purpose by the aforesaid Selyns, his minister, whose right and duty it is to exhort his members, timely and untimely, and to warn them in such instances in the name of love.

The Hon. Consistory - very displeased with the improper procedures mentioned above and with the unheard-of citation, and approving of what Henricus Selyns, minister, and Wilhelmus Bredenbend, elder, both very dear colleagues of ours and delegates for pastoral visits and for the customary invitation of our members, have said, dutifully and with permission, to the person of Gerrit Dircksen Croesen van Wynschoten [= of Winschoten] whom the afore-said rumors referred to - is of opinion that the afore-mentioned Henricus Selijns was unlawfully, untimely, and improperly cited in the Secular Court where, according to Christ's precepts, no Church disputes can nor may be settled, neither [those] among members, much less [those] between members and the consistory or its delegate, for the sake of Church discipline which Christ instituted for that purpose and which the aforesaid Croesen himself had promised to submit to at all times during the traditional confirmation ritual.

And [as to] what ought to be done next, it was decided to request that the afore-mentioned Selyns discuss the matter with the Rev., pious, and very learned father Domine Johannes Megapolensis, minister of the Word of God in Amsterdam in New Netherland, [namely] whether we should at once summon the aforesaid Gerrit Dircksen Crousen to the consistory or not; whether we should take action against him with Church censure or not; and whether we should appear in the Court in which we were cited or not.

Original

[19^V: "Pag. 37"]

't geene Henricus Selyns (ten besten van de gemeente, en ten versoeck van de Eerw^e kerckenraet, die 't voorschreven Citatie seer
gemoeyt heeft) heeft aengenoomen uyt Haer name te doen.

Den 5 dicto

Volgens Ordre en Commissie wiert van Henricus Selyns gerapporteert
't Advijs, en seer gesont oordeel, van den Eerw^e, Godtsalige, en
Hoog-geleerde Vader, D^o Johannes Megapolensis; dat wy Gerrit
Crousen metten eersten ontbieden souden, 't geen wy om Tegenwoordig te verschijnen, door den Gerechtsbode gedaen hebben: Dat hij
voor de aenstaende Tijdt behoorde van 't Avontmael te absenteeren,
Voor eerst, by forme van Excusatie, als hebbende ten tijde der
Visite gesproocken onbereyt te wesen, door de Tegenwoordige Geruchten mitsgaders andre particuliere Questien met Teunis Nijssen en
Albert Corñ. Wantenaer. En ten Tweeden, by forme van Suspensie,
door Particuliere Haet tegens syn wettige Predicant aengaende de
voorgeñ. Citatie, en streckende tot Suspensie ende ophoudinge des
Gantsche Gemeente van 't Avontmael des Heeren: door Verwerpinge
en cleynachtinge des Kerckenraet, met den Citatie voor den Politicen Raet, daer Civile ende geen kerckelijcke Saecke worden oft
kunnen worden gedecideert en afgedaen: door verbreeckinge syner
beloften, die men gewoon en gehouden is te belooven na de Belijdenisse des geloofs en met de aenneeminge tot Ledematen. Met serieuse vermaninge om Satisfactie te geeven van de geruchten tegens de
naestkoomende Vergaderinge des Eerw^e kerckenraet, Ten dien eijnde,
om dese loopende Ergernisse te weeren uyt de gemeynte des Heeren,
en naer goetgunstigheyt des kerckenraedt aengenoomen dan te worden
in de gemeente des leevendige Godts. Ende dat wy, om niet te
schynen 't Gerechte te verwerpen, soude Schryven aen de Selfde,
met Versoeck omme door den officier informatie te neemen van de
loopende geruchten, en voornamentlyck oft den Voornoemde Crousen
schuldig is, oft niet.
Den kerckenraet, Seer bedanckende den Hooggemelte D^o Johannes
Megapolensis voor Sijn Eerw^e Advijs en jnstructie, lieten Gerrit
Crousen, ontboden synde, binnenstaen, die gevraegt wiert, Uyt wat
cracht en waerom dat hy, die ledemaet was, syn Predicant (die hem
waerschouwde, met Wilhelmus Bredenbent, en die, sulcke Geruchten
loopende, niemant, die daermede beticht wort, soude kunnen tot het
gebruyck des Avontmaels noodigen ten ware naer diergelycke ondersoeckinge en waerschouwinge) geciteert hadde voor den Gerechte,
dat noyt gehoort en niet gebruyckelyck is. Oft so hy ten regarde
van kerckelycke saecke iets te seggen hadde, dat dit de plaetse
was om syn saecke te openbaren en beschuldinge by te brengen.
En hier op heeft de meergemelte Crousen geantwoort, dat het syn
botticheyts schult was, en niet beter en wiste, maer daer toe van
wijser geraden was, selfs ten dien eynde geweest was op de Manhatans, en meer als een halve dag gewacht om Henricus Selyns te
Spreecken, schreuwende tot den E: H^r Generaels te koomen, daer hy
woonde. Persisteerde in syn onschult, en versocht, dat de geene
niet mochten ten avontmael gaen, die sulcks hem nagaven. Mitsgaders, dat Femmetie Nyssens mochte compareeren voor den kerckenraet.
Nam syn reflexie, omdat geseijt was, Hout my voor de Man, daer op

Translation

Henricus Selyns took it upon himself to do this on the consistory's behalf (for the best of the congregation and at the request
of the Hon. Consistory which was very troubled by the aforesaid
citation).

[April] 5 [1662]

In accordance with his order and commission, Henricus Selyns
informed us of the advice and very sound judgement of the Rev.,
pious, and very learned father Domine Johannes Megapolensis,
[namely] that we should summon Gerrit Crousen at once (which we
did through the court-messenger: he will have to appear immediately); [and] that he ought to absent himself from the Lord's
Supper for the time being - first of all, as an apology, since
at the time of the pastoral visit he had voiced unwillingness
[to participate] in view of the current rumors as well as some
private quarrels with Teunis Nijssen and Albert Corn[elissen]
Wantenaer. And second, under a suspension: because of personal
hatred against his lawful minister, as is evident from the afore-
mentioned citation which was aimed at suspending the entire
congregation and withholding the Lord's Supper from them; because
of his rejection and contempt of the consistory, as shown in his
citation in the Secular Council where civil, not Church cases are
or can be decided and settled; [and] for breaking the promises
which one is customarily obligated to make in accordance with the
confession of faith and upon one's confirmation as a member.
In addition, [he should] seriously be admonished to refute the
rumors by the next meeting of the Hon. Consistory in order to
remove the current offense from the Lord's congregation and then
to be admitted, through the consistory's kindness, to the community of the living God. And lest we appear to reject the Court,
we should write them a letter with the request that the prosecutor hold an inquiry into the current rumors and especially into
[the question of] whether the aforesaid Crousen is guilty or not.
The consistory, thanking the afore-mentioned Domine Johannes
Megapolensis very much for his advice and instructions, summoned
Gerrit Crousen and made him appear. He was asked what justification and reason he, a member, had to cite his minister in Court
(who together with Wilhelmus Bredenbent had come to warn him, as
they were unable to invite anyone to the Lord's Supper who was
being accused of the kind of things that were alleged in the
rumors going around, unless after such an inquiry and warning),
which is unheard of and unusual. [We also told him] that, if he
had anything to say with regard to Church matters, this was the
place to make his case public and bring his accusations forward.
And the afore-mentioned Crousen replied to this that [the
citation] was due to his own dullness and that [he] did not know
any better, but that he had been advised by wiser people, even
had gone to Manhattan for that purpose, and had waited for more
than half a day to see Henricus Selyns, shouting he would come to
the Hon. Lord General's place where he [28] was staying. [He] persisted in his innocence and requested that those who pressed such
charges against him be barred from the Lord's Supper, and furthermore, that Femmetie Nyssens be allowed to appear in the consistory. [He] reflected a while upon the remark he [reportedly] had

Original

[20^V: "Pag. 39"]

geantwoort wiert, dat dit sag niet op de waerheyt, maer op de geruchte, want wy seyden, Ick en weet 'et niet, Godt weet 'et, my
kunt gy bedriegen, en godt niet, 't welcke den Voorñ Croesen niet
en ontkende van syn meergenoemde Predicant geseyt te wesen, socht
syn saecke ten laeste te rechtveerdigen met onbehoorlycke verwenschinge, en seggende, So 't waer is, moet ick versincken, ende
daer over bestraft synde, bleeft eeven sterck op den Voorgemelte
verwenschinge ende syns selfs vervloeckinge.
Vorders gevraegt synde, waerom hy voornoemt geciteert hadde Henricum Selijns voor 't Avontmael des Heeren, daer 't Gerechte van
Breuckelen niet en soude sitten voor dien tydt, gaff tot Antwoort,
dat hij gesocht hadde syn Eer, hoe eer hoe liever. ten tweeden,
Waerom Henricum Selyns, en niet den voorgemelte Femmetie ofte anderen die daer van daegelycks spraecken, seyde van niemant dies aengaende beschuldigt te wesen, als van de meer gem̃. Selyns; dat on-
warachtig was, want te vooren heeft hy gesproocken voor de volle
Vergaderinge, dat Femmetie hem voor een Boomdief uytgescholden
hadde. gevraegt ten derden Wanneer hij dan gehaelt soude hebben
uyt het Bosch (gelyck hij seyt) 't geboomte, dat geen Wilde maer
Fruytboomen waren, Seijde, Midden Meert, maer wist so nau niet,
daer op geantwoort wiert, wy 't seer wel te weten, dat 't op den
Verleden Beedag was, Hy tot antwoort geevende, van tegens den
avont geweest te sijn. Ende ten laesten gevraegt synde, Waer hy
den voornoemde Boomtiens in 't bosch gevonden en hoe veel dat hy
t'huys gebracht hadde, Seyde niet te willen seggen voor dat hy
overtuygt was, en dat hy 't niet en wist van hoe veel.
Alles den Bovengenoemde Kerckenraet overweegende in de Vreese des
Heeren, beslooten, den Meergemelte Crousen buyten gestaen hebbende,
volgens 't voorgaende Advys van den Eerw^e, Godtsalige, en Hooggeleerde Vader D^O Johannes Megapolensis, aenteseggen, dat hij voor
den Tegenwoordige tydt geexcuseert soude wesen om ten avontmael te
gaen, omdat hy, gelyck hy tot Henricum Selyns en Willem Bredenbent,
syn Predicant en ouderling, geseyt hadde, onbereyt was, so door de
geruchten als Particuliere questien, die boven verhaelt syn. Ende
voornamentlyck, dat wy den meergenoemde Croesen voor dese tydt
suspendeeren van 't Avontmael des Heeren, ten eersten, door de particuliere Haet tegens syn wettige Predicant met de voornoemde Citatie, die gestreckt heeft Om den geheele gemeente te onthouden
van 't Avontmael des Heeren. Ten tweeden, door de Verwerpinge en
vilipendentie van den kerckenraet met den citatie voor den Politiquen Raet, daer Civilijck geprocedeert, maer geen kerckelycke Saecken gedecideert oft afgedaen worden. Ende ten derden door de verbreeckinge van syn beloften, die hy met hantgeevinge gedaen heeft
voor de kerckenraet, om Haer t'syner tydt onderworpen te wesen.
Ende aengaende syn versoeck, dat de geene die hem beschuldigden
niet soude mogen ten Avontmael koomen, wort by den kerckenraet
goetgekeurt, dat hij ('t welck voornaemst is) hem eerst sal pur-
geeren na behooren voor den Gerechte van Breuckelen, daer hy den
Voornoemde Predicant geciteert heeft. En dan sal de kerckenraet
daer in doen, dat sy duncken oirbaer en billick te wesen. 't Geene den meergemelte Crousen, met Vermaninge om satisfactie te geeven van de Geruchten, voor geleesen is.

Ende aen de Scholtes en Scheepenen van de Durpe en jurisdictie van
Breuckelen, tot voldoeninge van de Citatie, wiert ter selfde stont

Translation

made: "Consider me the offender", and replied that this was not
based upon the truth but upon the rumors. We said: "I do not
know, God knows. You can deceive me but not God", which the
aforesaid Croesen did not deny he had been told by his minister
mentioned before. Eventually, [he] tried to justify his case
with indecent maledictions saying "If it's true, I'll be damned!",
and after he had been punished for that, [he] persisted equally
strongly in his afore-mentioned swearing and self-damnation.

When he was asked, furthermore, why he, the aforesaid, had
cited Henricus Selijns prior to the Lord's Supper whereas the
Court of Breuckelen would not be in session before that day, [he]
replied that he had sought his honor, the sooner the better.
When asked, secondly, why [he had cited] Henricus Selyns and not
the afore-mentioned Femmetie or others who were talking about it
every day, [he] said that he had not been charged with this
offense by anyone but the afore-mentioned Selyns - which was
untrue, because sometime earlier he had said in the presence of
the full meeting that Femmetie had called him a tree-thief. Upon
being asked, thirdly, when he had taken the trees (which were not
wild trees but fruit trees) from, by his own account, the woods,
[he] said [that it was] in the middle of March but that he did
not know for sure. We replied that we knew very well, namely
during the latest day of prayers; he answered that it was towards
evening. And upon being asked, finally, where in the woods he
had found the aforesaid trees and how many he had taken home,
[he] said he did not want to tell before he was absolutely sure
and that he did not know how many.

After the aforesaid consistory had taken everything into
consideration in the fear of the Lord, [we] resolved to tell the
afore-mentioned Crousen, who had been standing outside, that for
the time being, in accordance with the preceding advice of the
Rev., godly, and very learned father Domine Johannes Megapolensis,
he would be excused from partaking of the Lord's Supper because,
as he had told Henricus Selyns and Willem Bredenbent, his minister
and elder, he had been unwilling to do so in view of the rumors
as well as his private quarrels which have been related above.
And [we would tell him] especially, that we suspend the aforesaid
Croesen from the Lord's Supper for the time being, first, because
of his personal hatred against his lawful minister, as is evident
from the aforesaid citation which was aimed at withholding the
Lord's Supper from the entire congregation; second, because of
his rejection and contempt of the consistory as shown in his
citation in the Secular Court where civil lawsuits are conducted
but no Church matters can be resolved or settled; and third, for
breaking the promises he had made to the consistory while shaking
their hands, [namely] to be obedient to them in due time. And
with regard to his request that those who were accusing him not
be allowed to come to the Lord's Supper, it is decided by the
consistory that (most importantly) he will first clear himself
properly in the Court of Breuckelen where he cited the aforesaid
minister. And the consistory will then do what they consider
proper and reasonable. This was read to the aforesaid Crousen,
and he was exhorted to refute the rumors.

And at the same time, in order to settle the citation, the
following missive was sent to the schouts and schepens of the

Original

[21^V: "Pag. 41"]

dese Missive gesonden, die Schout Adriaen Hegeman, doe op Breuckelen sijnde, behandigt is. Ende luydt als volgt met 't naeste
bladt,

Copie van Missive aen de Scholtes
en Scheepenen van de durpe en
jurisdictie van Breuckelen

                  Den Heeren van de Gerechten wenst
                  de Kerckenraedt Vrede en Salicheijt.

Voorsienige, discrete, en Seer Besondere Heeren en Vrienden,

Dese weijnigen dienen tot Antwoort, jnformatie en satisfactie tegens de Citatie van Gerrit Dircksen Crousen, van Wijnschoten, ledemaet onser gemeente, en resorteerende onder UE jurisdictie:
Welcke met overgroote stoutigheyt en noyt gehoorde onbeschaemheyt
sig heeft derven (Godt betert) onderwinden, buyten alle kerckelycke Ordonnantien, buyten alle gewoonelycke Proceduuren, buijten
recht en reden, en buytens tijdts, self den Sabbath, die van Gode
tot den Godtsdienst verordineert ende ten selve dage ons diende
tot Voorbereijdinge en beproevinge ten aenstaende Avontmael, tot
dit onbeschaemt voorneemen misbruijckende; Omme den Persoon Henricus Selyns, in Qualite syn wettige Predicant en leeraer, ende gekoomen in Commissie van de kerckenraet, selfs van de Gemeynte, ten
tyde van de Visite en gewoonelycke noodinge tot den Tafel des Heeren, te citeeren, en doen citeeren, gelyck hij hem geciteert heeft
verleeden Rustdag door den Gerechtsbode: Uyt oorsaecke van
seeck're onbehoorlycke en t'eenemael onchristelycke Geruchten, die
wy hem plichtshalven, Conscienties wegen, en volgens kerckelycke
Resolutie bekentmaeckte, met Wilhelmus Bredenbend, onse ouderling
ende gedeputeerde tot de Visite; Niets binnen Huijs in de Tegen-
woordigheyt syns Huysvrouws tot sijner beschaminge, maer buytens
huys gaende, om ten bequaemste maniere en na behooren onderricht
te worden aengaende de Geruchten, die selfs bij de kinderen notoir
en openbaer sijn.
Gelyck wy dan verstaen, dat Henricus Selijns, die 't toekomt
plichtshalven syn ledematen tijdelijck en ontijdelyck te vermanen,
ende in sulcke voorvallen na de aert der liefde te waerschouwen,
onwettiglijck, ontijdelijck, en onbehoorlijck geciteert is voor
den Politiquen Rechtbanck, alwaer geen kerckelijcke geschillen oft
kunnen oft meugen na de jnstellinge J. Christi afgedaen worden van
ledematen tusschen ledematen, veel min dan van ledematen tegens de
kerckenraet ofte Gecommitteerde der Selfde, ten eynde der kerckelycke discipline, die Christus ten dien eynde ingestelt, en den
Voorn Croesen selfs belooft heeft na gewoonelycke maniere der aenneeminge sig t'alle tydt te onderwerpen.
So versoeckt de kerckenraet aen UE: gerechte, behoudens UE: gerech-
tigheyt en ordonnantien, omme den Voorgemelte Citatie te annihileeren, diergelycken na desen te beletten, en 't geene kerckelyck is,
te laten aen de kerckelycke Vergaderinge, welcke reets gedaen
heeft na rype deliberatie aen de meergenoemde Croesen naer eysch
van Saecken, en raeckende sijn particuliere partydschap, verwerpinge der kerckelycke Ordonnantien, en verbreeckinge der Beloften.

Translation

village and jurisdiction of Breuckelen, which was handed to
schout Adriaen Hegeman who was in Breuckelen then. And it reads
as follows, on the next page:

Copy of the missive to the schouts
and schepens of the village and
jurisdiction of Breuckelen

> The consistory wishes the Gentlemen
> of the Court peace and salvation.

Provident, Discreet, and Very Special Gentlemen and Friends,

These few words serve as a reply to, information on, and settlement of, the citation by Gerrit Dircksen Crousen, from Winschot-
en, a member of our congregation living under your jurisdiction;
Who has dared (may God mend his manners!) - with extreme wickedness and unheard-of impudence, in violation of all Ordinances
of the Church, in violation of all customary procedures, without
any right or justification, and at an inappropriate time,
abusing even the Sabbath for this impudent scheme, a day
reserved by God for the divine worship and for abstinence in
preparation of the imminent Lord's Supper - to cite, and to
have cited, as he had him cited by the court-messenger on the
latest holiday, the person of Henricus Selyns, his lawful minister and teacher who had come [to him] under commission of the
consistory, indeed, of the [entire] congregation, during his
pastoral visit for the customary invitation to the Lord's Table,
[a citation] in connection with certain improper and utterly
unchristian rumors that we [29] informed him [30] of dutifully,
conscientiously, and in accordance with Church resolutions,
together with Wilhelmus Bredenbend, our elder and deputy present
during the pastoral visit - not inside the house where he would
have been embarrassed in the presence of his wife, but after we
had gone outside, so that he was told in the most suitable and
proper way about the rumors which are notorious and public
knowledge even among the children.
As we understand, then, that Henricus Selijns, whose right and
duty it is to exhort his members timely and untimely and to warn
them in such instances in the name of love, has been cited unlawfully, untimely, and improperly in the Secular Court where, according to Jesus Christ's precepts, no Church disputes can nor may
be settled, neither [those] among members, much less [those]
between members and the consistory or its delegate, for the sake
of Church discipline which Christ instituted for that purpose
and which the aforesaid Croesen himself had promised to submit
to at all times during the traditional confirmation ritual;
Therefore, the consistory petitions your Court, with due respect
for your justice and ordinances, to annul the afore-mentioned
citation, to prevent such citations in the future, and to leave
those concerning Church matters to the Church meeting, which
after careful deliberation has already taken action against the
aforesaid Croesen as circumstances required, with regard to his
personal biases, rejection of the Ordinances of the Church, and
breach of promises. This does not mean that we prohibit you

Original

[23^r: "Pag. 44"]

Niets dat wy UE: mits desen verbieden, om de Saecken die hem nage-
geeven ende alreede van UE: Officier ondersocht worden te inquireeren, ofte te doen inquireeren: Maer wenschen en versoecken ter
contrarie, dat UE: naerstigheyt, Sorgvuldigheyt, en becommernisse
tot de gemelte ondersoeckinge dies te grooter en nauwer zij, ten
eijnde, so 't logentale is, dat de meergemelte Crousen gepurgeert
en gesuijvert werde aengaende de Geruchten van dieverije en ontroo-
vinge van Seeck're Boomen. Mitsgaders onse Gemeente bevryt werde
van loopende Ergernissen. So 't waer is, dat wij doen, dat ver-
eyst wort, volgens de kerckelycke Costuyme en discipline. Hier-
meede, Voorsienige, discrete, en seer besondere Heeren en Vrienden,
beveelen wij UE: Vergaderinge in de Protectie en beschermimge des
Alderhoogsten: verlatende ons selven op UE serieuse ondersoeckinge,
met Verlangen, dat de Gemelte Crousen syn saecke voor UE: gerechte
gesuyvert, oft niet gesuyvert sal hebben. Valete.

Uijt de Name des Kerckenraets,
   en bij laste
(Onderstont)

Actum Breuckelen,
in onse kerckelycke
Vergaderinge, den 5
April, 1662.

Henricus Selijns,
   Bedienaer des Euangeliums
Wilhelmus Bredenbend,
   Ouderling

Den 14 Maij

Is toegestaen en goet gevonden by de Kerckenraet, omme de twee
koeybeesten, van Harmen de Soldaet voor 315 guld. gekocht, te geeven aen Mr Carel d'Beauvois, onse Voorleeser, Voorsanger en Schoolmeester, en Mr Jeurie Probasco, op Halve aanteelinge, ten Profyte
van de Armen; maer dat den Voorn Mr Carel d'Beauvois, om sijn getrouwe dienst, en daer in wackerder te maecken, soude van Boterpacht exempt wesen, en dat de voorschreeven Mr Jeurie 't Eerste
jaer tien pont, en volgende jaeren sestien pont boter, ofte Seewant, 't geen Probasco versocht en toegestaen wiert, in plaets
van Boter te geeven, met beloften, om de schade (so de Beesten quuuaa-
men te sterven) Elck voor 't sijne te vergoeden. Volgens de Acte daer van gemaeckt, van Haer beyde onderteeckent, ende
jnde koffer der diaconen berustende, oft daer van copye gestelt
sal worden achter de Reeckening van Ontfang en Uytgift der diaconen.

Den 21 dicto

Naer behoorlijcke Confessie des Gelooft is lidmaet geworden, ende
tot onser gemeynschap aengenoomen,

Fijtie Martens, van Hamburg,
   Wiens getuygen sijn,
      Tryntie Hadders, en Lijsbeth Rossillon.

Translation

hereby from inquiring, or having someone inquire, into the things he is being accused of and which are already being investigated by your prosecutor. However, [we] desire and request on the other hand that you show greater and more scrupulous diligence, caution, and care than ever towards the said investigation so that, if it is all lies, the aforesaid Crousen will be cleansed and cleared of the rumors about thievery and theft of certain trees, and our congregation will be freed from the current aggravations; [but] that, if it is true, we will do what is required according to Church customs and discipline. Herewith, provident, discreet, and very special gentlemen and friends, we commend your assembly to the protection and shelter of the Most High, relying on your serious investigation and desiring that the said Crousen clear or fail to clear his case in your Court. Farewell.

On behalf and by order
of the consistory,
(underneath stood)

Done in Breuckelen
in our Church
meeting,
April 5, 1662.

Henricus Selijns,
Minister of the Gospel
Wilhelmus Bredenbend,
Elder

May 14 [1662]

The consistory gave permission and approval to give the two cows which had been purchased from Harmen the soldier for 315 guilders, to Mr. Carel d'Beauvois, our reader, precentor, and schoolmaster, and to Mr. Jeurie Probasco, at half the offspring [31] for the benefit of the poor. [We decided] however, that the aforesaid Mr. Carel d'Beauvois would be exempted from butter-lease in view of his loyal service and as an incentive to even greater enthusiasm, and that the aforesaid Mr. Jeurie would give ten pounds of butter in the first year and sixteen pounds in subsequent years or - upon Probasco's request which was granted - sewan instead of butter, with the promise that if the beasts come to die, either party will cover half of the loss. [All of this is] in accordance with the deed made thereof, signed by both of them, and deposited in the deacons' trunk, a copy of which will be registered after the Account of Receipts and Expenditures of the Deacons.

[May] 21

Upon a proper confession of faith, the following person became a member and was confirmed in our congregation:

Fijtie Martens, from Hamburg,
whose witnesses are:
Tryntie Hadders, and Lijsbeth Rossillon.

Original

[24^r: "Pag. 46"]

Den 30 dicto

Ten Versoecke van den E: Gerechte is wederom den Voorschreeven Gerechte van diaconies-middelen verschooten de Somme van Vierendertig
guld. en Ses stuyvers om Plancken te koopen tot het Predicantshuys.

Den 27 Septemb.

Jan Thomassen, wonende tot Uijtrecht in N. Nederl^t., versocht om
wederom aengenoomen te worden ende beneffens onse ledematen te tre-
den tot den Tafel des Heeren, waer van Hij onthouden was door seecker ongeluck van Mes-treckinge. Seijde ten dien eijnde met Jan
van Cleeft afgemaeckt te hebben.
Waer op wij, den Voorgemelte Jan Thomassen buyten staende, geresolveert hebben, en resolveeren, dat 't best was dese geleegentheyt
over te laten, en besonderlyck acht op hem te neemen, ende soo ten
tijden van berouw en leetwesen wederom tot onse Gemeente te ontfangen. 't geen hem binnen koomende aengeseyt is.
Lange Barent, ontboden synde om syn dagelijcksche droncckenschap,
en al te groote nalaticheijt van sorge te dragen voor syn kinderen,
die niet te eeten hadden en qualyck om van gecleedt te worden,
seyde, wat wy seyden, en godts straffe voorstelden, niet te kunnen
belooven sig van droncckenschap te onthouden, maer dat hy (so 't
mogelyck was) beteren soude, en meerder Sorge dragen voor syn kinderen.
Aucke Jans, op sijn Versoeck binnen staende, versocht, om 't kerckhof ten deele aftesetten, daer syn Huysvrouw, Magdaleen Pieters
van Langendyck, begraven leyt. Maer gaven tot Antwoort, geen
Eygendom aen 't kerckhof te hebben, maer dat wy Spreecken sullen
met den Rechtbanck van Breuckelen, om 't geheele kerckhof, dat
seer nootsaeckelyck is, met clapborden aftesetten, tegens de Verckens, die in de graven wroeten, en gewroet hebben.

Ende tot ledematen syn aengenoomen, so met Attestatien, als door
belydenisse, dese navolgende,

    Mechtelina Specht, van Uijtrecht,
        Met Attestatie van Uijtrecht.
    Marritie Thomas, Huysv. van Mr Paulus, en
    Marritie Willems, van Nieuw-Nederl^t.,
        Beyde met Attestatie van de Manhatans.
    Anneken Hans, van Nieuw-Nederl^t.,
        getuygen,
        Jan Jorissen, Brechtie Hans.
    Agnietie Jans, van Amsterdam,
        getuygen,
        Jan Thomassen, dien wij 't om redenen toegelaten
        hebben, Tryntie Agens.

Mr Carel d'Beauvois, onse Voorleser, Voorsanger en Schoolmeester,
wiert oock aengedient en toegestaen, dat hij boven de Exemptie van
Boterpacht, 't welcke ten minsten sestien ℔ boter na 't contract
met Mr Georgi Probasco opgericht beloopen soude, soude

48

Translation

[May] 30 [1662]

At the request of the Hon. Court, another sum, amounting to thirty-four guilders and six stuivers, was advanced to the aforesaid Court out of the deaconry's funds in order to buy planks for the minister's house.

September 27

Jan Thomassen, living in Utrecht in New Netherland, requested to be re-admitted and to partake of the Lord's Supper beside our members, which had been denied him because of a certain knifing incident. [He] said he had settled with Jan van Cleeft to that end. Whereupon we resolved, and do resolve, while the aforementioned Jan Thomassen was standing outside, that it would be best to let this opportunity pass and to keep a special watch on him, and then, at the time of repentance and regret, to re-admit him to our congregation; which was told him when he came in.

Lange [= Tall] Barent - summoned because of his daily drunkenness and great lack of care for his children who had nothing to eat and hardly anything to wear (which we told him, and [we] described to him God's punishment) - said he could not promise to refrain from drunkenness but that he would improve, if possible, and take better care of his children.

Aucke Jans, appearing at his own request, asked [permission] to fence part of the churchyard where his wife, Magdaleen Pieters van Langendyck, lies buried. [We] replied, however, that we do not have ownership of the churchyard but that we will talk to the Court of Breuckelen about fencing the entire churchyard with clapboards, which is very necessary, against the pigs that are rooting, and have rooted, in the graves.

And the following persons were confirmed as members, both on the basis of attestations and through confessions of faith:

Mechtelina Specht, from Utrecht,
    with an attestation from Utrecht.
Marritie Thomas, wife of Mr. Paulus, and
Marritie Willems, from New Netherland,
    both with an attestation from Manhattan.
Anneken Hans, from New Netherland;
    witnesses:
        Jan Jorissen, Brechtie Hans.
Agnietie Jans, from Amsterdam;
    witnesses:
        Jan Thomassen (whom we allowed [to be witness]
        for [certain] reasons), Tryntie Agens.

Mr. Carel d'Beauvois, our reader, precentor, and schoolmaster, was also announced, and it was granted that on top of the exemption from butter-lease, which would amount to at least sixteen lbs. of butter according to the contract made with Mr. Georgi Probasco, he would annually receive 4 schepels[32] of grain in his

Original

[25^r: "Pag. 48"]

's jaerelycks tot een vereeringe ontfangen 4 Scheepels koren, om
syn Persoon in syn dienst meer Encouragement te geeven. Welcke
Voorschreven Vier Scheepels van nu af ingaen sullen.

Den 25 Octob.

Met de doot van Teuntie Straetsmans, Huysvr. van Gabriel Corbesy,
woonende in haer leeven op de Cujanes, en die seer Ernstelyck op
haer Sterfbedde versocht hadde aen Henricus Selyns en Teunis
Janssen, Predicant en diacon, om sorg te dragen en opsicht te hebben voor Haer nagelatene Wesen, Laurens Haf en Anna Tienemans, syn
wij volgens Plicht en beloften (ende den Voorgemelte Teuntie ter
aerde geholpen hebbende) met den geheelen kerckenraet 's Woensdags
daer na na 't Sterfhuys gegaen, om ten besten van de kinderen seecker jnventaris te maecken van de Goederen, 't geen wij aldus bevonden hebben,

Inventaris van den Boel en Goederen van Teuntie Straetsmans,
gewoont hebbende op Cujanes, gestorven synde den 19 Octob.
des tegenwoordige jaers, 1662, ende nalatende,

1. Gabriel Corbesij, haer Weduwenaer
2. Margariet Meijring, dochter van Jan Meyring,
   en die se per donatie gemaeckt heeft, Een
   Swarte Borstrock, Een Swarte Schort, Een
   Voorschoot, Ende een ronde neusdoeck met een ⎫ Kinders
   neers stuck   ⎬ van 't
3. Laurens Haf, soon van Georg Haf, by syn   ⎪ Voorbedde
   leeven Velttrompetter in Brasilien   ⎭
4. Annatie Tienemans, dochter van Tieneman
   Jacobsen

Voor eerst, den voorgemelte Borstrock, Schort, Voorschoot, neusdoeck en neerstuck, tot den overledens lijf behoorende, ende oud-
ste dochter geproelegateert synde.
Ten tweeden, Sestig Guldens seewant, van seecker Huys op de Manhatans verkocht, welcke penningen soude wesen tot Hendrick Jansen
van de Ven.
Ten derden, twee lapiens wit linnen, t'samen bedragende vyfender-
tig Ellen, 't welck gedeelt wiert ten halven voor Gabriel Corbesij,
en ten halven voor de kinders, om wederom in drien verdeelt te worden, voor Margariet, Laurens, en Anna, en voor de twee laesten
Hembden te maecken, mitsgaders Anderhalf El. Blauw-linnen, dat Gabriel aen de kinders geschoncken heeft, en 't welcke voor Annatie
tot voorschooties gebruyckt soude worden.
Ten Vierden, Gesonden aen Barentie Straetsman, Huysvrouw van Hans
de Backer, wonachtig aen 't fort Orangien, om voor den overleede-
nen te verhandelen,

          155 Pompoenen,
           55 Waterlimoenen,
          200 Beetwortels,
           33 Calebassen,
           5½ schep Uijen.

Translation

honor to give him more encouragement in his service.   These aforesaid four schepels will become effective today.

October 25 [1662]

Upon the death of Teuntie Straetsmans, wife of Gabriel Corbesy,
in her lifetime living at the Gowanus, who on her deathbed had
urgently requested that Henricus Selyns and Teunis Janssen, minister and deacon, take care of and look after her orphans left
behind, Laurens Haf and Anna Tienemans, we interred the afore-
mentioned Teuntie and, on the following Wednesday, went to the
house of the deceased with the entire consistory, in accordance
with our duty and promises, in order to make a certain inventory
of the goods for the benefit of the children, which we found thus:

Inventory of the estate and goods belonging to Teuntie
Straetsmans, who lived at Gowanus, died on the 19th of
October of the present year, 1662, and left behind:

1. Gabriel Corbesij, her widower
2. Margariet Meijring, daughter of Jan
   Meyring, to whom she willed through a
   donation a black undershirt, a black
   apron, a smaller apron, and a round   children
   handkerchief with a linen undershirt   from previous
3. Laurens Haf, son of Georg Haf, in his   marriages [33]
   lifetime field-trumpeter in Brazil
4. Annatie Tienemans, daughter of Tieneman
   Jacobsen

[We found] first, the afore-mentioned undershirt, apron,
smaller apron, handkerchief, and linen undershirt, belonging to
the body of the deceased and willed to the eldest daughter.
Second, sixty guilders in sewan, from a certain house sold in
Manhattan; this money would be given to Hendrick Jansen van de
Ven.
Third, two small pieces of linen measuring thirty-five els [34]
altogether, which was divided in two: one half for Gabriel
Corbesij and the other half for the children; [this latter half]
will be subdivided in three: for Margariet, Laurens, and Anna,
for the latter two of whom shirts will be made from their
shares.   Also, one and a half els of blue linen, which Gabriel
has donated to the children and which would be used for aprons
for Annatie.
Fourth, sent to Barentie Straetsman, wife of Hans de Backer
[= the Baker], living at Fort Orange, to be sold on behalf of
the deceased:
        155   pumpkins
         55   waterlemons
       200   beetroots
        33   calabashes
        5½   schepels of onions

Original

[25^V: "Pag. 49"]

En daervan komende Vyfenveertig Guld ('t Resteerende onverkocht
synde), wiert gegeeven tot betalinge van Cors Jansen, Mr Carel
d'Beauvois, Aucke Jans, Mr Paulus, Wiggert Reyniersz., Mr Jeurie
Probasco, en Besie Beulings, volgens Quitancie van de meeste daer
van synde.
Ten Vijfden, ten huyse van den overleedene gevonden daerenbooven,
Vier Schepels Grote grauwe Erten, Vier Schepels witte Erten, Anderhalf Schepel cleyne grauwe Erten, ende Vierd'half Scheepel kooren.
't welcke, Provisie synde, goetgevonden wiert, te blyven voor de
meergemelte Gabriel en voor de wesen, die by geleegentheyt besteedt soude worden.
Ten Sesten, Twee Verckens, voor Gabriel ten Halven, en voor de
kinders ten halven.
Ten Seevenste, Een paer Vim Kooren voor de Pachter.
Ten Achsten, Vyf morgen Schoon Lant, Ende Ettelycke morgen-Bosch-
lant, t'samen gekocht van Bartel Claeszen voor   guld, te betalen in twee paijen, en daer van de Eerste paij soude wesen de
somma van 230 gld. 5 stuyv., maer nademael niet meerder op 't
Voorschreeven lant betaelt was dan Veertien scheepels Erten, die
aengenoomen syn voor de somma van 70 gld., wiert best geoordeelt
den voorn Bartel te ontbieden, om Gabriel 't lant over te doen, en
daer van de wesen te ontslaen. 't Welcke den Meergemelte Bartel
Claessen, van Middelwout gekoomen synde, geschiet is, hem daer toe
geevende seecker Myt Hoij, op 50 gl. en 5 st getaxeert, tot afkor-
tinge van de Eerste pay; met conditie, dat Gabriel sulcks ten
halven aen de Wesen vergoeden soude.
Ten Negenste, Keetels, Huysraet en Gantsche Tuyn, die den meergenoemde Gabriel voor Hondert en tachtentig lb tabacq overgenoomen
heeft.
Ende ten laesten, seecker Parthye Tabacq, naest Jan Pietersen
hangende op Cujanes, die wy gesien hebben, ende metten eersten
gestript en gedeelt soude worden.

Eodem

Gesproocken hebbende metten Gerechte van Breuckelen ten regarde
van 't Kerckenhof aftesetten na behooren, en dat Sy 't volkomelyck
gelaten hadden aen den Eerw. kerckenraet, die sulcks om de Gemeente te vergenoegen aengenoomen heeft, Vint den voorgemelte goet, om
beyde Henricus Selyns ende Jan Jorissen, Predicant en diacon, te
belasten, van 't kerckenhof metten eersten te besteeden, 't geen
sy gedaen hebben na dit navolgende Contract, ten dien eynde met
Aucke Janssen opgerecht,

Ick Ondergeschreeven bekenne, met de kerckenraet van Breuckelen in
Contract getreeden te syn, om 't kerckenhof ter Voorgemelte plaetse, gelyck als volgt, aftesetten voor de somma van Seeventig Guldens in Seewant, namentlyck met
          Klapborden van vyf voeten hoog, ende op malkanderen
          gespijckert,
          Posten en Richels, alles beslagen,
          Een deurkosyn, en frontispies,
          Plancken tot den deur.

Translation

This yielded forty-five guilders (the rest remained unsold),
which was set apart to pay Cors Jansen, Mr. Carel d'Beauvois,
Aucke Jans, Mr. Paulus, Wiggert Reyniersz, Mr. Jeurie Probasco,
and Besie Beulings, as per receipts that most of them have.
Fifth, found, moreover, in the house of the deceased: four
schepels of large yellow peas, four schepels of white peas, one
and a half schepels of small yellow peas, and three and a half
schepels of grain. Since these were provisions, it was decided
that they would remain there for the aforesaid Gabriel and for
the orphans and that they would be used in due time.
Sixth, two pigs, one for Gabriel and the other for the children.
Seventh, a couple of vims[35] of grain for the tenant.
Eighth, five morgens[36] of clear land and several morgens of
woodland, bought from Bartel Claeszen for ... guilders[37] altogether, to be paid in two installments, the first installment of
which would amount to 230 guilders 5 stuivers; but since for
the aforesaid land not more than fourteen schepels of peas had
been paid, which had been accepted for the sum of 70 guilders,
it was judged best to send for the aforesaid Bartel in order to
transfer the land to Gabriel and release the orphans from it.
This was done after the afore-mentioned Bartel Claessen had
come from Midwout, whom was given a certain stack of hay valued
at 50 guilders and 5 stuivers to redeem part of the first
installment, with the condition that Gabriel give half of it to
the orphans.
Ninth, kettles, furniture, and the entire garden, which the
aforesaid Gabriel took over for one hundred and eighty lbs. of
tobacco.
And finally, a certain lot of tobacco hanging at Gowanus next
to Jan Pietersen's, which we have seen and which would be
stripped and divided at the first opportunity.

Ibid. [= October 25, 1662]

After [we] had talked to the Court of Breuckelen about properly
fencing the churchyard, they left it entirely to the Hon. Consistory which agreed to do it to please the congregation. The afore-
mentioned [consistory] decided to instruct both Henricus Selyns
and Jan Jorissen, minister and deacon, to put the churchyard[-job]
immediately out to contract, which they did as is evident from
the following contract made up to that end with Aucke Janssen:

I, the undersigned, acknowledge to have entered into a contract
with the consistory of Breuckelen to fence the churchyard in
the afore-mentioned place as follows, for the sum of seventy
guilders in sewan, namely with
        clapboards, five feet tall and nailed together;
        posts and ledges, everything covered [with iron];
        a doorframe and pediment;
        planks for the door.

Original

[26^v: "Pag. 51"]

't Welcke ick beloove ter goeder trouwe binnen de tydt van drye
weecken voor de boven genoemde Penningen op te maecken. Actum,
den 25 octob. 1662.

(Was onderteeckent)

Aucke Jans

Den 29 dicto

Wiert voorgeslagen, dat men ten behoeve van 't Kerck Hof, 't welcke afgeset soude worden, seecker overslag maecken souden, omme
van ieder Huysgesin aftevorderen, Een oft Twee gulden Seewant,
alsser tot 't Afsetten nootsaeckelyck soude wesen. Ende daerenboven goetgevonden, datter sodanige collecten gedaen soude worden,
van Wilhelmus Bredenbend op de Cujanes, daer syn Eerw^e woont, van
Teunis Janssen tot Breuckelen en op 't Veer, ende van Jan Jorissen
in de walebocht, daer hy van gelycken woont.
Terwijle 't Predicants huys geen Inkomste heeft, en niet volkomentlyck voltoyt synde, voornamentlyck 't Een oft ander van nooden
heeft tot behoorlycke reparatie, oft diergelycke behoeften, 't welcke door de slechte tydt en tegenwoordige ongeleegenheyt der Huys-
lieden soude niet te wel bygebracht kunnen worden, wiert oock by
den kerckenraet gearresteert en vastgestelt, als wy stellen by
desen, dat ten behoeve van 't voorgemelte Huys gegeeven sal worden,
't geene voor Trougelt gegeeven wort van de geene, die de deser
plaetse trouwen sullen, sijn aenvang neemende van de laeste die
getrouwt is, te weten van Dirck Janssen Hooglant met Annetie Hans,
weduwe van Jan Clerck, heden over drie weecken getrouwt, en voorts
van de geene die volgen sullen, En daer wy toe stellen Henricus
Selyns om de Penningen te ontfangen, en t'syner Huyse te gebruycken, met bereytwillige aenneeminge om daervan ter geleegener tydt
reeckeninge te doen.

Den 26 Novemb.

Wiert voorgestelt, nademael Henricus Selyns meent wederom syn Predicatien met de korte Avonden ende aenstaende Winter te staecken
op de E: H. 's Generaels bouwerye, oft hij, als Voorgaende Jaer,
den namiddag van de dag des Heeren sal gebruycken tot gewoonelycke
Catechisatien, oft dat hy sdingsdag namiddag, 't welck alrede van
den 18 April des Tegenwoordige jaers tot deser geduurt, en Catechu-
menen daer toe willig en gewoon syn, soude voortgaen met Catechi-
seeren. Wort 't laeste geoordeelt om verscheyden redenen, en voornamentlyck door de yver en sonderlinge bereytwilligheijt der Cate-
chumenen alsoo bequaem, ende door 't tamelyck getal van de jonge
jeugt te pyne waert te wesen, want, die komen tot den voorgemelte
Catechisatien, syn de navolgende,

Catalyntie Teunis,   Aeltie Teunis Gijsbertsen,

Saertie Pieters,   Catharyn }
                                      Getruyd   } d'Beauvois,

[continued on p. 56]

Translation

Which I promise to build up loyally within three weeks for the
money mentioned above. Done, October 25, 1662.

(was signed)

Aucke Jans

[October] 29 [1662]

A proposal was made to raise a certain levy for the churchyard
which was going to be fenced, [namely] to exact from each family
one or two guilders in sewan depending on what the fencing would
require. And [it was] approved, moreover, that such collections
would be made, by Wilhelmus Bredenbend at Gowanus where he lives,
by Teunis Janssen in Breuckelen and at the Ferry, and by Jan
Jorissen in the Wallabout where he lives.
Since the minister's house has no income and, in its not
entirely finished state, is in urgent want of certain things for
proper repairs and similar needs (the money for which would be
hard to raise in view of the bad times and the present poverty
among the villagers), it was also decided and resolved by the
consistory, as we resolve hereby, that whatever is donated in
wedding-money by those who will get married in this place, will
be set apart for the benefit of the afore-mentioned house,
starting with the latest person who got married - namely Dirck
Janssen Hooglant, married more than three weeks ago to Annetie
Hans, widow of Jan Clerck - and henceforth all people who will
follow. And we appoint Henricus Selyns to collect the money and
use it for his house, who willingly takes it upon himself to
render an account of it in due time.

November 26

Since it is Henricus Selyns' intention, in view of the short
evenings and imminent winter, to suspend [his services] at the
Hon. Lord General's Bowery [= farm] again, a proposal was made
[to consider] whether he should use the afternoon of the Lord's
Day for the confirmation classes as in the previous year, or
continue catechizing on Tuesdays in the afternoon as he has been
doing since April 18 this year and to which the catechumens are
disposed and accustomed. It is resolved to do the latter for
several reasons, especially because it is justified by the diligence and extraordinary willingness on the part of the catechumens
and because the considerable number of the youngsters makes it
worthwhile; for the following persons are attending the confirmation classes mentioned above:

Catalyntie Teunis,	Aeltie Teunis Gijsbertsen,
Saertie Pieters,	Catharyn } d'Beauvois,
	Getruyd }

[continued on p. 57]

Original

Hendrickie Jans,

Saertie Teunis,

Hendrick Obee,

Pieter Pietersen,

Laurens Haf,

Jan Teunissen,

Anna Tielemans,

Joost Symonsen,

Hendrick Janssen,

Stoffel Probasco,

Lucas Teunissen,

Marie Hanssen,

Janneken Montfoort,

Janneken Teunis,

Aeltie Teunis Jansen,

Marten Reijersen,

Catharyn } Joosten,
Marritie

Jeurie Probasco,

Daniel Jorissen,

Jan Pietersen,

Cornelis Jansen,

Nys Teunis,

Jacob } Jorissen,
Willem

Ian Teunissen,

Cornelis Abramsen,

Joris Hansen,

Annetie Teunis,

Aecht Teunis,

Anneken Rems,

David de Potter,

Pieter Lambertsen.

Den 20 decemb.

Pieter Prae ontboden synde, om seecker Contract te maecken, belangende seecker koey-beest, 't Welcke hem mits desen gegeeven
wiert op Halve aenteelinge, en twalef pont boter, Maeckte swaricheyt omtrent de vergoedinge van de Halve Schade door seecker Gebreck by de Voorschr koey. daer wy op geantwoort hebben, dat wy
sulcks ten goede gekoomen hebben met de voornoemde Boterpacht van
Twalef Ponden, daer sestien ordinaris gegeeven wort. Ende heeft
daermede 't Contract by de diaconie berustende onderteeckent.
Sijmon Joosten, met syn Huysvrouw geciteert synde voor den Eerw^e
kerckenraet door den kercken bode, heeft alleen verscheenen, ende
ons aengedient, dat de Verschillen tusschen hun beyde geslecht en
geeffent waren, met vergeevinge van wedersyde; met versoeck, dat
de kerckenraet sig wilde daer mede vergenoegen, en dat sy gerust
synde van gemoede, den avontmale des Heeren mochte by woonen, 't
geen wy toegestaen, en vorders vermaent hebben tot Vrede, Een-
dracht, en liefde.
Alsoo Teunis Nijssen, Ledemaet deser Gemeynte, geciteert heeft
Aeltie Joris, Huysv. van Willem Gerritsen van Couwen-hoven, ter
oorsaecke van seeck're Scheltwoorden en misnoeginge, wiert onder
ons goetgevonden Eerst gecommitteerde te senden naer beijde Persoonen, om de saecke te middelen ende ter neder te leggen. En
daer wy toe verkosen hebben Wilhelmus Bredenbent, Ouderling, en
Jan Jorissen, diacon, die de saecke uytgevoert hebben tot een goet
eynde.
Ende met eene heeft de kerckenraet, als Uytvoerders des Uytterste
wille van wylen Teuntie Straetsman en opsienders van Hunne

Translation

Hendrickie Jans,	Catharyn
Saertie Teunis,	Marritie } Joosten,
Hendrick Obee,	Jeurie Probasco,
Pieter Pietersen,	Daniel Jorissen,
Laurens Haf,	Jan Pietersen,
Jan Teunissen,	Cornelis Jansen,
Anna Tielemans,	Nys Teunis,
Joost Symonsen,	Jacob
Hendrick Janssen,	Willem } Jorissen,
Stoffel Probasco,	Ian Teunissen,
Lucas Teunissen,	Cornelis Abramsen,
Marie Hanssen,	Joris Hansen,
Janneken Montfoort,	Annetie Teunis,
Janneken Teunis,	Aecht Teunis,
Aeltie Teunis Jansen,	Anneken Rems,
Marten Reijersen,	David de Potter,
	Pieter Lambertsen.

December 20 [1662]

Pieter Prae, summoned to make a certain contract for a certain cow, which was given him hereby at half the offspring[38] and for twelve pounds of butter, raised objections against [his obligation to] cover half of [possible] losses because of a certain ailment with the aforesaid cow. We replied that we compensated him for that with the aforesaid butter-lease of twelve pounds which is usually fixed at sixteen [pounds]. And herewith [he] signed the contract, which is deposited with the deaconry.

Sijmon Joosten, cited with his wife to the Hon. Consistory by the church-messenger, appeared on his own and notified us that the quarrels between the two of them had been leveled and smoothed with mutual forgiveness; and he requested that the consistory be satisfied with that, and that they, with peace in their hearts, be allowed to partake of the Lord's Supper. This was granted by us, and furthermore we exhorted [him] to [show] peace, union, and love.

Since Teunis Nijssen, member of this congregation, has cited Aeltie Joris, wife of Willem Gerritsen van Couwen-hoven, on account of certain abusive language and displeasure, it was approved among us first to send delegates to both persons to arbitrate in the affair and settle it. And we chose for this Wilhelmus Bredenbent, elder, and Jan Jorissen, deacon, who carried the affair to a happy conclusion.

And at the same time, the consistory, as executors of the late Teuntie Straetsman's last will and as supervisors of her minor

Original

onmondige kinders, besteedt Laurens Haf, Soon van wylen Georgie
Haf, Trompetter, aen Henricus Selyns, Predicant te deser Plaetse,
omme t'Syner Huyse te woonen, ende ten dienste te wesen voor de
Tydt van Ses achtervolgende Jaeren. Ten welcke voorschreeven Jaren den Voornoemde Selyns belooft heeft, en belooft, desen Laurens
van behoorlycke kost en klederen te versien, Hem 's Winters oft
t'Schole te senden, ofte selfs te onderwysen na behooren, en met
hem te handelen als betamelyck is.
Ende diergelyck Contract te maecken met Gerrit Corñ. van Niekerck,
wonachtig in 't Vlacke Bosch, daer Anna Tielemans van de voorschreven kerckenraet besteet is.

Den 25 dicto

Naer Voorgaende Attestatien, soo van de Manhatans, als 't Fort
Orangien, en elders, syn tot ledematen ontfangen,

> Joris Janssen Rappalje,
> Catharina Jeronijmus,
> Catharina Joris Rappalje, van Nieuw-Nederlant,
> > Met Attestatie van de Manhatans.
> Frederick Lubbertsen,
> Tryntie Hendricks,
> > Met Attestatie van de Manhatans.
> Paulus Dircksen,
> > Met Attestatie van 't Fort Orangien.
> Jan Pieterszen,
> Marie Hoogeboom,
> > Met Attestatie van Bunninck.

A^O 1663

Den 21 Februar

Na de Aenroepinge des Alderhooghsten tot Verkiesinge van Ouderling
en Diaconen, docht ons met de doot van Jan Jorissen, die den
28 Januar. des tegenwoordige Jaers gestorven is, seer nootsaeckelyck te wesen, Wilhelmus Bredenbent, wonachtig op de Cujanes, in
syn dienst te continueeren voor een Jaer lang, ende neffens hem
tot Ouderling te verkiesen, Teunis Jansen Coevors, die tegenwoordig diacon was, 't geen sy beyde toegestaen en aengenoomen hebben;
maer om wederom te vervullen 't Getal der diaconen, syn dese navolgende, die te Breuckelen ende in de Bocht wonachtig syn, gebracht
op de nominatie, om van beyde Plaetsen een diacon te verkiesen,

> Van Breuckelen,

> Albert Cornelissen Wantenaer,
> Willem Gerritsen van Couwenhoven,
> Teunis Nijssen,
> Johannes Marcus,
> Jan Martyn, van Campen.

[continued on p. 60]

Translation

children, placed Laurens Haf, son of the late Georgie Haf,
trumpeter, in the custody of Henricus Selyns, minister in this
place, in order to live in his house and to serve him for a
period of six consecutive years. The aforesaid Selyns promised,
and promises, to provide this Laurens with proper board and
clothing during the aforesaid years, to send him to school in
winter or teach him properly himself, and to treat him in a
proper way.
[He also promised] to make a similar contract with Gerrit
Corn[elissen] van Niekerck [= of Niekerk], living in Vlackebos,
in whose custody Anna Tielemans was placed by the aforesaid
consistory.

December 25 [1662]

On the basis of attestations, both from Manhattan and Fort
Orange and elsewhere, the following persons were accepted as
members:

    Joris Janssen Rappalje,
    Catharina Jeronijmus, [and]
    Catharina Joris Rappalje, from New Netherland,
        with an attestation from Manhattan.
    Frederick Lubbertsen, [and]
    Tryntie Hendricks,
        with an attestation from Manhattan.
    Paulus Dircksen,
        with an attestation from Fort Orange.
    Jan Pieterszen, [and]
    Marie Hoogeboom,
        with an attestation from Bunnik.

A.D. 1663

February 21

Upon the invocation of the Most High for the election of an
elder and deacons, we deemed it very necessary, after the death
of Jan Jorissen who died on January 28 this year, to continue
Wilhelmus Bredenbent, living at the Gowanus, in his service for
one year and to elect as elder beside him Teunis Jansen Coevors
who up to now was a deacon, which both agreed to and accepted.
However, in order to fill the number of deacons, the following
persons, living in Breuckelen and at the Wallabout, were nominated so that from either place a deacon could be elected:

    from Breuckelen,

    Albert Cornelissen Wantenaer
    Willem Gerritsen van Couwenhoven
    Teunis Nijssen
    Johannes Marcus
    Jan Martyn, from Kampen   [continued on p. 61]

Original

[30^r: "Pag. 58"]

Uijt de Walebocht,

Teunis Gysbertsen Bogaert,
Rem Jansen,
Joris Rappalie.

En daer uyt sijn eendrachtelyck de stemmen gevallen op Willem Gerritsen van Couwenhooven, scheepen tot Breuckelen, en Teunis Gysbertsen Bogaert, 't geene haer E: van stonden aen uyt de name des
kerckenraets soude aengeseyt, en metten eersten de Gemeynte voorgestelt worden. Desen dan sijnde tot Ouderlingen en diaconen ge-
continueert en verkosen, als volgt met deser,

Ouderlingen,

Wilhelmus Bredenbent,
Teunis Janssen Coevors.

Diaconen,

Willem Gerritsen van Couwenhoven,
Teunis Gysbertsen Bogaert.

Den 11 Mart.

Heeft de Kerckenraet opgenoomen de Reeckeningen der Diaconen, so
ten aensien van 't geen se ontfangen, als uytgegeeven hebben van
den 2 Mart. des Jaers 1661, tot den 4 Mart. 1663. Ende, 't geen
wy te samen onderteeckent hebben, aldus bevonden,

Bij de Diaconie van Breuckelen,

1. Ontfangen

Van den 2 Mart tot Ultim. dēc. 1661	Gld.	673- 4
Van prim͠ Jan. tot ult. decemb 1662	Gld.	623-15
Van primo Jan. tot 4 Mart. 1663	Gld.	63- 2
Somma	Gld.	1360- 1

2. Uijtgegeeven en Verschooten

Van den 16 Apr. tot ult. decemb. 1661	Gld.	188- 0
Van Primo Jan. tot ult. dēc. 1662	Gld.	782-17- 8
Van Primo Jan. tot 9 Mart. 1663	Gld.	266-18- 4
Somma	Gld.	1237-15-12

3. Overgeschooten

Van den Voorgemelte penningen	Gld.	122- 5- 4
Stelt hier bij van Uytgift en Verschot	Gld.	1237-15-12
t'Samen bedragende	Gld.	1360- 1

[continued on p. 62]

Translation

from the Wallabout,

Teunis Gysbertsen Bogaert
Rem Jansen
Joris Rappalie

And the votes were unanimously cast for Willem Gerritsen van Couwenhooven, schepen in Breuckelen, and Teunis Gysbertsen Bogaert, which would be announced to them as soon as possible on behalf of the consistory, and which would be presented to the congregation at the first opportunity. These persons, then, were continued and elected as elders and deacons, namely the following:

elders,

Wilhelmus Bredenbent
Teunis Janssen Coevors

deacons,

Willem Gerritsen van Couwenhoven
Teunis Gysbertsen Bogaert

March 11 [1663]

The consistory checked the accounts of the deacons, both with regard to what they have received and to what they have spent, from March 2 of the year 1661 until March 4, 1663. And we signed them together upon finding them as follows:

Deaconry of Breuckelen

1. Received,

From March 2 until the last of Dec., 1661:	Gld.	673- 4
From the first of Jan. till the last of Dec., 1662:	Gld.	623-15
From the first of Jan. till March 4, 1663:	Gld.	63- 2
Total:	Gld.	1360- 1

2. Spent and advanced,

From April 16 till the last of Dec., 1661:	Gld.	188- 0
From the first of Jan. till the last of Dec., 1662:	Gld.	782-17- 8
From the first of Jan. till March 9, 1663:	Gld.	266-18- 4
Total:	Gld.	1237-15-12

3. Surplus,

From the afore-mentioned money:	Gld.	122- 5- 4
Add to this, in expenditures and advances:	Gld.	1237-15-12
Totaling:	Gld.	1360- 1

[continued on p. 63]

Original

[31^r: "Pag. 60"]

4. Contra bevonden In Cassa

Seecker Testament van Barent Balde	Gld.	50- 0
Aen Gereedt seewant,	Gld.	93-13
Ende aen silvergelt, 7-15-0 - Naer waerdye	Gld.	18-14
Somma	Gld.	162- 7

Eodem, 11

Sijn binnengestaen, Willem Gerritsen van Couwenhoven en Teunis
Gysbertsen Bogaert, dien wy tot diaconen verkosen en bevestigt
hebben, en dien wy naer Voorgaende Geluckwenschinge en verwelle-
kominge, dit navolgende overgeleevert hebben, Seecker koeybeest
met een Bulkalf tot Carel d'Beauvois, noch een tot Mr Georgie
Probasco, noch een koeybeest met een bulkalf tot de Weduwe van
Pieter Prae sal^r, Baldees-Testament, Verschooten Penningen aen de
Gerechte van Breuckelen, 't Tinwerck tot 't Avontmael des Heeren,
kerckbancken, en so voort, daer wij besondere Specificatie van gemaeckt hebben in de Reeckeninge der diaconen, en 't geene den
Voorschr diaconen Willem Gerritsen en Teunis Gysbertsen, als ontfangen te hebben, met haer eygen handen onderteeckent hebben.

Den 25 dicto

Met den Tegenwoordige Paeschen syn tot ledematen aengenoomen, en
tot 't Gebruyck des H. Avontmaels toegelaten, dese twee navolgende
persoonen,

Marten Reijersen, van Amsterdam,
     Met Attestatie van 't Vlacke-bosch.
Anneken Duurkoop, Huysvrouw van Michiel Zyperus,
     Met Attestatie van N. Amsterdam.

Den 1 April

Wiert ons van de Gerechte van Breuckelen ter hande gestelt, om de
Gemeynte voor te stellen, seeck're Uytschrijvinge van Een Algemeene Vast en Bededag, die door last van den Grootachtb. H. Di-
rect^r Generael en Raden van Nieuw-Nederlant, met den aenstaende
Woensdag ten regarde van Verscheyden besoeckinge en Castydinge,
't welck Nieuw-Nederlant tot Groote droeffenisse geleden heeft,
gehouden sal worden, den voorgemelte Uytschryvinge, als volgt,
luydende,

Eersaeme, Lieve, Besondere,

Dat den alleen Barmhertigen en niet min rechtvaerdigen Godt, gelyck andere, oock dese eerst opluyckende Provintie en des Selfs
inwoonderen tot Boetvaerdigheyt en bekeeringe heeft soecken te

Translation

4. Instead of that [39], found in the treasury,

A certain bequest, Barent Balde's: Gld. 50- 0
In ready sewan: Gld. 93-13
And in silver money, [nominally [40]
   Gld.] 7-15-0, market value: Gld. 18-14

                           Total: Gld. 162- 7

[March] 11 [1663]

Willem Gerritsen van Couwenhoven and Teunis Gysbertsen Bogaert
appeared [in the consistory] whom we elected deacons and confirmed
in that position. And upon congratulating and welcoming them, we
handed them the following: a certain cow with a bull-calf at
Carel d'Beauvois' [place], another one at Mr. Georgie Probasco's,
another cow with a bull-calf at the late Pieter Prae's widow's,
Baldee's bequest, advances to the Court of Breuckelen, the pewter-
ware for the Lord's Supper, pews, and so on; we made a special
specification of this in the Account of the Deacons, which was
signed by the aforesaid deacons, Willem Gerritsen and Teunis
Gysbertsen, with their own hands in confirmation of the transfer.

[March] 25

Today, Easter, the following two persons were confirmed as
members and admitted to the Lord's Supper:

    Marten Reijersen, from Amsterdam,
          with an attestation from Vlackebos.
    Anneken Duurkoop, wife of Michiel Zyperus,
          with an attestation from New Amsterdam.

April 1

We were handed by the Court of Breuckelen a certain ordinance
to be presented to the congregation, calling for a general day of
fasting and prayers which will be held this Wednesday by order of
the Highly Esteemed Lord Director-General and Councillors of New
Netherland, in view of several visitations and castigations which
New Netherland suffered with great sorrow; the afore-mentioned
ordinance reads as follows:

   Respectable, Dear, [and] Special [People],

The only merciful and no less righteous God sought to induce this
nascent province and its inhabitants, like other provinces, to
penitence and repentance, [on the one hand] through ordinary

Original

[32^V: "Pag. 63"]

brengen door de Ordinarie middelen, als syn de Basuyne synes
Woorts en vercondinge des Selfs door sijn getrouwe dienaers, als
Vrede gesanten van Godt tot desen Volcke uytgesonden, om hen van
Christi wegen te bidden, datse haer met Godt soude laten versoenen,
ten anderen door de stemme Syner Seegeningen en weldaden over desen Volck uytgegoten, betoont in de Verlossinge en redderinge van
dit lant en Volck uyt gedreygde Oorlogen met de nabueren, gevoelde
en geleden Massakres van de Barbarische Naturellen, goet doende desen Volcke van den Hemel, hen Vruchtbare tyden geevende, vervullende hun Herten met Spyse en Vrolyckheijt, van den Welcken den Apos-
tel uytroept, weet gy niet, dat de goedertierentheyt Godts, u tot
bekeeringe leijt,   den goede Godt op dese twee manieren nu by nae
dese veertig jaren tot dit lant en Volck te vergeeft en vruchte-
loos geroepen hebbende, wie hoort, wie weet, en wie siet niet, dat
Godt nu begint, en al een tydt lang begonnen heeft, over dit Volck
en lant te donderen door de Stemme Van syn Rechtvaerdigen Oordeelen, het selve rontom en door besoeckende met (onder andere Castydinge so geen Straffen) de seer besmettelycke Sieckte der kinderpocken, so generael en Gemeen, dat weynig plaetsen, jae seer weynig Huysgesinnen, daer van vrij syn gebleeven, en of eenige haer
des mochten beroemen, hebben te gedencken, dat EENEN, jae meer,
dat VEELE overkomt, kan een iegelyck toekoomen, en wie en siet
niet des Heeren Straffende Hant noch daegelycks daer in Continueeren, door die en andere plaegen daegelycks nu desen en dan genen
sonder onderscheyt van Jaeren in een meerder getal dan oyt voor desen uyttet lant der leevendige wechrucken, en eerse des Gedachten
voor de Oogen der leevendigen ten graeve voeren. Welcke Oordeelen
en Gerichten Godts over anderen geoeffent, ons, die syne goedertierentheyt voor een Corten tydt noch in 't leeven gelieft te spaeren,
doen vermanen en waerschouwen, soo wy ons van de sonden, die wy
met alle geplaegde gemeen hebben, niet en bekeeren, de dreygende
wolcke van het selfde oordeel niet en sullen ontvlieden: want het
is niet alleen te vreesen, maer seeckerlyck te verwachten, waer
een Corte en haest passeerende naelde van de sonde voor en door-
gaet, datter (Sonder oprechte boetvaerdigheyt en bekeeringe des
leevens) een lange draet van meerder en swaerder besoeckinge, so
geen straffen, sal opvolgen; als connen syn Pestilentiale Sieckte,
dochters, als het Spreeckwoort seyt, en gemeenelyck gebeurt, van
den besmettelycke Moeder der Pocken: Hier en daer onvruchtbare tyden, Neeringloosheijt, oorlogen, beroovinge van de Predicatien des
Goddelycke Woorts, en dienvolgens van de tydt en middelen der Bekeeringe en Salicheyt, en wat diergelycke ontallijcke wel verdiende lantstraffen meer syn,   alle 't Welcke om van den alleen Barmhertigen Godt door ootmoedige Gebeeden, oprechte Boetveerdigheijt,
en bekeeringe des leevens, door Vasten, Rouw, en Weeclagen af te
bidden, Het heeft den Directeur Generael en Raden van N. Nederlant
nootsaeckelyck gedacht te beraemen en uytteschryven, Een Algemeene
Vast, en Bededag, die alomme binnen dese Provintie gehouden sal
worden op den Eersten Woensdag in den Maent April, sijnde den 4
dag der selver Maent,   oversulcks worden alle jngeseetenen deser
Provintie, so wel Officieren als Onderdaenen, by desen Gelast ten
Voorschr. dage in de kercke oft daermen gewoon is Godts Woort te
predicken ofte voor te leesen, te verschijnen, omme nae aenhooringe des Selfs met deemoedige en Verslagene Herten de Name des
Heeren vieriglyck aente roepen, Hem te bidden en te smeecken,
dattet syne Goddelycke

Translation

means like the trumpet of His Word and the preaching of the
Gospel by His loyal ministers, dispatched by God as peace-deleg-
ates to this people to beg them on Christ's behalf to reconcile
themselves with God; [and] on the other hand, through the voice
of His blessings and benefits strewn over this people, which He
showed by delivering and rescuing this country and people from
the threat of wars with our neighbors and from the massacres
felt and suffered at the hands of the barbaric natives, by
conferring benefits upon this people from heaven, by giving them
fruitful times, [and] by filling their hearts with food and joy,
causing the Apostle to exclaim: "Don't you know that it is God's
loving-kindness which leads you to repentance?" Now that the
good God has been calling vainly and fruitlessly upon this
country and people in the aforesaid two ways for almost this
entire period of forty years, [is there anybody] who does not
hear, know, or see, that God is now beginning - and has already
begun for quite a while - to thunder over this people and
country through the voice of His righteous judgements, visiting
every corner of the country with (among other castigations, if
not punishments) the very contagious disease smallpox, so general
and widespread that few places, indeed few families, remained
free from it? And in case some people take a pride in this[41],
[they] should keep the following in mind: what happens to one
person, indeed to many people, can happen to anybody. And [is
there anybody] who does not notice the Lord's punishing hand,
continuing every day through those and other plagues, tearing
people away from the land of the living - daily, at complete
random, regardless of age, [and] in a greater number than ever
before - and carrying them off to the graves under the very eyes
of the living before they even realize it? These judgements and
trials, carried out by God against others, exhort and warn us,
whom His mercy choses to keep alive for a while longer, that, if
we do not turn away from the sins which we have in common with
all the afflicted people, [we] will not escape from the threatening cloud of the same judgement, because it is not only to be
feared but certainly to be expected that, wherever a short and
hasty needle of sin is passing through (without sincere penitence
and conversion of life), a long thread of more and heavier
visitations, if not punishments, will follow; for instance:
pestilential diseases - as the proverb says (and as it usually
happens): "daughters of the contagious mother smallpox" -, here
and there fruitless periods, lack of trade, wars, deprivation of
the preaching of the Word of God and as a consequence, of the
time and means needed for conversion and salvation, and whatever
other similar, countless, and well-deserved punishments there
are for the country. In order to beseech the only merciful God
to turn all these [punishments] away from us, through humble
prayers, sincere penitence, and conversion of life, [and] through
fasting, mourning, and lamenting, the Director-General and
Councillors of New Netherland have deemed it necessary to plan
and prescribe a general day of fasting and prayers, which will
be held everywhere in this province on the first Wednesday in the
month of April, being the 4th day of that month. For this reason,
all inhabitants of this province, both administrators and
subjects, are hereby ordered to appear in church on the aforesaid
day, or wherever one is accustomed to preach or read the Word of
God, in order to hear the Word of God, to invoke ardently the

65

Original

[33^V: "Pag. 65"]

Majesteyt gelieve syne Rechtvaerdige Plaegen ende welverdiende
straffen van ons afte wenden ende te doen Cesseren, de Vrede en
goede Correspondentie onder ons ende onse nabueren te continueren,
ende ons, ende dese eerst opluyckende Provintie in sijn Vaderlycke
Bescherminge aen te neemen, ende tegens alle quade Practycken te
mainteneeren, de vruchten der Aerde met vroegen ende spade Regen
te seegenen, ende voor al onder ons te doen wassen ende toeneemen
Synes Naems Vrese ende kennisse, ende onse eygener sonden haet,
't welcke op dat te beter gepractiseert ende naergecomen mach worden, Den direct.^{r} Generael en Raden voorgemelt verbieden ten voorsch. Vast ende bededag alle Exercitie ende Oeffeninge, Hanteeringe
ende Neeringe, hoe deselve oock soude mogen werden genaemt. Mitsgaders oock alle ongeoorlofde speelen, dobbelen, ende droncken
drincken, op d'Amende Voormaels daer op beraemt, en worden de dienaren van Godes Heylige Woort binnen dese Provintien versocht Hare
Predicatien ende Gebeeden ten voorschr eynde te willen formeeren.
Aldus gedaen ter vergaderinge van den E: Heere Direct.^{r} Generael en
Raden van N. Nederlant, gehouden in't Fort Amsterdam, den 1 Mart.
A^o 1663.

(Onderstont)

P. Stuijvesant

Ter Ordonnantie van den E: H.^{re} Dr Gener̃l En Raden van N. Nederl.^{t},

(leger Stont)

C: V: Ruijven, Secr̃ets.

Den 18 Dicto

Pieter Prae van Diepe, den Sesten des Verleeden maent overleeden,
bij de diaconie ter aerde gestelt, ende twee kinders van syn Eerste bedde nalatende, heeft ons, die schuldig syn voor de Arme Wesen te sorgen, nootsaeckelyck gedacht, den Nalatene Weduwe Catharina Letie, die wederom verlooft was met Joost Casparsen van Groeningen, woonende tot Boschwyck, te ontbieden naer de Ses weecken
voor de kerckenraet, ende te verneemen, wat den Voorschreven Pieter mochten nagelaten hebben; maer niet of weynig vindende van
jmportantie, heeft den Voorgemelte Kerckenraet voor de onmondige
Wesen eens voor al met den Voornoemde Weduwe uytkoop gedaen voor
tachtgentig guld. Seewant, daer wy mede van Wedersyde te vreden
waren.
Vorders gevraegt naer voorgaende Bestraffinge, wat haer beweegen
mochten, omme (Haer voorgaende Man, die seer Christelyck van leeven was, qualyck overleeden sijnde) sig metten eersten te begeeven
tot huwelycksche Beloften, dat onfatsoenelyck was, Gaft tot Antwoort en Verontschuldinge, datse anders soude koomen ten laste van
de Armen, en datter, die een Vrouw was ende een jong kint hadde,
onmogelyck soude wesen, om te planten, ploegen, sayen, wieden, oft
't lant, dat leeg soude leggen, te gebruycken. 't welck alles met
dit Twede Huwelyck haer ten Goede, ende ons tot ontlastinge konde
strecken. Ende als wij seijden, dat sulcks ongeoorlof was,

Translation

Name of the Lord with a humble and submissive heart, and to beg
and beseech Him, if His Divine Majesty pleases, to turn His
righteous plagues and well-deserved punishments away from us
and to put an end to them; to continue the peace and good harmony between us and our neighbors; to take us and this nascent
province under His paternal protection and to preserve us from
all evil practices; to bless the fruits of the earth with early
and late rains; and especially, to make the fear and knowledge
of His Name, and the hatred of our own sins, grow and increase
among us. For the sake of optimum compliance [with our orders],
the afore-mentioned Director-General and Councillors prohibit
all exertion and exercise, labor and trade, no matter how it is
called, on the aforesaid day of fasting and prayers, as well as
all illegal pastimes [such as] playing dice and getting drunk,
on the penalties laid down in the past; and the ministers of
the Holy Word of God within this province are requested to word
their sermons and prayers to the aforesaid end. Done in the
meeting of the Hon. Lord Director-General and Councillors of
New Netherland, held in Fort Amsterdam, March 1, 1663.

(underneath stood)

P. Stuijvesant

By order of the Hon. Lord Director-General and Councillors of
New Netherland,

(underneath stood)

C. V. Ruijven, Secretary

[April] 18 [1663]

Pieter Prae van Diepe [= of Dieppe], who died on the sixth of
the previous month and was interred by the deaconry, had left
behind two children of his first marriage, and [for that reason]
we, whose duty it is to look after the poor orphans, deemed it
necessary after these six weeks to summon to the consistory the
widow he left behind, Catharina Letie, who was engaged again to
Joost Casparsen van Groeningen [= of Groningen], living in Boswijck, and to learn what the aforesaid Pieter might have left
behind. However, upon finding little or nothing of importance,
the afore-mentioned consistory made a once-and-for-all settlement
with the aforesaid widow with regard to the minor orphans for
eighty guilders in sewan, to the satisfaction of both parties.
Furthermore, we reprimanded her and asked her what ever moved
her to have her banns proclaimed so soon which was indecent
(since her previous husband, who had led a very Christian life,
had just died). [She] apologized and replied that otherwise she
would become a burden to the poor and that it would be impossible
for her, a woman with a young child, to plant, plow, sow, weed,
or use the land, which would lie barren; this second marriage
could turn all of this for the better for her and lighten our
burdens. And when we said that this was unallowed because she

67

Original

[35^r: "Pag. 68"]

omdatse swaer mochte syn, van haer overleeden man, welcke gisteren
over ses weecken gestorven, en schielyck sieck geworden was,
Sprack seer hoog en leeg, dat se ons verseeckerde van niet swaer
te wesen, ende noemende ten dien eynde Verscheyden Vrouws personen,
die ledematen syn, en sulcks, als sy seyde, wel wisten.
Heeft oock binnen gestaen, Jan Martyn van Campen, Ledemaet, ende
jnwoonder tot Breuckelen, ende versocht van den E: Kerckenraet,
dat Annetie Prae, Dochter van Pieter Prae sal^r, mochte tot synent
woonen, met beloften van alles te doen, 't Welcke harenthalven billick en behoorlijck soude wesen. Daer van met malckanderen spreeckende, ende ten vollen verseeckert sijnde van syn bescheydentheyt
en godtvruchtigheyt des leevens; niet twyffelende, of de Voorgemelte Annetie sal 't allenthalven ten besten strecken, Heeft de Kerckenraet, tot Welvaert en opsichte van de Arme Weesen ende voornamentlyck der ledematen verplicht synde, sulcks den Voornoemde Jan
Martyn geconsenteert en toegestaen, met hem treedende in dit Accoort, dat sy van de diaconie, ofte van 't geen haer van Catharina
Lethie toegewesen is, met een kleetie uytgereet, soude t'sijner
dienste wesen van de tydt van ses achtervolgende jaren: En dat
hy van synent weegen den Voorgemelte Annetie Prae vorders versien
sal van kost en kleeren, en 's winters tot het Avontschool te senden, naer 't Contract daer van gemaeckt, en van hem onderteeckent.
Heeft Mr Carel d'Beauvois, Schoolmeester en Voorsanger tot Breuckelen, versocht, dat hy den koey (van den diaconie Verleeden Veer-
tiende Maij des jaers 1662 ontfangen ten halven aenteelinge met
Exemptie van Boterpacht) mochte, door de Groote Swackheyt en weynig melcks van den Voorgemelte koeij, tegens den Aenstaende Middel-
maij wedergeeven, 't geen hem bij de Broeders toegestaen is, die
oock goet gevonden hebben den Voorschreven koey in 't Bosch vet te
laten loopen, en met den Herfst te verkoopen.

Den 1 Julij

Door 't Alderdroevigste Ongeluck en moetwillige Massacre van de
Esopische Wilden, die met voorbedachte raet getracht hebben den
Esopus onder schyn van Vrientschap afteloopen, ende middelerwijle
tot Groote droeffenisse verleden 7sten Juny verscheyden persoonen
in de Esopus gedoot, sommige gequest, Veele gevangen, Huysen verbrant, ende 't gantsche Nieuwe dorp verwoest hebben, wiert ons
tegenwoordig gegeeven, en bevoolen den Gemeynte voor te leesen,
desen (om den Almachtigen te bewegen tot ontferminge en barmhertigheyt, en N. Nederl^t tot boetvaerdigheyt en bekeeringe) Navolgende
Uytschryvinge van Algemeene en Ordinarische vast en Bededagen die,
van den Vierden des Tegenwoordige beginnende, sullen alle maenden
op den Eerste woensdag door last van den E: H. Generl. en Raden
van N. Nederl^t gehouden worden, wiens Copye is,

Eersame, lieve, Besondere,

Het is UL: soo niet alle, immers het meerendeel bekent, hoe dat
den Almachtigen Godt, den Rechtveerdigen Richter des Heemels ende
der Aerden, weijnig maenden geleeden over dit lant en Volck heeft

Translation

might be pregnant from her deceased husband who died six weeks ago yesterday after a sudden illness, [she] assured us with great emphasis that she was not pregnant, and to that end she mentioned several women, members, who knew this, according to her.

Jan Martyn van Campen [= of Kampen], a member living in Breuckelen, also appeared and asked the Hon. Consistory to allow Annetie Prae, daughter of the late Pieter Prae, to live with him, with the promise to do everything that would be fair to her and proper. After discussing this among ourselves and fully ascertaining his modest and pious conduct, not doubting that it would be beneficial to the afore-mentioned Annetie in every respect, the consistory, whose duty it is to care for and look after the poor orphans and especially the members, gave the aforesaid Jan Martyn consent and permission and entered into the following agreement with him: that she will be provided with a little frock, [either] by the deaconry or from what has been granted her by Catharina Lethie, and that she will serve him for a period of six consecutive years; and that he on his part from now on will provide the afore-mentioned Annetie Prae with board and clothing and will send her to evening-school in winter - [all of this] in accordance with the contract made on this occasion and signed by him.

Mr. Carel d'Beauvois, schoolmaster and precentor in Breuckelen, requested permission to return the cow (received from the deaconry on May 14 last, in 1662, at half the offspring[42] while exempted from butter-lease) by the middle of the imminent month of May, in view of the serious weakness of the afore-mentioned cow and its low milk-yield. This was granted by the brethren, who also decided to fatten the aforesaid cow in the woods and sell it in the fall.

July 1 [1663]

On account of the extremely distressing calamity and wanton massacre by the Esopus savages - who with malicious intent tried to walk down the Esopus [River] under the pretence of friendship and in the meantime, on June 7 last, killed several persons in Esopus, wounded some, took many prisoner, burned down houses, and destroyed the entire new village, to [our] great sorrow - we were given today and ordered to read to the congregation (in order to induce the Almighty to pity and mercy, and New Netherland to penitence and repentance) the following ordinance calling for general and ordinary days of fasting and prayers, which will be held every month on the first Wednesday, beginning on the fourth of the present [month], by order of the Hon. Lord General and Councillors of New Netherland; a copy of which reads as follows:

Respectable, Dear, [and] Special [People],

It is known to you - if not to all, in any case to the majority - that a few months ago, God Almighty, the righteous judge of heaven and earth, thundered over this country and

Original

[36^r: "Pag. 70"]

gedondert, door de stemme van syn Rechtvaerdige Oordeelen, het
selve rontom besoeckende met de Seer besmettelycke Sieckte der
kinderpocken, waerdoor veele sonder onderscheyt van jaeren in een
meerder getal dan oyt voordesen uyt de landen der leevendige (Eerse des gedachten) syn weg geruckt, welcke gerichten en oordelen
Godts over anderen geoeffent, of wel ons (die syne Goedertierentheyt noch voor een korten tydt heeft gelieven te sparen) hadde behooren te dienen ende te brengen tot opmerckinge en waerschouwinge,
dat wij alle des gelijcks sullen vergaen, so wij ons niet en bekeeren, so syn wij echter in onse voorgaende sonden, als daer syn
traegheyt en lauwicheyt in den Godtsdienst, lasteringe synes Heyligen Naems, Schendinge des Sabbaths, dronckenschap, wulpsheyt, Hoer-
erye, overspel, Haet, nyt, leugen, bedriegerijen, pracht, mis-
bruyck der Gaven Godts, en andere gruwelycke sonden meer gecontinu-
eert en voortgegaen, en dewyle wy Godt tegenwandelen in onse Sonden, Soo gaet hy ons oock tegen met sijn Straffen, gelyck Godt
Spreeckt by den Propheet, daeromme (te weten, omdatse syn gebooden
verwierpen) is den toorne des Heeren Ontsteecken tegens sijn Volck,
ende hij heeft tegens het selve syne hant uytgestreckt, ende hy
heeft het geslagen, so dat de Bergen hebben gebeeft, &c. Ende
alsoo wij nu wederomme de Toorne des Heeren swaerlyck tegens ons
brandende sien met syn opgeheeven hant, niet alleen dreygende een
Lantverdervende Oorlog, nemaer ons reets doende gevoelen de daede-
lycke Vruchten des Selfs in 't gevangen neemen, moorden, en bran-
den van onse Vrunden, Lantsgenooten, en mede ingeseetenen door de
Cruellen en wreede barbaren in de Esopus, Alle 't welcke dan
sijnde een Rechtveerdige Vergeldinge en huysbesoeckinge van onsen
Godt over onse Gruwelycke en Godttergende Sonden en al te groote
ondanckbaerheijt voor veele genooten seegeningen en weldaeden,
Het heeft daeromme den Direct? Generael en Raeden van Nieuw-nederlant nootsaeckelyck gedacht (omme sulck van den alleen Barmhertige
Godt door ootmoedige gebeeden, Vasten, Rouw- en Weeclaegen aftte
bidden) te beraemen en uyt te schryven Een Algemeene Vast en bede-
dagh, die alomme binnen dese Provintie gehouden sal werden op den
Eersten woensdag in de maent July synde den 4^e dag der selver
maent, en vervolgens alle maenden op den Eersten woensdag in de
maent. Oversulcks worden alle ingeseetenen deser Provintie, so
wel officiers als onderdaenen, by desen gelast ten voorschreven
dage in de kercke, ofte daermen gewoon is Godts woort te preedicken Ende voor te leesen, te verschijnen, omme na aenhooringe des
Selfs met een bekeert gemoet en een needrig verslagen herte den
name des Heeren vieriglyck aen te roepen, hem te bidden ende te
smeecken, dattet syne Goddelycke Majesteyt gelieve syne Rechtvaerdige plagen, daer mede wij alreets syn en worden aengetast, van
ons weg te neemen, syn roede, die over ons bloeyt, van ons afte-
wenden, ende syne toorne uyt te storten over de Heijdenen, die
syne Naeme niet en kennen, Voor al ende voornamentlyck, dattet
syne goddelycke Majesteyt gelieve, de aengewende middelen tot los-
singe van de Gevangenen dier maten te seegenen, dat se weder in
vrijheyt mogen werden gestelt, en sy neffens ons den Heere daer
voor loff en danck mogen toebrengen, en vorders dattet syne Goddelycke Majesteijt gelieve dese Eerst opluyckende Provintie en des
selfs inwoonderen in syn Vaderlycke beschuttinge en bescherminge
aenteneemen, de selve te mainteneeren tegens de Cruelle Barbaren,
en haere Raetslagen te verydelen, daerentegen onse Overicheyt en

Translation

people through the voice of His righteous judgements, visiting
every corner of the country with the very contagious disease
smallpox, by which many people, regardless of age [and] in a
greater number than ever before, were torn away from the lands
of the living (before they even realized it). These trials and
judgements, carried out by God against others, should have served
as a reminder and warning to us (whom His mercy chose to spare
for a while longer) that all of us will fare likewise if we do
not repent. However, we continued and persisted in our sins of
the past, such as sluggishness and lukewarmness in the divine
worship, blasphemy of His Holy Name, breaking the Sabbath,
drunkenness, lasciviousness, fornication, adultery, hatred, envy,
lying, deceiving, pomp, abuse of God's gifts, and other horrible
sins. And while we act against God through our sins, He on His
part takes action against us with His punishments, as God speaks
through the Prophet: "It is for that reason (namely, because
they rejected His commandments) that the Lord aimed His wrath
against His people, and He stretched His hand out against them,
and He struck them, so that the mountains trembled", etc. And
since we are now again seeing the Lord's wrath burning severely
against us, with His hand raised, not only threatening [us] with
a war that will ruin the country, but also making us already feel
the immediate consequences of such a war - [namely] the capture,
murder, and burning of our friends, fellow-countrymen, and co-
inhabitants by the cruel and ferocious barbarians in Esopus, all
of this being a righteous retaliation and visitation by our God
for the horrible sins by which we irritate Him and for [our] all
too great lack of gratitude for many blessings and benefits
received -; Therefore, the Director-General and Councillors of
New Netherland have deemed it necessary (in order to beseech the
only merciful God, through humble prayers, fasting, mourning and
lamenting, to turn these [punishments] away from us) to plan and
prescribe a general day of fasting and prayers, which will be
held everywhere in this province on the first Wednesday in the
month of July, being the 4th day of that month, and subsequently
on the first Wednesday of every month. For this reason, all
inhabitants of this province, both administrators and subjects,
are hereby ordered to appear in church on the aforesaid day, or
wherever one is accustomed to preach and read the Word of God,
in order to hear the Word of God, to invoke ardently the Name of
the Lord with a repentant, humble, and submissive heart, and to
beg and beseech Him, if His Divine Majesty pleases, to take away
from us His righteous plagues by which we already were, and are
being, affected, to turn away from us His birch which is bleeding
over us, and to pour out His wrath over the pagans who do not
know His Name; [we should beg Him] above all and especially, if
His Divine Majesty pleases, to bless the means employed to free
the captives, to such an extent that they will be liberated and
together with us will praise and thank the Lord for that; and
furthermore, if His Divine Majesty pleases, to take this nascent
province and its inhabitants under His paternal shelter and
protection, to preserve them from the cruel barbarians and thwart
their attacks, and, on the other hand, to confer common sense,

Original

[37^r: "Pag. 72"]

Regenten des Lants te begaven met Verstant, Wysheyt, Voorsichtig-
heijt en Godtsalicheyt, dat se mogen resolveeren, beoogen, ende
cloeckmoediglyck uytvoeren het geene, dat welstant des Lants ende
der Goede Ingeseetene na Lichaem en siele mach dienstig syn.
't Welcke op dat te beter gepractiseert en naer gecomen mag werden,
Den Direct! Generael en Raeden Voorgemelt verbieden ten Voorschreven Vast en Bededagen alle Exercitien en oeffeningen, Hanteeringe
ende Neeringe, hoe de selve oock soude mogen werden genaemt, mitsgaders alle ongeoorlooffde Speelen, Dobbelen en dronckendrincken,
op d'Amende Voormaels daer op beraemt, en worden de Dienaren van
Godes Heyligh woort versocht hare Predicatien ende gebeden ten
voorschreeven eijnde te willen formeeren. Aldus gedaen ter Vergaderinge van den E: Heere Direct! Generael en Raeden van Nieuw-
Nederlant in 't Fort Amsterdam, den 26 junij, A? 1663.

                (Was onderteeckent)

                        P. Stuijvesant

        Den 23 Septemb.

Sijn, als Ledematen van de Ware Gereformeerde kercke, tot onser
Gemeynte aengenoomen en ingeschreeven, naer behoorlycke Attestatie
en getuygenisse, dese navolgende Persoonen,

        Pierre Parmentier,
        Thonnet Terrin,
                Met Attestatie van Manheim.
        Roelof Willemssen,
        Willemken Thyssen,
                Met Attestatie van Beverwyck.

Ten regarde van de kinderen van Teuntie Straetsmans wiert ingegee-
ven, dat Hendrick Janssen van der Vin, burger van N. Amsterdam, volgens syn uytgeschreeven reeckening veel van den Voorgemelte kinderen pretendeerende, door Henricus Selyns, als last van den Kerckenraet hebbende, verleden 6sten August van der kinders wegen ten Vollen voldaen is. Ende ontfangen hebbende Seecker Sog met een
keutie, nagelaten by Teuntie Straetsmans, ende loopende op de Cujanes, van Estime omtrent 45 guld., den navolgende Quitantie daer op
passeerende,

Ick ondergeschreeven bekenne, deugdelyck voldaen te sijn wegens
't geen hadde te pretendeeren op de kinderen van Teuntie Straetsmans in haer leven aen myn Schuldig geweest, ende voor het Part
van de Voorschr. kinderen bedragende omtrent 45 guld. Daer voor
aengenoomen een Sog en een keutie daer by, synde een beertge:
Waer over den voorn kinderen hier mede ten vollen quiteere, en
voor namaninge beloove te bevryden. Amsterd. in N. Nederl!, den
6. Augusti, 1663.

        (leger Stont)   .

't Bovenstaende gedaen, en ontfangen van de diaconie ten dorpe

                        72

Translation

wisdom, carefulness, and piety upon the government and regents
of this country, so that they may determine, pursue, and execute
bravely whatever might be conducive to the well-being of the
country and its good inhabitants, in body and mind. For the
sake of optimum compliance [with our orders], the afore-mentioned Director-General and Councillors prohibit all exertion and
exercise, labor and trade, no matter how it is called, on the
aforesaid days of fasting and prayers, as well as all illegal
pastimes [such as] playing dice and getting drunk, on the
penalties laid down in the past; and the ministers of the Holy
Word of God are requested to word their sermons and prayers to
the aforesaid end. Done in the meeting of the Hon. Lord Director-General and Councillors of New Netherland in Fort Amsterdam,
June 26, 1663.

(was signed)

P. Stuijvesant

September 23 [1663]

On the basis of proper attestations and upon confessions of
faith, the following persons were confirmed and registered in our
congregation as members of the true Reformed Church:

Pierre Parmentier, [and]
Thonnet Terrin,
        with an attestation from Mannheim.
Roelof Willemssen, [and]
Willemken Thyssen,
        with an attestation from Beverwijck.

With regard to Teuntie Straetsmans' children, notice was given
that on August 6 last, Hendrick Janssen van der Vin, burgher of
New Amsterdam, whose claims on the afore-mentioned children were
considerable according to the bill he had made out, was fully
satisfied on behalf of the children by Henricus Selyns, by order
of the consistory; and that he received a certain sow with a
little hog, left behind by Teuntie Straetsmans and feeding at the
Gowanus, worth an estimated 45 guilders, as per the following
receipt:

I, the undersigned, acknowledge to have been satisfied properly
for the claims [I] had on the children of Teuntie Straetsmans,
who in her lifetime owed me approximately 45 guilders, which is
what the children's debt amounted to. In return, [I] received
a sow, and with it a little hog, a young boar. Herewith, [I]
fully absolve the aforesaid children and promise to free them
from future claims. Amsterdam in New Netherland, August 6,
1663.

(underneath stood)

The above having been done and received from the deaconry in

Original

[38^V: "Pag. 75"]

van Breuckelen in N. Nederl^t dato als boven, oirconde dit met myn
Eygenhant onderteeckent.

(Ende was onderteeckent)

Hendrick Janssen Van der Vin

Mitsgaders dat wij Hendrick Marten van Coppenhagen, die de Man was
van Margariet Meyrinck en schoonsoon van wylen Teuntie Straetsman,
met den Tegenwoordige Oorlog gevangen van de Esopische Wilden en
verlost van de Onsen, Ende welcke soude toekoomen 't derde part
van Teuntie Straetsmans Boel (den Dootschulden en gemeene Schulden
by de kerckenraet verschooten, ofte elders geborgt, daer van afge-
trocken sijnde), toegeleyt hebben, boven 't linnen by 't Sterfhuys
gevonden, so aen linnen als Procuratien op Barentie Straetsman,
des overleedene Suster, ende Gabriel Corbesij, des overleedene man:
de Somma van 65 gl. 19 st.; met beloften van synent wegen, omme
Satisfactie te geeven, naer proportie van de wesen, so der, 't
geen wy niet vertrouwen sullen, andre crediteuren als voldaen syn,
mochte voor den dag komen. Ende met aenneeminge van onsent weegen,
omme den Heer Olof Stephensen te betalen Een Tonne Biers, daer den
Voorschreev. Hendrick Martensen, die 't derde deel van syn Schoon-
moeders wegen Schuldig was, van bevrydt soude wesen. Met syn
merck heeft Hendrick Martense 't voorgaande onderteeckent.
Om te koomen tot de Verschootene Penningen voor 't Sterfhuys en
wesen van Teuntie Straetsman, was 't Tabacq by de diaconie verkocht aen Fredrick Philipsen, en daer te ontfangen, namentlyck
    370 lb tabacq à 10 st lb, ende
    134 lb tabacq à 5 st lb, komt met 't Aftrecken van 't waeg-
loon 218-10.
Ende met deser Geleegentheijt wort de Reeckening van Ontfang en
Uytgift ten regarde van de Boel en sterfhuys van Teuntie Straetsman aldus bevonden;

Kerckenraet Van Breuckelen

Ontfangen van 't Voorgemelte Sterfhuijs,

35 el. osenbrugs linnen, met Gabriel Corbesy gedeelt		
1½ el. Blaeuw linnen	Gld.	.. ..
Een Sog met een Ceutie	Gld.	45- 0
Van Barentie Straetsman, van verkochte Pom-		
poenen &c.	Gld.	45- 0
Van dicto Barentie, van diergelycke	Gld.	30- 0
Van Tabacq, aen Fredrick Philipsen jn See-		
want verkocht	Gld.	218-10
Van Seecker Myt Hoijs, 't welck Gabriel		
toegestaen was om naderhant te vergoeden	Gld.	16-13
	Somma Gld.	355- 3

Contra Uijtgegeeven, voor 't Voorsch. Sterfhuijs,

't gedeelde 35 ellen, 't welck 17½ el. was, aen Laurens Haf, Anna
Tienemans, en Hendrick Martensen, elck voor 1/3 deel
aen Anna Tienemans, 1½ el Blaeuw linnen   Gld. .. ..

[continued on p. 76]

Translation

the village of Breuckelen in New Netherland on the date as above, [I] confirm this officially by signing with my own hand.

(and was signed)

Hendrick Janssen van der Vin

Furthermore, [it was made known] that we granted Hendrick Marten van Coppenhagen [= of Copenhagen] - who was Margariet Meyrinck's husband and the late Teuntie Straetsman's son-in-law; [who was] captured during the present war by the savages of the Esopus and liberated by our forces; and to whom is due one-third of Teuntie Straetsmans' estate (after deducting the debts of the deceased and the ordinary debts advanced by the consistory or given on credit elsewhere) - in addition to the linen found at the house of the deceased, the sum of 65 guilders 19 stuivers, both in linen and in warrants made out to Barentie Straetsman, sister of the deceased, and to Gabriel Corbesij, husband of the deceased; with the promise on his part to give satisfaction, in proportion to the orphans, if creditors might show up other than the ones who were satisfied, which we do not expect. And we on our part took it upon ourselves to pay Sir Olof Stephensen a barrel of beer, from which the aforesaid Hendrick Martensen would be absolved who owed one-third on his mother-in-law's behalf. Hendrick Martense signed the above with his mark.

In order to pay back the money that had been advanced for the house of the deceased Teuntie Straetsman and to [her] orphans, the tobacco had been sold by the deaconry to Fredrick Philipsen, for which [we] will receive:

370 lbs. of tobacco at 10 stuivers a lb., and
134 lbs. of tobacco at 5 stuivers a lb., which, after deducting the weighing expenses, amounts to [Gld.] 218-10.

And on this occasion, the account of receipts and expenditures with regard to the estate and house of the deceased Teuntie Straetsman was found as follows:

Consistory of Breuckelen

Received from the afore-mentioned house of the deceased,

35 els[43] of osnaburg[44] linen, shared with Gabriel Corbesy;		
1½ els of blue linen:[45]	Gld.	.. ..
A sow with a little hog:	Gld.	45- 0
From Barentie Straetsman, for pumpkins etc.:	Gld.	45- 0
From the same Barentie, for similar items:	Gld.	30- 0
From tobacco, sold to Fredrick Philipsen in sewan:	Gld.	218-10
From a certain stack of hay, which Gabriel was permitted to pay for later:	Gld.	16-13
Total:	Gld.	355- 3

Spent, on the other hand, for the aforesaid house of the deceased,

The share in the 35 els, amounting to 17½ els for Laurens Haf,

[continued on p. 77]

75

Original

Aen Hendrick Jansen van den Vin, een sog met een Ceutie	Gld.	45
Aen Gabriel Corbesy, tot betalinge van M.[r] Carel de Beauvois, voor 't graf en aenspreecken	Gld.	11-14
van Wiggert Reyniersen, voor seeckre Restant	Gld.	11
van M.[r] Jeurie de smit	Gld.	6
Van Besie Beulings	Gld.	3
Van 't kerckhoft	Gld.	2
Ende van verscheyden kladschulden, mits-gaders Kors Janssen van 't gelt onthouden heeft, alles van Barentie Straetsmans ge-sonden	Gld.	11- 6
Somma	Gld.	90- 0

Comt van 't Voorgaende bladt uytgegeeven	Gld.	90- 0
Verschooten bij de kerckenraet, so tot doot-schulden als Nagelaten Wesen, Laurens Haf en Anna Tienemans, mitsgaders van ver-scheijden oncosten, ten regarde van 't coren te dorschen, Tabacq te strippen en Packen, 't Tabacqsvat te maecken, &c, naer de Reeckening van de diaconie	Gld.	163- 8-8
Aen Hendrick Martense van Coppenhagen, 12 ell. osenbrugs gebleeckt linnen ã 32 st.	Gld.	19- 4
Op Barentie Straetsmans, procuratie van	Gld.	30- 0
Op Gabriel Corbesije, van het Hoij, pro-curatie van	Gld.	16-13
Voor Anna Tienemans, een paer schoenen be-steedt	Gld.	7-10
Aen Burgerm. Olof Stephensen, een ton bier aengenoomen voor de Erfgenamen te betalen	Gld.	24- 0
Somma	Gld.	350- 5-8

Resteert voor den Voorschr Laurens Haf en Anna Tienemans,

Van den kerckenraet	Gld.	4-17-8
Van Gabriel Corbesij, van 't Hoij	Gld.	8-12
Met een Ceutie, van 't Vercken, haer toebe-hoort hebbende, voortgekoomen	Gld.	.. .. .
Somma	Gld.	13- 9-8

Den 28 Octob.

Wiert goetgevonden M.[r] Carels d'Beauvois Tractement te verbeeteren, ende voor de Vier Schepels Cooren, die wy hem toegeleyt hadden, 's jaerelycks te geeven Vyftig guldens seewant, 't Welcke volgens Accoort van Vyfentwingtig Guldens t'samen bedraegt Vyfenseeventig Guldens Seewant, boven Vrij huyshuur, en boven van den E: H. Ont-fanger Generael Van Ruyven en deser Gerechte tot syn Tractement gecontribueert wort. Ende 't Welcke, om syn Persoon te yveriger

Translation

Anna Tienemans, and Hendrick Martensen, 1/3 each;
To Anna Tienemans, 1½ els of blue linen:[46]   Gld.   .. ..
To Hendrick Jansen van den Vin, a sow with a
    little hog: Gld.   45
To Gabriel Corbesy, in order to pay Mr. Carel
    de Beauvois for the grave and [his funeral]
    oration: Gld.   11-14
    [to pay] Wiggert Reyniersen a certain
    balance: Gld.   11
    [to pay] Mr. Jeurie the smith: Gld.   6
    [to pay] Besie Beulings: Gld.   3
    [to pay] for the churchyard: Gld.   2
And [to pay off] several trifling debts, as
well as [what] Kors Janssen withheld from
the money, everything sent by Barentie
Straetsmans: Gld.   11- 6
                                      Total: Gld.   90- 0

Spent as per the preceding page: Gld.   90- 0
Advanced by the consistory, both to the deceas-
    ed and to the orphans left behind, Laurens
    Haf and Anna Tienemans, as well as several
    expenses made for threshing the grain,
    stripping and packing tobacco, repairing
    the tobacco-barrel, etc., in accordance
    with the deaconry's account: Gld. 163- 8-8
To Hendrick Martense van Coppenhagen [= of
    Copenhagen],
    12 els of bleached osnaburg linen at
    32 stuivers [per el]:   Gld.   19- 4
    A warrant made out to Barentie Straetsmans
    to the amount of: Gld.   30- 0
    A warrant made out to Gabriel Corbesije,
    for the hay: Gld.   16-13
Spent for Anna Tienemans, on a pair of shoes: Gld.   7-10
To Burgomaster Olof Stephensen, a barrel of
    beer, which [we] offered to pay on behalf
    of the heirs: Gld.   24- 0
                                      Total: Gld. 350- 5-8 [47]

    Left for the aforesaid Laurens Haf and Anna Tienemans,

From the consistory: Gld.   4-17-8
From Gabriel Corbesij, for the hay: Gld.   8-12
With a little hog, offspring of the pig which
    belonged to them:[48]   Gld.   .. .. .
                                      Total: Gld.   13- 9-8

October 28 [1663]

    It was approved to improve Mr. Carel d'Beauvois' salary and to
give him annually, instead of the four schepels[49] of grain which
we had awarded him, fifty guilders in sewan, which together with
the [existing] arrangement of twenty-five guilders adds up to
seventy-five guilders in sewan, in addition to free house-rent

Original

[40^V: "Pag. 79"]

te maecken in syn bedieninge en meer Encouragement te geeven, Hem
aengeseyt synde, den kerckenraet voor den Voorgemelte Verbeete-
ringe bedanckt heeft.

Den 23 Decmb.

Tot Ledematen syn den Navolgende na de aenroepinge van de Name des
Heeren aengenoomen,

    Cornelis Van Bossum,
        Getuygen,
            Jan Hybon, Dirck Janssen.
    Geertie Gijsbert,
          wiens getuijge was,
            Grietie Jans.
    Jean Messural,
    Jenne Carton,
        Met Attestatie van Manheim.

A^O 1664

Den 17 Februar.

Den Kerckenraet bericht sijnde, door seecker Engelsman David Hopkims, dat Tieleman Jacobssen (die geseyt was op 't Eijlant Gardelupe gebleeven, en naderhant gestorven te wesen, ende wiens dochter, by wijlen Teuntie Straetsmans nagelaten, van ons tot Gerrit
Corñ. van Niekerck besteedt is) soude op 't Eylant Jamaica in 't
leeven sijn ende sig met cleermaecken geneeren, docht naer de
Warachtige beschryvinge van syn Persoon, wesen, en maniere van leeven, niet ongeraetsaem te wesen, derwaerts met den Voorgemelte
David Hopkims te schryven, syn persoon bekent te maecken van
Teuntie Straetsmans doot, ende overgebleevene Anna Tielemans,
't zij om haer te halen, oft iets te senden tot een teecken van Vaderlycke Affectie. Ende met Eene om den Eerwaerd^e, Godtsalige, en
seer geleerde d^o Samuel Drisius, bedienaer des Goddelycke Woort
tot Amsterdam in N. Nederl^t, te versoecken, dat syn Eerw^e, die met
Teuntie Straetsman, als den meergemelte Tieleman daer gebleeven is,
van Gardelupe gekoomen was, soude gelieven tot versterckinge te
onderteeckenen. 't geen wy dan geschreeven hebben, was dit volgende,

                    Copie van den Brieff geschreeven
                    aen Tieleman Jacobsen van den
                    kerckenraet tot Breuckelen

    Goede Vrunt, Tieleman Jacobsen,

Alsoo wij tot Verwonderinge bericht syn van den Brenger deses,

Translation

and on top of [what] is contributed to his salary by the Hon. Lord
Receiver-General Van Ruyven and the Court in this place. And after
this was told him, in order to make him even more diligent in his
service and to give him more encouragement, [he] thanked the consistory for the afore-mentioned raise.

December 23 [1663]

   Upon the invocation of the Name of the Lord, the following
people were confirmed as members:
      Cornelis Van Bossum;
                 witnesses:
                      Jan Hybon, Dirck Janssen.
      Geertie Gijsbert,
                 whose witness was:
                      Grietie Jans.
      Jean Messural, [and]
      Jenne Carton,
                 with an attestation from Mannheim.

A.D. 1664

   February 17

   The consistory - notified by a certain Englishman, David
Hopkims, that Tieleman Jacobssen (who was said to have stayed behind
on the island of Guadeloupe and to have died later on, and whose
daughter, left behind by the late Teuntie Straetsmans, had been
placed by us in the custody of Gerrit Corn[elissen] van Niekerck
[= of Niekerk]) reportedly was alive on the island of Jamaica and
made his living as a tailor - deemed it not inexpedient, judging
from the true description of his person, character, and way of
living, to write to him via the afore-mentioned David Hopkims,
[and] to inform him of Teuntie Straetsmans' death which had left
Anna Tielemans behind, so that he either could call for her or
send her something as a token of paternal affection. And at the
same time, [we would] ask the Rev., godly, and very learned Domine
Samuel Drisius, minister of the Word of God in Amsterdam in New
Netherland, who had come from Guadeloupe along with Teuntie Straetsman when the afore-mentioned Tieleman had stayed behind there, to
be so kind as to add weight [to the letter] by [co-]signing it.
This, then, is what we wrote:

                        Copy of the letter written to
                        Tieleman Jacobsen by the consistory
                        of Breuckelen

   Dear Friend, Tieleman Jacobsen,

   Since we were informed to our surprise by the bearer, David

79

Original

[41^r: "Pag. 80"]

David Hopkims, Engelsman, UL. (Als hy seyt) goede bekende en sonderlinge Vrunt, dat gij, die lang doot geschreeven waert, in 't
leeven en noch wel te passe zijt, UL: tot Jamaica met Cleêrmaecken
geneerende, en dat gij, omdat gy gehoort hadde, dat Teuntie
Straetsman getrouwt was, niet begeerig waert na Nieuw-Nederlant te
trecken, So dient dit alles tot uwer onderrichtinge, dat sy tot
verscheyden reijse bericht was, dat gy, die op 't Eylant Gardelupe
gebleeven syt, gestorven waert, en dat sij ten laesten met consent
van den E: H^r Generael Petrus Stuyvensant wederom tot den Echten
staet getreeden is met Gabriel Corbesij, soldaet van den Hooggemelte Generael. Maer sy, die gemeent heeft, dat gy voor haer gestorven waert, heeft UL de Weg gewesen door de doot, die niemant
verschoont, namentlyck den 19 Octob. 1662. 't Geense nagelaten
heeft, was seer weynig van jmportantie, en neffens dien Margariet
Meyringk, die voor den tweedemael getrouwt is met Hendrick Martensen van Coppenhagen, en drie kinderen heeft; Laurens Haf, die wy
besteet hebben tot Henricus Selyns, predicant op den Voorgemelte
Generaels-Bouwerye en tot Breuckelen; Ende Anna Tielemans, UL.
dochter, die wy tot Middelwout, oft anders 't Vlackebosch genaemt,
verhuurt hebben tot Gerrit Cornelissen, en daer se dick en vet
wort, tot een teecken dat sy der beter aert als sy t'Huys gedaen
heeft, Ende weest Daer van verseeckert, dat de lieden wel syn, en
dat sy uw dochter so wel lyden meugen als haer eijgen kinderen.
Schoon wij dan gedaen hebben naer ons vermoogen, en voortaen
harent halven sullen doen, so hebben wy niettemin niet kunnen na-
laten als UL., die de Vader syt, te adverteeren met den Tegenwoordige, dat uw dochter leeft, opdat so gy se iets te maecken oft te
senden hebt tot een teecken van Vaderlijcke Affectie, dat gy
sulcks doen kunt, ofte so gy se selfs begeert, omdat gij de naeste
syt, niet dat se ons tot overlast is, dat gy se sout kunnen halen,
oft by haer koomen, oft senden Volmachtige met behoorlycke Procura-
tie, en seecker blyck van UE: Gouverneur oft Magistraten, ten
eynde dat wy seecker weten, oft gy leeft, en oft uw wille en be-
geerte is, om den Voorschr. Anna Tielemans tot haer Verresene Vader te senden, so tot uwer vergenoeginge, als voldoeninge onser
Conscientie. Vale. Actum Breuckelen in N. Nederlant, den 17 Feb.
1664.

(onderstont)

Uyt name en laste van onse kerckelycke
Vergaderinge,

(was oock onderteeckent by)	(onderteeckent)
Samuel Drisius,	Henricus Selijns, V D M
predicant op de Man- hatans in N. Amsterdam, die met uw Huysvrouw van Gardelupe gekomen ben, Testis.	Willem Bredenbend, Ouderling
	Teunis Janssen, Ouderling
	Teunis Gysbertsen, diacon

Translation

Hopkims, an Englishman and (according to himself) an old acquaint-
ance and special friend of yours, that you, who were considered
dead for a long time, are alive and well, making a living as a
tailor in Jamaica, and that you are not eager to go to New Netherland because you have heard that Teuntie Straetsman got married,
this serves to notify you that she had been told several times
that you, who had stayed behind on the island of Guadeloupe, had
died, and that eventually, with the Hon. Lord General Petrus
Stuyvensant's consent, she entered into matrimony again, with
Gabriel Corbesij, soldier of the afore-mentioned General. However,
she, who assumed you had died before her, showed you the way
through death (which spares nobody), namely on October 19, 1662.
What she left behind, was of very little importance, but in addition to that, [the following persons]: Margariet Meyringk, who is
married for the second time, to Hendrick Martensen van Coppenhagen
[= of Copenhagen], and [who] has three children; Laurens Haf, whom
we placed in the custody of Henricus Selyns, minister at the
afore-mentioned General's Bowery [= farm] and in Breuckelen; and
Anna Tielemans, your daughter, whom we hired out to Gerrit Cornelissen in Midwout, also called Vlackebos, where she is getting
plump and fat, an indication that she is thriving better there
than she did at home. And you can be assured that the people are
fine and that they like your daughter as much as their own
children. Although we acted to the best of our abilities and
will continue to do so on her behalf, we nonetheless could not
refrain on this occasion from advising you, who are the father,
that your daughter is alive, so that, if you have something to
make for her or send to her as a token of paternal affection, you
can do so, or if you want her yourself since you are her closest
relative (not that she is a burden to us), you could come and get
her or come to her, or send a warrant with a proper procuration
and a certain statement from your governor or magistrates so that
we know for certain whether you are alive and whether it is your
wish and desire that the aforesaid Anna Tielemans be sent to her
risen father, both to your contentment and to the satisfaction of
our conscience. Farewell. Done in Breuckelen in New Netherland,
February 17, 1664.

(underneath stood)

On behalf and by order of our church
meeting,

(was also signed by)   (signed)

Samuel Drisius,   Henricus Selijns, Minister of the
                                          Word of God
Minister in Manhattan
in New Amsterdam,   Willem Bredenbend, Elder
who came along with your
wife from Guadeloupe;   Teunis Janssen, Elder
    as a witness.
                                      Teunis Gysbertsen, Deacon

Original

[42^V: "Pag. 83"]

Den 27 dicto

Syn op de nominatie van ouderlingen en diaconen gebracht, om daer
uyt te verkiesen een ouderling en diacon, dese navolgende Persoonen, Van

Breuckelen,

Albert Cornelissen Wantenaer
Roelof Willemssen
Pierre Parmentier

Cujanes,

Jan Pieterssen
Thomas Verdon
Willem Willemssen

Walebocht,

Rem Janssen
Paulus Dircksen
Marten Reyerssen

't Veer

Frederick Lubbertsen
Dirck Janssen
Cornelis van Bossum

Maer naer verscheijden Debatten wiert door Pluraliteyt van Stemmen
goetgevonden, dat Teunis Gysbertsen, tegenwoordig Diacon, soude
van den Kerckenraedt versocht worden tot Ouderling in de plaetse
van Wilhelmus Bredenbend, wiens tydt naer seer loffelycke en getrouwe Bedieninge geexpireert was, En dat men een Verkiesen soude
van de Cujanes, om de plaetse te vervullen van Teunis Gijsbertsen,
die 't Beroep op syn Eerw.^{e} gedaen aengenoomen heeft. Ende de
Stemmen tot een Diacon colligeerende, syn eendrachtelyck gevallen
op Willem Willemssen, dien wy 't met een Briefken verwittigt hebben door Wilhelmus Bredenbend, daer met hem woonende, om met den
naeste Sondag syn geneegentheyt tot 't Voorgemelt beroep te openbaren. So gebleeven, als verkosen synde den navolgende tot Ouderlingen en Diaconen,

Ouderlingen,

Teunis Janssen Coevors
Teunis Gysbertsen Bogaert

Diaconen,

Willem Gerritsen van Couwenhoven
Willem Willemssen

Translation

[February] 27 [1664]

For the functions of elder and deacon, the following persons were nominated, from among whom one elder and [one] deacon will be elected:

from Breuckelen,

Albert Cornelissen Wantenaer
Roelof Willemssen
Pierre Parmentier

Gowanus,

Jan Pieterssen
Thomas Verdon
Willem Willemssen

Wallabout,

Rem Janssen
Paulus Dircksen
Marten Reyerssen

the Ferry,

Frederick Lubbertsen
Dirck Janssen
Cornelis van Bossum

After several debates, however, it was approved by a majority of the votes that Teunis Gysbertsen, currently deacon, would be asked by the consistory [to become] elder in place of Wilhelmus Bredenbend, whose term had expired after very laudable and loyal service, and that one person from the Gowanus would be elected to fill the place of Teunis Gijsbertsen, who accepted the call made on him. And when the votes for a deacon were collected, they turned out to have been cast unanimously for Willem Willemssen, whom we notified of his election in a note via Wilhelmus Bredenbend, who is living there[50] with him, [and we asked him] to inform us this Sunday of his decision regarding the afore-mentioned call. The following persons remained or were elected elder or deacon:

Elders,

Teunis Janssen Coevors
Teunis Gysbertsen Bogaert

Deacons,

Willem Gerritsen van Couwenhoven
Willem Willemssen

Original

[43^V: "Pag. 85"]

Den 26 Mart.

Sijn Verscheenen den nieuwe Verkoosen ouderlingh, Teunis Gysbertsen Bogaert, ende diacon, Willem Willemssen, die Verleeden Sondag
bevestigt sijn, en dien wy naer den ontfang en uytgift by den oude
kerckenraet onderteeckent, dit navolgende overgeleevert hebben,
seecker koeybeest met een Veers tot Mr Jeurie Probasko, dito koeybeest met een Bulkalf tot Pieter Prae sal^r, 't Testament van Barent Balde met een jaer renten, 't Verschot aen den Gerechte van
Breuckelen, aen Fytie Dircks, wed. van Jan Martyn, aen Teunis
Janssen, ouderling, ende aen Jan Jacobsen, tinwerck tot 't Avontmael en kerckbancken, Restant van Hendrick Janssen van der Vin ten
regarde van syn Gekochte koey, seecker obligatie van Marcus Suson
op syn lant van de wesen van Pieter Prae, Ende gereedt seewant,
met Silvergelt, &c, alles bedragende de somma van duysent vier-
hondert en twee guld. 14 st̃. Ende 't welcke Willem Gerritsen en
Willem Willemssen naer voorgaende onderteeckeninge ontfangen hebben.
Wiert oock Wilhelmus Bredenbend, die ons was t'allentijden seer be-
hulpsaem en stichtelyck ten besten van de gemeente J. Christi,
voor syn getrouwe dienst van ouderlingschap van de gantsche vergaderinge bedanckt, ende den Almachtige bevolen met toewenschinge
van genade en Vrede.

Den 9 April

Tot ledematen sijn den Navolgende aengenoomen, ende t'onser gemeynte ingeschreeven,

    Meijnart Jorneij,
         Met Attestatie van Manheim.
    Jacob Leendertsen,
    Rebecca Fredericks,
         met Attestatie van Middelwout.
    Albert Coningk,
    Tryntie Jans,
         met Attestatie van Middelwout.
    Aert Teunissen Middag, van Heijkoop,
         Getuijgen,
            Teunis Gysbertsen Bogaert, Janneken Joris.
    Janneken Jans, van Almeloo,
         getuygen,
            Paulus Dircksen, Geertie Gijsberts.
    Judith Joris, van N. Nederlant,
         getuygen,
            Catharina Joris, Teunis Gysbertsen.
    Janneken Montfoort, van N. Nederl^t,
         Getuijgen,
            Sara de Plancke, Fytie Dircks.
    Anneken Rems, van N. Nederlant,
         Getuygen,
            Janneken Joris, Catharina Jeronymus.

[continued on p. 86]

Translation

March 26 [1664]

The newly elected elder, Teunis Gysbertsen Bogaert, and deacon,
Willem Willemssen, who were confirmed last Sunday, appeared [in
the consistory], whereupon we handed them the following, as per
the receipts and expenditures signed by the old consistory:
a certain cow with a heifer at Mr. Jeurie Probasko's [place];
another cow with a bull-calf at the late Pieter Prae's; Barent
Balde's bequest with a year's interest; the advances to the Court
of Breuckelen, to Fytie Dircks, widow of Jan Martyn, to Teunis
Janssen, elder, and to Jan Jacobsen; pewter-ware for the Lord's
Supper and pews; the balance [to be received] from Hendrick
Janssen van der Vin for the cow purchased by him; a certain
obligation owed to Pieter Prae's orphans by Marcus Suson
for his land; and ready sewan, with silver money, etc., everything amounting to the sum of one thousand four hundred and two
guilders 14 stuivers. And this was received by Willem Gerritsen
and Willem Willemssen after they had signed it.
Furthermore, Wilhelmus Bredenbend, who at all times had been
very helpful to us and edifying, for the benefit of the congregation of Jesus Christ, was thanked by the entire assembly for his
loyal service as elder, and commended to the Almighty with wishes
of grace and peace.

April 9

The following people were confirmed as members and registered
in our congregation:
    Meijnart Jorneij,
        with an attestation from Mannheim.
    Jacob Leendertsen, [and]
    Rebecca Fredericks,
        with an attestation from Midwout.
    Albert Coningk, [and]
    Tryntie Jans,
        with an attestation from Midwout.
    Aert Teunissen Middag, from Heikop;
        witnesses:
            Teunis Gysbertsen Bogaert, Janneken Joris.
    Janneken Jans, from Almelo;
        witnesses:
            Paulus Dircksen, Geertie Gijsberts.
    Judith Joris, from New Netherland;
        witnesses:
            Catharina Joris, Teunis Gysbertsen.
    Janneken Montfoort, from New Netherland;
        witnesses:
            Sara de Plancke, Fytie Dircks.
    Anneken Rems, from New Netherland;
        witnesses:
            Janneken Joris, Catharina Jeronymus.

[continued on p. 87]

Original

[44^{v}: :Pag. 87"]

Neeltie Jans, van N. Nederlant,
        Getuygen,
            Gerrit Crousen, Willem Gerritsen van Couwen-
        hoven.

        Den 1 Jun:

Metten bedroefden staet van N. Nederl^{t}, so ten aensien van de Wilden, die sommige gedoot, sommige gequest, en sommige van de Onse
gevangen, ja verscheyden huysen verbrant hebben in de Esopus, als
voornamentlyck van de Engelsche, welcke verclaert hadden ons dorp
met 't gantsche Lange Eijlant voor den koning met 't Vliegende
Vaendel, heeft men van Julio laestleden den Eersten woensdag van
de maent gehouden tot een Vast en bededag, ten Eynde om den Almachtigen seer Ernstelyck te beweegen tot Vaderlycke ontferminge en
mededoogentheyt. Maer alles heeft de goede Godt, die gepresen sy,
gebracht ten besten met dit laeste arrivement der Schepen, de
Engelsche tot stilte, en wilden tot Vreede, onse weeclagen tot lof-
sangen, en de maendelycke Vastdagen tot een dag van danckseginge,
die volgens 't besluyt en volgende Ordre van d'E: H^{re} Direct^{r} Generael en Raden van N. Nederl^{t} metten Aenstaende woensdag sal gehouden worden, Van den Heer Secretaris Cornelis van Ruijven alleene
gewaerschouwt, dat wij, die sochtens te Breuckelen en savonts op
den Hooggemelte Generaels-Bouwerye preedicken, soude, metten afkondinge, de woorden van Ende na middag, die in 't origineel staen,
achter wegen laten en overslaen, 't geen wy belooft en aengenoomen
hebben omte doen:

                        Copie van den Algemeene danckdag,
                        door Ordre van de E: H^{r} Dr Generael
                        en HH. Raden van N. Nederlant

Nadien het den Alleen goede Godt, uyt syn sonderlinge Barmhertigheyt, gelieft heeft, tegens alle menschelycke verwachtinge, de
Gevangen Christenen uyt der Barbaren handen te verlossen, ende met
de Verlossinge ons te geeven ende te verleenen een Eerlycke ende
profytelijcke Vreede met den Esopische Wilden, isset niet alleen.
betamelyck, maer ten hoogsten nodig, dat den alleen goede Godt
daer voor geloeft, gedanckt, ende gepreesen werde, niet alleen van
de Verloste Christenen, nemaer oock van allen en een ieder, die
dus lange hare gebeeden voor de Gevangenen tot Godt hebben opgeof-
fert, Het welck, op dattet te beter ende te gesamentlycker werde
gepractiseert ende naergekoomen, wort het de Christelycke gemeente
by desen bekent gemaeckt, dat wy op de Ordre ende aenschryvens van
onse hooge Overicheden, de gewoonelycke Maentlycke Bededag sullen
eyndigen ende besluyten met een Algemeene Danckdag, die gehouden
sal worden op den Eersten woensdag in Junij synde den 4 der selver
maent, ten welcke dage alhier des voor ende naemiddag sal gepredickt worden. Een ieder bereyde syn herte tot ware ende oprechte
danckbaerheyt.

Translation

Neeltie Jans, from New Netherland;
      witnesses:
          Gerrit Crousen, Willem Gerritsen van Couwen-
          hoven.

June 1 [1664]

In view of the distressing condition of New Netherland - both
with regard to the savages who killed some people, wounded others,
took some of our people prisoner, and even burned down several
houses at the Esopus; and especially on account of the English who
with flying banners had claimed our village with all of Long
Island for the King - the first Wednesday of every month since
last July has been observed as a day of fasting and prayers in
order to induce the Almighty very urgently to [show] paternal pity
and compassion. However, the good God - praised be the Lord! -
turned everything for the best through the recent arrival of the
ships: [He turned] the English to silence, the savages to peace,
our lamenting into hymns of praise, and the monthly day of fasting
into a day of thanksgiving, which will be held this Wednesday
according to the resolution and subsequent order by the Hon. Lord
Director-General and Councillors of New Netherland. The Lord
Secretary Cornelis van Ruijven, however, told us that during the
proclamation [of the ordinance], we, who preach in Breuckelen in
the morning and at the afore-mentioned General's Bowery [=farm] in
the evening, should omit and skip the words "and in the afternoon"
which are written in the original; we promised and accepted to do
so.

                    Copy of the general day of thanks-
                    giving, by orders of the Hon. Lord
                    Director-General and Lords
                    Councillors of New Netherland

Since the only good God, in His extraordinary mercy, and against
all human expectation, chose to free the captured Christians
from the hands of the barbarians and to give and grant us, in
addition to the liberation, an honest and profitable peace with
the savages at Esopus, it is not only proper but highly imperative that the only good God be lauded, thanked, and praised for
that, not only by the freed Christians but also by every single
person who remembered the prisoners in his prayers to God for
such a long time. For the sake of optimum compliance, the
Christian congregation is hereby notified that by order 'and
instruction of our high authorities we will end the customary
monthly day of prayers and conclude with a general day of
thanksgiving, which will be held on the first Wednesday in June,
being the 4th of this month, on which day a sermon will be given
in the morning and in the afternoon. Let everyone prepare his
heart for true and sincere gratitude.[51]

Original

[46^r: :Pag. 90"]

Den 23 July

Naer de aenroepinge van de Name des Heeren, en met 't Vertreck van
Henricus Selijns, predicant te deser Plaetse, daer van gesproocken
sal worden, heeft den Voorschreeven Henricus Selyns dit geheele
Prothocol den Vergaderinge voorgelesen, van den beginne totten eynde, om van de Broeders mitsgaders van Willem Bredenbent, out ouderling, gesamentlyck onderteeckent te worden, en vorders te beraet-
slagen, 't welck tot welstant en profyt van de gemeente tot Breuckelen mochte nootsaeckelyck wesen. Neffens Seecker Authentyck
Copie, 't welck gelesen en nagesien wiert, dan van Teunis Gysbertsen Bogaert, Ouderling, en dan van Willem Gerritsen, diacon, alles
volkomentlyck en punctuelyck metten Prothocolle accorderende ende
overeenkomende.
Heeft oock Henricus Selyns sijn Reeckeninge gedaen van 't Trouwgelt by hem ontfangen ende overgeleevert na den navolgende lyste,

Copie van de Reeckeninge van 't
Trouwgelt van Breuckelen, sedert
den 29 Octob. 1662, Van

Dirck Janssen Hooglant	Gld.	5-17-8
Arie Willemsen	Gld.	6- 8
Marten Jansen Meyer	Gld.	6
Lambert Jansen Bosch	Gld.	6
Somma	Gld.	24- 5-8
Comt van 't Voorgaende Bladt	Gld.	24- 5-8
Paulus Heymans	Gld.	6- 7
Claes Teunissen Appeldoorn	Gld.	6
Arie Huybertsen	Gld.	6
Joost Caspartsen	Gld.	6
Jan Corñ. Buys	Gld.	5-18
Pieter Lambertsen	Gld.	6
Marten Reyersen	Gld.	6
Symon Hansen	Gld.	6
Jan Pietersen	Gld.	6
Somma	Gld.	78-10-8

(Was Onderteeckent)

Henricus Selijns

Den Voorgemelte Reeckening opgenoomen hebbende, bevinden naer
Waerheyt te wesen, en bekennen ontfangen te hebben, Actum 23 Jul.
1664.
(Onderstont)

Willem Gerritsen van Couwenhooven

Willem Willemsen

Translation

July 23 [1664]

In view of the [imminent] departure of Henricus Selijns, minister in this place, which will be discussed later, the aforesaid
Henricus Selyns, after the invocation of the Name of the Lord,
read this entire Protocol to the meeting, from beginning to end,
in order to have it signed by all the brethren as well as by
Willem Bredenbent, former elder, and furthermore, to discuss whatever might be needed for the well-being and benefit of the congregation in Breuckelen. [He] also [showed] a certain certified copy,
which was read and checked first by Teunis Gysbertsen Bogaert,
elder, and then by Willem Gerritsen, deacon, who found everything
in perfect and punctual accordance and agreement with the [origin-
al] Protocol.
Henricus Selyns also made out his account of the wedding money
received by him, and handed it over as per the following list:

Copy of the account of wedding
money in Breuckelen, since
October 29, 1662

From Dirck Janssen Hooglant:	Gld.	5-17-8
Arie Willemsen:	Gld.	6- 8
Marten Jansen Meyer:	Gld.	6
Lambert Jansen Bosch:	Gld.	6
Total:	Gld.	24- 5-8

Transferred from the preceding page:	Gld.	24- 5-8
Paulus Heymans:	Gld.	6- 7
Claes Teunissen Appeldoorn:	Gld.	6
Arie Huybertsen:	Gld.	6
Joost Caspartsen:	Gld.	6
Jan Corn[elissen] Buys:	Gld.	5-18
Pieter Lambertsen:	Gld.	6
Marten Reyersen:	Gld.	6
Symon Hansen:	Gld.	6
Jan Pietersen:	Gld.	6
Total:	Gld.	78-10-8

(was signed)

Henricus Selijns

Upon checking the afore-mentioned account, [we] find it to be in
accordance with the truth and acknowledge to have received it.
Done, July 23, 1664.   (underneath stood)

Willem Gerritsen van Couwenhooven

Willem Willemsen

Original

[47^r: "Pag. 92"]

Syn binnen gestaen, die gelt geleent en opgenoomen, oft koeijen
van de diaconie ontfangen hadden, ende geresolveert;
Dat Teunis Jansen, Ouderling, van syn opgenoomen Vyftig Guld. soude tien ten hondert, oft Vyf guld. 's jaerlycks geeven, 't welck
syn E: onderteeckent heeft.
Dat Jan Jacobsen van Rheenen, door 't ongeluck van syn afgebrant
huys en kooren, niet verplicht sal wesen, om Renten te geeven;
maer simpelyck bekennen sal, met behoorlycke onderteeckinge, van
de diaconie de somma van Hondert guld. seewant ontfangen te hebben,
't welck geschiet is.
Dat Catharina Lethie soude 's jaerlycks van Boterpacht geeven de
somme van Veertien gl. 8 stuyv., 't geen se aengenoomen heeft.
En dat Heyltie Probasco, die veel swaricheyts maeckte van dat haer
koey geen melck gaf, en dat sy by de voorschreͤv koeij veel schade
leed, 's jaerlycks soude geeven als van een Veerkoeij, tot dat den
voorschreͤv. Heyltie Probasko sal van een ander versien wesen.
Maer Jenne Carton, die belooft hadde, om de tachtgentig guld. van
de wesen van Pieter Prae sal^t met kooren van den Tegenwoordige Bou
te betalen, claegde, dat, wat sy geeven moeste van 't lant van
Marcus Soisson, daer de voorschr̅. 80 gl., als per obligatie blyckt,
op stont, door Timotheus Gabrij, scheepen van Amsterdam in N. Ne-
derl^t, gearresteert was: Niet van harent wegen, die bereijt was te
betalen, maer van den Voornoemde Soissons wegen, die veel op 't
meergemelte lant opgenoomen hadde. de kerckenraet heeft dies aengaende aen de diaconen gerecommandeert, dat sy daervan spreecken
soude voor den gerechte, en soo se ten regarde van den voornoemde
Sr Gabry oft anderen niet en wierden, 't geen wy niet vertrouwen
sullen, geprefereert, omdat het weesgoet en bewesen van haer Va-
ders wegen is, dat sy pretendeeren sullen op de dootschulden, die
sy den Vader verschooten hebben ende aen de kinderen op sulcke manier geeven souden, 't geen se aengenoomen hebben.

Heeft oock Henricus Selijns, die aengenoomen was van 't Eerw^e.
Classis van Amsterdam met Approbatie van de HH. Bewinthebberen, om
vier jaren 't Predickampt te bedienen, volgens syn jnstructie daer
van synde, aen de kerckenraet na Verloop van de Voorschreͤv jaren syn
dimissie versocht, en daer toe ingeleevert, so 't Consent van de
Hooggem̅. HH Bewinthebberen, 't welck uyt 't dagregister van de
Voorgem̅ Heeren geextraheert en by C. Van Seventer onderteeckent
was; als 't Apostil van de H. Dr Generael en HH. Raden van N. Ne-
derl^t tot favorabele ontslaginge, 't welck op dit Request was,

                         Copie van 't Request aen de
                         Eedelen, Grootachtbaren H^r D^r
                         Generael en H. H. Raden van
                         N. Nederl^t

    Mijn Heeren,

Geeft met Eerbiedigheijt te kennen, Haer E: Grootachtbaerhedens
Suppl^t en Onderdaen, dat hij naer besondere Hulpe en bystant des
Alderhoogsten, Syn Gemeynte, beyde van de Byeenwooninge van en omtrent syn E: Grootachtb^rs Generaels-Bouwerije en tot Breuckelen,
t'samen bedient, ende ten aenstaende Expiratie van Verbantjaren,
die tegenwoordig voldaen syn, van de E: E: HH. Bewinthebberen syn

90

Translation

Those who had borrowed and taken up money or had received cows
from the deaconry, appeared [in the consistory]. And it was
decided:
That Teunis Jansen, elder, would give ten per one hundred, or
five guilders annually, for the fifty guilders borrowed by him;
which he signed.
That Jan Jacobsen van Rheenen [= of Rhenen], in view of his
misfortune caused by the fire that burned down his house and
grain, would not be obliged to pay interest, but would simply
acknowledge with a proper signature that he received the sum of
a hundred guilders in sewan from the deaconry; which was done.
That Catharina Lethie would annually give in butter-lease the
sum of fourteen guilders 8 stuivers; which she accepted.
And that Heyltie Probasco, who made a big fuss about the fact
that her cow did not produce any milk and that she was suffering
a considerable loss on the aforesaid cow, would annually make the
[lower] payments that are due for a heifer, until the aforesaid
Heyltie Probasko would be provided with another cow.
Jenne Carton, however, who had promised to pay with grain from
the present harvest the eighty guilders that were owed to the
late Pieter Prae's orphans, complained that what she was obliged
to give from Marcus Soisson's land, where the aforesaid 80 guilders [in grain] were located as it appears from an obligation,
had been distrained by Timotheus Gabrij, schepen of Amsterdam in
New Netherland, not on her behalf, since she was willing to pay,
but on behalf of the aforesaid Soisson, who had borrowed a great
deal on the afore-mentioned land. The consistory advised the
deacons to discuss the matter in Court; and in case they[52] would
not be given priority over the aforesaid Sir Gabry or others
since there were [merely some] orphans involved without a father
(we trust [though] that that will not happen), they would lay
claim on the money which they had advanced to the father now
deceased, and in so doing, [they would] transfer the advances to
the children. They took it upon themselves to do so.

Furthermore, Henricus Selijns, who had been engaged by the Rev.
Classis of Amsterdam, with the approval of the Lords Directors[53],
to hold the ministry for four years in accordance with his
instructions, asked the consistory after the aforesaid years to
be relieved of his office, and for that purpose he submitted not
only the afore-mentioned Lords Directors' consent, which had been
abstracted from the aforesaid Lords' daybook and signed by C. Van
Seventer, but also the apostil by the Lord Director-General and
Lords Councillors of New Netherland accepting his resignation,
which was granted upon the following request:

> Copy of the request to the Honor-
> able Highly Esteemed Lord Director-
> General and Lords Councillors of
> New Netherland

My Lords,

Your Hon. Highly Esteemed Lordships' petitioner and subject
informs you respectfully that with the special help and assistance of the Most High, he has served his dual congregation,
both the hamlets in and around the Hon. Highly Esteemed General's Bowery [= farm] and Breuckelen, and that in view of the

Original

[48^r: "Pag. 94"]

dimissie versocht heeft: 't Welcke ten regarde van de Voorgemelte
Expiratie, en besonder met de Hoge Ouderdom van Haer E: Suppl^{ts}
Vader (die 't Voorschreeven Versoeck met den Eerw^e D^o Jacobus Triglandius, predicant tot Amsterdam, van den Hooggemelte H. H. verkregen, en daervan aen syn E: Grootachtb^t Generael geschreeven
heeft), toegestaen is.
Ende Versoeckt, Oft oock Haer E: Grootachtb^{en} gelieve tot sijn dimissie te consenteeren, en ten aensien der zeylreetleggende scheepen toelaten met 't Schip de Bever te vertrecken, metten welcken
Haer E: Grootachtbaerh^{ens} Suppl^t gekomen is; Niet twyffelende Of
met de komste van den Eerw^e D. Samuel Megapolensis, Predicant en
Medinæ doct^r, sullen Haer E: Grootachtb^{en} seer bequaeme gelegentheyt hebben, syn Plaetse te vervullen, en door een goetgunstig
Apostil den Suppl^t te verplichten, die van gantscher herten is

Actum, Amsterd.
in N. Nederl^t
den 17 Jul. 1664.

Haer E: Grootachtbaerhedens
Ootmoedigste Suppl^t en onderdaen,

(onderstont)

Henricus Selijns

't Apostil was dese,

FIAT, QUOD PETITUR

Actum Fort Amsterd. in N. Nederl^t
Adij, 17 Jul. 1664.

(Onderstont)

Ter Ordonnantie van de E: Heeren Dr Generael en Raden van N. Nederlant,

(Ende was onderteeckent)

C. V. Ruijven, Secrets.

Den Kerckenraet van Breuckelen, alles overweegende in de Vreese des
Heeren, hebben, 't geen toegestaen was by de H. H. Bewinthebberen
en d^r Generael en Raden van N. Nederl^t, ten laesten van harent wegen geconsenteert, ende den meergem Henrico Selyns, Haer Predicant
en leeraer, gegeeven den navolgende Attestatie, Van den Eerw^e,
Godtsalige, en Seer geleerde D. Samuel Drisius, Predicant tot Amsterdam in N. Nederl^t, op ons versoeck geschreeven, en met ons onderteeckent,

Copie van den Voorgemelte
Attestatie

Wij, ondergeschreeven Samuel Drisius, predicant tot Nieuw-Amsterdam in Nieuw-Nederlant, ende kerckenraedt van het dorp genaemt
Breuckelen op het Lange Eylant in N. Nederlant voornoemt, geeven
getuygenisse aen die geene, die dese onse Attestatie mag vertoont

Translation

imminent expiration of the years of the contract, which as of now have been fulfilled, he has asked the Hon. Lords Directors[54] to be relieved of his office. This was granted because of the afore-mentioned expiration, and especially in view of the very old age of Your Hon. Lordships' petitioner's father (who obtained the aforesaid permission from the afore-mentioned Lords [Directors] through the Rev. Domine Jacobus Triglandius, minister in Amsterdam, and who wrote about it to the Hon. Highly Esteemed General).
And [the petitioner] requests that Your Hon. Highly Esteemed Lordships, too, accept his resignation, and that you allow him, now that the ships lie ready to sail, to leave on the ship "Bever" [= "Beaver"] with which Your Hon. Highly Esteemed Lordships' petitioner arrived here. [The petitioner] does not doubt that with the arrival of the Rev. Domine Samuel Megapolensis, Minister and M.D.,[55] Your Hon. Highly Esteemed Lordships will have an excellent opportunity to fill his place and to oblige the petitioner by a favorable apostil. He remains with all his heart,

Your Hon. Highly Esteemed Lordships'
most humble petitioner and subject,

Done in Amsterdam
in New Netherland,
July 17, 1664.   (underneath stood)

Henricus Selijns

The apostil read as follows:

REQUEST GRANTED

Done in Fort Amsterdam in New Netherland,
July 17, 1664.[56]

(underneath stood)

By ordinance of the Hon. Lords Director-General and Councillors of New Netherland,

(and was signed)

C. V. Ruijven, Secretary

The consistory of Breuckelen, taking everything into consideration in fear of the Lord, finally consented on their part to what the Lords Directors[57] and the Director-General and Councillors of New Netherland had given permission for, and they gave the afore-mentioned Henricus Selyns, their minister and teacher, the following attestation, which was written and co-signed at our request by the Rev., godly, and very learned Domine Samuel Drisius, minister in Amsterdam in New Netherland:

Copy of the afore-mentioned attestation

We, the undersigned Samuel Drisius, minister in New Amsterdam in New Netherland, and the consistory of the village called

93

Original

[49^r: "Pag. 96"]

worden in hollant, ofte Elders, dat d^o Henricus Selyns, Herwaerts
gesonden van de E: E: Geoctroyeerde Westindische Comp.^{ie}, onse Pa-
tronen, om hier de dienst van de Gemeynte te Breuckelen voor vier
jaer waer te neemen, sig neerstig ende getrouwelyck heeft gedragen
in syn ampt, in twee plaetsen, namelyck te Breuckelen ende op de
Bouwerey (gelyck wy het hier noemen) elcken sondag predickende,
ende Catechiseerende in de weecke Op den dingsdag te Breuckelen
ende donderdag op den voorgemelte Bouwerije: Het Avontmael des Heeren op beyde Plaetsen ter bequamer tydt uytrichtende, de ongereegelde Vermanende, de siecke ende bedrucke besoeckende ende ver-
troostende, de verschillende vereenigende, en met een stichtelyck,
nederig, ende sachtmoedig Exempel syne kudde ende andere voorlich-
tende. Daerom wy oock gewenst hadden, dat hy onder ons hadde mogen continueeren, ende zyn droevig, dat hy van ons moet scheyden,
doch siende, dat het om de outheyt van syne Vader ende Moeder den
wille Godts niet en is, dat hy hier langer onder ons soude blijven,
so bidden wy Hem, die de winden ende wateren in syne macht heeft,
dat hy hem wille geleyden, ende beveelen hem Gode ende den woorde
syner genade, die ons alle machtig is op te bouwen ende een Erf-
deel te geeven onder alle de geheyligde. Ende versoecken de E:
Broederen, dat dese onse Attestatie voor de waernt mag aengenoomen
worden tot voordeel van d^o Selyns in syn beroep of andersints.
Actum, Breuckelen in N. Nederl^t den 23 Jul. A^o 1664.

Ita Attestor, (was onderteeckent)

Samuel Drisius, Eccles.

Teunis Janssen, ouderling

Teunis Gysbertsen, ouderling

Willem Bredenbent, oudt ouderling

Willem Gerritsen, diacon

Willem Willemsen, diacon

Wiert ten laesten voorgeslagen en geresolveert, dat men de gemeente by malckanderen soude houden, tot nader ordre van de E: H. Generael, die gesegt heeft tot den meergemelte Henricus Selyns van
ordre te sullen stellen; mitgaders van de EE: H.H. Bewinthebbers, die ten deele geresolveert waren om wederom met 't Vertreck
van den voorn Henricus Selyns een Predicant naer N. Nederl^t te
senden.
Dat d'Eerwaerdege, Godtsalige, en seer Geleerde D. Johannes Megapolensis, predicant tot Amsterdam in N. Nederl^t, gepresenteert heeft,
als 't tydt was, 't Avontmael tot Breuckelen voor de ledematen uyt-
tedeelen, oft dat sulcks geschieden koft door belet van syn Eerw.
door den Eerw^{en}, Godtsaligen, en Hoog geleerden D. D. Samuel Drisius en d^r Samuel Megapolensis.
Dat Mr Carel d'Beauvois, onse Voorleser, Voorsanger, en Schoolmeester, 's Sondags soude leesen Een Predicatie voor de Gemeente uyt-
ten Postil van Mr Abraham Schultetus buyten de gebeeden en Psalmen
voor en naer de voorgemelte Predicatie: Wiens gagie ten dien eynde, als oock met de slechte prys van 't Seewant, verhoogt is, om
eens voor al te krygen van den kerckenraet de somma van Hondert

Translation

Breuckelen in Long Island in aforesaid New Netherland, certify
for [all] the people to whom this our attestation may be shown,
in Holland or elsewhere, that Domine Henricus Selyns, sent here
by the Hon. Chartered West-India Company, our patrons, to hold
the ministry of the congregation of Breuckelen here for four
years, has acquitted himself diligently and loyally of his
office in two places, namely by preaching every Sunday in
Breuckelen and at the "Bouwerey" [= "Bowery"[58]] (as we call it
here); by having confirmation classes on weekdays: on Tuesdays
in Breuckelen and on Thursdays at the afore-mentioned Bowery;
by administering the Sacrament of the Lord's Supper on the
appropriate occasions in both places; by exhorting the unruly,
visiting and comforting the sick and dejected, reconciling the
quarreling, and instructing his herd and others by setting an
edifying, humble, and gentle example. For those reasons, we
wish he could have stayed among us, and we are sad that he will
have to part from us. Realizing, however, that because of his
father's and mother's old age it is not God's will that he stay
longer among us here, we pray to Him, who holds the winds and
waters in His power, to guide him. And [we] commend him to God
and to the words of His mercy, which has the power to give
strength to all of us and to give us a share among all saints.
And [we] request that the Rev. Brethren accept this our attestation as the truth, for the benefit of Domine Selyns in his
ministry or otherwise. Done in Breuckelen in New Netherland,
July 23, 1664.

Attesting to this: (was signed)

Samuel Drisius, Minister

Teunis Janssen, Elder

Teunis Gysbertsen, Elder

Willem Bredenbent, former Elder

Willem Gerritsen, Deacon

Willem Willemsen, Deacon

Finally, it was proposed and resolved, that the congregation
would be held together until further notice both from the Hon.
Lord General, who had told the afore-mentioned Henricus Selyns
that he would put things in order, and from the Hon. Lords Directors[59], some of whom had decided to send another minister to New
Netherland now that the aforesaid Henricus Selyns was leaving.
[It was also noted] that the Reverend, godly, and very learned
Domine Johannes Megapolensis, minister in Amsterdam in New Netherland, had offered to administer the Sacrament of the Lord's Supper
to the members in Breuckelen on the appropriate occasions; and in
case the Rev. was prevented from coming, this could be done by
the Rev., godly, and very learned Domines Samuel Drisius and
Dr. Samuel Megapolensis.
[Furthermore, it was decided] that on Sundays, Mr. Carel
d'Beauvois, our reader, precentor, and schoolmaster, would read
a sermon to the congregation from the Postil[60] by Mr. Abraham
Schultetus, in addition to the prayers and psalms before and
after the afore-mentioned sermon. For that purpose, as well as
in view of the low price of sewan, his salary was raised so that

Original

[50^r: "Pag. 98"]

guld. Seewant in plaetse van de 75 gld. die hem toegeleyt was, en
boven van de E: H D.r Generael en Raden en van de gerechte van de
durpe Breuckelen gecontribueert wert. Welcke voorschreṽ. Penning-
en soude betaelt Werden, ten halven Prim⁰ Januar. en ten halven
Primo Jul. Ende daerenboven wiert sijn Versoeck toegestaen, so
van ons als van de Gerechte van Breuckelen, om voortaen te woonen
in 't Predicants huys (nademale 't Huys daer hy woont, staet om
verkocht te worden met den toebehoorende Bouwerye), maer soo de
HH. Bewinthebberen en HH. d.r Generael en Raden van N. Nederlant te
bewegen syn om de Tegenwoordige gemeente met een leeraer te versien, dat voor den voorschr̃. Schoolmeester een ander Huys be-
schairt sal worden, t geen hy, ende voornamentlyck van 's Sondags
voor te leesen, aengenoomen heeft, met beloften, om syn best en
uytterste devoir te doen.
Ende alsoo den meergenoemde M.r Carel d'Beauvois soude woonen in 't
Voorschreṽ. Huys, wiert den gerechte toegestaen, voor dien tydt
geen renten te sullen geeven van de penningen, die wy aen de Hooggemelte gerechte verschoten hebben tot de opbouwinge van 't meergenoemde Predicantshuys.

Den 30 dicto

Wij, Ondergeschreeven, bedienaer des H. Euangeliums, Ouderlingen
en diaconen van de Gemeynte Tot Breuckelen, geeven van onsent wegen Getuygenisse, dat dit Prothocol, van den Beginne tot den Tegenwoordige dato toe voor onse kerckelycke Vergaderinge geleesen,
naer waerheyt is, 't geen wij tot bevestinge met ons allen onderteeckent hebben. Actum Breuckelen, in onse kerckelycke Vergaderinge, datum als boven, 1664.

> Henricus Selijns, predicant Te
>   Breuckelen en̄ op 's Generaels
>   bouwerye
>
> Teunis Janssen, ouderlingh
>
> Tunis Gijsbertsen, ouderlingh
>
> Willem Bredenbent, out ouerlingh
>
> Willem Gerretsen Van Couwehoven
>
> Willem Willemsen

Translation

henceforth he will receive the sum of one hundred guilders in
sewan from the consistory (instead of the 75 guilders awarded to
him [earlier]), on top of what he is being paid by the Hon. Lord
Director-General and Councillors. Half of the aforesaid money
would be paid on the first of January and the other half on the
first of July. Moreover, both we and the Court of Breuckelen
granted his request for permission to live in the minister's
house henceforth (since the house where he is living [now] is
about to be sold with the farm belonging to it). If, however,
the Lords Directors and the Lords Director-General and Councillors
of New Netherland can be persuaded to provide the present congregation with a teacher, another house will be procured for the
aforesaid schoolmaster. He accepted this, and especially [his
assignment] to read on Sundays, with the promise to do his best
and highest duty.

And since the afore-mentioned Mr. Carel d'Beauvois was going
to live in the aforesaid house, the Court was permitted for the
time being not to pay any interest on the money advanced by us
to the afore-mentioned Court for fixing up the afore-mentioned
minister's house.

[July] 30 [1664]

We, the undersigned, minister of the Holy Gospel [and] elders
and deacons of the congregation in Breuckelen, certify on our
behalf that this Protocol, read to our church meeting from the
beginning to the present date, corresponds with the truth, and
all of us have signed it in confirmation. Done in Breuckelen
in our church meeting, dated as above, 1664.

> Henricus Selijns, Minister in
>   Breuckelen and at the General's
>   Bowery [= farm]
>
> Teunis Janssen, Elder
>
> Tunis Gijsbertsen, Elder
>
> Willem Bredenbent, former Elder
>
> Willem Gerretsen Van Couwehoven
>
> Willem Willemsen

Original

[51^V: "101"]

den 13 Maij Anno 1670

Sijn Tot Leedemaetten aengenoomen om Meede Te $\tilde{v}$schijnen jn de
gemeente Tot Breuckellen jn het gebruijck des H: Avontmaels op
dese Pinxteren, dese nae volgende persoonen,

1 Dirck Storm,
         met Attestatie van S Hertoogenbosch ende Vrijheijt
         Osch
2 Jan Pieterssen Mackelijck en
3 Stijntien Janssen, sijn Huijsvrouw,
         Ter presentie Van Dom:^{S} Polhemius, Predikant,
         Thonis Gijsberts, Ouderlingh, Willem Willemsse
         Bennit, Ouderlingh.

Deese Getransporteert op het volgende Register Der Leedemaaten.

A$^{\underline{o}}$ 1676 (op den 9$^{\underline{e}n}$ Junij)

Alsoo het den Almachtigen Godt gelieft heeft den Erw: godtsaaligen
Joh: Theodoris Polheemius uijt deese bedroefde weerelt te verlossen ende jn syne Heemelsche koninckrijcke te ontfangen: waer door
onse Christelijcke Gemeijnte sigh Ontbloodt bevinden te sijn,
weegens sijne Gedachte Leersaeme ende Stichtelijcke Predicatie
ende jn sonderheyt van D:^{e} bedieninge van des Heeren Heijlige
Sacrament des Avontmaels, Ooversulckx met den Eerw: Welgeleerde
Dom:^{S} Nieuwenhuijsen, Predicant tot N: Jorcke, naer goede Deliberatie hebbende goetgevonden ende vast gestelt, Dat het Hooghwaer-
digh Heijligh Avontmael Door den welgemelten Dom:^{S} Nieuwenhuijse
viermael des jaers tot Breuckelen alhier op het langh Eylant Door
des Heeren genaede aen sijne gemeente sal werden bedient.
Ende js meede door de Voorgedachte Onse Gemeijnte vastgestelt ende
belooft dat den Meergemelten Dom:^{S} ..... Nieuwenhuijse voor Sijne
Salaris ontfangen sal tot 200 gulden jn het Jaer t'weeten zewants
wardije, ende t'selve te betaelen in Taruw Marcksgangh, den
jnganck beginnende ende Eijndigende naer Experientie vantijt als
hier naer volght, alles tot opbouwinge van de dierre gekochte
gemeijnte Jesu Christij ende tot Lof en grootmaeckinge des Heijligen Naame Goodes.

A$^{\underline{o}}$ 1676 den 7$^{\underline{e}}$ Augustij

heeft den Welgemelten E Erw: Dom:^{S} Nieuwen Huijsen, Predikant tot
N: Jorck: het H: Sacrament des Avontmaels tot onsse Gemeente jn
het Dorp Breuckelen bedient, naer gedaene Loffelijcke Predicatie
ende Aenroepinge van des Heeren Heijligen Naeme.

Translation

Entries after Henricus Selijns' ministry in Breuckelen

May 13, 1670

In order [to be able] to appear in the congregation in Breuckelen to partake of the Lord's Supper this Whitsuntide, the following persons were confirmed as members:

1. Dirck Storm,
               with an attestation from 's-Hertogenbosch and
               the jurisdiction of Oss;
2. Jan Pieterssen Mackelijck and
3. Stijntien Janssen, his wife;
               in the presence of Domine Polhemius, minister,
               Thonis Gijsberts, elder, [and] Willem Willemsse
               Bennit, elder.

These people [were] transferred to the following Register of
Members.[61]

June 9, 1676

Since Almighty God chose to release the Rev. [and] godly
Joh[annes] Theodoris Polheemius from this sad world and receive
him in His heavenly Kingdom, as a consequence of which our
Christian congregations[62] find themselves destitute of his well-
considered, instructive, and edifying preaching, and especially,
the administration of the Holy Sacrament of the Lord's Supper,
- therefore, [we] have approved and resolved, upon good deliberation with the Rev. [and] very learned Domine Nieuwenhuijsen,
minister in New York, that through the Lord's mercy, the
Consecrated Holy Supper will be administered four times a year
to His congregation here in Breuckelen in Long Island by the
afore-mentioned Domine Nieuwenhuijse.
And it was also resolved and promised by our aforesaid congregation that the afore-mentioned Domine ..... Nieuwenhuijse[63] will
annually receive a salary of up to 200 guilders (sewan value),
beginning and ending as the future will show; it will be paid in
wheat at the current market price - all of this in order to build
up the precious congregation of Jesus Christ and to laud and
praise God's Holy Name.

August 7, 1676

The afore-mentioned Hon. [and] Rev. Domine Nieuwen Huijsen,
minister in New York, administered the Holy Sacrament of the
Lord's Supper to our congregation in the village of Breuckelen,
after a laudable sermon and upon the invocation of the Lord's
Holy Name.

Original

[73^V: "143"]

A? 1677 den 19 maert

Is tot voorsanger der gemijnte van Brueckelen met meerderheijt
van steme Beroepen,

Henderick Slecht,

Welcke inde beroepinge aennemende belooft heeft den dienst als
bij Constabel en opsienders hem voorgestelt is te sullen waer-
nemen, geen boecken als Conform de leeren der gereformeerde
kercke in sijn kercken dienst te gebruijcken, hem onderwerpende
de kerckelijck disciplijne volgens de artijculen van het synodus
nation: tot dordrecht gehouden 1618 en gelijck inde nederduijt-
sche gereformeerde kercke gebruijckelyck is, en soo het daer
voor valt dat de voornoemde H: Slecht soude koomen ter voorschreeven dorpen Brueckelen t:eeniger tyt school te houden, neemt hey
aen geen anderen Boecken dan beij de reformeerde schoole gebruy-
ckelijck is de Jeught te sullen onderweijsen.

[54^r: "106"]

Anno 1684 den 3 october

heeft Maria Baddia aen de kercke van breukelen vereert een
zilvere beecker om het Avontmael uijt te delen.

[73^V: "143"]

den 28 meij 1693

sijn wij ouderlingen en diakenen bevesticht,

Hendrick Slecht

Daniel de Rappaljee

Joris Hansen tot ouderlinge,

en Jan Gerritsen

Folkert Hendricksen

en Barent Slecht tot diakenen.

den 30 Juny 1695

heeft Folkert Hendericksen zijn twe Jaeren Wel en duedelijck
uijt gedient en zijn dienst opgeseijt en daer voor bedanckt.

Translation

March 19, 1677

By a majority of the votes,

Henderick Slecht

was called to be precentor of the congregation of Breuckelen. Accepting his call, he promised to hold his office as it was presented to him by the constable and supervisors; to use no other books in his church service than the ones that are in conformity with the doctrines of the Reformed Church; [and] to subject himself to Church discipline in accordance with the articles of the National Synod of Dordrecht held in 1618, and with the customs of the Dutch Reformed Church. And if the aforesaid H. Slecht finds an opportunity some day to keep school in the aforesaid village of Breuckelen, he pledges he will teach the youth with no other books than the ones that are common in the Reformed schools.

October 3, 1684

Maria Baddia presented the Church of Breuckelen with a silver cup for the administration of the Lord's Supper.

May 28, 1693

We, elders and deacons, were confirmed:

Hendrick Slecht,

Daniel de Rappaljee, [and]

Joris Hansen as elders; and

Jan Gerritsen,

Folkert Hendricksen, and

Barent Slecht as deacons.

June 30, 1695

Folkert Hendericksen has served his two years reliably and well, has terminated his service, and was thanked for it.

Original

[71^v: "139"]

Kerken=Raads Handelingen

beginnende met 't Jaer 1750

Kerken-Raad gehouden den 3 Jannuari 1750

De vergadering geopent zynde met een gebeede tot Godt, Zoo is
bij die gelegentheijdt van de Eerwaarde Vergaderinge besloten,
dat in vervolg van tijdt niemant tot het Eerwaerdig ampt van het
Ouderlinschap Sal bevestigt worden ten sij na voorafgaande betui-
ginge dat hij voor het opgeregte Coetus is (van het classis van
Amsterdam opgerigt in den jaere 1747, Dog na verloop van eenige
jaren weder verbroken in twee deelen dat veel ongenoegen heeft
veroorsaekt &c:) en de kerkelyke wetten is te Dordregt gemaakt
in den Jaere 1618, 1619.

Uijt naam en last van onse kerkelijke vergaderinge ondertekent

Vlakbos den 3 Januar: 1750	U: van Sinderen
	Abraham Loth
	Louwerens Ditmarsen
	Pieter Leffertsen
	Karel de Beauvois
	Jacob Sebering
	Pieter van der Voot
	Jan Loth
	Willem Kouvenhove
	Steven Schenk
	Jan van der Bilt
	Willem van Nuys
	Andries Emans
	Jan Miserol
	Hendrick van de Water

Kerken Raad gehouden den 9 Mey 1750

Over het protesteren van een Ouderling en een Diaken aldaar
verkoren den 15 April deses jaers. De vergaderinge heeft geoordeelt, dat er [.....]° reeden toe waren om sulks te doen, en
dat deselve Ouderling, met Name Hendrick van de Water, en Joost

---

[° Brackets [] followed or preceded by ° mark passages which
       are illegible because of the poor quality of the original
       handwriting.]

Translation

Proceedings of the Consistory

beginning in the year 1750

Consistory meeting held January 3, 1750

After the meeting was opened with a prayer to God, the Hon. Consistory resolved on that occasion that henceforth, no one will be confirmed in the honorable office of elder without a declaration of loyalty to the Coetus (instituted in 1747 by the Classis of Amsterdam but broken up in two parts after some years, causing a great deal of displeasure etc.[64]) and to the Church Laws made in Dordrecht in the years 1618, 1619.

Signed on behalf and by order of our Church meeting,

Vlackebos,
January 3,
1750.

U. van Sinderen

Abraham Loth

Louwerens Ditmarsen

Pieter Leffertsen

Karel de Beauvois

Jacob Sebering

Pieter van der Voot

Jan Loth

Willem Kouvenhove

Steven Schenk

Jan van der Bilt

Willem van Nuys

Andries Emans

Jan Miserol

Hendrick van de Water

Consistory meeting held May 9, 1750,

because of objections raised against an elder and deacon, elected there on April 15 of this year. The assembly decided that there were [..... [65]]° reasons to do so, and that this elder, namely Hendrick van de Water, and deacon, Joost S[chilman?]°, would be

---

[°   Brackets [] followed or preceded by ° mark passages which are illegible because of the poor quality of the original handwriting.]

Original

[72^r: "140"]

S[chilman?]° als Diaken, sullen bevestigt worden soo aldaar niet
nader teegen geprotesteert [wert?]°, waer op de vergaderinge na
een Danksegginge tot God gescheyden is.
Waer op de bovengemelde perzonen den 4 Juni in haar dienst bevestigt zyn.

Kerken Raad gehouden den 10 Septr 1750:

de vergaderinge geopent zijnde met den Gebede tot God, zoo is van
de vergaderinge tot Lidt van het Coetus verkoren, Abr: Loth,
regerend ouderling tot Vlakbos &c:

Kerken-Raad gehouden Woensdag den 5 Septr 1751

De vergaderinge geopent zijnde met den gebede tot Godt, soo is
tot een Mede Lidt van 't Coetus verkoren, Abraham Loth, regerend
Ouderling tot Vlakbos, dog soo die bovengenoemde niet in Staat
moghte wesen, Willem Kouwenhove, Mede Richter en Ouderling van
Nieuw Amersvoort.

Kerken Raad gehouden Donderdag den 10 October

en zyn by die gelegentheydt na den Gebeede tot God tot Gecommitteerde verkoren (over de groote verschillen, voor het grooste
gedeelte ontstaen door het onwettig inkruijpen van Johannes
Arundeus, in den jaere 1748 voorgevallen) Abraham Loth, regerend
Ouderling tot Vlakbos, en Bernardus Reyder, Ouderling tot
Gravesant en Mede Richter in Kings Contij, en hebben over die
saken tot N: York by het Extraordinaar Coetus geseten den 16, 17,
18, 21, 22, 23 October 1751, en is by het Coetus besloten dat
[...]° drie Gecommitte[erden]* na het Lange Eylant sullen gesonden worden tegens den 26 November, Namelyck Johannes Ritsema,
Lambertus de Ronde; en Johannis Frielinhuysen, om soo de verschillen, soo het mogelyck is, weg te nemen,
dog de [..........]°
                        U: van Sinderen
                        Bedienaer van het H: Euan[gelium]*
                        in Kings Conty

[°   Brackets [] followed or preceded by ° mark passages which
       are illegible because of the poor quality of the original
       handwriting.
  *   Brackets [] followed or preceded by an asterisk * mark
       passages which are illegible because of damage to the
       original manuscript.]

25

Translation

confirmed if no further objections were raised against them
- whereupon the assembly dispersed after having thanked God.
   Consequently, the persons mentioned above were confirmed in
their services on June 4.

Consistory meeting held September 10, 1750

After the meeting was opened with the prayer to God, Abr[aham]
Loth, currently elder in Vlackebos etc., was elected a member of
the Coetus by the assembly.

Consistory meeting held Wednesday, September 5, 1751[66]

After the meeting was opened with the prayer to God, Abraham
Loth, currently elder in Vlackebos, was elected a member of the
Coetus. However, should the afore-mentioned not be able [to
accept], Willem Kouwenhove, co-justice and elder of New Amersfoort, [would be appointed].

Consistory meeting held Thursday, October 10 [1751]

On this occasion, upon the prayer to God, the following persons
were elected delegates (in view of the great differences caused
for the most part by Johannes Arundeus' unlawful meddling, which
occurred in the year 1748[67]): Abraham Loth, currently elder in
Vlackebos, and Bernardus Reyder, elder in Gravesend and co-justice
in Kings County. And [they] attended the Extraordinary Coetus
held about these matters in New York on October 16, 17, 18, 21,
22, [and] 23, 1751.[68] The Coetus resolved that by November 26,
[...]° three deleg[ates]* will be sent to Long Island, namely Johannes Ritsema, Lambertus de Ronde, and Johannis Frielinhuysen,
in order to settle the differences, if possible.
   However, [..........[69]]°

                    U. van Sinderen,
                    Minister of the Holy Gos[pel]*
                    in Kings County

[° Brackets [] followed or preceded by ° mark passages which
     are illegible because of the poor quality of the original
     handwriting.
  * Brackets [] followed or preceded by an asterisk * mark
     passages which are illegible because of damage to the
     original manuscript.]

Original

[72^V: "141"]

Woensdag den 13 November 1751

zyn de Algemene Kerken Raden vergadert geweest om in overweginge
te nemen wat haer te doen zy over de besluyten van het laeste
gehouden Coetus October gemaekt, hoe men sig gedragen sal als de
Gecommitteerde op den 26 November en den 27 hier in Vlakbos
zullen komen &c, namelyck Johannes Ritzema, L: de Ronde en Jan
Frielinhuysen met hun respective Ouderlingen, en is by die tydt
besloten dat men hen dit onderstaende sal opdragen indien zy hun
besluyten gelieven uyt te voeren,
dogh niet geschiet is om reden &c: en daerom ook hier niet ge-
boekt is.

Woensdag den 8 April 1752

Kerken Raad gehouden over de Saeke van Arundeus by het Coetus,
dat den 14 April Staat gehouden te worden: En zyn by die gele-
gentheydt van de E Vergaederinge tot Gecommitteerde verkoren
Pieter Leffertse van Vlakbos, Willem Kouwenhoove van Amersvoort,
Bernardus Reyder van Gravesant, Willem van Nuys van Utregt,
Pieter van der Voort van Breukelen, Hendrick van der Water van
Boswyck.
Bij welke gelegentheydt Arundeus volgens de Classicale Resolutie
van den 12 Jannuarij 1751 onwettig is verklaart.
Dog in plaats van daer na te luysteren Soo heeft hy des Saterdags
den 25 April getrouwt de Dochter van Johannis Loth &c, als ook de
Dochter van Abr. Brouwer, en des Zondaghs den 26 tot Jamaïca ge-
predikt en daar op den derden Meij tot N: Amersvoort, en heeft
aldaer drie kinderen gedoopt, Sc: het kent van Dirk Remsen,
Marten Schenk en Jan Suydam, als Vrijdag den 15 Mey heeft hy de
Doghter van Roelof Voorhees [.....]° getrouwt.
°[? Hemelsvaart]dag den 7 Meij heeft hy de [dienst?]° tot Uytregt
laten openstaen gelyck mede tot Vlakbos den 10 dito als mede te
pinxster zondag en maandag den 17 en 18 mey.
[Vrijdag?]° den 29 mey heeft hy weder tot N: Uytregt gepredickt.

[° Brackets [] followed or preceded by ° mark passages which
     are illegible because of the poor quality of the original
     handwriting.]

Translation

Wednesday, November 13, 1751

   The consistories met in a general session in order to consider
what ought to be done about the resolutions that were made by the
latest Coetus [held] in October, [and] how one should act when on
November 26 and 27, the delegates - namely Johannes Ritzema,
L[ambertus] de Ronde, and Jan Frielinhuysen with their respective
elders - will come here to Vlackebos etc. And on that occasion,
it was decided that if they [70] wish to carry out their resolutions,
they will be instructed to do the following:
   For [certain] reasons etc., this did not happen, however; and
therefore, it has not been registered here.

Wednesday, April 8, 1752

   Consistory meeting - convened because of the Arundeus-affair
in the Coetus which is scheduled to be held on April 14.[71] And
on that occasion, the following persons were elected delegates
by the Hon. Assembly: Pieter Leffertse from Vlackebos, Willem
Kouwenhoove from [New] Amersfoort, Bernardus Reyder from Gravesend, Willem van Nuys from [New] Utrecht, Pieter van der Voort
from Breuckelen, [and] Hendrick van der Water from Boswijck.
   In accordance with the resolution of the Classis of January 12,
1751[72], Arundeus was declared unlawful on that occasion.
   However, instead of being obedient, he married Johannis Loth's
daughter on Saturday, April 25, as well as Abr[aham] Brouwer's
daughter; and on Sunday the 26th, he preached in Jamaica; and
thereupon, on May 3, in New Amersfoort, where he baptized three
children, namely those of Dirk Remsen, Marten Schenk, and Jan
Suydam; on Friday, May 15, he married Roelof Voorhees' daughter
[.....]°; on [Ascension?]° day, May 7, he held a public
[service?]° in [New] Utrecht, as well as in Vlackebos on the 10th
of the same month and on Whit Sunday and Whit Monday, May 17 and
18; [on Friday?]° May 29, he preached again in New Utrecht.

[° Brackets [] followed or preceded by ° mark passages which
     are illegible because of the poor quality of the original
     handwriting.]

Translation

BAPTISMAL REGISTER OF BREUCKELEN

First List[1]

1660, October 31:

- Helena; parents: Adam Brouwer, Magdaleen Jacobs, "by the
      mill".

1660, December 5:

- Janneken (died December 26, 1660); parents: Simon Claesse,
      Anneken Lodowijcks, "at the Poor Bowery";
      witness: Dirck Janssen.
- Jeuriaen (died December 15, 1660); parents: Hendrick
      Volckerssen, Geertien Claess, "near the ferry";
      witness: Hermanus Van Bossum.

1661, January 16:

- Susanna; parents: Hendrick Jorisz, Claesie Cornelis, "from
      Middelwout"; witnesses: Cornelis Janssen, Susanna
      Dubbels, Gijsbertie Willems.

1661, January 23:

- Femmetie; father: Barent Gerritsen van Swol, "from Mispadt";
      witness: Reijck Leijdecker.

1661, February 6:

- Adam (died February 8, 1661); parents: Pieter Pra, Catharina
      Letie, "at the Creupelbosch"; witnesses: Adam Brouwers,
      Trijntie Hadders.

1661, April 3:

- Stephen; father: Jan Carvoij, "from Nieuw Haerlem"; witness:
      Stephen de Oude [= the Elder].

1661, June 6:

- Harmtie; parents: Dirck Janssen, Marritien Teunis, "from the
      ferry"; witnesses: Teunis Nijssen, Sijmon Claessen.

Translation

[75^{v}: "147"]

1661, June 12:

- Aefie; parents: Joris Jacobsen, Trijntie Claes, "from the
    ferry"; witnesses: Pieter Wolphertsen, Hester.

1661, June 26:

- Anna Maria; father: Matthijs Boon, "from N[ieuw] Haerlem";
    witness: Jeurie Probasko.

1661, July 24:

- Marta; parents: Jan Dame, Fijtie Martens, "from Breuckelen";
    witnesses: Michiel Tatens, Annetie.

1661, August 28:

- Annetie; parents: Teunis Janssen, Barber Lucas, "from Breuck-
    elen"; witnesses: Joost Goderis, Jacomijntie Franse.

1661, September 18:

- Maria; parents: Jan de Bon, Getruijt Barents, "from the
    ferry"; witnesses: Jacobus Backer, Hendrick Obee,
    Catrijntie Verbrugge.

1661, October 9:

- Lowijs; parents: Lowijs Bijose, Annetie Jeuriaens;
    witnesses: Louseijn Brijel, Marij Brontijn.

1661, November 6:

- Jeuriaen; parents: Hendrick Volckerssen, Geertie Claes,
    "from the ferry"; witnesses: Sijmen Janssen, Hermanus
    van Bossum, Trijntie Claes.

1661, November 13:

- Aeltie; parents: Teunis Gijsbertse, Sara Joris, "from the
    Walebocht"; witnesses: Rem Janssen, Maria Fredericks.

1661, November 27:

- Claes; parents: Sijmon Claessen, Annetie Lodewijcks, "at
    the Poor Bowery"; witnesses: Dirck Janssen, Margrietie
    Teunis.

Translation

[76^r: "148"]

1661, December 18:

- Elsje; parents: Pieter Jansen, Annetie Jans, "from Cujanes";
      witnesses: Gerrit Croesen, Trijntie Jans, Grietie Jans.

1661, December 26:

- Joosje; parents: Barent Joosten, Cijtie Laurents, "from
      Boswijck"; witnesses: Jan Janssen, Engeltie Laurens.

1662, January 15:

- Gerrit; parents: Willem Gerritsen, Aeltie Joris, "from
      Breuckelen"; witnesses: Elbert Albertsen, Hendrick
      Joriszen, Aeltie Cornelis.

1662, February 19:

- Rebecca; parents: Willem Traphagel, Joostie Willems, "from
      Boswijck"; witnesses: Roelof Janssen, Magdaleentie
      Walincks.

1662, February 26:

- Petrus; parents: Jan Martijn, Fijtie Dircks, "from Breuckelen";
      witnesses: Albert Cornelissen, Gardijntie de Silla.

1662, March 5:

- Abraham; parents: Pieter Pra, Catrina Abrahams, "from the
      Creupelb[osch]"; witnesses: Adam Brouwer, Maria Fredericks.

1662, March 12:

- Femmetie; parents: Aucke Jans, Magdaleen Pieters, "from the
      ferry"; witnesses: Wijnant Pieterszen, Anneken Auckens.

1662, March 19:

- Jacob; parents: Rem Janszen, Janneken Joris, "from the Wale-
      bocht"; witnesses: Jan Joriszen de Rappalie, Teunis
      Gijsbertsen Bogert, Catharina Joris de Rappalie.

1662, April 30:

- Frederick (died July, 1662); parents: Jan Joriszen de Rappalie,
      Maria Fredericks, "as above" [= "from the Walebocht"];
      witnesses: Joris de Rappalie, Aeltie Claes.

Translation

[76^V: "149"]

1662, May 18:

- Adam;   parents: Adam Brouwer, Magdaleentie Jacobs; witness:
  Neeltie Jans.

1662, June 4:

- Janneken;   parents: Jan Corneliszen, Janneken Pieters;
  witnesses: Wessel Gerritsen, Clara Leijdeckers.

1662, July 16:

- Annetie;   parents: Carel Fonteyn, Catharina de Balie;
  witnesses: Jacques Kartiou, Annetie Vincent.

1662, July 23:

- Dirck;   parents: Gerrit Croesen, Neeltie Jans; witnesses:
  Adam Brouwers, Grietie Jans.

1662, September 24:

- Hendrick;   parents: Gerrit Hendrickze, Anna Johannis;
  witnesses: Gijsbert Teuniszen, Magdaleentie Walinx.

1662, October 8:

- Jacobus (died December, 1662);   parents: Jan Jacobsen, Geertie
  Gijsberts, "from Breuckelen"; witnesses: Mr Carel de
  Beauvois, Teeuwis Cornelisz, Sara de Plancke.

1662, December 3:

- Sara;   parents: Jan Pieterszen, Grietie Jans, "from Cujanes";
  witnesses: Frederick Lubbertzen, Annetien Jans.
- Jan;   parents: Hendrick Jansze Been, Jannetie Duurkop, "from
  Breuckelen"; witness: Annetie Duurkop.

1662, December 17:

- Jannetie;   parents: Marcus Soisson, Lijsbet Nachtegael, "from
  Breuckelen"; witnesses: Claes van Elslant d'Oude [= the
  Elder], Fijtie Dircks.

1662, December 24:

- Jan;   parents: Aert Anthonisze Middag, Brechtie Hans, "from
  the Walebocht"; witnesses: Jan Hanssen, Catarina
  d'Rappalie.

Translation

[77^V: "151"]

1663, January 7:

- Jan;   parents: Willem Willemszen, Getruijd van Mullem, "[from]
  Cujanes"; witnesses: Willem Bredenbent, Aeltie Brackunee,
  Janneken Boons.

1663, January 28:

- Joost;   parents: Barent Joosten, Eijtie Laurents; witnesses:
  Sijmon Hansen, Laurens Pieterszen, Magdaleentie Walingx.

1663, February 11:

- Cornelis;   parents: Jan Damen, Fijtie Martens, "[from] Breuckelen"; witnesses: Willem Gerritszen, Susanna Dubbels.

1663, March 11:

- Jacobus;   parents: Jan Pieterszen, Marijtie Hogeboom, "[from]
  Breuckelen"; witness: Lijsbeth Harmensz.
- Johannes;   parents: Barent Gerritsen, Geertie Dirckx;
  witnesses: Volckert Dirckzen, Sara Vernier.

1663, April 22:

- Jan;   parents: Pieter Claeszen, Grietie Cornelis; witnesses:
  Jan Corszen, Hendriekie.

1663, July 8:

- Pieter;   parents: Pieter Janszen, Annetie Jans; witnesses:
  Dirck Stillewil, Anneken Booms.

1663, September 9:

- Pieter;   parents: Wijnant Pietersz, Annetje Auckens, "[from]
  Blommendael"; witnesses: Aucke Jans, Geertie Gijsberts.

1663, September 30:

- Gijsbert;   parents: Jan Laurensze Bogaert, Cornelia Everts;
  witnesses: Teunis Gijsbertse Bogaert, Sara de Rapalie.

1663, December 5:

- Maurits;   parents: Teunis Janszen Coevors, Barber Lucas,
  "[from] Breuckelen"; witnesses: Willem Bredenbend,
  Grietie Jans.

113

Translation

[78^r: "152"]

1663, December 23:

- Trijntie; parents: Tijte Siericks, Jannetie Teunis, "[from] Breuckelen"; witnesses: Jan Buys, Femmetie Jans.

1663, December 26:

- Barent; parents: Jan Hendrickzen, Grietie Barents, "[from] Boswijck".

1664, January 6:

- Femmetie; parents: Dirck Janssen, Marritie Teunis, "[from] the ferry"; witnesses: Isaaqk Foreest, Anneken Lodowijxs.

1664, February 3:

- Trijntie; parents: Willem Willemsen, Agnietie Jans, "[from] Cujanes"; witnesses: Mr Paulus Verbeeck, Teunis Janssen, Tryntie Agens.
- Lidia; parents: Carel Fonteijn, Catharina de Balie; witnesses: Amadoor Fochie, Lidia Mitteroo.

1664, February 17:

- Sara; parents: Pieter Lambertsen, Fijtie Dircks, "[from] Breuckelen"; witnesses: Adriaen Vincent, Marritie Lamberts.

1664, May 11:

- Geertruijt; parents: Barent Joosten, Sijtie Laurens; witnesses: David Jochemsen, Gijsie Hendricks.

1664, May 18:

- Jacques; parents: Lovys Biosie, Anneken Jeuriaens; witnesses: Jacques Corsiou, Hester Vincent.
- Harmen; parents: Joris Jacobsen, Tryntie Claes, "[from the] ferry"; witnesses: Jan Buytenhuysen, Hillegont Joris.

1664, May 22:

- Lijsbeth; parents: Simon Claessen, Anneken Lodowijcx, "[from] Breuckelen"; witnesses: Joost Koekuit, Lysbeth Jans.

1664, July 20:

- Johannes; parents: Barent Gerritsen, Grietie Dircks; witnesses: Jan Licoye, Magdaleentie Walingx.

Translation

[79^r: "154"]

1666, October 10:

- Rijck, and
- Jacob, his younger brother; parents: Heyndrick Rycke, Jtie
        Jacobs; witness: Heylte Aertse.

1667, March 6:

- Aeltie; parents: Louwerens Coleuert, Sara Walderom; witnesses:
        Resolfus Walderom, Willemtie, wife of Roelof Willemse.

1667, July 17:

- Niestie; parents: Tuenis Dirckse, Lysbet Tuenis; witness:
        Mentie Rutgers, maiden.

1667, October 30:

- Stintie; parents: Jan Mackelyck, Stintie Jans; witnesses:
        Claes Arentse, Grietie N., wife of Jan Pieters.

1670, September 22:

- Arien; parents: Dirck Corn? Hooglant, Lijsbeth Jorissen D. Rap-
        alie, "[from] Breuckellen"; witnesses: Joris Jacopssen,
        Catharina Jeronimus.
- Ghielliam; parents: Jan Lequieer, Rachgel Dirckx de Noorman
        [= the Norman], "[from] Boschwijck"; witnesses: Barent
        Geridtssen, Annitie Flipssen.

1671, January 12:

- Jan; parents: Sijmon Claessen, Annitie Lodewijckx, "[from]
        Breuckellen"; witnesses: Willem Janssen, Maritien Claessen.

1672, April 19:

- Maritie; parents: Lambert Janssen Dorlant, Hermtien Pieters,
        "[from] Breuckellen"; witnesses: Wouter Gijssen, Fytien
                                                        Martensse.

1672, April 20:

- no name recorded; parents: Eevert N., Lijsbeth Tonissen,
        "[from] Neuten Eijlant" [= "Nuts Island"]; witness:
        Trijntien Harders.

1673, June 1:

- Petranelle; parents: Dirck Storm, Maria Petersse, "[from]
        Breuckelen"; witnesses: Jeronimus De Rapalie, Hendrica

[continued overleaf]

115

Translation

[79^V: "155"]

Hainelle, Neeltien Careljouw.

1674, May 14:

- Margriet; parents: Sijmon Claessen, Annitie Lodewijckx, "[from] Breuckelen"; witnesses: Jan Claesse Van Huijsse, Marietie Claesse v. Huijse.
- Michiel; parents: Michiel Hainelle, Hendricka Strockels, "[from] Breuckelen".

1674, August 19:

- Sophija; parents: Jan Cornelissen Damen, Fijtie Martens, "from Boswijck"; witnesses: Gerrit Huijgen, Jan de Foreest, Susanna Verledt.
- Geertje; parents: Jan Geritsen Dorlant, Anna Remsen, "from Breukelen"; witnesses: Rem Janssen, Hille Remsen.

1676, August 7:

- Isaack; parents: Borgenson Brokaerd, Cathalijn Leeffeber; witness: Michiel Permentier.
- Aeltje; mother: Mardaleen Hendricks; witness: Hendrick Thijnussen.

1677, June 11:

- Aertje; parents: Hendrick Jansen, Geurtjen Hendricks; witnesses: Jan Keersen, Hendrickje Stevens.

1677, September 30:

- Roelof; parents: Arent Isaacksen, Stijntjen Lourens; witnesses: Hendrick Slecht, Jannitjen Roemers.
- Margriet; parents: Jan Pieterssen, Stijntjen Jans; witnesses: Willem Jorrissen, Hermjen Jans.

1677, October 14:

- Elsje; parents: Willem Jorrissen, Hendrickje Johannes; witnesses: Johannes Marcus, Trijntjen Klaessen.
- Lammitje; parents: Jan Cornelissen Bogaert, Angenietje Strijkers; witnesses: Pieter Strijcker, Sara Strijker.

1677, December 9:

- Jan; parents: Jan Fredericksen, Aeltje Jans; witnesses: Klaes Arensen, Dina Jans.
- Anitjen; parents: Gerrit Kroes, Neeltjen Jans; witnesses: Annitjen Jans, Jan Van Cent.

Translation

[81^r: "158"]

1677, December 27:

- Jakobus; parents: Marten Reijersen, Anitje Jorissen;
  witnesses: Jeronimus Rappalji, Mrs. van Suren.

1678, February 10:

- Sara; parents: Poulus van der Beeck, Sara Schouten; witnesses:
  Meester [= Mr.] Poulus van der Beeck, Sara Schouten.

1678, April 1:

- Jan; no parents recorded; witnesses: Jeronimus Rappalje,
  Kathalijntje Jeronimussen Rappalje.

1678, April 28:

- Aeltje; parents: Jan Geritsen van Couwenhoven, Gedijne de
  Sille; witnesses: Lourens de Sille, Archonia Hillegonde,
  his wife.

1678, June 2:

- Jakobus; parents: Evert Hendricksen, Fijtjen Adams;
  witnesses: Jakop Pietersen, Aeltje Brouwer.
- Katharina; parents: Abraham du Toiet, Jannitjen Reronimus
  Bockqui; witnesses: Bourgon Broucar, Katharini, his wife.
- Saertje; parents: Michiel Hansen, Femmitje Teunis;
  witnesses: Teunis Ghijsbert Bogaert, Sara Jorissen.

1678, June 31:^{2}

- Willem, and
- Merritje; parents: Joris Wolseij, Rebecka Wolseij.

- Jan; parents: Jan Cornelissen Buijs, Machtel Buijs;
  witnesses: Jan Buijs, Cristiaen Jakopsen Wolf.
- Neeltje; parents: Cornelis Verweij, Hendrickje Jans;
  witnesses: Michiel Hansen, Merritje Teunis.

1678, July 28:

- Denijs; parents: Dirck Jansen, Merritje; witnesses: Nijs
  Teunissen, Femmitje Teunis.
- Aeltje; parents: Johannis Christoffel, Marrij Johannes;
  witnesses: Klaes Jansen, Khatarina van der Beeck.

1678, August 25:

- Khatarijnje; mother: Stijntjen Hansen; witnesses: Tieleman
  Jakopsen, Elsje Barens.

117

Translation

[82^r: "160"]

1679, June 22:

- Hendrick; parents: Hermen Hendricksen, Mergriet Sodder;
    godfather: Ferdenandes van Sichelen; godmother:
    Stijntje Hendricks.

1679, July 20:

- Merria, sixteen or seventeen years of age, and
- Samuel, ten or eleven years of age; parents: Clement
    Sallomons, Johanna Salamons.

1679, August 16:

- Jan; parents: Jeurien Blanck, Hester van der Beeck;
    witnesses: Nicklaes Blanck, Klaesje Blanck.
- Jan; parents: Cornelis Jansen Seeuw, Geertje Colfs;
    witnesses: Pieter Jansen Seeuw, Saertje Colfs.

1679, September 14:

- Pieter; parents: Cornelis Pietersen, Geertje Sijmens;
    witnesses: Pieter Klaessen, Grietje Hendricks.
- Machdalena; parents: Willem Brouwer, Betje Brouwer;
    witnesses: Josius Stracken, Aeltjen Brouwer.

1679, October 12:

- Magriet; parents: Cornelis Buijs, Machtel Gerrits;
    witnesses: Jan Buijs, Willemje Thijssen.

1679, December 14:

- Daniel; parents: Denten, Abigael; witnesses: Jan Buijs,
    Cornelis Verwije.
- Ragel; parents: Jan Leurst, Raguel Dircks; witnesses:
    Michiel Hainel, Jannitje Jamiserol.

1680, January 17:

- Sara; parents: Folkert Dircksen, Annitjen Flipsen;
    witnesses: Jeurien Jansen, Lijsbet Jansen.

1680, March 14:

- Margriet; parents: Jan Fredericksen, Aeltje Jans;
    witnesses: Klaes Arensen, Lummitje van Vechten.

Translation

[83^r: "162"]

1680, May 23:

- Johannes, and
- Wilhelmus; parents: Dirck Poulussen, Eechtje Teunis; witnesses: Teunis Jansen Coevors, Arent Fredericksen, Jannitjen Teunis, Jannitjen Klaes van Leendersloot.

1680, June 13:

- Pieter; parents: Michiel Palmetier, Neeltje Jansen Damen; witnesses: Piter Palmentier, Fijtjen Marten Damen.

1680, August 8:

- Sophia; parents: Jan Cornelissen Damen, Sophia Martens; witnesses: Lijsbedt Jansen Damen, Jan Coesjee.
- Femmitje; parents: Jan Theunissen, Cathalijntje Teunis; witnesses: Theunis Ghijsbersen, Sara Jorissen.

1680, October 31:

- Aeltje; parents: Dirck Storm, Marritje Pieters; witnesses: Jan Gerritsen, Fijtjen Martens.
- Adriaen; parents: Joseph Hegeman, Femmitje Remsen; witnesses: Henderikes Hegeman, Catrijna Hegemans.

1680, November 28:

- Hendrick; parents: Cornelis Barensen "from de Nes", Karnelia Hendricks; witnesses: Cornelis Roelofsen, Machdaleen van Ghijsen.
- Krijntje, "the younger [child]"; parents: same as above; witnesses: Rinier van Gijsen, Annemari.

1681, January 9:

- Johanna; parents: Pieter Schamp, Jannitje Dircks; witnesses: Joseph van Bosleijdingh, Marriken Lucas.
- Jannitje; parents: Ares Jansen Vandebilt, Hillitje Remsen; witnesses: Jan Remsen, Marritje Jans.

1681, February 6:

- Catrijn; parents: Joost Caspersen, Machdalena Jansen; witnesses: Johannes Caspersen, Maria Teuniss.

1681, April 17:

- IJsaack; parents: Jan Haesbroeck, Andogo; witnesses: Abraham du Bois, Maria Lorijn.

Translation

[83^V: "163"]

1681, April 17 (continued):

- Cristiaen; parents: Pieter du Joo, Angeniet Nickee;
  witnesses: Cristiaen du Joo, Sian Wiboo.
- Jeuriaen; parents: Melckgert Caspersen, Geertruijt Bartels;
  witnesses: Casper Jansen, Teuntje Jeuriaens.

1681, June 1:

- Marij; parents: Jakop Larsiljeer, Marrij Granson;
  witnesses: Bergon Brokaer, Neeltje Jans Damen.

1681, August 13:

- Cornelis; parents: Pieter Galjamsen, Margrietje Verschuer;
  witnesses: Cornelis Steenwijck, Grietje Steenwijcks.
- Cornelia; parents: Cornelis Corsen Vroom, Merritje Jakops
  Vroom; witnesses: Hendrick Corsen Vroom, Annitje
  Jakops van der Grift.

1681, September 11:

- IJsaack; parents: Thomis Jansen van Dijck, Marrij Andriessen;
  witnesses: Pieter Jansen, Annitjen Jans.

1681, November 6:

- Sara; parents: Sijmen Hansen, Marij Fredericks; witnesses:
  Cornelis Jan Berrien, Jannitje Strijkers.
- Poulus; parents: Poulus van der Beeck, Sara Schouten;
  witnesses: Coenrades van der Beeck, Sara Schouten.

1681, December 11:

- Marije; parents: Cornelis Pietersen, Geertje Sijmen;
  witnesses: Sijmen Jansen, Pieterje Klaes.
- Anthonetta; parents: Joost Duiere, Madleen Duiere; witnesses:
  Jan Miserol d[e] J[onge] [= the Younger], Leja Fonteijn.
- Adriaentje; parents: Jan Hansen Bergen, Jannitje Teunis;
  witnesses: Hans Teunissen, Annitje Teunis.

1682, January 1:

- Daved; parents: Cornelis Jansen de Zeeuw, Geertje Colfs,
  "[from] Boswijck"; witnesses: Wouter Ghijsbersen,
  Doorthee, his wife.

1682, February 26:

- Ledia; parents: Folkert Dircksen, Annitje Flippsen;
  witnesses: Willem Aertsen, Ledia Kasjaert.

Translation

[84^V: "165"]

1682, February 26 (continued):

- Mijndert; parents: Gerbrant Klaessen, Marritje Klaessen;
     witnesses: Arien Klaessen, Marritje Cornelis.
- Willemje; parents: Mathijs Brouwer, Marritje Brouwer;
     witnesses: Pieter Brouwer, Eegtje Joris.
- Abigael; parents: Willem Appelbeij, Divertje Jans;
     witnesses: Jan Buijs, Willemje Thijssen.

1682, April 2:

- Eeght; parents: Jan Thijssen, Grietje Jans; witnesses:
     Thomas Lammersen, Jannitje Jeuriaens.
- Lijntje; parents: Marten Reijersen, Annitje Jorissen;
     witness: Kathelijntje Joris.

1682, April 30:

- Willem; parents: Jakop Verdon, Femmije Verdon; witnesses:
     Johannes Willemsen, Jannitje Boons.

1682, July 9:

- Abraham; parents: Jan Fredericksen, Aeltje Jans; witnesses:
     Frederick Hendricksz, Gerritje Reijniersen.
- Annitje; parents: Stoffel Jansz, Geertje Pieters;
     witnesses: Roelof Mertensz Schenck, Annitje Pieters.
- Jakop; parents: Stoffel Parabaski, Eijtje Strijkers;
     witnesses: Jakop Strijcker, Cornelis Jansen,
     Mrs. Potters.
- Anna; parents: Cornelis Barensen, Annitje Polhemius;
     witnesses: Cornelis Jansen Seubering, Marritje Willems.

1682, August 6:

- Susanna; parents: Hendrick Jansen, Marritje Joris;
     witnesses: Jan Ariaensz, Marritje Hendricks.

1682, September 3:

- Anenietje; parents: Arien Willemsen Bennet, Anenietje Jans;
     witnesses: Thomas Verdon, Marritjen Andries.

1682, October 29:

- Annitje; parents: Roelof Jansen Verkerck, Catharina Sijmens;
     witnesses: Barent Jansen Verkerck, Geertje Verkerck.

121

Translation

[85^V: "167"]

1682, December 24:

- Barbar; parents: Achijas Jansen, Jannitje Lammers; witnesses:
  Jan Jansen van Dijck, Anenietje Jans.

1683, January 28:

- Jannitje; parents: Willem Huijken, Annitjen Huijken;
  witnesses: Pieter Sinkam, Debora Sinkam.
- Gerrit; parents: Athoni de IJck, Anthe Bocque; witnesses:
  Thijs Lubbersen, Trijntje Thijssen.

1683, March 8:

- Lijsbeth; parents: Jan Masten, Geertje Fransen; witnesses:
  Wouter Ghijsbersen, Elisabeth Jans.

1683, May 7:

- Hendrick; parents: Hendrick Corsen, Jesijna Pieters;
  witnesses: Pieter van Nest de Jonge [= the Younger],
  Jakemijntje Pieters.
- Tijs; parents: Hendrick Thijssen, Annitje Tielemans;
  witnesses: Ghijsbert Tijssen, Theuntje Tijssen.

1683, June 24:

- Poulus; parents: Jeurien Blanck, Heester van der Beeck;
  witnesses: Dirck Jansen, Aeltje van der Beeck.

1683, September 23:

- Jannitje; parents: Hendrick Rijcken, Eijtje Jakops;
  witnesses: Engelbaert Lot, Hendrickje Verplanck.
- Jannitje; parents: Willem Appelbeij, Divertje Jans;
  witnesses: Jan Jansen Buijs, Trijntje Jans.
- Thomas; parents: Jakop Verdon, Femmitje Willems;
  witnesses: Maritje van der Beeck, Abram Willemsen.

1683, October 21:

- Rem; parents: Jan Remsen, Martha Jans; witnesses: Jan
  Cornelisse Damen, Jannitje Rappallee.

1683, December 30:

- Lijsbet; parents: Melbert Caspersen, Geertruij Bartelsen;
  witnesses: Willemje Hendricks, Hendrick Jansen.
- Jakop; parents: Jakop Jorissen, Lijsbet Thommissen;
  witnesses: Jakobus van de Water, Hendrickje Johannes.

Translation

[87^r: "170"]

1684, January 20:

- Sara; parents: Jesaijs Draeck, Aeltje Brouwers; witnesses:
  Michiel Hansen, Sara Strijcker.
- Jakop; parents: Jakop Hansen, Elsje Fredericks; witnesses:
  Joris Hansen, Catalijn Bogaert.
- Annitje; parents: Roelof Verkerck, Catrijn Zijmens;
  witnesses: Jan Dircksen van der Vliet, Geertje Verkerck.
- Jakop; parents: Dirck Zutvin, Elisabet Jans; witnesses:
  Auke Jans, Geertje Aukes.
- Jan; parents: Leffert Pietersen, Abigael Aukessen;
  witnesses: Jakobus Aukessen, Femmitje Aukes.

1684, February 17:

- Johannes; parents: Cornelis Neefjes, Eechtje Joris; witnesses:
  Joris Jakopsen, Jan Aertsen, Ariaenje Potters.
- Elisabeth; parents: Randolf Evens, Margriet Evens; witnesses:
  Jakobus van de Water, Elisabeth Lee.

1684, March 16:

- Jan; parents: Jan Jansen, Annitje Pieters; witnesses: Pieter
  Jansen, Annitje Jans van Dijck.

1684, April 6:

- Catrijn, and
- Jannitje; parents: Joost Caspersen, Macdaleenje Jans; witness-
  es: Johannes Caspersen, Casper Jansen, Marrij Teunissen,
  Teuntje Jeuriaens.

1684, June 15:

- Annitje; parents: Dirck Jansen Woertman, Marritje Teunis;
  witnesses: Jan Teunissen, Cathalijntje Teunis.

1684, August 10:

- Wilhelmus; parents: Garardes Beeckman, Machdaleentje Abiels;
  witnesses: Marrijtje Abiels, Wilhelmus Beeckman.
- Elisabeth; parents: Pieter Schamp, Jannije Dircks;
  witnesses: Folckert Dircks, Elisabet Kockuijt.
- Jan; parents: Pieter Strijker, Annitje Strijker; witnesses:
  Swaentje Strijkers, Jan Strijker, Hendrick Stijker.
- Adolfus; parents: Willem Brouwer, Elisabeth Brouwer;
  witnesses: Cornelis Seuberingh, IJda Seuberingh.

1684, October 3:

- Geertje; parents: Jan Vliet, Geertje Verkerck; witnesses:
  Hendrick Vliet, Barentje Verkerck.

Translation

[88^r: "172"]

1684, November 30:

- Jeuriaen; parents: Jakobus van de Water, Engeltje Jeuriaens; witnesses: Thomas Lammarsen, Elisabeth Thomas.
- Jakop; parents: Jakop Brouwer, Annitje Bogardus; witnesses: Jesaijas Dreets, Aeltje Brouwer.
- Jannitje; parents: Evert Hendricksen, Fijtje Brouwer; witnesses: Mathijs Brouwer, Marritje Brouwer.

1684, December 25:

- Willem; parents: Randolf Evens, Margriet Evens.

1685, January 7:

- Johannes; parents: Albert Hendricksen, Grietje Arens; witnesses: Jaques Fonteijn, Lea Fonteijn.

1685, February 1:

- Kornelia; parents: Hendrick Jansen, Marritjen Jans; witnesses: Arien Jansen, Gerritje Smit.
- Zara; parents: Jan Teunissen, Cathalintje Teunis; witnesses: Nijs Teunissen, Aertje Teunis.

1685, March 29:

- Marijje, and
- Aeltje, twins; parents: Adriaen Laforge, Jannitje Jansen; witnesses for Marijje: Geertje Colfs, Jaques Fonteijn; witnesses for Aeltje: Wouter Ghijsen, Doorethee Caljers.
- Marritje; parents: Jan Hansen, Jannitje Teunis; witnesses: Jannitje Teunis, Neeltje Teynis.
- Jakobus; parents: Hendrick Jorissen, Claesje Cornelis; witnesses: Gerrit Willemsen, Joris Abramsen.
- Kathalijn; parents: Jeronimus de Rappalee, Annitje Teunis; witnesses: Nijs Teunissen, Marritje Teunis.

1685, April 20:

- Willem; parents: Dirck Poulussen, Sara Willems.

- Grietje; parents: Jan Fredericksen, Aeltje Jans; witnesses: Jakop Hansen, Annitje Pieters.

1685, July 20:

- Johannes; parents: Theodorus Polhemius, Aertje Teunis; witnesses: Teunis Ghijsbertsen, Katrijna Polhemius.

Translation

[89^r: "174"]

1686, April 29:

- Gosen; parents: Arien Reijersen, Annitje Martens; witnesses:
    Hendrick Willemsen, Marija Adriaensen.
- Elisabeth; parents: Willem Heuijken, Annitjen Andries;
    witnesses: Jan Darval, Elisabeth Hegemans.
- Anna Marij; parents: Frederick van Leeuwen, Dina Jans;
    witnesses: Geertreut Willem, Gerrit Lubbertsen.
- Jakoba; parents: Cornelis Jansen, Trijntje Jillis;
    witnesses: Daniel Polhemius, Catharijna Polhemius.
- Marija; parents: Pieter Galjamsen, Margrietje Verschuer;
    witnesses: Garardes Beeckman, Machdeleentje Beeckman.
- Annitje; parents: Lukas Stevensen, Cathalijntje Hansen;
    witnesses: Jan Martentensen [should probably be: Mart-
    ensen], Jannitje Stevens.
- Angenietje; parents: Jan Jansen, Teuntje Tijssen; witnesses:
    Arien Bennet, Anenietje Jans.
- Anna; parents: Anthoni de Eijcke, Anna Bokee; witnesses:
    Hendrick Tijssen, Annitje Tielemans.

1686, May 2:

- Jan; parents: Jan Stevensen, Femmitje Aukes; witnesses: Jan
    Aukes, Annitje Aukes.
- Lourens; parents: Arien Pietersen Kume, Willemje Peeters;
    witnesses: Joost de Baen, Katrijn van Leeuw.
- Albert; parents: Klaes Jansen Romijn, Stijntjen Alberts;
    witnesses: Dirck Jansen, Aeltje van der Beeck.

1686, August 1:

- Annitje; parents: Jakop Jansen, Anna Fonteijn; witnesses:
    Jan Jansen, Lea Foteijn.

1686, August 29:

- Rem; parents: Ares Jansen van de Bilt, Hillitje Remsen,
    "[from] Vlackebos"; witnesses: Jan Aertsen van de Bilt,
    Jannitje Remsen.^{3}
- Dirck; parents: Dirck Poulussen, Sara Jeets, "[from] Simmeko";
    witnesses: Poulus Dircksen, Elisabeth Poulussen.

1686, November 21:

- Willemje; parents: Jan Hendricksen, Machtel Roelofsen;
    witnesses: Jan Buijs, Grietje Jakops.
- Jakop; parents: Joost Dulje, Madleen Delefeebre; witnesses:
    Folkert Dircksen, Elisabeth Lodowijcks.
- Marritje; parents: Dirck Jansen Woertman, Marritje Teunis;
    witnesses: Cornelis Teunissen, Harmjen Dircks.

Translation

[90^r: "176"]

1687, January 27:

- Sarai; parents: Cornelis Klaessen, Aertje Teunis; witnesses: Claes Jansen van Hasijmes, Aertje Teunis.

1687, January 30:

- Jannitje; parents: Hendrick Klaessen Vechten, Gerritjen Rieniers; witnesses: Pieter Cornelissen, Lummitjen Hendricks.

1687, March 25:

- Dina; parents: Jan Fredericksen, Aeltje Jans; witnesses: Jan Jansen, Elsje Frederick.

1687, April 17:

- Neeltje; parents: Jan Jansen, Annitje Pieters; witnesses: Pieter Pra, Neeltje Jans.
- Thomas; parents: Achijas Jansen, Jannitje Lammers; witnesses: Jan Darval, Catharina Darval.
- Jan; parents: Jan Remsen, Marta Jans; witnesses: Rem Remsen, Annitje Remsen.
- Anna; parents: Pieter Loijs, Sara Loijs; witnesses: Wouter Ghijsen, Annitje Rosendal.

1687, May 8:

- Willem; parents: Jakop Brouwer, Annitje Bogardus; witnesses: Willem Bogardes, Helena Verbrugge.

1687, June 8:

- Johannes; parents: Wouter Teunissen van Pelt, Marij van Pelt; witnesses: Alexander Johannessen, Marija Willemsen Bennet.
- Elisabeth; parents: Jan Roelofsen Seubering, Ariaentje Polhemius; witnesses: Cornelis Barentsen, Margriet Polhemius.

1687, June 26:

- Aeltje; parents: Stoffel Parabaski, Eijtje Strijkers; witnesses: Gerrit Jakopsen Strijker, Teuntje Strijkers.
- Hans; parents: Gerrit Hansen, Jannitje Remsen; witnesses: Jan Remsen, Kathalijntje Hansen.

1687, August 21:

- Joseph; parents: Joseph Hegemans, Femmitje Remsen; witnesses: Ares van de Bilt, Hillitje Remsen.

Translation

[91^{V}: "179"]

1687, September 16:

- Neeltje; parents: Jakobus van de Water, Engeltje Jeuriaens;
    witnesses: Theunis Lammerse, Jannitje Jeuriaens.

1687, September 18:

- Johannes; parents: Willem Brouwer, Elisabeth Brouwer;
    witnesses: Barent Jansen, Marritje Korsen.

1687, November 13:

- Sara; parents: Jeronimus Rappalje, Annitje Teunis;
    witnesses: Femmitje Teunis, Cornelis Teunissen.
- Eijtje; parents: Jeurien Hendricksen, Anenietje Barens;
    witnesses: Folkert Hendricksen, Albertje Barens.

1687, December 11:

- Jan; parents: Jesaijas Dreets, Aeltje Brouwer; witnesses:
    Adam Brouw de Jonge [= the Younger], Antje Brouwer.

1688, May 6:

- Aert; parents: Carel Jansen van Dijck, Lijsbeth Aersen van
    Hert; witnesses: Jan Jansen van Dijck, Teunje Tijssen.

1688, May 27:

- Jannitje; parents: Joris Hansen, Sarai Strijckers;
    witnesses: Jakop Hansen, Eijtje Stijckers.
- Sara; parents: Dirck Poulussen, Sara Jitee; witnesses:
    Willem Pos, Geertje Poulus.

1688, July 29:

- Merritje; parents: Hendrick Jansen, Marritje Jans;
    witnesses: Jochom Woutersen Verschuer, Annitje Jans.
- Margriet; parents: Willem Huijken, Annitje Huijken;
    witnesses: Willem Leijnes, Andrel Tammessen, Marrij
    Leijnes, Marrij Tammes.

1688, August 26:

- Jakop; parents: Pieter Stijcker, Annitje Barens; witnesses:
    Jan Stijcker, Sara Strijckers.

Translation

[92^r: "180"]

1688, September 28:

- Jan; parents: Pieter Usiel, Kornelia Damen; witnesses: Jan
  Damen, Fijtje Mertens.

1688, September 30:

- Maria; parents: Pieter Pra, Marike Heij; witnesses: Kasper
  Joosten, Annitje Pra.

1688, October 28:

- Elsje; parents: Willem Jorissen, Hendrickje Willems;
  witnesses: Hermen Jorissen, Marritje Joris.
- Johannes; parents: Anthoni Salm, Lijsbeth Thijssen;
  witnesses: Johannis Hartman, Annitje Hartmans.

1688, November 25:

- Pieter; parents: Jan de Conselje, Fijtje Schuts;
  witnesses: Michiel Palmentier, Marritje Barens.

1689, February 24:

- Barbera; parents: Willem Pos, Aeltje Coevors; witnesses:
  Hans Teunissen, Berbara Covors.

1689, September 11:

- Frans; parents: Dirck Croes, Elisabeth Croes; witnesses:
  Pieter Jansen, Katrijna Bogardes.
- Jakap; parents: Lourens Haf, Kaniertje Haf; witness: Grietje
  Jillissen.

1689, October 11:

- Barbara; parents: Gerrit Spronk, Annitje Spronk; witnesses:
  Sara Kovors, Arent Fredericksen.
- Pieter; parents: Adriaen de la Forse, Jannitje Loije;
  witnesses: Michiel Palmentier, Sara Loije.
- Jannitje; parents: Johannes van Eekelen, Trijntje van Ekelen;
  witnesses: Jeronimus de Rappalle, Jannitje Teunis.

1689, November 10:

- Elsje; parents: Jan Fredericksen, Aeltje Jans; witnesses:
  Femmitje Teunis, Pieter Jansen.

Translation

[93^r: "182"]

1689, December 8:

- Everardes; parents: Jakop Brouwer, Annitje Bogardes;
  witnesses: Cornelis Hoijer, Cornelia Bogardes.
- Jannitje; parents: Jeurien Hendricksen, Angenietje Barens;
  witnesses: Elsje Prevoost, Ghijsbert Bogaert.

1690, January 12:

- Arien; parents: Hendrick Jansen, Marritje Jans; witnesses:
  Annije Jans, Jochom Verschuer.
- Geertje; parents: Cornelis Jansen Schers, Geertje Colfs;
  witnesses: Maritje Miserol, Jan Sjerol.

1690, March 9:

- Sara; parents: Evert Hendricksen, Fijtje Brouwer;
  witnesses: Abram Brouwer, Sara Brouwer.
- Annitje; parents: Joris Hansen, Sara Strijkers; witnesses:
  Annitje Strijkers, Pieter Strijker.

1690, April 6:

- Thomas; parents: Dirck Poulussen, Sara; witnesses: Luijkas
  Coevers, Marie.
- Katrijna; parents: Hendrick Corsen, Jesijna Pieters;
  witnesses: Aeltje Fredericks, Pieter van Nest.

1690, May 25:

- Johanna; parents: Jakobus de Beavoijs, Maria Carels;
  witnesses: Jakop Hendricks, Katrijna Beavoijs.
- Ariaentje; parents: Anthoni van Pelt, Maddalena Joosten;
  witnesses: Gerrit Strcker, Weijntje Strijckers.

1690, August 3:

- Pieterjen; parents: Pieter Schamp, Jannitje Schamp;
  witnesses: Michiel Palmentier, Macdalena.
- Ariaentje; parents: Hans Teunissen Coevors, Jannitje Boka;
  witnesses: Teunis Jansen Coevors, Barbar Luijkes.

1690, August 24:

- Sara; parents: Ghijsbert Bogaert, Jannitje Bogaert;
  witnesses: Theunis Ghijbertsen, Aertje Teunis.
- Matijs; parents: Anthoni Salm, Lijsbeth Tijssen; witnesses:
  Klaes Barensen, Lijsbeth Poulus.
- Trijntje; parents: Claes Tomissen van Dijck, Trijntje Reijn-
  iers; witnesses: Rijn Arens, Marritje van Dijck.

Translation

[94^r: "184"]

1691, April 11:

- Daniel; parents: Daniel de Rappalje, Sara Klock; witnesses:
    Michiel Hansen, Trijntje Abrams.

1691, May 3:

- Sophija; parents: Pieter Usielle, Cornelia Damen; witnesses:
    Jan Damen, Fijtje Damen.

1691, June 29:

- Mijndert; parents: Gerbrant Klaessen, Marritje Klaes;
    witnesses: Harmen Jorissen, Ariaentje Michielse.
- Marijtje; father: Thomis Hickam; witness: Hillitje Jans.

1691, July 28:

- Debora; parents: Samuel Berrij, Kathalijntje Berri;
    witnesses: Jakobus Berrij, Annitje Rappalje.
- Jannitje; parents: Johannes van Ekelen, Trijntje van Ekelen;
    witnesses: Jeronimus Rappalje, Jannitje Teunis.

1691, August 23:

- Cornelis; parents: Cornelis Jansen Seeuw, Geertje Colfs;
    witnesses: Michiel Palmentier, Neeltje Jans.
- Marijtje; parents: Jan Bibou, Metje Beeckman; witnesses:
    Neeltje Beeckman, Pieter Jansen Staets.

1691, October 18:

- Jan; parents: Jakop Jansen Buijs, Marritje Joris; witnesses:
    Jan Buijs, Trijntje Klaes.
- Abram; parents: Leendert van der Grift, Stijntje van der Grift;
    witnesses: Johannes van der Grift, Stijnge van der Grift.
- Jan;[4] parents: Jakop Jansen Buijs, Maritje Joris; witnesses:
    Trijntje Klaes, Jan Buijs.

1691, November 22:

- Andries; parents: Jan Dircksen Woerman, Anna Marija;
    witnesses: Jan Jansen, Harmje Dircks.

1692, March 13:

- Jannitje; parents: Johannes Jansen, Elbertje Barens;
    witnesses: Jan Pitersen, Annitje Jans.
- Neeltje; parents: Dirck Kroesen, Elisabeth Cregiers;
    witnesses: Folkert Hendricksen, Annitje Para.[5]

Translation

[95^r: "186"]

1692, March 13 (continued):

- Jan; parents: Dirck Poulussen, Sara Jeets; witnesses: Teunis
    Jansen Coevers, Elisabeth Hedlock.
- Cornelia; parents: Pieter Brouwer, Pieternelle Uldricks;
    witnesses: Cornelis Seeberingh, Aeltje Fredericks.
- Elisabeth, "an elderly woman who has several children,
    from Vlissinge".

1692, April 2:

- Sijmen; parents: Klaes Sijmense, Hillitje Jans; witnesses:
    Jan Buijs, Grietje Sijmens.
- Teunis; parents: Nijs Teunissen, Helena Kerteljou;
    witnesses: Jan Teunissen, Annitje Teunis.
- Maddaleentje; parents: Adam Brouwer, Marritje Hendricksen;
    witnesses: Volckert Hendricksen, Hillegont Hendricks.

1692, May 1:

- Cornelis; parents: Anthoni Salm, Elisabeth Tijssen;
    witnesses: Jan Gerritse Dorlant, Annitje Remse.

1692, May 16:

- Jannitje; parents: Wouter Jansen, Rijntje Hendricks;
    witnesses: Jan Woutersen, Gerritje Spiegelaers.

1692, August 27:

- Brechje; parents: Gerrit Middach, Cornelia Jans; witnesses:
    Michiel Hansen, Annitje Middach.

1692, September 4:

- Abram; parents: Leffert Pietersen, Abigel Aukes; witnesses:
    Auke Reijniersen, Margriet Polhemius.

1692, October 30:

- Aeltje; parents: Jan Jansen, Annitje Pra; witnesses: Jan
    Dircksen, Aeltje Jans.
- Rensje; parents: Albert Minnes, Mincke Jans; witnesses:
    Lukas Stevense, Lijsbeth Minnes.

1692, November 27:

- Jan; parents: Gerrit Sprong, Annitje Teunis; witnesses:
    Willem Pos, Barber Sprong.

Translation

1693, April 2:

- Susanna; parents: Joris Abramse, Annitje Teunis; witnesses: Marten Roelofse, Aeltje Strijker.
- Cornelia; parents: Pieter Usile, Cornelia Damen; witnesses: Michiel Palmentier, Neeltje Damen.

1693, April 23:

- Maijke; parents: Hendrick Tijssen, Marij van der Beeck; witnesses: Wouter van Pelt, Marija Johannes.
- Lummitje; parents: Hendrick Klaessen Vechten, Gerritje Pieters; witnesses: Machdalena Vechten, Gerret Klaessen Vechten.

1693, May 14:

- IJsaack; parents: Cornelis Sebering, Aeltje Fredericks; witnesses: Theodorus Polhemius, Aert Teunis Bogaert.
- Willemmijntje; parents: Mathijs Brouwer, Marritje Pieters; witnesses: Nicklaes Brouwer, Rachel Brouwer.

1693, June 11:

- Cristijnje; parents: Barent Slecht, Hilitje Jans; witnesses: Cornelis Slecht, Elsje Barens.
- Aert; parents: Aris Janse van de Bilt, Hillitje Remse; witnesses: Jakop Remsen, Sara Remsen.

1693, July 23:

- Hendrikus; parents: Marten Hendrickse Wils, Marrij van der Wijck; witnesses: Theodorus van der Wijck, Catrijna Polhemius.
- Kathalina; parents: Jakobus de Beavoijs, Marrijtje Jooste; witnesses: Jan Damen, Trijntje Sijmens.

1693, August 13:

- Jan; parents: Gerrit Middach, Cornelia Middach; witnesses: Gerdijna de Zilla, Jan Gerritse Couwenoven.

1693, September 3:

- Annitje; parents: Hendrick Jansen, Hester Janse; witnesses: Jan Thijssen, Wolfje Jans.
- Jannitje; parents: Stoffel Gerritse, Annitje Stoffels; witnesses: Lourens Jansens, Elisabeth Gerritse.

Translation

[97^r: "190"]

1693, October 15:

- Adam; parents: Nicklaes Brouwer, Jannitje Brouwer; witnesses:
  Abram Brouwer, Maddaleentje Brouwer.
- Marritje; parents: Lourens Koeck, Margriet Barens; witnesses:
  Michiel Palmentier, Neeltje Palmentier.

1693, November 5:

- Elisabeth; parents: Theodorus Polhemius, Aertje Polhemius;
  witnesses: Daniel Polhemius, Annitje Bogaert.
- Sijmen; parents: Ghijsbert Bogaert, Jannitje Bogaert;
  witnesses: Sijmen Jansen, Joris Abramse.

1693, November 26:

- Sijmen; parents: Joost Duljee, Maddaleen Lafeber; witnesses:
  Pieter Pra, Marrijtje Heij.
- Dirck; parents: Jan Woertman, Anna Marrij; witnesses: Dirck
  Janse Woertman, Engeltje van de Water.

1694, January 21:

- Damen; parents: Michiel Palmentier, Neeltje Damen; witnesses:
  Jan Damen, Elisabeth Damen.

1694, February 11:

- Jannitje; parents: Claes Barensen Blom, Elisabeth Poulus;
  witnesses: Jan Gerritsen Dorlant, Annitje Remsen.

1694, March 4:

- Elisabeth, and
- Pieter, twins; parents: Thomis Killeman, Annitje Killeman;
  witnesses: Elisabeth Booch, Elsje Killemans, Pieter
  Siaeck, Cobus Pietersen.
- Metje; parents: Willem Jorissen, Hendrickje Jans; witnesses:
  Cornelis Neefjens, Hennitje Lammers.
- Jooris; parents: Jakop Janse Buijs, Marritje Jooris;
  witnesses: Jeronimus de Rappaljee, Annitje Teunies.

1694, April 9:

- Gerrit; parents: Gerrit Claessen Vechten, Maddaleentje Vechten;
  witnesses: Hendrick Claesse Vechten, Gerritje Vechten.
- Catrijntje; parents: Johannes Jansen, Metje Johannes; witnesses: Frederick Sijmense, Catrijntje Jans.

133

Translation

[98^r: "192"]

1694, April 29:

- Abram; parents: Jeurien Blanck, Hester Blanck; witnesses:
  Jakop Hansen, Elisabeth Witte.
- Hendrick; parents: Jan Frederickse, Aeltje Jans; witnesses:
  Hendrick Klaessen, Lummitje Klaesse.
- Aeltje; parents: Thobijas de Nijck, Elisabeth de Nijck;
  witnesses: Benjemin Hegeman, Jannitje Hegemans.
- Cornelis; parents: Theodorus van der Wijck, Mergrietje van
  der Wijck; witnesses: Cornelis Barense van der Wijck,
  Catrijna Polhemius.
- Catrijntje; parents: Pieter Wijnanse, Anna Marij; witnesses:
  Catrijna Vroom, Joris Hoochlant.

1694, May 17:

- Jan; parents: Joris Hansen, Sara Strijker; witnesses: Stoffer
  Parabako, Femmitje Teunis.

1694, July 29:

- Teunis; parents: Gerrit Sprong, Annitje Teunis; witnesses:
  Gabriel Sprong, Maritje Sprong.

1694, December 9:

- Dina; parents: Frederick van Leeuwen, Dina Jans; witnesses:
  Hendrikes Hegeman, Ariaentje Hegemans.
- Dirck; parents: Willem Aersen, Stijntje Aersen; witnesses:
  Maddaleen Rosekrans, Giljam Likuje.
- Joris; parents: Gerret Hansen, Jannitje Remsen; witnesses:
  Joris Remsen, Femmitje Joris.

1695, May 4:

- Jan; parents: Willem Willemsen, Jannitje Willemse; witnesses:
  Claes Tomussen van Dijck, Marritje Andriessen.
- Klaes; parents: Gerrit Klaessen, Marritje Ariaensen; witness-
  es: Jan van Ditmarsen, Ariaentje van Ditmarsen.
- Cornelis; parents: Mathijs Cornelissen, Fijtje Brouwer;
  witnesses: Thomis Lammerse, Elisabeth Thomis.
- Gerrit; parents: Stoffel Gerritse, Annitje Stoffels; witness-
  es: Gerrit Stoffelse, Hendrickje Jakops.
- Jan Evertse Bout; parents: Jan Woertman, Anna Marij Woertman;[6]
  witnesses: Pieter Woertman, Annitje Wijnans.
- Catrijn; parents: Pieter Tijssen, Barber Jans; witnesses:
  Jakop Cassou, Marij Meijnders.
- Marijtje; parents: Adam Brouwer, Marritje Brouwer; witnesses:
  Willem Nasareth, Lena Nasareth.
- Willem; parents: Denijs van Duijn, Marritje Huijke; witness-
  es: Abram van Duijn, Annitje Sijmens.
- Sijbregh; parents: Roelof Verkerck, Katrijna Verkerck;
  witnesses: Barent Jansen, Annitje Jansen.

Translation

[99^r: "194"]

1695, May 4 (continued):

- Cristijna; parents: Joost de Bane, Elijsabeth de Bane;
      witnesses: Cornelis van der Werf, Marij Karteljou.
- IJsaack; parents: Abram Bokee, Jannicken Bokee;
      witness: Maddaleentje Schenck.
- Wijnant; parents: Pieter Wijnans, Anna Marij; witnesses:
      Johannes Richou, Annitje Woertman.

1695, May 5:

- Sara; parents: Walter, son-in-law of Leijsenaer, Katharina
      Leijsenaer.
- no name recorded; parents: Jan Teunisse, Cathalijntje Teunis;
      witness: Ghijsbert Bogaert.
- Jan; parents: Andries Jansen, Geertje Andriessen; witnesses:
      Albert Jansen Steenwijck, Aeltje Alberts.
- no name recorded; parents: Elbert Ariaensen, Cathalijntje
      Remsen; witnesses: Jakobus Hegeman, Jannitje Ariaens.
- Annitje; parents: Gabriel Sprong, Geertruij Sprong;
      witnesses: Arent Vredericks, Hester Arense.
- Abram; parents: Joris Abramsen, Annitje Jorissen; witnesses:
      Abram Jorissen, IJda Abramsen.

1695, October 19:

- Marija,
- Katrijna, and
- Elisabeth; parents: Joris Cimmer, Marij Cimmer; witnesses
      for Marija: Jannitje Caspers, Hendrick Janse; witnesses
      for Katrijna: Frans Abramse, Engelje van de Water;
      witnesses for Elisabeth: Mathijs Bofi, Katrijna Barwa.
- Jeremijas; parents: Aris Janse van de Bilt, Hillitje Remse;
      witnesses: Jeremijas Remsen, Martha Jans.

1695, October 20:

- Dirck; parents: Goris Storm, Engelje Tomis; witnesses:
      Kasper Janse, Fransijntje.
- Kornelia; parents: Cornelis Seberingh, Aeltje Seuberingh;
      witnesses: Roelof Seberingh, Katrijn Seberingh.
- IJsaack; parents: Jan Auke, Eefje Jans; witnesses: Jakop
      Remsen, Geertruijt Dircks.
- Jakop; parents: Bartel Jakopsen, Helena Donlus; witnesses:
      Jakop Hendricksen, Katrijntje Beavoijs.
- Johanna; parents: Pieter Couwenoven, Peesjiens Daes;
      witnesses: Willem Couwenoven, Jannitje Couwenoven.

1696, March 27:

- Helena; parents: Pieter Usiel, Kornelia Usiel; witnesses:
      Samuel Berrij, Martha Jans.
- Jannitje; parents: Pieter Loijissen, Sara Loijis; witnesses:

[continued overleaf]

135

Translation

[100^r: "196"]

1696, March 27 (continued):

Johannis Fonteijn, Annitje van Cleef.
- Hendrick; parents: Barent Slecht, Hillitje Jans; witnesses:
Hendrik Slecht, Hendrika Strockels.

1696, March 29:

- Annitje; parents: Davidt Sprong, Ragel Sprong; witnesses:
Teunis Woertman, Katrijn Sprong.
- Johannes; mother: Divertje Tijssen; godmother: Trijntje
Tijssen.
- Jan; parents: Jan Bennit, Aeltje Bennit; witnesses: Leffer
Pietersen, Abigael Leffersen.
- Adam; parents: Jakop Brouwer, Annitje Brouwer; witnesses:
Cornelis Fiele, Katrijna Bogardes.
- Teunis; parents: Rijn Arens, Jannitje Ryeniersen;
witnesses: Johannes Tibont, Teuntje Tibont.
- Marija; witnesses: Hendrikus Frees, Marijtj Frees;
godmother: Femmitje.[7]
- Hendrick; parents: Jakop Hendrickse, Sijtje Jakops;
witnesses: Rijck Hendrickse, IJda Hendricks.
- Katrijna; parents: Chaerlis Fonteijn, Leentje Fonteijn;
witnesses: Jaques Fonteijn, Marijtje Reijnierse.
- Sara; parents: Jan Monfoor, IJda Monfoor; witnesses: Joris
Abramse, Lammitje Abramse.
- Katrijna; parents: Jan van ter Veer, Femmitje van ter Veer;
witnesses: Cornelis van der Veer, Trijntje van der Veer.
- Bragon; parents: Hans Coevors, Jannitje Coevors;
witnesses: IJsaack Brokaer, Marritje Coevors.
- Sijtje; parents: Jan Hoochlant, Jakoba Hoochlant;
witnesses: Marten Schenck, Elisabeth Schenck.
- Marritje; parents: Tijs Pietersen, Conelia Tijssen;
witnesses: Hendrikus Kip, Sara Neefjens.
- Jakobus; parents: Jan Stevense, Femmitje Jans; witnesses:
Jan Keersen, Hendrickje Jans.
- Cornelis; parents: Gerrit Dorlant, Kornelia Dorlant;
witnesses: Gerrit Janse Dorlan, Catrijna Jakops.
- Cornelis; parents: Barent Follemon, Trijntje Follemon.

1696, August 9:

- Andries; parents: Arent Andriessen, Maddalena Jans;
witnesses: Dirck Andriessen, Elisabeth Jan.
- Trijntje; parents: Cornelis Jorissen, Annitje Pieters;
witnesses: Pieter Jansen Staets, Trijntje Klaes.
- Daniel; parents: Pieter Wijnans, Anna Marija; witnesses:
Poulus Richou, Cathalijntje Richou.

1696, October 18:

- Gerritje; parents: Hendrick Klaessen, Gerritje Rijnierse;
witnesses: Jillis Provoost, Marija Provoost.
- Jannitje; parents: Hendrik Jansen, Geertje Andriesse;
witnesses: Benjamin Hegeman, Geertruijt Hegeman.

Translation

[101^r: "196"]

1696, October 18 (continued):

- Annitje; parents: Joris Rappaljee, Neeltje Rappalje; 8
  witnesses: Jeronumus Rappalje, Annitje Rappalje.

1696, November 15:^{9}

- Gerbrant; parents: Folkert Hendrikse, Elisabeth Poulus;
  witnesses: Pieter Janse Staets, Annitje van Sent.

1696, December 13:^{9}

- no name recorded; parents: Cornelis van Duijn, Machtel van
  Duijn.
- Elisabeth; parents: Jan Frederickse, Aeltje Jans;
  witnesses: Cornelis van Duijn, Annitje Staets.
- Eeghtje; parents: Gabriel Sprong, Geertruijt Sprong;
  witnesses: Gerrit Sprong, Annitje Sprong.

1696, December 27:^{9}

- Marritje; parents: Teunis Woertman, Catharijna Woertman;
  witnesses: Dirck Janse Woertman, Barbar Coevors.
- Jeuriaen; parents: Jochom Caljer, Marritje Caljer;
  witnesses: Jeuriaen Caljer, Geertruijt Caljer.
- Hillegont; parents: Adam Brouwer, Marritje Brouwer;
  witnesses: Ariaen Claessen, Rachel Brouwer.

1697, February 21:

- Leendert; parents: Harmen de Grauw, IJbitje de Grauw;
  witnesses: Jakop Buijs, Hillitje Uijthuijsen.

1697, March 19:

- Abram; parents: Theodorus Polhemius, Aertje Polhemius;
  witnesses: Ariaenje Sebering, Michiel Hansen Bergen.
- Cornelia, "an elderly spinster baptized by Domine Lupardus".

1697, March 21:

- Machdalena; parents: Abram Brouwer, Cornelia Brouwer;
  witnesses: Nicklaes Brouwer, Jannitje Brouwer.
- Pieter; parents: Pieter Strijker, Annitje Strijker;
  witnesses: Joris Hansen Bergen, Angenietje Strijkers.

1697, May 9:

- Teunis; parents: Joris Abramsen, Annitje Teunis;
  witnesses: Ghijsbert Bogaert, Cathalijntje Teunis.

Translation

1697, May 9 (continued):

- Dina;   parents: Gerrit Middach, Cornelia Middach; witnesses:
    Abram Remsen, Neeltj Rappalje.

1697, May 24:

- Sophija;   parents: Jakobus de Beavoijs, Marijtje Beavoijs;
    witnesses: Hendrick Klaessen Vechten, Sara Klock.

1697, June 7:

- Arien;   parents: Jan Bennit, Femmitje Bennit; witnesses:
    Arien Bennit, Angenietje Bennit.

1697, August 15:

- Jonathan;   parents: Jonathan Marel, Judith Marel; witnesses:
    Pieter Pra, Marijtje Pra.

1697, September 10:

- Willem;   parents: Pieter Willemse, Catharijna Kips;
    witnesses: Cornelis Willemse, Lammitje Abrams.

1697, September 12:

- Jakoba;   parents: Thomas Luwes, Franssijntje Luwwes;
    witnesses: Jakop Lookermans, Geesjen Luwwes.
- Catrijna;   parents: Thomas Boudi, Marrij Boudi; witnesses:
    Mathijs de Maree, Catrijna Kadt.

1697, October 10:

- Jan;   parents: Jan Hebbelem, Sara Bergen; witnesses: Jan
    Hanse Bergen, Jannitje Berget.

1697, November 5:

- Jacop;   parents: Cornelis Sueberingh, Aeltie Sueberingh;
    witnesses: Daniel Polhemijus, Neltie Polhemijus.

1697, December 26:

- Annitje;   parents: Cornelis Pauelsen, Jannitje Andrissen;
    witnesses: Jan Pietersen Staets, Anne Marija Andrissen.

Translation

1697, December 27:

- Zara; parents: Mourus Koevers, Annetje; witnesses: Jaqes
  Fonteijn, Anneke, his wife.
- Folkert; father: Jurien Naghel; witnesses: Frederick Cijmonse,
  Grietje Folkertse.

1698, April 10:

- Maergrieta; parents: Tobijas de Nijck, Lijsbet de Nijck;
  witnesses: Cobus Hegheman, Loeckreesje Hegeman.
- Femmetje; parents: Jacob Buijs, Marretje Buijs; witnesses:
  Michiel Hanse, Femmetje, his wife.
- Samuel; parents: Samuel Berrij, Catelijntje Berrij;
  witnesses: Daniel Rapalje, Zara, his wife.

1698, May 1:

- Cristina; parents: Pieter Para, Maria Para; witnesses:
  Juriaen Anderiesse, Lijsbet Anderiesse.
- Lijsbet; parents: Pieter Lowijse, Zara; witnesses: Cornelis
  Lowyse, Geertje, his wife.
- Cornelis; parents: Jan Berrien, Rutje; witnesses: Pieter
  Berrien, Jannetje Etcel.

1698, May 9:

- Maria; parents: Jan Gancel, Judick; witnesses: Jan Miserol
  de Jonghe [= the Younger], Marretje, his wife.

1698, June 13:

- Cornelis; parents: Dirck Middagh, Catelijntje; witnesses:
  Gerridt Middagh, Marretje van Neste.

1698, July 10:

- Hendrick; parents: Albartus van de Water, Heijltje;
  witnesses: Willem Bennet, Ariaentje, his wife.
- Annitje; parents: Hendrick Janse, Marretje; witnesses:
  Barnardus Smit, Lena Verschuere.

1698, August 7:

- Arie; parents: Jsaeck Bennet, Lena; witnesses: Arie Bennet,
  Angenietje, his wife.

1698, September 30:

- Pieter; parents: Jan Woertman, Anne-Marij; witnesses: Machiel

[continued overleaf]

Translation

[103^V: "201"]

Hanse, Femmetje Remse.

1698, October 2:

- Maria; parents: Daniel Polemus, Neeltje; witnesses: Cornelis
  Ceberingh, Maria van der Veer.

1698, October 30:

- Jan; parents: Barent Slecht, Hilletje Sleght; witnesses: Jan
  Waggelom, Blandina Waggelom.
- Annetje; parents: Cornelis Jorisse, Annetje; witnesses:
  Harmen Jorisse, Annetje Staets.

1698, November 27:

- Cathrina; parents: Leendert Huijge de Klijn, Madeleetje;
  witnesses: Barent Hendrickse, Cathrina Waters.
- Jan; parents: Gabriel Sprongh, Geertruij; witnesses: Klaes
  Barentse Blom, Lijsbet, his wife.
- Cornelis; parents: Cornelis Verhoeve, Lijsbet; witnesses:
  Thomas Lammertse, Metje Bibout.

1698, December 25:

- Neeltje; parents: Folckert Hendrickse Bries, Lijsbet;
  witnesses: Michiel Hanse, Jannetje Poulisse.
- Mourus; parents: Gerridt Sprongh, Annetje; witnesses: Hans
  Coevers, Antje Fonteijn.

1699, January 15:

- Jakemijntje; parents: Gerridt Couwenoven, Lijsbet;
  witnesses: Jan Gerritsz Couwenoven, Gerardina, his wife.
- Abram; parents: Mathijs Corneliss, Fijtje; witnesses:
  Nicklaes Brouwer, Jannetje, his wife.
- Hendrick; parents: Adam Brouwer, Marretje; witnesses: Willem
  Brouwer, Angenietje, his wife.
- Bettij; parents: Jeseijas Drets, Aeltje; witnesses: Willem
  Hiltin, Johana Kaer.

1699, February 12:

- Fredrick; parents: Fredrick Sijmonse, Ledia; witnesses:
  Jacobus Boubyn, Annetje, his wife.

1699, March 12:

- Marytje; parents: Abram Brouwer, Cornelia; witnesses:
  Cornelis Caljer, Margrietje Pieters.

Translation

[104^V: "203"]

1699, April 9:

- Lucas; parents: Lucas Coevers, Barber; witnesses: Gerrit
  Sprong, Annetje, his wife.

[56^r: "110"]

1699, April 9 (continued):

- Teuntje; parents: Daniel Hendrikze, Trijntje; witnesses:
  Gerardus Beekman, Magdaleentje, his wife.

1699, May 28:

- Jan; parents: Jeems, Grietje; witnesses: Barent Slegt,
  Hilletje Slegt.
- Jan; parents: Johannes Fijn, Anna Fijn; witnesses: Jacob
  Fijn, Hester Fijn.
- Tys; parents: Dirck Tyssen, Annetje; witnesses: Tijme
  Valentijn, Trijntje Lubberts.
- Ysaak; parents: Joris Abramse, Annetje; witnesses: Theodurus
  Pollemus, Aertje, his wife.

1699, June 18:

- Lijsbet; parents: Niclaas Brouwer, Jannetje; witnesses:
  Cornelis Caljer, Geertruit Caljer.
- Antje; parents: Jacob Casjouw, Anne Maria; witnesses: Joris
  Daniels Rapalje, Angenietje, his wife.

1699, July 16:

- Maria; parents: Joris van Neste, Maria; witnesses: Rinier
  Aernoutze, Jannetje, his wife.
- Lijsbet; parents: Michiel van der Voort, Christina;
  witnesses: Claas Barentze Blom, Lijsbet, his wife.
- Lijsbet; parents: Michiel Parmentier, Neeltje; witnesses:
  Jeems Simson, Marta, his wife.

1699, August 20:

- Wijntje; parents: Cornelis Paulisse, Jannetje; witnesses:
  Johannes Paulisse, Jannetje Paulisse.

1699, September 17:

- Rem; parents: Yzaak Remze, Sara; witnesses: Pieter Monfoort,
  Jannetje Remze.
- Gerbrandt; parents: Pieter Gerbrandtze, Stijntje; witnesses:

[continued overleaf]

Translation

[56^V: "111"]

1699, September 17 (continued):

Gerbrandt Claasse, Maritje, his wife.
- Ariaantje; parents: Aart Aarsen, Lijsbet; witnesses: Jan
  Aarzen, Jannetje Poulisse.
- Christiaan; parents: Jacob van Dooren, Maritje; witnesses:
  Pieter van Dijk, Maayke van Deventer.

1699, October 13:

- Abram; parents: Abram van Duyn, Geertje; witnesses: Cornelis
  van Duyn, Machtel, his wife.

1699, October 15:

- Reinier; parents: Charel Fontein, Leena; witnesses: Aucke
  Reinierze, Ida, his wife.

1699, November 12:

- Engeltje; parents: Cornelis Slegt, Johanna; witnesses:
  Jacobus van de Water, Engeltje, his wife.
- Pieter; parents: Johannes Pieterse, Annetje; witnesses:
  Roelof Pieterse, Aeltje Boekhoute.
- Elisabet; parents: Cornelis Sybrich, Aaltje; witnesses:
  Theodorus Polemus, Annetje Barents.

1699, December 26:

- Pietronelletje; parents: Gysbert Bogaart, Jannetje;
  witnesses: Evert Janzen, Metje, his wife.

1700, January 14:

- Jacomijntje; parents: Cornelis van Duyn, Machtel;
  witnesses: Abram van Duyn, Aeltje van Duyn.

1700, March 10:

- Margrietje; parents: Dirck Andriesse, Femmetje; witnesses:
  Arent Andriesse, Margrietje Lork.
- Lijsbeth; parents: Theunus Woertman, Catharijntje;
  witnesses: Joris Remze, Lijsbeth Woertman.

1700, April 1:

- Hieronymus; parents: Jan Bennet, Femmetje; witnesses:
  Theunus Rapalje, Saartje, his wife.

Translation

[57^V: "113"]

1700, May 19:

- Hendrick; parents: Cornelis Bries, Saartje; witnesses:
  Folkert Bries, Lijsbet, his wife.
- Cornelis; parents: Arje Bennet, Berbertje; witnesses: Henrie
  Filkin, Magdaleentje van Dijck.
- Fytje, "born first", and
- Divertje, twins; parents: Cobus Evertze, Diwertje; witnesses
  for Fytje: Gabriel Sprong, Fijtje Cornelisse; witnesses
  for Divertje: Willem Thijsse, Trijntje Lubberts.

1700, June 9:

- Isaak; parents: Isaak Bennet, Leëna; witnesses: Michiel van
  der Koek, Saartje, his wife.

1700, July 7:

- Jan; parents: Thijs Buys, Lijsbet; witnesses: Jan Buys,
  Hilletje Simense.

1700, August 11:

- Johannes; parents: Johannes Sybrink, Aaltje; witnesses:
  Roelof Sybrink, Abigel Pieters.
- Hendrick; parents: Aucke Reinierse, Yda; witnesses: Hendrik
  Reinierse, Alida Vonk.
- Geertje; parents: Hendrick Janze, Hester; witnesses: Corn-
  elis Lowize, Geertje, his wife.
- Tammes; parents: Paulus Dirkse, Rachel; witnesses: Gabriel
  Sprong, Geertruy, his wife.
- Engeltje; parents: Benjamin van de Water, Engeltje;
  witnesses: Cobus van de Water, Lijsbet van de Water.

1700, September 8:

- Willem; parents: Cornelis Couwenhove, Margrietje;
  witnesses: Willem Couwenhove, Jannetje, his wife.
- Samuel; parents: Jan Berry, Rutje; witnesses: Klaas Berry,
  Trijntje Remze.
- Angenietje; parents: Jacob Bennet, Barbara; witnesses: Arje
  Bennet, Angenietje, his wife.
- David; parents: David Sprong, Rachel; witnesses: Henricus
  Fereest, Femmetje, his wife.
- Joosje; parents: John Bahnham, Wolfje; witnesses: Hendrick
  Janze, Helena Gijsberts.

1700, October 6:

- Pieter; parents: Joris van Neste, Marijtje; witnesses:
  Klaas Arisen, Jacomijntje, his wife.
- Hendrick; parents: Daniel Polemus, Neeltje; witnesses:
  Johannes Wijk, Hendrickje van der Veer.

Translation

[59^r: "115"]

1700, October 6 (continued):

- Aaltje; parents: Isaak Broekaar, Hilletje; witnesses: Roelof
  Bas, Catalijntje Broekaar.
- Jan; parents: Jacobus Lowysse, Lijsbet; witnesses: Cornelis
  Lowijsse, Grietje Tilburgh.

1700, November 1:

- Johannes; parents: Pieter Cornel, Catrina; witnesses:
  Johannes Cornel, Anna van Wijk.

1700, December 1:

- Metje; parents: Cornelis van der Hoeve, Lijsbet; witnesses:
  Benjamin van de Water, Elsje van der Hoeve.

1700, December 25:

- Marijtje; parents: Isaak Remse, Saartje; witnesses: Joris
  Remze, Marytje Monfoor.

1701, February 2:

- Hendrick; parents: Rijk Hendrickze, Jannetje; witnesses:
  Jan Dorlandt, Eytje Hendrickze.
- Mearcy; parents: Thomas Schilman, Annetje; witnesses: Isaak
  Broekaar, Mearcy van Hove.

1701, March 2:

- Reinier; parents: Hendrick Vechte, Gerritje; witnesses:
  Joris Bergen, Sara, his wife.
- Jacomyntje, and
- Aaltje, twins; parents: Gerrit Couwenhove, Lysbet; "witnesses
  for the elder one" [= Jacomyntje]: Steven Richard, Mar-
  ica, his wife; "witnesses for the younger one": Abram
  Jorize, Aaltje, his wife.

1701, March 30:

- Andries; parents: Cornelis Paulisse, Jannetje; witnesses:
  Jurje Andriese, Lijsbet Bordan.
- Jurje; parents: Niclaas Brouwer, Jannetje; witnesses: Jurie
  Case, Lena Nazaret.
- Casparis; parents: Jesaias Draake, Aaltje; witnesses:
  Niclaas Brouwer, Sara Neyt.
- Margrietje; parents: Arent Andriesse, Lena; witnesses: Thijs
  Buyl, Femmetje Andriesse.

Translation

[60^r: "117"]

1701, April 21:

- Maria; parents: Jan Arianse, Vrouwtje; witnesses: Thys
      Buyl, Annetje Bas.

1701, May 1:

- Lijsbet; parents: Pieter Uziele, Cornelia; witnesses: Samuel
      Philips, Celetje Dame.
- Marrytje; parents: Cornelis Wijkhof, Geertje; witnesses:
      Hendrick Wijkhof, Marrytje, his wife.

1701, June 8:

- Wijntje; parents: Folkert Bries, Lijsbet; witnesses:
      Johannes Paulisse, Marrytje Paulisse.
- Echje; parents: Gerrit Sprong, Antje; witnesses: Jan Hanze
      Bergen, Jannetje, his wife.

1701, June 27:

- Lucas; parents: Gabriel Sprong, Geertruy; witnesses:
      Theunus Woertman, Berbertie Coevers.

1701, July 27:

- Antie; parents: Joris Remze, Femmetje; witnesses: Izaak
      Remze, Antje Woertman.
- Jan; parents: Jan Dorlandt, Marytje; witnesses: Jan Dorlandt,
      Trijntje van der Veer.
- Jannetje; parents: Jacob Remse, Geertruy; witnesses: Joris
      Remze, Annetje Dorlandt.
- Johannes; parents: Engelbart Lot, Cornelia; witnesses:
      Abraham Lot, Geertje, his wife.

1701, August 24:

- Annetje; parents: Aart Aarzen, Lijsbet; witnesses: Jan
      Staats, Lena Hooglandt.

1701, September 21:

- Lijsbet; parents: Matheus Aerzen, Marytje; witnesses: Aert
      Aerzen, Debora Schecerla.
- Andries; parents: Dirk Andriesse, Femmetje; witnesses:
      Johannes Verscheur, Trijntje Albertze.
- Marrytje; parents: Joris Remze, Lammetje; witnesses: Rem
      Remze, Marrytje, his wife.
- Jan; parents: Tomas Aete, Elsie; witnesses: Jan Aete,
      Lijsbet Schilman.
- Johannes; parents: Jacob Casjouw, Marytie; witnesses: Theunus

[continued overleaf]

Translation

[61^r: "119"]

Rapalje, Saartje, his wife.

1701, November 16:

- Jacob;   parents: Antoni Couzaar, Lijsbet; witnesses: Gijsbert
  Bogaart, Jannetje, his wife.
- Hendrick;   parents: Jan Aerisen, Yda; witnesses: Jacob
  Hendrikze, Eytje Hendrickze.

1701, December 14:

- Annetje;   parents: Johannes Pietersen, Annetje; witnesses:
  Ysaak Broekaar, Hilletje, his wife.
- Annetje;   parents: Pieter Wijnantze, Anna Maria; witnesses:
  Jan Bennet, Aaltje, his wife.

1702, January 18:

- Jannetje;   parents: Willem Brouwer, Marta; witnesses: Steven
  Beduew, Maria, his wife.
- Marrytje;   parents: Michiel de Gree, Catrina; witnesses: Jan
  Miserol, Marrytje, his wife.

1702, May 14:

- Dirck;   parents: Teunus Rapalje, Saartje; witnesses: Gabriel
  Tamze, Catalijntje Rapalje.
- David;   parents: Pieter Nevius, Jannetje; witnesses: Marten
  Schenk, Lijsbet, his wife.
- Elsje;   parents: Jan van der Vliet, Geertje; witnesses: Jan
  Verkerk, Elsje, his wife.
- Willemijntje;   parents: David Aerzen, Heyltie; witnesses:
  Jan Aerzen, Helena Hogelandt.
- Hendrick;   parents: Cornelis Slegt, Johanna; witnesses:
  Johannes Slegt, Anna Catrina Slegt.
- Claas;   parents: Jochum Verscheure, Catrina; witnesses:
  Dirck Andriesse, Kuyertie Loch.
- Martha;   parents: William Eldrets, Elizabet; witnesses:
  Tammes Davids, Margriet Dolstein.

1702, June 16:

- Annetje;   parents: Jacob Martenze, Stijntje; witnesses: Jan
  Dorlant, Annetje, his wife.
- Pieter;   parents: Lourens Koek, Margrietje; witnesses: Joost
  Duerje, Madaleentje, his wife.
- Maria;   parents: Gijsbert Bogaert, Jannetje; witnesses:
  Daniel Rapalje, Sara, his wife.

1702, October 26:

- Alida;   parents: Benjamin Hegeman, Barentje; witnesses: Neyus

146

Translation

[62^r: "121"]

1702, October 26 (continued):

Hegeman, Marytje van Sicklen.
- Jacobus; parents: Jan Snedeker, Hilletje; witnesses:
  Jacobus Herckze, Sara Snedeker.
- Adriaan; parents: Hendrick Hogelandt, Sara; witnesses:
  Adriaan Reyersen, Annatje, his wife.
- Willempje; parents: Thijs Buys, Lijsbet; witnesses: Jan
  Ariaanse, Annetje Pieters.
- Joost; parents: Michiel van der Koek, Sara; witnesses:
  Yzaak Bennet, Lena, his wife.
- Cornelis; parents: Joris Rapalje, Angenietje; witnesses:
  Hieronymus Remze, Trijntje, his wife.
- no name recorded; parents: Jacob Buys, Marytje; witnesses:
  Abram Metzelaar, Haremtje, his wife.
- Sara; parents: Cornelis Martenze, Sara; witnesses: Joris
  Hanzen Bergen, Zara, his wife.

1703, April 27:

- Jacob; parents: Jacob van Doorn, Marytje; witnesses: Arien
  Bennet, Angenietje Bennet.
- Rachel; parents: Thomas Nigt, Sara; witnesses: Tomas
  Davvids, Sara Dreafs.

1703, October 7:

- Anna; parents: Klaas Folkertze, Neeltje; witnesses: Gerrit
  Couwenhove, Machtelt Folkertze.
- Johannes; parents: Roelof Sibering, Cristyntje; witnesses:
  Cornelis Sibering, Rachel Folkertze.
- Annetje; parents: Arent Andriesse, Lena; witnesses:
  Johannes Pieterse, Annetje, his wife.
- Adriaan; parents: Abram Bennet, Jannetje; witnesses:
  Adriaan Bennet, Angenietje, his wife.

1704, April 18:

- Aaltie; parents: Joris Abramze, Annetje; witnesses: Jan
  Abramze, Lammetje Cornel.
- Lijsbet; parents: Aert Aerzen, Lijsbet; witnesses: Matheus
  Aersen, Elsje Staats.
- Elsje; parents: Hendrick Hendrikze, Bennetje; witnesses:
  Rijk Hendrikze, Marytje Dorlandt.
- Jannetje; parents: Michiel van der Voort, Stijntje;
  witnesses: Jan van der Voort, Madaleentje, his wife.
- Mechiel; parents: Jan Blaauw, Marytje; witnesses: Mathijs
  de Mat, Grietje Blaauw.
- Jannetje; parents: Tomas Aten, Elsje; witnesses: Tomas
  Schilman, Marytje Aten.
- Abram; parents: Tomas Schilman, Annetje; witnesses: Jan
  Aten, Sara Brees.
- Hendrick; parents: Jan Hansen, Willempje; witnesses:
  Hendrik Willemze, Aaltje Willemze.

Translation

[63^V: "124"]

1704, April 18 (continued):

- Elijsabeth; parents: Ferdinandus van Sichelen, Geertje;
    witnesses: Marten Schenk, Jannetje Schenk.
- Annetje; parents: Hieronymus Rapalje, Hilletje; witnesses:
    Hieronymus Rapalje, Femmetje Bennet.
- Willem; parents: Isaak Bennet, Lena; witnesses: Leffert
    Pieters, Abigel, his wife.
- Ariaantie; parents: Matheus Aersen, Marytie; witnesses:
    David Aersen, Jennitie Colies.
- Jurrie; parents: Philippus Nagel, Annatje; witnesses:
    Jurrie Nagel, Annetje van Wijk.
- Margarietje; parents: Daniel Polhemus, Neeltje; witnesses:
    Minicus van der Veer, Maria, his wife.
- Catrijntje; parents: Theunus Woertman, Catrijntie;
    witnesses: Abram Metzelaar, Harmtje, his wife.
- Nicolarus; parents: Hendrik Vechte, Gerritje; witnesses:
    Jan Snedeker, Hillitje, his wife.

1704, November 14:

- Cornelis; parents: Cornelis van Duin, Machtel; witnesses:
    Antoni Haar, Annetje Haar.
- Annetje; parents: Gerrit Dorlandt, Marrytie; witnesses:
    Jan Dorlandt, Lena Dorlandt.
- Pieter; parents: Cornelis Jorisse, Annetje; witnesses:
    Pieter Gerbrandtze, Stijntje, his wife.

1705, May 29:

- Sara; parents: Jan Chellwer, Sara Luwiss; witness: Marta
    Brouwers.
- Marijtje; parents: Willem Thijsse, Jannetje; witnesses:
    Martem Salm, Trijntje Salm.
- Cornelis; parents: Jan Lowise, Marijtje; witnesses: Gerrit
    Hoeck, Geertje Lowise.
- Sytje; parents: Jan Verkerk, Elsje; witnesses: Barent Wijck,
    Antje Verkerk.
- Andries; parents: Lambert Andriesse, Lea; witnesses:
    Benjamin van de Water, Engeltje van de Water.
- Elsje; parents: Abraham Slegt, Jannetje; witnesses:
    Cornelis Slegt, Elsje van der Hoeve.
- Jurrie; parents: Casparus Blank, Angenietje; witnesses:
    Cornelis Barentze, Annetje, his wife.
- Catalina; parents: Marten Schenk, Jannetje; witnesses:
    Lucas Stevenze, Annetje Lucas.
- Sara; parents: Jan Ammerman, Sara; witnesses: Claas Wijkhof,
    Willempje Wijkhof.
- Angenietje; parents: Jacob van Dooren, Marijtie; witnesses:
    Isaak Bennet, Lena, his wife.
- Jannetje; parents: Albert Ammerman, Geertje; witnesses:
    Theunus Ammak, Aaltje Amak.
- Madaleentje; parents: Joost Duerje, Lena; witnesses:
    Joost Duerje de Oude [= the Elder], Antenette Duerje.
- Willem; parents: Arje Boermark, Sara; witnesses: Matijs
    Smarck, Lijbet, his wife.

Translation

1705, May 29 (continued):

- Abraham; parents: Joris Rapalje, Angenietje; witnesses:
  Jan Berjen, Jannetje Essel.
- Aaltje; parents: Jan Schenk, Sara; witnesses: Jan Couwenhove,
  Coba, his wife.
- Jannetje; parents: Hendrick Hendrikze, Trijntje; witnesses:
  Claas van Dijk, Jannetje van Dijk.
- Neeltje; parents: Cornelis van Couwenhove, Margrieta;
  witnesses: Jan Luikasse, Maeike, his wife.
- Jannetje; parents: Johannes Coerte, Berbara; witnesses:
  Hendrick van Dijk, Trijntje van Dijk.
- Lijsbet; parents: Benjamin van Cleef, Hendrikje;
  witness: Jacob van Sutphen.
- Aaltje; parents: Gerrit Schenk, Neeltje; witnesses: Joost
  van Brunt, Aaltje, his wife.
- Joris; parents: Jan Brinkerhof, Catrina; witnesses: Joris
  Rapalje, Antje Brinkerhof.
- Johannes; parents: Willem Hendrikze, Willemptje Lane;
  witnesses: Stoffel Schar, Geesje van Hekel.

1705, August 7:

- Gerardina; parents: Nicasius van Couwenhove, Elsje;
  witnesses: Jan Staats, Gerardina van Couwenhove.
- Marytje; parents: Gabriel Sprong, Geertruit; witnesses:
  Theunus Hof, Maritje Titis.
- Richard; parents: Jan Berjan, Ruth; witnesses: Hieronumus
  Remze, Angenietje Rapalje.
- Jan; parents: Giliam Lerue, Catrijntje; witnesses: Jan
  Lerue, Maria Sevenhove.
- Folkert; parents: Abram Bennet, Jannetje; witness: Johannes
  van Oostrant.
- Adriaan; parents: Hendrick Hogelandt, Sara; witnesses:
  Adriaan Reyerze, Annetje, his wife.
- Catrijntje; parents: Jan Dorlant, Marijtje; witnesses:
  Jan Van der Veer, Annetje Dorlant.
- Jannetje; parents: Jacob Rijk, Cytie; witnesses: Daniel
  Remze, Jannetje, his wife.

1706, February 3:

- Jan; parents: Cymen Blom, Geertie; witnesses: Jan Auckes,
  Evertje, his wife.

1706, February 10:

- Elysabet; parents: Paulus van der Voort, Neeltje;
  witnesses: Jan Staats, Lysbet Blom.

1706, March 3:

- Harpert; parents: Pieter Gerbrantze, Stijntje; witnesses:
  Harpert Gerbrantze, Metje Gerbrandts.

Translation

[66^r: "128"]

1706, March 10:

- Lijsbet; parents: Wouter van Pelt, Marytje; witnesses:
       Benjamin Oldis, Aaltje, his wife.
- Rem; parents: Jan Remze, Lijsbet; witnesses: Rem Remze,
       Antje Remze.

1706, April 21:

- Catrijntje; parents: Steven Budet, Marytje; witnesses:
       David Potman, Lijsbeth van de Water.

1706, July 21:

- Catrina; parents: Paulus van den Enden, Jannetje;
       witnesses: Jacobus Cortlant, Catrina Philips.

1706, August 25:

- Samuel; parents: Willem Brouwer, Marta; witnesses: Jacob
       Swaan, Susanna Bourdet.

1706, September 8:

- Jannetje; parents: Isaak Remze, Hendrikje; witnesses:
       Jeremias Remze, Jannetje Remse.
- Marijtje; parents: Carel de Beautois, Margrietje;
       witnesses: Jacobus de Beautois, Marytje, his wife.
- Neeltje; parents: Joris Abramze, Annetje; witnesses:
       Theodorus van Wijk, Margrietje, his wife.

1706, October 13:

- Richard; parents: Jan Berjan, Rutje; witnesses: Hieronymus
       Remze, Angenietje Rapalje.
- Hendrick; parents: Hieronymus Rapalje, Hilletje; witnesses:
       Hendrik Vechte, Gerrytje, his wife.

1706, November 17:

- Johannes; parents: Abraham Lefoij, Anna Maria; witness:
       Johannes Elberts.
- Jacob; parents: Isaak Bennet, Magdalena; witnesses: Corn-
       elis van Brunt, Trijntje, his wife.

1706, December 15:

- Abraham; parents: Abraham Brouwer, Cornelia; witnesses:
       Jan Hendrikze, Magdaleentje Blaauw.

Translation

[67^r: "130"]

1707, March 9:

- Aert; parents: Gerridt Middagh, Cornelia; witnesses:
  Gerridt van Couwenhove, Aeltje, his wife.

1707, March 16:

- Nicolaas; parents: Niclaas Brouwer, Jannetje; witnesses:
  Joris Hora, Lena Douscon.

1707, May 22:

- Geertje; parents: Jacob Martenze, Stijntje; witnesses:
  Cornelis Martense, Geertje Lot.

1707, June 22:

- Cornelis; parents: Matheus Aersen, Marytje; witnesses:
  Pieter Nevius, Sara Nevius.

1707, July 27:

- Cornelis; parents: Pieter Berjan, Elisabet; witnesses:
  Hieronymus Remze, Trijntje, his wife, Claas Berjan.
- Cornelis; parents: Flip Nagel, Ana; witnesses: Cornelis
  van Wijk, Janetje Nagel.

1707, August 17:

- Trijntje; parents: Minicus Janse, Johanna; witnesses:
  Daniel Polemus, Neeltje, his wife.
- Abram; parents: Abram Bennet, Jannetje; witnesses: Cornelis
  van Brundt, Trijntje, his wife.

1707, August 24:

- Aaltje; parents: Jan Abramze, Catrina; witnesses: Dirk
  Abramze, Aeltje, his wife.

1707, September 14:

- Stijntje; parents: Jacob Wijkhof, Lammetje; witnesses:
  Gerrit Strijker, Aeltje Strijker.

1707, October 26:

- Cristina; parents: David Sprong, Rachel; witnesses: Pieter
  Para, Cristina Sibering.

Translation

[68^r: "132"]

1707, December 7:

- Brechje; parents: Abram Remse, Anna; witnesses: Jacob
  Remse, Cornelia Middagh.
- Metje; parents: Jacobus van de Water, Elsie; witnesses:
  Cornelis van der Hoeve, Susanna van der Hoeve.
- Jan; parents: Nicasius van Couwenhove, Elsie; witnesses:
  Pieter Staats, Annetje Staats.
- Marijtje; parents: Lambert Andriesse, Lea; witnesses:
  Tomas Bouman, Angenietje Andriesse.

1707, December 14:

- Elbert; parents: Benjamin van de Water, Engeltje;
  witnesses: Elbert Jansen, Trijntje, his wife.

1708, February 22:

- Cornelis; parents: Abram Slegt, Jannetje; witnesses:
  Cornelis van der Hoeve, Metje Bibou.

1708, February 29:

- Jurjen; parents: Fredrick Blaauw, Lena; witnesses: Abram
  Blaauw, Jannetje Brouwer.

1708, March 9:[10]

- Ysaak; parents: Jan Auckes, Lena; witnesses: Jan Auckes'
  father, Eva, his wife.

1708, March 14:

- Annitje; parents: Gosen Adrieaanse, Femmitje; witnesses:
  Aris van der Bildt, Annitje Adrianse.

1708, March 21:

- Annatje; parents: Jacob Casjou, Anna Maria; witnesses:
  Jisaak Remse, Hendrikje, his wife.

1708, April 5:

- Ysabelle; parents: Frans Abrahamse, Ysabelle;
  witnesses: Willem Daij, Susanna Salomons.
- Hendricus; parents: Claas van Dijk, Fransijntie;
  witnesses: Antoni Rutgers, Antje Caros.

Translation

[68^V: "133"]

1708, May 24:

- Femmetje; parents: Rem Jorise, Aaltje; witnesses: Joris
  Hanse, Femmetje Remse.

1708, May 30:

- Folkert; parents: Johannes Folkerts, Angenietje;
  witnesses: Abram Bennet, Jannetje, his wife.

1708, July 25:

- Catrina; parents: Jan Quitans, Elijzabet; witnesses:
  Jacobus van de Water, Catrina van der Veer.

1708, August 1:

- Willem; parents: Steven Janze, Ctrina; witnesses: Cornelis
  van Duyn, Annetje Aersen.

1708, August 22:

- Jeremias; parents: Jeremias Remze, Heyltje; witnesses:
  Hieronymus Remze, Trijntje, his wife.

1708, September 19:

- Tijs; parents: Jan Tijsse, Jannetje; witnesses: Barent
  Cool, Feytje Matijsse.

1708, October 24:

- Elizabet; parents: Steven Budet, Marijtje; witnesses:
  Cornelis Post, Marijtje Caljer.

1708, December 12:

- Jacob; parents: Hans Bergen, Sara; witnesses: Jacob Hanze
  Bergen, Elsje, his wife.

1709, January 9:

- Debora; parents: Teunus Wilze, Diewertje; witnesses:
  Jacobus Cranheidt, Elyzabeth, his wife.

1709, February 20:

- Cornelia; parents: Cornelis van Duyn, Machtel; witnesses:
  Jacob Hanse, Elsje, his wife.

Translation

[69^V: "135"]

1709, March 13:

- Hendrick; parents: Joris Brinkerhof, Antje; witnesses:
  Dirck Brinkerhof, Aaltje, his mother.

1709, March 20:

- Jacobus; parents: Carel Bevois, Margriete; witnesses: Jan
  Miserol, Marytje, his wife.
- Engeltje; parents: Cornelis van de Water, Dorithea;
  witnesses: Jurjan Andriesse, Helena Levise.

1709, April 24:

- Antje; parents: Antoni de Mot, Elsje; witnesses: Jan
  Blaauw, Dina Blaauw.

1709, May 1:

- Maria; parents: Willem Brouwer, Martha; witnesses: Barent
  van Tilburg, Annetje Brouwer.

1709, May 8:

- Margrieta Willemze Falentijn, and
- Antje van den Burgh, "two maidens baptized upon their
  confession".

1709, July 31:

- Neeltje; parents: Claas Folkertze, Neeltje; witnesses:
  Philippus Folkertze, Sara Folkertze.

1709, August 7:

- Jannetje; parents: Joost Springhstien, Maria; witnesses:
  David Louwrenze Akkerman, Sara Colve.

1709, October 9:

- Jan; parents: Jacob Martenz, Stijntje; witnesses:
  Hieronimus Remze, Jannetje Hendrikz.

1710, May 14:

- Berbertje; parents: Frans Abramz, Elyzabeth; witnesses:
  Jacob Salomonz, Elyzabet, his wife.

Translation

[70^V: "137"]

1710, May 28:

- Jan;   parents: Steven Janz, Catrijna; witnesses: Jan Janz,
     Madalena Janz.

1710, July 2:

- Joseph;   parents: Adriaan Hegeman, Marytje; witnesses:
     Joseph Hegeman Jr., Jannetje Cornel.
- Jannetje;   parents: Jan Barenz, Anna; witnesses: Abraham
     Hegeman, Geerttruydt, his wife.

1710, September 24:

- Jacob;   parents: Jacob Brouwer, Pieternelle; witnesses:
     Sybrandt Brouwer, Antje Brouwer.

1710, October 15:

- Ysaak;   parents: Ysaak Remze, Hendrikje; witnesses:
     Hieronimus Remze, Trijntje, his wife.

Translation

Second List of Baptisms[11]

[* Brackets [] followed or preceded by an asterisk * mark
passages which are illegible because of damage to the
original manuscript.]

In the year 1676, Thursday, the 8th of June, at about nine
o'clock in the evening, our dear, loyal old shepherd and teacher
Domine Joanus Polhemius piously passed away. He was buried here
in the baptistry on the 11th last, right in front of the pulpit.

1676, August 25:

Domine Wilhellmus Nieuwenhuijs, minister in N[ieuw] Jorck,
administered the Sacrament of the Lord's Supper here for the
first time, and further baptized [some] children, namely:

- Fransijna; father: Arent Pral, from "Staten Eijlandt";
    godfathers: Isack Culjouw, Lovies Laeckeman,
    godmother: Martha Stilwil.
- Jannetie; father: Jan Clement, from "Nieuw Wtrecht";
    godfather: Michiel Haijnel, godmother: Treijntie
    Ruthgers.

1677, April 2:

- Jannetie; father: Anthonie van der Wijck; godfather: Abram
    "ditto" [= van der Wijck], godmother: Jannetie.
- Albert; father: Willem Gerritsz van Couwenhov[en];
    godmother: Heijltie Elberts.
- Dirck; father: Abram Jorissen; godfather: *[?Piet]er
    Strijcker, godmother: Susanna Dubbels.
- Catharina; father: Dirck Jansz; godfathers: Jacob Perdon,
    Poulis van der Beeck, godmother: Steijntie Al[berts?]*.
- Willemeijntie; father: Albert Albertsz; godfather: Steven
    Coerten, godmother: Willempie Roel[ofs?]*.

1677, Whitsuntide:

baptized by Domine Gidion Schaets:

- Pieter; father: Laurens Juriaensz; godfather: Pieter Jansz,
    godmother: Sara Strijckers.
- Cornelis; father: Jan Buijs.

- Joannes; father: Laurens Janz; godfather: Joannes Jillisz,
    godmother: Treijntie Gillis.
- Aeffie; father: Jan Aertsz; godfather: Elbert Elbertsz,
    godmother: Helena Aertss.
- Aeltie; father: Jan Theunisz van Dyckhuijs; godfather:
    Capt. Elbert Elbertsz Stoothoff, godmother: Aeltie
    Elberts.

Translation

[144^r]

1677, September 16:

Domine Casparis van Sueren gave his first sermon here in Midwout in the church, and baptized the following children:

- Willemeijntie; father: Gijsbert Thijsen.

- Abram; father: Gerrit Snedecker.

- Steven; father: Luijcas Stevensz.

- Lambert; father: Aggias Jansz van Dij[...]*.

1677, December 25:

- Luijcas; parents: Eldert Luijcasz, Stijntie; godfather: Gerrit Snedecker, godmother: Egbertie.

1678, February 3:

- Helena; father: Willem Davidtz.

1678, March 31:

- Maritie; father: Adriaen Hendrickz; godfather: Hendrick van Doesborgh, godmother: Maritie van Doesb[orgh].
- Reijer; father: Adriaen Reijerz.

- Margriet; father: Abram Marlet; godfather: Jan Crosseron Jr., godmother: Marigriet Crosseron.
- Davidt; father: Willem van Barculo; godfather: Stoffel Jansz, godmother: Steijntie Alberts.

1678, April 21:

- Willemina; father: Jan Gillissen.

1678, May 12:

- Elsie; father: Lammert Dorlant; godfather: Thomas Lammertsz, godmother: Annetie Remss.
- Hans; father: Jacob Hanz; godfather: Theunis Gijsbertsz, godmother: Sara Rapalie.
- Catharina; father: Melchert Caspersz; godmother: Maria Theunis.
- Heijltie; father: Gijsbert Janz; godfather: Jan Aucus, godmother: Elsie Barents.
- Jacobus, 5 1/3 years of age,
- Judith, 2 5/6 years of age, and
- Jan, 1 1/4 years of age; father: Jan Woutersz; "have come from Straicfort in the north".

157

Translation

[144^V]

1678, June *[.]3:

- Cornelis; father: Coert Stevensz; godfather: Thomas Willet, godmother: Heijltie Elberts.

1678, July 14:

- Thijs; father: Barent Thijsen; godfather: Wolfert Jansz, godmother: Adriaentie van Deventer.
- Anna,
- Catharijn, and
- Rebecka; father: Niclaes Stilwil; godfathers: Daniel and Rithsart Stillewil, Adam Mathe[...]*, Jan Margen, godmothers: Annetie, Martha, and Marij Stillewil.
- Lovies; father: Rithsart Machielsz; godfather: Lovies Laeckeman, godmother: Marij Walte.
- Thomas, 2 years of age, and
- Marigriet; father: Tho[...]* Margen; godmother: Catharina Stillewil.
- Marij, 31 years of age, wife of Willem Britte, from "Staten Eijlant"; also:
- Willem, 15 years of age,
- Nathaniel, 13 years of age,
- Rithsart, 11 years of age,
- Joseph, 9 years of age,
- Benjamen, 7 years of age,
- Jan, 5 years of age, and
- Daniel, 1½ years of age; parents: Willem Britte, Marij; godfathers: Ananias Torner, Joris Commens, Nathaniel Britten, Pieter Pietersz, Pieter Coljouw, Thomas Stillew[il]*, Jan Oucus, Daniel Stillewil.

1678, August 11:

- Jan; father: Aris Jansz van de Bilt; godfather: Jacob Ja[nsz?]* van de Bilt, godmother: Jannetie Remss.

1678, August 18:

- Jacob; father: Cornelis Berrien; godfathers: Stoffel Prob[asco?]*, Pieter Strijcker, godmother: Heyltie Kloppers.

1678, October 13:

- Mahitebel; father: Jan Elsen; godfather: Dirck Jansz van der Vliet.

1678, October 20:

- Aeltie; father: Dirck Storm; godfather: Lourens Ackerman, godmother: Jannetie Titus.

158

Translation

[136^r]

Third List of Baptisms[12]

[* Brackets [] followed or preceded by an asterisk * mark
passages which are illegible because of damage to the
original manuscript.]

*[1688, Oct]ober 7:

- Annetje; parents: Hendrik Jansen, Hester Cortois;
    witnesses: Hendrik Claasen, Jannetje Cortois.

[1688], November 4:

- Geurtje; parents: Jaques Cardeljouw, Maritje Hendriks;
    witnesses: Cornelis Cardeljauw, Geurtje Hermansen.

[1688], December 25:

- Jan; parents: Aart Laanen van Pelt, Neeltje van Tuil;
    witnesses: Jochem Gulik, Geertruit Jans.

1689, February 3:

- Maria; parents: Jan Staats, Catarina Corssens; witnesses:
    Pieter Staats, Maritje van der Grift.

1689, March 3:

- Marij; parents: Gijsbert Thijssen, Jannetje Adriaans;
    witnesses: Aart van Pelt, Neeltje van Thuil.

1689, March 31:

- Geertje; parents: Dirk van Zutphen, Lijsbeth Janse;
    witnesses: Gerrit Holla, Maritje Hendriks.

1689, April 21:

- Isaak; parents: Salomon de Leever, Annetje Le Cluse;
    witnesses: Gijsbert Thijssen, Jannetje Adriaansen.
- Jannetje; parents: Theunis Janse, Jannetje Brouwers;
    witnesses: Hendericus Brouwer, Magtelt Brouwer.
- Jan; parents: Lambert Janse, Fijtje Barens; witnesses:
    Roelof Verkerke, Catarina Simons.

Translation

[136^r]

1689, June 2:

- Catarina;   parents: Gerardus Beekman, Magdalena Abeel;
  witnesses: Johannis Beekman, Elisabeth Abeel.

1689, June 30:

- Agnietje;   parents: Cornelis van Brunt, Trijntje Bennet;
  witnesses: Joost van Brunt, Agnietje van Dijk.

1689, July 28:

- Elisabeth;   parents: Cornelis Gerritse, Dirkje Juriaansen;
  witnesses: Dirk Jansen, Elisabeth Jansen.

1689, September 22:

- Karel;   parents: Johannis Fontein, Remmerich Simonse;
  witnesses: Simon Hansen, Maria Frederiks.
- Sara;   parents: Marten Pietersen, Hanna Willems;
  witnesses: Johannis Brouwer, Sara Willems.
- Pieter;   parents: Jochem Gulik, Jacomijntje Theunisse;
  witnesses: Jan Theunisse, Lijsbet Janse.
- Theunis;   parents: Reinier Aardse, Jannetje Aukes;
  witnesses: Auke Reiniersen, Trijntje Reiniers.
- Neeltje;   parents: Dionijs Theunissen, Helena Cardeljouw;
  witnesses: Jaques Cardeljouw, Maria Cardeljouw.

*[16]89, *[Oct]ober 20:

- *[J]osijntje;   parents: Gerrit Stoffelse, Lijsbet Cornelis;
  witnesses: Stoffel Gerritsen, Josijntje van Haagen.
- Neeltje;   parents: Michel Parmentier, Neeltje Dame;
  witnesses: Pieter Insiel, Aaltje Daame.

1689, November 15:

- Grietje;   parents: Wilhem Bennet, Ariaantje van de Waater;
  witnesses: Jan Bennet, Grietje van de Waater.

1690, February 16:

- Pieter;   parents: Pieter Staats, Lijsbet Arensen;
  witnesses: Pieter Staats, Agnietje van Dijk.

1690, March 16:

- Meindert;   parents: Isaak le Fevre, Weintje Meinders;
  witnesses: Meindert Courten, Marij, his wife.
- Theunis;   parents: Wouter van Pelt, Marijtje Schaars;
  witnesses: Hendrik Thijssen, Margrietje Jansen.

Translation

[136^V]

1690, April 13:

- Pieter;   parents: Pieter Franciscus, Susan Sar Dee;
  witnesses: Abraham Jansen, Susanne Ritsers.

1690, May 4:

- Maijke;   parents: Joost de Baane, Elisabeth Drabbe;
  witnesses: Cornelis Wijnhart, Maijke Cornelis.

1690, May 29:

- Jan;   parents: Isaak Goedink, Geertruid Jansen; witnesses:
  Jan Hansen, Marij Frederiks.

1694, November 14:

- Sara;   parents: Jan van der Vliet, Geertje Verkerke;
  witness: Jan Verkerke.
- Wouter;   parents: Hendrik Janse, Maritje Jans; witnesses:
  Juriaan Nagel, Dorothea Verscheur.
- Gerritje;   parents: Gerrit Strijker, Wijntje Bogaart;
  witnesses: Hendrik Wijcof, Ida Strijkers.

1694, November 15:

- Coert;   parents: Steven Coerten, Eegje Jans; witnesses:
  Coert Stevensen, Maritje, his wife.
- Antje;   parents: Gerrit Schenk, Neeltje Coerten; witnesses:
  Roelof Martense, Trijntje, his wife.
- Neeltje;   parents: Pieter Cardeljouw, Diewertje de Wit;
  witnesses: Dirk Volkerse, Maria Cardeljouw.
- Willemtje;   parents: Lucas Stevense, Jannetje Minne;
  witnesses: Marten Schenk, Femmetje Aukes.
- Annetje;   parents: Cornelis van Duin, Machteltje Huiken;
  witnesses: Pieter Staats, Annetje Huiken.
- Geesje;   parents: Claas van Dijk, Francijntje Hendriks;
  witnesses: Wilhem Hendrikse, Antje Staats.
- Jacob;   parents: Pieter Brouwer, Pieternelle Cleine;
  witnesses: Jacob Fardon, Geertruid Jansen.
- Anna Elisabet;   parents: Jacob Brouwer, Annatje Bogardus;
  witnesses: Lambert Sachariassen, Maritje Jansen.

1694, December 10:

- Pieter;   parents: Gerrit Coerten, Willemtje Pieters;
  witnesses: Joost van Brunt, Aaltje Coerten.
- Sijdtje;   parents: Pieter Strijker, Annetje Barends;
  witnesses: Johannes Swart, Femmetje Barends.
- Maria;   parents: Cornelis van Brund, Trijntje Bennet;
  witnesses: Jacob Christiaansen, Maria Cardeljouw.

Translation

[137^r]

1695, May 4:

- Catarina; parents: Joost de Baane, Elisabeth Drabbe;
      witnesses: Cornelis van der Werf, Maria Cardeljouw.

1695, May 29:

- Helena; parents: Antonij van Pelt, Magdaleentje Joosten;
      witnesses: Joseph Hageman, Femmetje Remse.
- Annetje; parents: Willem Willemse, Maijke Pieters;
      witnesses: Samuel Gerritsen, Geertje Pieters.
- Pieter; parents: Marten Pieterse, Hanna Willems;
      witnesses: Willem Willemse, Maijke Pieters.
- Femmetje; parents: Johannis Willemse, Magdalena Winants;
      witnesses: Jacob Fardon, Femmetje Fardon.

1695, May 30:

- Ariaantje; parents: Wilhem Bennet, Ariaantje van de Water;
      witnesses: Johannis van de Water, Marijtje van de
      Water.
- Harmtje; parents: Gerrit Dorland, Marijtje Dorland;
      witnesses: Rem Dorland, Bennetje Dorland.

[1695, ...]*:

- [.....]*; parents: [.....]*; witnesses: Elias de Hart,
      Claasje de Hart.

[1695], November 9:

- Catelijn; parents: Aart van Pelt, Neeltje van Tuil;
      witnesses: Hendrik Gulick, Catalijn Gulick.

[1695], November [..]*:

- Elisabeth; parents: Albert Coerten, Sara Willemsen;
      witnesses: Gerrit Coerten, Catarina Polhemius.
- Anna Maria; parents: Hendrik Jansen, Hester Jansen;
      witnesses: Hieronimus Remsen, Trijntje Berrien.
- Margrietje; parents: Jan Barense, Jannetje Willems;
      witnesses: Johannis van Sichelen, Sara Emans.
- Daniel; parents: Daniel Polhemius, Neeltje van der Veer;
      witnesses: Johannis Seubering, Femmetje Michiels.

1696, April 25:

- Abraham; parents: Dirk van Zutphen, Lijsbet Jansen;
      witnesses: Joost van Brunt, Aaltje Coerten.

Translation

[137^V]

1696, April *[2]6:

- Jan;   parents: Johannis Richou, Maijke van Dijk;
    witnesses: Jan van Dijk, Theuntje van Dijk.
- Dirk;   parents: Jacob van der Bilt, Marijtje Vliet;
    witnesses: Dirk Jansen van der Vliet, Geertje Verkerk.
- Helena;   parents: Jaques Cardeljouw, Maritje Hendriks;
    witnesses: Mathijs Smal, Helena Cardeljouw.
- Jannetje;   parents: Laurens Janse, Hendrikje Jacobse;
    witnesses: Stoffel Gerritje, Annetje Jans.
- Laurens;   parents: Cornelis van Cleef, Femmetje van Deventer;
    witnesses: Quirijn Jans, Neeltje van Cleef.
- Daniel;   parents: Jan Leek, Neeltje Claasen; witnesses:
    Claas Thomasse, Francijntje Hendriks.
- Jan;   parents: Abraham Leek, Claasje Langestraat;
    witnesses: Dirk Langestraat, Janna Havens.
- Dirk;   parents: Stoffel Langestraat, Maijke Laanen;
    witnesses: Dirk Langestraat, Claasje Langestraat.
- Antje;   parents: Andries Emans, Rebecca van Cleef;
    witnesses: Quirijn Jans, Engeltje van Cleef.
- Meindert;   parents: Andries Jansen, Hendrikje Meinders;
    witnesses: Meindert Coerten, Gerritje Spiegelaars.
- Cornelis;   parents: Dionijs Theunissen, Helena Cordeljouw;
    witnesses: Jeronimus Rapailje, Elsje Snediker.

1696, *[M]ay 8:

- Cornelis, "baptized by me, W. Lupardus";[13]   parents: Jan
    Laurensen, Marrijtje Vonk; witnesses: Achias van Dijk,
    Magdaleentje Vonk.

1696, *[Aug]ust 9:

- *[F]erdinandus;   parents: Samuel Gerritse, Ida Barends;
    witnesses: Barent Juriaanse, Aaltje Steevens.
- no name recorded;   parents: Pieter van Pelt, Saartje Bogardus;
    witnesses: Hendrik van Pelt, Annetje Keijserrijk.

163

Translation

[146^r]

Fourth List of Baptisms[14]

[* Brackets [] followed or preceded by an asterisk * mark
    passages which are illegible because of damage to the
    original manuscript.]

1719, May 18:[15]

- IJannete; parents: Adoleves Brouwer, IJannetie; witnesses:
  Jan Pessen, Leena, his wife.

1719, July 19:

- IJacob; parents: Frerick Bergen, Gerrettije; witnesses:
  IJacob Hanse, Elsje, his wife.
- IJacob; parents: Vijllem Verdon, Lis[...]*; witnesses:
  IJohannes Verdon, Aeltije B[.....]*, his [wife?]*.

1719, August 9:

- Abram; parents: Hendrick van [.....]*; witnesses: Abram
  Brouver, [.....]*.

1719, September 20:

- Goise; parents: Vijnan[.....]*; witnesses: IJohan[.....]*.

1719, December 13:

- Sara; parents: IJsack IJanse, IJannete; witnesses:
  IJohannes Hartenbrock, Sara Hijijer.

RECEIPTS AND EXPENDITURES

of the

DEACONS OF BREUCKELEN

in

NEW NETHERLAND

Translation

[105^V: "P. 1"]

RECEIPTS

A.D. 1660

	Found in the treasury, along with Balde's bequest:	Gld. 99- 5
Sept. 5	Received:	Gld. 20- 4
Sept. 12	Received:	Gld. 8-10
Sept. 19	Received:	Gld. 6-15
Sept. 26	Received:	Gld. 9- 3
Oct. 3	Received:	Gld. 6
Oct. 10	Received:	Gld. 6- 4
Oct. 17	Received: along with a certain silver coin.	Gld. 7-10
Oct. 24	Received:	Gld. 6- 1
	From the Lord's Supper:	Gld. 11-15
Oct. 31	Received:	Gld. 8- 5
Nov. 7	Received:	Gld. 4
Nov. 14	Received:	Gld. 4-10
Nov. 21	Received:	Gld. 5- 3
	With the interest on the aforesaid bequest:	Gld. 5
Nov. 28	Received:	Gld. 5-10
Dec. 5	Received:	Gld. 6-12
Dec. 15	Received:	Gld. 3- 1
Dec. 19	Received:	Gld. 10-10
ibid.	Received:	Gld. 2- 2
Dec. 25	Received:	Gld. 3-15
ibid.	Received from the Lord's Supper:	Gld. 9
ibid.	Received:	Gld. 1- 5
Dec. 26	Received:	Gld. 4
ibid.	Received:	Gld. 1- 5

Total: Gld. 255-5

A.D. 1661

Jan. 1	Received:	Gld. 4-10
Jan. 2	Received:	Gld. 4
ibid.	Received:	Gld. 1- 1
Jan. 9	Received:	Gld. 3-11
ibid.	Received:	Gld. 1-15
Jan. 16	Received:	Gld. 6-10
[?]^1	Received:	Gld. 1-17
[?]	Received:	Gld. 6
[?]	Received:	Gld. 1-14
[?]	Received:	Gld. 6-10
ibid.	Received:	Gld. 1
Febr. 6	Received:	Gld. 5
ibid.	Received:	Gld. 1- 6
Febr. 19	Received:	Gld. 7- 4
ibid.	Received:	Gld. 3
Febr. 20	Received:	Gld. 3
Febr. 27	Received:	Gld. 4

Total: Gld. 61-18

Translation

[106^r: "P. 2"]

EXPENDITURES

A.D. 1660

Oct. 20	Advanced to the Court of Breuckelen:	Gld. 50
Oct. 24	For the Lord's Supper, for bread and wine:	Gld. 5
Nov. 8	To the poor-box, for the iron:	Gld. 8
Dec. 24	For the Lord's Supper, for bread and wine:	Gld. 3-15
	Total:	Gld. 66-15

A.D. 1661

Jan. 6	To Hendrick Dirckzen:	Gld. 10
Febr. 6	To the same Hendrick Dirckzen:	Gld. 10
ibid.	To Pieter Pra "in the Creupelbosch":[2]	Gld. 15
Febr. 27	To the same:	Gld. 15
	Total:	Gld. 50

BALANCE

Received,		Spent,	
in the year 1660:	Gld. 255- 5	in the year 1660:	Gld. 66-15
in the year 1661:	Gld. 61-18	in the year 1661:	Gld. 50
Total:	Gld. 317- 3	Total:	Gld. 116-15

Remaining in the treasury,

in cash:	Gld. 151
in bequests:	Gld. 50
Total:	Gld. 201

Receipts:[3]	Gld. 317- 3	Expenditures:	Gld. 116-15
Found in excess		Surplus:	Gld. 201
of receipts:	Gld. -12	Total:	Gld. 317-15
Total:	Gld. 317-15		

This account of receipts, expenditures, and money advanced in the years as above with regard to the Deaconry of the Congregation of Breuckelen, has been found faithful as it is above, and hereby closed by

Breuckelen,
March 2, 1661.

Henricus Selijns, Minister of God's
Word in Breuckelen
Willem Bredenbent, as Deacon

Translation

[106^V: "P. 3"]

RECEIPTS [continued from p. 166]

A.D. 1661

March 2	Found in the treasury, as it appears, in cash:	Gld.	151
	Barent Balde's bequest:	Gld.	50
	Advance to the Court of Breuckelen:	Gld.	50
March 6	Received:	Gld.	6-14
March 13	Received:	Gld.	6
March 20	Received:	Gld.	4-11
April 4	Received:	Gld.	6
April 10	Received:	Gld.	6-15
April 17	Received:	Gld.	7-13
ibid.	From the Lord's Supper:	Gld.	11- 4
April 18	Received:	Gld.	7-15
April 24	Received:	Gld.	6
May 1	Received:	Gld.	6-13
May 8	Received:	Gld.	6-15
May 15	Received:	Gld.	6-10
May 22	Received:	Gld.	5-14
May 26	Received:	Gld.	7- 4
May 29	Received:	Gld.	8
June 5	Received:	Gld.	6-15
ibid.	Received from the Lord's Supper:	Gld.	14
June 6	Received:	Gld.	13- 5
June 13	Received:	Gld.	8-12
June 21	Received:	Gld.	7-16
June 28	Received:	Gld.	6- 8
July 3	Received:	Gld.	10
July 10	Received:	Gld.	11-14
July 17	Received:	Gld.	7- 8
July 24	Received:	Gld.	7-16
July 31	Received:	Gld.	6- 6
Aug. 7	Received:	Gld.	5- 8
Aug. 14	Received:	Gld.	6- 7
Aug. 21	Received:	Gld.	3
Aug. 28	Received:	Gld.	8-10
Sept. 4	Received:	Gld.	7-12
Sept. 11	Received:	Gld.	5
Sept. 18	Received:	Gld.	9-11
	With a piece of eight:[4]	Gld.	6
Sept. 25	Received:	Gld.	7
Oct. 2	Received:	Gld.	8- 4
ibid.	From the Lord's Supper:	Gld.	16-17
ibid.	Received:	Gld.	6- 1
Oct. 9	Received:	Gld.	6- 4
Oct. 11	In wedding money:	Gld.	6
Oct. 16	Received:	Gld.	6- 7
Oct. 23	Received:	Gld.	7
Oct. 30	Received:	Gld.	8-15

Total: Gld. 578-4

Translation

[107^r: "P. 4"]

EXPENDITURES   [continued from p. 167]

A.D. 1661

April 16	For the Lord's Supper, for bread and wine:	Gld.	3-14
May 15	To Tjerck:	Gld.	10
May 29	To the same Tjerck:	Gld.	10
June 4	For the Lord's Supper, for bread and wine:	Gld.	4
June 12	To Tjerck mentioned above:	Gld.	9- 8
ibid.	In expenses:	Gld.	2- 8
June 28	To Pieter Prae:	Gld.	40
July 13	To Gabriel Corbesij:	Gld.	12
Aug. 14	For the hymn-board:	Gld.	-12
Sept. 29	For the Lord's Supper, for a pewter bowl and pewter cup:	Gld.	14
Oct. 1	For the Lord's Supper, for bread and wine and other expenses:	Gld.	9- 6

Total: Gld. 115-8

Translation

RECEIPTS   [continued from p. 168]

A.D. 1661

	Received as per the preceding page:	Gld.	578- 4
Nov. 6	Received:	Gld.	4-12
Nov. 13	Received:	Gld.	7- 2
Nov. 20	Received:	Gld.	2-10
ibid.	In wedding money:	Gld.	6
Nov. 27	Received:	Gld.	8
Dec. 4	Received:	Gld.	7- 8
ibid.	From the confirmation classes:	Gld.	3-14
Dec. 11	Received:	Gld.	5-15
ibid.	Received:	Gld.	4-10
Dec. 18	Received:	Gld.	5
ibid.	Received:	Gld.	2-16
Dec. 25	Received:	Gld.	6- 9
ibid.	Received from the Lord's Supper:	Gld.	17- 4
ibid.	Received:	Gld.	4-10
Dec. 26	Received:	Gld.	7-10
ibid.	Received:	Gld.	2

Total: Gld. 673-4

A.D. 1662

Jan. 1	Received:	Gld.	6
ibid.	From the confirmation classes:	Gld.	3-16
Jan. 7	Received out of the poor-box:	Gld.	10-19
Jan. 8	Received:	Gld.	5-14
ibid.	Received:	Gld.	3- 4
Jan. 15	Received:	Gld.	6-14
ibid.	Received:	Gld.	3-13
Jan. 22	Received:	Gld.	4-14
ibid.	Received:	Gld.	3-16
Jan. 29	Received:	Gld.	4-17
ibid.	Received:	Gld.	2-12
Febr. 5	Received:	Gld.	4- 9
ibid.	Received:	Gld.	2
Febr. 12	Received:	Gld.	8- 5
ibid.	Received, along with the third part of a pig:	Gld.	11-10
Febr. 19	Received:	Gld.	7
ibid.	Received:	Gld.	2-12
Febr. 26	Received:	Gld.	8-10
	In wedding money:	Gld.	6
ibid.	Received:	Gld.	3-12
March 5	Received:	Gld.	7-10
ibid.	Received:	Gld.	1-14
March 12	Received:	Gld.	6
March 15	Received:	Gld.	4-11
March 19	Received:	Gld.	7- 7
March 26	Received:	Gld.	7- 8
ibid.	In wedding money:	Gld.	6

Total: Gld. 150-7

Translation

[108^r]

EXPENDITURES   [continued from p. 169]

A.D. 1661

	Spent as per the preceding page:	Gld.	115- 8
Nov. 15	For the Lord's Supper, for a pewter wine-ewer:	Gld.	15
Dec. 23	Given to Marcus Susoij, to provide for his needs,		
	for 1½ els^5 of dozen-cloth^6:	Gld.	12
	for 2 pairs of shoes at 5 glds. a pair:	Gld.	10
	for 1 pair of women's stockings:	Gld.	3
	for 1 skein of yarn and 9 dozen buttons:	Gld.	1-10
	with a schepel^7 of rye:	Gld.	4
Dec. 23	To Gabriel Corbesij, a p[air] of shoes:	Gld.	5
ibid.	To Mr.^{8} Carel d'Beauvois, for the half-year expired:	Gld.	13
Dec. 24	For the Lord's Supper, for bread and wine:	Gld.	9- 2

Total: Gld. 188

A.D. 1662

Jan. 27	To the Deaconry of N[ew] Amsterdam, for the cost of supporting Tjerck Thomas, as it appears from bills signed by Daniel van Donck and received:	Gld.	111
Febr. 20	Providing Marcus Suson with 2 schepels of rye, for the third part of a certain pig reverted to the poor:	Gld.	8
April 8	For the Lord's Supper, for bread and wine, and money for the ferry:	Gld.	9- 2

Total: Gld. 128-2

Translation

RECEIPTS [continued from p. 170]

A.D. 1662

	Received in the current year as per the preceding:	Gld.	150- 7
April 2	Received:	Gld.	10-10
April 9	Received:	Gld.	6-16
ibid.	From the Lord's Supper:	Gld.	16
April 10	Received:	Gld.	6- 4
April 16	Received:	Gld.	7- 9
April 23	Received:	Gld.	7- 8
April 30	Received:	Gld.	6-10
May 7	Received:	Gld.	7
May 14	Received:	Gld.	1-16
May 18	Received:	Gld.	6
May 21	Received:	Gld.	4-15
May 28	Received:	Gld.	7-16
ibid.	Received from the Lord's Supper:	Gld.	15- 6
May 29	Received:	Gld.	6-12
June 4	Received:	Gld.	3-18
June 11	Received:	Gld.	5-10
June 18	Received:	Gld.	10-19
June 25	Received:	Gld.	9
ibid.	From a pig:	Gld.	8-10
July 2	Received:	Gld.	11- 6
	With a half-ducatoon:[9]	Gld.	4
July 9	Received:	Gld.	9-18
July 16	Received:	Gld.	9- 4
July 23	Received:	Gld.	6
July 25	Received:	Gld.	15-15
July 30	Received:	Gld.	4-15
Aug. 6	Received:	Gld.	8-17
ibid.	Received in wedding money:	Gld.	14
Aug. 13	Received:	Gld.	8- 7
ibid.	In wedding money:	Gld.	6
Aug. 20	Received:	Gld.	6-11
Aug. 27	Received:	Gld.	7- 5
Sept. 3	Received:	Gld.	5-13
Sept. 10	Received:	Gld.	7-11
Sept. 17	Received:	Gld.	12- 8
	With a piece of eight:[4]	Gld.	6
ibid.	In wedding money:	Gld.	6
Sept. 24	Received:	Gld.	6-16
Sept. 27	Out of the poor-box, from Albert Cornelisz:	Gld.	10
ibid.	Out of the poor-box, from Corn[elis] van Bossum:	Gld.	4
		Total: Gld.	468-12

Translation

EXPENDITURES   [continued from p. 171]

A.D. 1662

	Spent in the current year as per the preceding:	Gld. 128- 2
May 6	To Marcus Suson:	Gld. 12
May 27	For the Lord's Supper, for bread and wine etc.:	Gld. 6- 4
May 30	Advanced to the Court of Breuckelen, for planks for the Minister's house:	Gld. 34- 6
June 6	To Harmen the soldier, for two cows:	Gld. 315
June 10	To Gabriel the cowherd:	Gld. 10
July 5	To Marcus Suson:	Gld. 10
Sept. 27	To Willem Gerritsen, house-rent for Mr. Carel:	Gld. 30
Sept. 30	For the Lord's Supper, for bread and wine:	Gld. 7-12
	Total: Gld. 553-4	

Translation

[109^v]

RECEIPTS   [continued from p. 172]

A.D. 1662

	Received in the current year as per the preceding:	Gld. 468-12
Oct. 1	Received:	Gld. 14
ibid.	From the Lord's Supper:	Gld. 15-17
ibid.	Received:	Gld. 4- 7
Oct. 8	Received:	Gld. 5- 6
Oct. 15	Received:	Gld. 6-12
Oct. 22	Received:	Gld. 7- 2
Oct. 29	Received:	Gld. 6-13
Nov. 5	Received, with 2 years of interest from Dirck Jansen:	Gld. 12
Nov. 12	Received:	Gld. 5- 7
Nov. 19	Received:	Gld. 5-19
Nov. 26	Received:	Gld. 6-13
Dec. 3	Received:	Gld. 7-12
Dec. 10	Received:	Gld. 7- 9
Dec. 17	Received:	Gld. 5- 5
Dec. 24	Received:	Gld. 7- 5
Dec. 25	Received:	Gld. 6- 8
	From the Lord's Supper:	Gld. 15-14
ibid.	Received:	Gld. 5- 3
Dec. 26	Received:	Gld. 6- 5
Dec. 31	Received:	Gld. 4- 6

Total: Gld. 623-15

A.D. 1663

Jan. 1	Received:	Gld. 5
Jan. 7	Received:	Gld. 4-15
Jan. 14	Received:	Gld. 4-16
Jan. 21	Received:	Gld. 4
Jan. 28	Received:	Gld. 7-10
Febr. 4	Received:	Gld. 4-16
Febr. 11	Received:	Gld. 3-13
Febr. 18	Received:	Gld. 2-13
Febr. 21	Out of the poor-boxes:	Gld. 17- 4
Febr. 25	Received:	Gld. 4- 2
March 4	Received:	Gld. 4-13

Total: Gld. 63-2

Translation

[110^r]

EXPENDITURES [continued from p. 173]

A.D. 1662

	Spent in the current year as per the preceding:	Gld.	553- 4
October	Advanced to the Court of Breuckelen, for nails for the Minister's house:	Gld.	8-12
Oct. 25	To Aucke Jans, for Teuntie Straetsmans' coffin:	Gld.	12
	Advanced to Teunis Straetsmans' children left behind,		
Nov. 20	in dozen-cloth^6, stockings, shoes, buttons, yarn etc.:	Gld.	62- 6-8
Nov. 28	in wages for cutting the said cloth:	Gld.	1- 5
Dec. 2	To Pieter Lamberts, for stripping tobacco:	Gld.	15
	To the same, for threshing grain:	Gld.	2
	To Joost and Harmen, for threshing the same grain:	Gld.	4
Dec. 4	To Laurens Haf, for serge^{10}, a pair of stockings etc.:	Gld.	40- 6
	To Anna Tienemans, a pair of stockings and ribbon etc.:	Gld.	7-10
	To Haf mentioned above, for a hat:	Gld.	6
	In money for the ferry:	Gld.	-16
Dec. 6	To Mr. Carel, for a schepel^7 of rye:	Gld.	5
Dec. 7	To Jacob Stephenszen, for a barrel of tobacco:	Gld.	6
Dec. 13	To Marcus Suson, for a schepel of rye:	Gld.	5
Dec. 13	To Heijltie Probasko, for sewing shirts:	Gld.	3
Dec. 13	For Teuntie's children:	Gld.	9- 5
Dec. 20	To Marcus Suson, for a schepel of rye:	Gld.	5
Dec. 23	For the Lord's Supper, for bread and wine:	Gld.	11-10
Dec. 28	To Mr. Carel, for a schepel of rye:	Gld.	5
ibid.	Advanced to the Court, for 1000 bricks for the Minister's house:	Gld.	20

Total: Gld. 782-17-8^{11}

A.D. 1663

Jan. 19	To Marcus Suson, for two schepels of rye:	Gld.	10
Jan. 22	To Schout Hegeman, for a cow:	Gld.	134- 5
	In money for driving:^{12}	Gld.	6-14-4
Jan. 22	To Pieter Pra, a pair of shoes:	Gld.	12
Febr. 8	To Mr. Carel, for a half[-year of^{13}] service:	Gld.	13
Febr. 19	To Jan Pieterszen, for half a cask of beer:	Gld.	12-10
Febr. 27	For 6 pews:	Gld.	15-15
March 6	To Pieter Prac, for ½ cask of beer and sugar:	Gld.	14-14
March 7	To the same, for planks and nails for a coffin:	Gld.	3-15
March 9	Advanced to the Court for iron work:	Gld.	7-10

Translation

RECEIPTS [1663, continued from p. 174]

[110^V: "P. 11"]

BALANCE

Received,

A.D. 1661:	Gld. 673- 4	
A.D. 1662:	Gld. 623-15	
A.D. 1663 until March 4:	Gld. 63- 2	
	Total:	Gld. 1360- 1

Spent and advanced,

A.D. 1661:	Gld. 188	
A.D. 1662:	Gld. 782-17-8	
A.D. 1663 until March 9:	Gld. 266-18-4	
	Total:	Gld. 1237-15-12

Surplus should be:	Gld. 122- 5- 4	
	Total:	Gld. 1360- 1

Instead of that,[14]
and found in the treasury:

Balde's bequest:	Gld. 50	
ready sewan:[15]	Gld. 93-13	
silver money, nominally[16]		
[Gld.] 7-15:	Gld. 18-14	
	Total:	Gld. 162- 7

[We] have found these accounts of receipts, expenditures,
and money advanced, as above, in accordance with the truth,
and undersigned them at once in confirmation of the same.
Done in Breuckelen, March 11, 1663.

Henricus Selijns, Minister of
the Holy Gospel in
Breuckelen
Willem Bredenbent, as Elder
Teunis Janssen, Deacon

Translation

[110^r]

EXPENDITURES   [1663, continued from p. 175]

[Mar. 9]   To Olof Stephensze, for
½ cask of good beer and ¼ [cask] of small beer[17] for Teuntie Straetsmans:	Gld. 14
½ cask of good beer for Marcus Suson:	Gld. 12
In excise on the beer mentioned above, etc.:	Gld. 1-15
To Mr. Carel, for a schepel[7] of rye:	Gld. 5
To Pieter Lambertsen, for packing tobacco:	Gld. 2
To Teunis Jansen, for carrying and packing the barrel of tobacco:	Gld. 2

Total: Gld. 266-18-4

[111^r: "P. 12"]

TRANSFER

Handed over to the undersigned Deacons,
A cow with a bull-calf at Carel Beauvois' [place]:	Gld. 150
A cow at Jeurie Probasko's:	Gld. 165
A cow with a bull-calf at the late Pieter Pra's:	Gld. 140-19
Barent Balde's bequest:	Gld. 50
Advance to the Court of Breuckelen:	Gld. 50
Advance to the aforesaid Court:	Gld. 90
Advance to the same, with the interest on etc.:	Gld. 90-18
Pewter-ware for the Lord's Supper:	Gld. 29
Six pews:	Gld. 15-15
Advance for Teuntie Straetsmans' funeral and children, Laurens and Anna:	Gld. 163- 8-8
In ready sewan:[15]	Gld. 93-13
In silver money, [nominally[16]] Gld. 7-15:	Gld. 18-14

Total of everything: Gld. 1057-7-8

We, the undersigned, acknowledge hereby, that we
received the afore-mentioned and found it as above
- everything belonging to the poor of the Congregation
of Breuckelen; which we sign to that end in the
presence of the old Consistory.
Done in Breuckelen, March 11, 1663.

Willem Gerretsen
Tunis Gijsbertsen Bogaert

Translation

RECEIPTS   [continued from p. 176]

1663

	Received as per the preceding page, which we checked, as it appears herewith:	Gld.	1057- 7-8
March 11	Received:	Gld.	7- 5
March 18	Received:	Gld.	7- 6
March 25	Received:	Gld.	4-18
	From the Lord's Supper:	Gld.	16- 9
March 26	Received:	Gld.	7- 3
April 1	Received:	Gld.	9-13
April 4	Received:	Gld.	6-18
April 8	Received:	Gld.	7- 2
April 15	Received:	Gld.	5- 4
April 18	Received on a certain occasion:	Gld.	9- 8
April 22	Received:	Gld.	6-12
April 29	Received:	Gld.	2-10
May 3	Received:	Gld.	4-15
May 6	Received:	Gld.	2-15
May 13	Received:	Gld.	6-15
	From the Lord's Supper:	Gld.	13
May 14	Received:	Gld.	5- 3
May 20	Received:	Gld.	2
May 27	Received:	Gld.	7-17
June 3	Received:	Gld.	5-15
June 10	Received:	Gld.	8- 8
June 17	Received:	Gld.	6
June 24	Received:	Gld.	3-16
July 1	Received:	Gld.	5-15
July 4	Day of prayer - received:	Gld.	5
July 8	Received:	Gld.	6
July 15	Received:	Gld.	4
July 22	Received:	Gld.	4-18
July 29	Received:	Gld.	4-13
Aug. 1	Received - day of prayer:	Gld.	6
Aug. 5	Received:	Gld.	6
Aug. 12	Received:	Gld.	3-17
Aug. 19	Received:	Gld.	6-10
Aug. 26	Received:	Gld.	5-11
Sept. 2	Received:	Gld.	3- 6
Sept. 5	On the day of prayer:	Gld.	7
Sept. 9	Received:	Gld.	8-10
Sept. 16	Received:	Gld.	5
Sept. 23	Received:	Gld.	6- 5
	From the Lord's Supper:	Gld.	11-15
	In the afternoon, during the sermon of thanks:	Gld.	4
Sept. 30	Received:	Gld.	4- 5
Oct. 3	Received on the day of prayer:	Gld.	5- 2
Oct. 7	Received:	Gld.	4- 2
Oct. 14	Received:	Gld.	5
Oct. 21	Received:	Gld.	4- 6
Oct. 28	Received:	Gld.	5- 2

Total: Gld. 1345-16-8

Translation

[112^r]

EXPENDITURES [continued from p. 177]

<u>1663</u>

March 11	Spent for Pieter Prae's funeral:	Gld.	12
March 23	For the benefit of the Lord's Supper:	Gld.	11- 5
March 25	For a certain plank for Pieter Prae's coffin:	Gld.	1
April 5	To Jean Martijn, Frenchman:	Gld.	12
April 18	To Mr. Carel de Beauvois, for a schepel[7] of rye:	Gld.	5
ibid.	For two pews:	Gld.	5-10
April 27	For the late Pieter Prae's orphans, 2 3/4 els[18] of white kersey[19] at 6 glds. an el:	Gld.	17- 5
	2 1/2 els of white duffel[20] at 8 glds. an el:	Gld.	20
	8 1/4 els of osnaburg[21] linen at 30 stvs. an el:	Gld.	12- 7-8
	yarn, hooks and eyes:	Gld.	2- 4
	cost of ferrying:	Gld.	- 8
May 1	To Jan Pieterszen, tailor, in mending wages:	Gld.	1-16
May 4	To Mr. Carel, for a schepel of rye for his cow:	Gld.	5
May 5	To Oloff Stephensze, for 1 el of duffel:	Gld.	8
May 12	For the benefit of the Lord's Supper:	Gld.	11-19
	Lent to Fijtie Dircks, because of Jan Martijn's misfortune:[22]	Gld.	50
June 24	Lent to Catharina Joris:	Gld.	50
July 28	To Mr. Carel d'Beauvois, for a half[-year of[13] service:	Gld.	13
Sept. 22	For the benefit of the Lord's Supper:	Gld.	11-12
	To Jan Pietersen, in mending wages:	Gld.	4
Sept. 19	To Hendrick Martense van Coppenhagen [= of Copenhagen], for his inheritance from his wife's mother, Teuntie Straetsman,		
	5 7/8 els of osnaburg linen for a shirt, found in the house of the deceased:[23]	Gld.	....
	12 els of the same linen, bleached, for shirts, at 32 stvs. [an el]:	Gld.	19- 4
	A warrant of 30 glds. made out to Barentie Straesman,	Gld.	30
	A warrant made out to Gabriel Corbesy:	Gld.	16-13
Aug. 6	To Hendrick Jansen van der Vin, a sow with a little hog, in settlement of his bill and claim on the children of Teuntie Straetsman who left the sow behind - and which are valued at:	Gld.	45
Oct. 29	To Anna Tienemans, 1 pair of shoes:	Gld.	7-10
Oct. 30	To Mr. Carel d'Beauvois, whom we have awarded henceforth, on top of his salary, instead of the grain given him every year, 50 glds. in sewan[16] - [which] for half a year amounts to:	Gld.	25

Total: Gld. 397-13-8

Translation

RECEIPTS [1663, continued from p. 178]

	N.B., in addition to the aforesaid,		
Aug. 6	A sow and little hog for Teuntie Straetsman's children:	Gld.	45
Sept. 19	2 warrants, made out to Gabriel Corbesy and Barentie Straetsman:	Gld.	46-13
	5 1/8 [els^{24}] of osnaburg^{21} linen, from the house of the deceased Teuntie Straetsman:^{25}	Gld.	.....
	Total: Gld. 91-13		

Nov. 1	Received from Fredrick Philipszen, for tobacco sold to him for Teuntie Straetsman's children:	Gld.	218-10
Nov. 4	Received, including the ensuing day of prayer, Nov. 7:	Gld.	10- 4
Nov. 11	Received:	Gld.	3- 8
Nov. 18	Received:	Gld.	4
Nov. 25	Received:	Gld.	3
Dec. 2	Received:	Gld.	9- 2
Dec. 5	Received - day of prayer:	Gld.	3- 5
Dec. 9	Received:	Gld.	4- 6
Dec. 16	Received:	Gld.	6- 7
Dec. 23	Received:	Gld.	5- 7
Dec. 25	Received:	Gld.	6-15
	From the Lord's Supper:	Gld.	13
ibid.	Received:	Gld.	3-12
Dec. 26	Received:	Gld.	5
Dec. 30	Received:	Gld.	4- 2
Dec. 31	Received from Catharina Joris, our money lent out:	Gld.	50
	For compensation of the poor:	Gld.	3
ibid.	From Jean Martyn, Frenchman, the money lent out:	Gld.	12
	With interest on it:	Gld.	1
	Total: Gld. 365-18		

A.D. 1664

Jan. 2	Received - day of prayer:	Gld.	6- 5
Jan. 6	Received:	Gld.	2-14
Jan. 13	Received:	Gld.	5
Jan. 20	Received:	Gld.	4-17
Jan. 27	Received:	Gld.	2-18
Feb. 3	Received:	Gld.	5
Feb. 6	Received - day of prayer:	Gld.	5- 5
Feb. 10	Received:	Gld.	5-14
Feb. 17	Received:	Gld.	7- 4
March 2	Received:	Gld.	4- 9
March 5	Received - day of prayer:	Gld.	3- 5

Translation

[112^r]

EXPENDITURES   [<u>1663</u>, continued from p. 179]

	Nota Bene,[26]	
May 18	Sold to Fredrick Philipsen, for Teuntie's children,	
	370 lbs. of tobacco at 10 stvs. [a lb.],	
May 25	134 lbs. of tobacco ground leaves at 5 stvs. [a lb.],	
	[which,] after deducting the expenses paid by Fredrick Philipsen, amounts to:	Gld. 218-10

[113^r]

Nov. 6	To Teunis:	Gld. 6
Nov. 12	To the same:	Gld. 6
Dec. 24	For the benefit of the Lord's Supper:	Gld. 12
ibid.	Given to Teunis Janssen Coevors, at interest:	Gld. 50
Nov.	Sold to Hendrick Janszen van der Ven, a certain cow which Mr. Carel d'Beauvois had at half the offspring:[27]	Gld. 145
	Total: Gld. 219	

A.D. 1664

Jan. 1	To Anna Tienemans, a deuvekater[28] on the occasion of a New Year:	Gld. 2-16
ibid.	To Annetie Prae, a similar deuvekater:	Gld. 2-16
Feb. 11	Lent to Jan Jacobsen, because of misfortune, [viz.] that his house burned down:	Gld. 100
Feb. 16	To Mr. Carel d'Beauvois, for a half-year of service:	Gld. 13
ibid.	For mending the Deaconry's little chime:	Gld. 1
March 19	To Mr. Harmen, surgeon[29], on behalf of Teunis[30]:	Gld. 10

Translation

[112^V]

RECEIPTS   [1664, continued from p. 180]

March 9	Received:	Gld.	5-13
March 16	Received:	Gld.	4-12
March 19	Received from Hendrick Janszen van der Ven, on the cow sold to him:	Gld.	32- 7
March 22	Out of the poor-boxes:	Gld.	7-18
March 23	Received:	Gld.	4-19
	A certain title-deed held by the late Pieter Prae's children on Marcus Suson's land - paid Nov. 1, 1665:^{31}	Gld.	80

Total: [Gld.] 183-1^{32}

[113^V]

Of the aforesaid account,

RECEIVED,

1663

The surplus of the preceding years until Oct. 28:	Gld.	1345-16-8
From the late Teuntie Straetsmans:	Gld.	91-13
From the first of Nov. till the last of Dec.:	Gld.	365-18

1664

From the first of Jan. till the closing of the account:	Gld.	183- 1

Total: Gld. 1986-8-8

SPENT,

1663

From the last of March till Oct. 30:	Gld.	397-13-8
Sold in tobacco:	Gld.	218-10
From Nov. 6 till the last of Dec.:	Gld.	219

1664

From the first of Jan. till March 19:	Gld.	176-12

Total: Gld. 1011-15-8

HANDED OVER,

To the new Deacons:	Gld.	1402-14

Translation

[113^r]

EXPENDITURES [1664, continued from p. 181]

March 26 To Willem Gerritsen van Couwenhooven, house-
            rent for Mr. Carel, more than a year overdue: Gld. 30
March 19 To Burgom[aster] Olof Stephenszen, in
            complete settlement of his claim on Teuntie
            Straetsmans' children, a cask of beer: Gld. 24

                    Total: Gld. 176-12^{33}

[114^r]

TRANSFER

Handed over to the undersigned Deacons,
A cow with a heifer, at Jeurie Probasco's
  [place]:   Gld. 165
One cow with a bull-calf, at the late
  Pieter Pra's: Gld. 140-19
Barent Balde's bequest with a year's
  interest: Gld. 55
Advance to the Court of Breuckelen, with
  last year's interest: Gld. 244-18
Pewter-ware for the Lord's Supper: Gld. 29
Eight pews: Gld. 21- 5
Advance to Fytie Dircks, widow of Jan
  Martyn: Gld. 50
Given to Teunis Janszen Coevors, at
  interest: Gld. 50
Advance to Jan Jacobsen: Gld. 100
To be received from Hendrick Janse van der
  Ven, the balance of a certain cow sold to
  him: Gld. 114-13
To be received, butter-lease on the cows
  mentioned above: Gld. 22
From Pieter Prae's children on Marcus
  d'Suson's land: Gld. 80
In ready sewan:[15]   Gld. 298-19
In silver money, [nominally[16]] 7 glds.
  15 stvs., at the current value of sewan: Gld. 31
                    Total: Gld. 1402-14

183

Translation

[113^V]

RECEIPTS   [1664, continued from p. 182]

[We] have found this account of receipts, expenditures,
and money advanced, as above, in accordance with the
truth, and signed it at once in confirmation.
Done in Breuckelen, March 26, 1664.

> Henricus Selijns, Minister in
>   Breuckelen
> Willem Bredenbent, Elder
> Teunis Janssen, Eld[er]
> Willem Gerretsen, Deacon
> Tunis Gijsbertsen, Deacon

[114^V]

A.D. 1664

March 26	Received as per the preceding page:	Gld.	1402
	From Heyltie Probasko, butter-lease:	Gld.	10
March 30	Received:	Gld.	5
April 2	Day of prayer:	Gld.	3-17
April 6	Received:	Gld.	3-17
April 13	Easter:	Gld.	6- 8
	From the Lord's Supper:	Gld.	12-10
	With a piece of eight:[4]	Gld.	9-12
April 14	Received:	Gld.	7-17
April 20	Received:	Gld.	5- 3
April 27	Received:	Gld.	2-11
May 4	Received:	Gld.	6- 1
May 7	Day of prayer:	Gld.	4
May 11	Received:	Gld.	5-15
May 18	Received:	Gld.	14
May 22	Received:	Gld.	5-18
May 25	Received:	Gld.	9
June 1	Whitsuntide:	Gld.	9-10
	From the Lord's Supper:	Gld.	15-15
	With a piece of eight:	Gld.	9-12
June 2	Received:[34]	Gld.	7- 3
June 4	Day of thanksgiving:	Gld.	8- 2
June 8	Received:	Gld.	4
June 15	Received:	Gld.	5- 7
June 22	Received:	Gld.	5- 6
June 23	Received from Hendrick Janssen van der Vin, an installment for the cow:	Gld.	49- 4
June 29	Received:	Gld.	
July 6	Received:	Gld.	8-10
July 13	Received:	Gld.	5- 3
July 20	Received:	Gld.	6- 3
July 27	Received:	Gld.	24-12

Translation

[114^r]

EXPENDITURES   [1664, continued from p. 183]

> We, the undersigned, acknowledge hereby, that we
> received the afore-mentioned and found it so -
> everything belonging to the poor of the Congregation
> of Breuckelen; which we signed to that end in the
> presence of the old Consistory.

Done in Breuckelen,   Willem Gerretsen van
March 26, 1664.   Couw[enhooven]
                              Willem Willemsen

[115^r]

A.D. 1664

April 11	For the benefit of the Lord's Supper:	Gld. 13-10
April 17	To Mr. Carel d'Beauvois, what has been awarded him:	Gld. 25
June 2	To Gerrit Segertsen of "N[ieuw] Uytrecht":	Gld. 9
ibid.	For the benefit of the Lord's Supper:	Gld. 11-16
July 10	To Mr. Carel d'Beauvois, for a half-year of service:	Gld. 13
July 23	To Willem Gerritsen van Couwenhooven, house-rent for Mr. Carel:	Gld. 30
	To Mr. Carel de Beauvois:	Gld. 13
	Total: Gld. 115-6	

Translation

[115^v]

DEACONS' ACCOUNTS [1664, continued from pp. 184 and 185]

BALANCE

of the aforesaid account

of the Deacons

A.D. 1664

Received,^{35} Spent,

From March 26   From April 11 till July 23: Gld.   115- 6
till July 27: Gld. 1674-1   Left from the receipts: Gld. 1558-15
                                            Total: Gld. 1674- 1

    [We] have found this account of receipts, expenditures, and money advanced, as per the preceding balance, in accordance with the truth, and signed it all of us in confirmation. Done in Breuckelen during our Church meeting, July 27, 1664.

                    Henricus Selijns,
                        Minister in Breuckelen
                    Teunis Janssen, Elder
                    Teunis Gijsbertsen, Elder
                    Willem Bredenbent, former Elder
                    Willem Gerretsen, Deacon
                    Willen Willemsen, Deacon

[116^r]

    I, the undersigned Hendrick Martensz van Coppenhagen [= of Copenhagen], acknowledge to have received from the Deaconry of Breuckelen, out of the estate of the late Teuntie Straesman, widow of Jan Meyring and Georg Haft, and wife of Gabriel Corbesy, for and on behalf of Margariet Meyring, heir-at-law and daughter of the deceased, and wife of the aforesaid undersigned: osnaburg^{21} linen for a man's shirt, 12 more els^5 of the same bleached linen for shirts, with a warrant of 30 glds. in sewan^{15} made out to Barentie Straetsman, sister of the deceased and living at Fort Orange, for pumpkins, onions, beetroots, water-lemons etc., sent by the aforesaid Teuntie to the afore-mentioned Barentie in order to sell everything on her behalf; with which I, the undersigned, acknowledge to be satisfied for my and my wife's part of the estate mentioned above, and thank the afore-said Deaconry for their trouble and careful supervision; with the promise - if after this date creditors might show up other than the ones we have satisfied, which we do not expect - to give satisfaction therefrom, [viz.] out of the inheritance received, proportionally from the orphans and minor children.

Translation

[116^r]

DEACONS' ACCOUNTS [1664, continued]

Done in Amsterd[am] in N[ew] Netherl[and], Sept. 19, 1663.

[I] acknowledge to have received, in addition to the afore-
mentioned, a certain order for payment of 16 glds. 13 stvs., in
the name of Gabriel Corbesy, because of the hay [and] peas which
had been given on the land, etc. Done, as above.

The mark of ⌇⌇ Hendrick Martensse van
Coppenhagen

[116^v]

I, the undersigned Jan Jacobsen van Rheenen [= of Rhenen],
acknowledge to have borrowed from the Deaconry of Breuckelen the
sum of a hundred guild[ers] in sewan[15], with the promise to give
it back on the first opportunity. Done in Breuckelen, July 23,
1664.

The mark of ⏀ Jan Jacobsen van Rheenen

I, the undersigned Teunis Janssen Coevors, acknowledge to
have taken on interest from the Deaconry of Breuckelen the sum
of fifty guild[ers] in sewan, on the understanding that I
promise to give for the aforesaid money ten per hundred, or five
guild[ers] a year. Done in Breuckelen, July 23, 1664.

Teunis Janssen[36]

I, the undersigned Pieter Lambertsen de Heest, acknowledge to
owe the Deaconry of Breuckelen the sum of fifty guild[ers] in
sewan, which was advanced to my wife, Fytie Dircks, because of
the misfortune[37] of her deceased husband, the late Jan Martyn,
and on which the Consistory does not want interest; which [I]
promise to give back to the aforesaid Deaconry in due time.
Done in Breuckelen, July 28, 1664.[38]

Translation

[140^r]

Other financial records

Hendrick Jansen van de Vin's "Account for Teuntge Straetm[an]s and Gabriel Carbosie" [39]

DEBIT

__1657__

Feb. 5	11½ els[5] of black plets[40] at 2 glds.:	Gld. 23	
	6 els of blue linen at 4 els per beaver reduced to sewan[15] at 12 glds. per beaver - amounts to:	Gld. 18	
			Gld. 41
April 28	for her daughter, 1 pair of shoes and 1 pair of mules - total:		Gld. 9
May 28	sewan lent:	Gld. 6	
	7¼ lbs. of Leiden cheese at 12 stvs.:	Gld. 4- 7	
	2 one-vaen jugs[41] - total:	Gld. 4	
			Gld. 14- 7
	1 oxhooft[42] of French wine, to be paid in beavers or silver money:		Gld. 106
	2 small pewter jugs - total:		Gld. 4
July 4	sewan lent:	Gld. 6	
	purchased in lace:	Gld. 6-16	
	1 schepel[7] of maize:	Gld. 2- 6	
	some time ago, 1 schepel of wheat:	Gld. 3-10	
	1 pair of men's stockings:	Gld. 7	
	2 scarves at 3 glds. each:	Gld. 6	
	2 schepels of wheat at 4 glds.:	Gld. 8	
			Gld. 39-12

__1658__

Oct. 31	lent on interest to Gabriel Carb- osie (her husband), one hundred glds. in sewan at 10 percent a year, as it appears from an oblig- ation sanctioned by notary Matheus d'Vos:	Gld. 100

__1659__

Jan. 2	2½ schepels of wheat at 4 glds.:	Gld. 10
	at Hermen Jansz' funeral, ½ barrel of good beer with excise:	Gld. 12-10

__1660__

Oct. 31	interest for 2 years on the one hundred glds. lent in 1658 - see above:	Gld. 20

__1661__

Jan.	sewan lent:	Gld. 50

[continued on p. 190]

188

Translation

[141^r]

"Account for Teuntge Straetm[an]s"

CREDIT

1657

June 7 paid for 1 oxhooft^{42} of French wine
which was bought on credit,
20 pieces of eight^4 at 3 glds.: Gld. 60

Aug. 4 paid by Jacob Moesman for the same,
4 complete and 3 half beavers with
2 glds. in sewan - which amounts
to: Gld. 46

1659

Nov. paid, a year's interest on the
obligation: Gld. 10

1660

Dec. 30 paid off by Gerrit Jansz van Aernhem [= of Arnhem], the obligation
signed Oct. 31, 1658, with a
year's interest, [as part] of the
purchase price for the house: Gld. 110
in addition, by the same: Gld. 23-10
Gld. 133-10

1662

Jan. 21 [paid] by Gerrit Jansz, the balance
for the house, which was Gld. 125;
deducted herefrom:

to Gabriel:	Gld. 20
for the deed:	Gld. 14
in expenses:	Gld. 8
to Gerrit Jansz:	Gld. -14
in trifles:	Gld. -14
Remainder:	Gld. 81-12

March 27 [paid] by Gerrit Jansz for the farmyard bill: Gld. 20

May 8 paid in sewan by the same Gerrit
Jansz van Aernhem for his farmyard
bill: Gld. 40

Sept. 9 paid, 2 schepels of buckwheat at
3 glds.: Gld. 6

Sept. 23 ⎧ supplied, 6 schepels of yellow peas
NB ⎨ at .. glds. [and] 2 schepels of
⎩ white peas at .. glds.:^{43}

Translation

[140^V]

"Account for Teuntge Straetm[an]s"

DEBIT [continued from p. 188]

1662

Feb. 18	in yarn:	Gld.	1		
	sewan lent:	Gld.	2		
	vinegar:	Gld.	1		
	3 lbs. of lard at 20 stvs.:	Gld.	3		
				Gld.	7
March 10	lent: 6 stvs. in sewan; ½ barrel of good [beer and] ½ barrel of small beer^{17} - total:			Gld.	15-16
April 7	sewan lent:			Gld.	4
April 15	NB: 2½ schepels of white } peas to be				
	2 schepels of yellow } sown^{44}				
May 8	sewan lent:	Gld.	1		
	in white bread:	Gld.	-10		
	3¾ lbs. of smoked pork:	Gld.	3-15		
				Gld.	5- 5
	for the transport from the farmyard:			Gld.	4
May 13	sewan lent:	Gld.	1		
	in fresh fish:	Gld.	2		
	1 skein of yarn:	Gld.	- 8		
	½ schepel of salt:	Gld.	2-10		
				Gld.	5-18
May 23	sewan lent for fish:	Gld.	3-10		
	1 skein of silk:	Gld.	-10		
	2 schepels of white peas at 4 glds.:	Gld.	8		
				Gld.	12
June 25	sewan lent:	Gld.	1-10		
[.....................................Gld.	12?............]^{45}				
				Gld.	13-10
[.........4¾ lbs. of smoked?] pork at 20 stvs.:	Gld.	4-15			
Sept. 11	2 lbs. of frying-fat at 20 stvs.:	Gld.	2		
				Gld.	6-15
	2 skeins of yarn:			Gld.	-16
Sept. 23	8 els of ribbon at 2 stvs.:	Gld.	-16		
	½ packet of pins, 10 stvs.:	Gld.	-10		
				Gld.	1- 6
	Total:^{46}			Gld.	..-..

4½ schepels { The above-mentioned total excludes 2½ schepels of white peas and 2 schepels of yellow peas for sowing, as is evident from the entry dated April 15, 1662.

Amst[erdam] in N[ew] Netherland, October 23, 166[2]^{47}

Your Obliging   Hend[rick] J[ansen] vand[e] Vin

Translation

[5^r: "Pag. 9"]

Frederick Philipsen's transaction[48]

May 18 [1663[49]]   received: a barrel of tobacco, net [weight]:
                    370 pounds [at] 10 stuivers [per] pound in sewan;
May 25   received: 134 pounds [at] 5 stuivers [per] pound
                    [which] together amounts to, in sewan:

                                              [Gld.] 218-10

          Paid in sewan: 218-10

                    Frederijck Flijpsen

                                              [143^r]

From another fragment of text,[50] it appears that on May 15, 1676, the treasury of the church[51] contained Gld. 27-2 in cash, Gld. 8-11 in silver money, Gld. 750-5 in obligations (including two obligations of Gld. 50 each from Jan van Rossu[m]), and Gld. 53[-..?] in sewan.

ORPHANS

OF THE DEACONRY

Original

[119^r]

DIACONIES

WEESKINDERS

I

Laurens Haff, van Brasilien,
van Ouderdom omtrent 13 jaren,
en soon van wijlen

Den 22 Nōv.
1662.

Georgh Haff, van Auspurg,
veltrompetter der H.H. Staten
der Vereenigde Nederlanden,
onder Capt Claessen; van de
welcke den voorgem Georgh ont-
slagen wiert naer behoorlycke
paspoort van dato 23 Jun. 1649.
Teuntie Straetsmans, van Culenburg, weduwe van Jan Meijr-
inck, en Huijsvrouw van Gabriel Corbesij: ende gestorven
den 19 Octob. 1662.

Besteed-Ceel

Wij, Ondergeschreven, bekennen mits desen, dat wij, als Uijtvoer-
ders des uijtterste wille van wijlen Teuntie Straetsmans en Opsienders van Hunne onmondigen kinderen, besteedt hebben, en besteeden, Laurens Haff, soone van wijlen Georgie Haff, Trompetter,
om te woonen ten Huijsen van Henricus Selijns, Bedienaer des H.
Euangeliums in sijn Gemeijnte tot Breuckelen in N. Nederlant, ende
hem ten dienste wesen voor de tijdt van ses achtervolgende jaeren:
ten welcke voorschr. jaren den voorgemelte Henricus Selijns belooft heeft, en belooft met eijgen onderteeckinge, desen Laurens
van behoorlijcke kost en klederen te versien, hem 's winters oft
t'schole te senden, ofte selfs te onderwijsen na behooren, en met
hem te handelen als betamelijck is. Actum in onse kerckelijcke
vergaderinge, den 20 dec. 1662.

(Onderteeckent)

Henricus Selijns, predicant te
Breuckelen

Willem Bredenb̃., ouderling

Teunis Jansen

Jan Jorisse Rappalie

Translation

ORPHANS

OF THE DEACONRY

<table>
<tr>
<td>

I

Laurens Haff, from Brazil,
about 13 years of age,
and son of the late

November 22,
1662.

</td>
<td>

Georg Haff, from Augsburg,
field-trumpeter of the Hon.
States of the United Nether-
lands under Captain Claessen,
by whom the afore-mentioned
Georgh was dismissed [from
military service] as it app-
ears from a proper notice of
dismissal dated June 23, 1649;
Teuntie Straetsmans, from Cul-
emborg, widow of Jan Meijr-
inck and wife of Gabriel Corb-
esij, and who died on October
19, 1662.

</td>
</tr>
</table>

Custody Contract

We, the undersigned, acknowledge hereby that we, as executors
of the late Teuntie Straetsmans' last will and as supervisors of
her minor children, have placed, and do place, Laurens Haff, son
of the late Georgie Haff, trumpeter, in the custody of Henricus
Selijns, minister of the Holy Gospel in his congregation in
Breuckelen in New Netherland, in order to live in his house and
to serve him for a period of six consecutive years. The afore-
mentioned Henricus Selijns promised, and promises with his own
signature, to provide this Laurens with proper board and clothing
during the aforesaid years, to send him to school in winter or
teach him properly himself, and to treat him in a proper way.
Done in our church meeting, December 20, 1662.

(signed)

Henricus Selijns, Minister in
Breuckelen

Willem Bredenb[ent], Elder

Teunis Jansen

Jan Jorisse Rappalie

Original

[119^V]

II

Anna Tienemans,
    van ouderdom 8 jaren,
    en dochter van

Den 22 Nov.
    1662.

Tieneman Jacobszen, kleêrmaecker,
    ende gebleeven door 't haestig ver-
    trecken van d'Heer Generael Petrus
    Stuijvesant op 't Eijlant Gardulypen.
Teuntie Straetsman, van Culenborg,
    weduwe van Jan Meijring en Georg Haff,
    ende Huijsvrouw van Gabriel Corbesij;
    gestorven dato als boven.

Besteed-Ceel

Wij, Ondergeschreven, bekennen mitsdesen, dat wij, als uijtvoer-
ders des uijtterste wille van wijlen Teuntie Straetsmans ende
Opsienders van hunne Onmondige kinders, besteedt hebben, en besteeden, Anna Tienemans, Dochter van Tieneman Jacobsen, kleer-
maecker, om te woonen ten huijsen van Gerrit Cornelissen, woonende op Secretaris-Bouwerije te Middelwout, ende hem ten dienste te
wesen voor de Tydt van ses achtervolgende jaeren: ten welcke
voorschr. jaren den voorgemelte Gerrit Cornelissen van Niekerck
belooft heeft, en belooft met eijgen onderteeckeninge, dit Meijsie
van behoorlijcke kost en kleeren te versien, haer 's Winters met
de Avonden t'Schole te senden, en met haer, als 't betamelijck is,
te handelen. Actum te Breuckelen: den 1 dec. 1662.

Uijt name des kerckenraedts en opsien-
    ders der voors kinderen,

Henricus Selijns,
    Predicant op 's Generaels
    Bouwerije en te Breuckelen

Het merck van Gerrit Cornelissen

III

Annetie Prae,
    van Ouderdom omtrent
    .. jaeren, en
    dochter van

Pieter Prae, van Diepe,
    man van Catharina Lethie,
    ende gestorven den 6 mart. 1663.

Besteed-Ceel

Wij, Ondergeschreven, bekennen mitsdesen, dat wij, als uijtvoer-
ders des uijtterste wille van wijlen Pieter Prae ende opsienders
van sijne onmondige kinders, besteedt hebben, ende besteeden,
Annetie Prae, dochter van   , om te woonen ten huijsen
van Jan Martijn van Campen, woonende tot Breuckelen, ende hem

[continued on p. 198]

Translation

II Anna Tienemans, 8 years of age, and daughter of November 22, 1662.	Tieneman Jacobszen, tailor, who had stayed behind on the Island of Guadeloupe owing to the Lord General Petrus Stuijvesant's hurried departure; Teuntie Straetsman, from Culemborg, widow of Jan Meijring and Georg Haff, and wife of Gabriel Corbesij, and who died on the date as above.

Custody Contract

We, the undersigned, acknowledge hereby that we, as executors
of the late Teuntie Straetsmans' last will and as supervisors of
her minor children, have placed, and do place, Anna Tienemans,
daughter of Tieneman Jacobsen, tailor, in the custody of Gerrit
Cornelissen, living at the Secretary's farm in Midwout, in order
to live in his house and to serve him for a period of six consecutive years. The afore-mentioned Gerrit Cornelissen van Niekerck
[= of Niekerk] promised, and promises with his own signature, to
provide this girl with proper board and clothing during the
aforesaid years, to send her to school during the winter evenings,
and to treat her in a proper way. Done in Breuckelen, December 1,
1662.

On behalf of the consistory and supervisors of the aforesaid children,

Henricus Selijns,
Minister at the General's Bowery [= farm] and in Breuckelen

The mark of Gerrit Cornelissen

III Annetie Prae, about .. years of age,[1] and daughter of	Pieter Prae, from Dieppe, husband of Catharina Lethie, and who died on March 6, 1663;

Custody Contract

We, the undersigned, acknowledge hereby that we, as executors
of Pieter Prae's last will and as supervisors of his minor
children, have placed, and do place, Annetie Prae, daughter of
,[2] in the custody of Jan Martijn van Campen [= of
Kampen], living in Breuckelen, in order to live in his house and

[continued on p. 199]

Original

[120^r]

ten dienste te wesen voor de tijdt van ses achtervolgende jaeren:
ten welcke voorschr. jaren den voorgemelte Jan Martijn belooft
heeft, en belooft met eijgen Onderteeckeningen, dit meijsie van
behoorlijcke kost en kleeren te versien, haer 's Winters met de
Avonden t'Schole te senden oft selfs te onderwysen na behooren,
en met haer, als 't betamelijck is, te handelen. Actum in onse
kerckelijcke vergaderinge, den 18 April. 1663.

        Henricus Selijns, V.D.M.

        Willem Bredenbent, oudterlingh

        Tunis Gijsbertsz Bogaert, diacon

        Jan Mar-tyn

        Van

      Laurens Haf

    Tweede Besteed-Ceel

Wij, Ondergeschreeven, bekennen mitsdesen, dat wij, als Uytvoerders des Uytterste wille van wijlen Teuntie Straetsman ende opsienders van hunne onmondige kinders, besteedt hebben, en besteeden, (met het vertreck van Henricus Selyns, predicant, na 't
vaderlant) Laurens Haf, die tot synent by de 19 maenden gewoont
en sig seer trouw gedragen heeft, om te woonen ten huysen van
Willem Gerritsen van Couwenhooven, diacon en Schepen te deser
plaetse, ende hem ten dienste te wesen voor de tijdt van drie
Achtervolgende jaeren; ten welcke Voorschrev. Jaren den voorgemelte Willem Gerritsen belooft heeft, en belooft voor de volle
Vergaderinge, metten voornoemde Laurens te handelen als betamelyck is, hem 's winters Schole te senden oft selve te onderwijsen,
van kost en kleeren te versien, en so hem uyttesetten naer Expiratie van Verbantjaren als Willem Gerritsen hem van den meergemelte Henricus Selyns ontfangen heeft, naer de lyste daer van
volgende, ende daeren boven te geeven aen den voornoemde Laurens,
Een pinck van een jaer, 't welck wedersyds aengenoomen is.
Actum te Breuckelen, in onse kerckelycke Vergaderinge, den 23 Jul.
1664.

      Uyt name des kerckenraets

        Henricus Selijns

        Willem Gerretsen Couwehouen

Translation

to serve him for a period of six consecutive years. The afore-
mentioned Jan Martijn promised, and promises with his own signature, to provide this girl with proper board and clothing during
the aforesaid years, to send her to school during the winter
evenings or teach her properly himself, and to treat her in a
proper way. Done in our church meeting, April 18, 1663.

> Henricus Selijns, Minister of
> the Word of God
>
> Willem Bredenbent, Elder
>
> Tunis Gijsbertsz Bogaert, Deacon
>
> Jan Mar-tyn

Second Custody Contract

for

Laurens Haf

We, the undersigned, acknowledge hereby that we, as executors
of the late Teuntie Straetsman's last will and as supervisors of
her minor children, have placed, and do place, (in view of the
departure of Henricus Selyns, minister, for the fatherland)
Laurens Haf, who lived with him[3] for about 19 months and behaved
very loyally, in the custody of Willem Gerritsen van Couwenhooven,
deacon and schepen in this place, in order to live in his house
and to serve him for a period of three consecutive years. The
afore-mentioned Willem Gerritsen promised, and promises in the
presence of the entire assembly, to treat the aforesaid Laurens
in a proper way during the aforesaid years, to send him to school
in winter or teach him himself, to provide him with board and
clothing, and to release him from custody upon the expiration of
the years of the contract in the same material circumstances that
he was in when Willem Gerritsen received him from the afore-mentioned Henricus Selyns, in accordance with the following list;
and [Willem promises] to give the aforesaid Laurens then in addition to that, a one-year-old yearling. This was accepted by both
parties. Done in Breuckelen in our church meeting, July 23, 1664.

> On behalf of the consistory,
>
> Henricus Selijns
>
> Willem Gerretsen Couwehouen

Original

[121^r^]

Lijste van de Cleederen, linnen, kousen,
Schoenen, &c, Van Laurens Haf, als hij
tot Willem Gerritsen besteedt wiert

Een Sarge Jnnocent, die weynig gedragen is

Een Sarge Broeck

Nieuwe Hemb-rock, van root Carzaij

Roode Bercaense Broeck

Witte linnen Broeck

Leere Broeck

Paer Sy-jette kousen, half nieuw en onversoolt

Paer nieuwe Yslantse kousen

Paer Nieuwe Schoenen

Paer Halfsleeten Schoenen

Nieuwe Swarte Hoet

dito Swarte Hoet

Sargie Muts

Paer Nieuwe Hantschoenen

Vier nieuwe Hembden

Twee neusdoecken

Twee dasiens

Pampieren van Syn Vader Sal^r^

Copie van d'Obligatie van Jan
Laurensse Bogaert, ten regarde van
Seecker Vercken, 't welck Laurens
Haf gegeeven is, en daer van Willem Gerritsen aengenoomen heeft,
't geen voor den voorschr Laurens
van de aentelinge komt, te sullen
by syn Verckens laten loopen

Ick, ondergeschreeven, bekenne van Henricus Selyns, Predicant tot
Breuckelen, ontfangen te hebben, seecker Sog, swart van Coleur,
die den Voorschrev. Henricus Selyns aen syn Jongen Laurens Haf
gegeeven heeft, met beloften, dat ick den Voornoemde Haf, ofte
syn opsienders, den diaconen van Breuckelen, van synent wegen,
's jarelycks uyt de Aenteelinge Een sal laten kiesen, te weten
voor kerstydt, Ende so 't Vercken quam te sterven, dat ick met
eene van de Eerste aenteelinge sal bestaen kunnen. Actum ter
presentie der voorgemelte diaconen, den 23 Jul. 1664.

(onderteeckent)

Jan Laurenssen

Translation

>List of the clothes, linen, stockings,
>shoes, etc., belonging to Laurens Haf when he
>was placed in the custody of Willem Gerritsen

a serge[4] innocent[5], hardly worn,

a pair of serge trousers,

a new dress-coat, made of red carsay[6],

a pair of red barracan[7] trousers,

a pair of white linen trousers,

a pair of leather trousers,

a pair of .....[8] stockings, half-new and unmended,

a new pair of Iceland stockings,

a new pair of shoes,

a half-worn pair of shoes,

a new black hat,

a similar black hat,

a serge cap,

a new pair of gloves,

four new shirts,

two handkerchiefs,

two scarves,

papers from his late father.

>Copy of Jan Laurensse Bogaert's
>obligation with regard to a certain
>pig given to Laurens Haf; Willem
>Gerritsen has agreed that whatever
>offspring of this pig will belong
>to the aforesaid Laurens, will be
>allowed to feed along with his own
>pigs.

I, the undersigned, acknowledge to have received from Henricus Selyns, minister in Breuckelen, a certain sow, black-colored, which was given by the aforesaid Henricus Selyns to his boy, Laurens Haf; with the promise that each year I will let the afore-said Haf - or his supervisors, the deacons of Breuckelen, on his behalf - chose one of the offspring, namely before Christmas. And [I promise] that, if the pig comes to die, I will live on one of the first offspring. Done in the presence of the afore-mentioned deacons, July 23, 1664.

(signed)

Jan Laurenssen

COWS

OF THE DEACONRY

Original

[124^r]

DIACONIES

KOEIJEN

d'Eerste

Kost 150 gld. seewant.

Ick, Ondergeschreven Mr Carel d'Beauvois, Schoolmeester en Voorsanger der Gemeente van Breuckelen, bekenne uijt Handen van de
kerckenraedt ontfangen te hebben voor de Armen ter voorschr
plaetse, Seecker Koeij, namentlijck vrij van Boterpacht: maer
vorders achtervolgens de gewoonelijcke Conditien van Halve Aentelinge; en Beloften, om de Schade ten halven, oft 't Beest quam
te Sterven, te vergoeden. Actum, ter Kerckelijcke Vergaderinge
des Voorgemelte Plaetse, den 14 Maij. 1662.

(Onderteeckent)

Carel de Beauvois

Van welcke Voorsch koey gekoomen is
den 4 Febr. 1663, Een Bulkalf, ende   gestorven.

Mr Carel d'Beauvois, veel tegenspoets en ongeleegenthz vindende
in de voorn. koeij met de langduerende Winter, versocht na 't
volkomen Jaer ontslaginge, dat hem vergunt en toegestaen is:
waer door dan geresolveert wiert om den voorsch vet te laten
loopen.
Aen Hendrick Jansen van de Vin is de voorschr koeij vkocht voor
de somme van 145 gl. seewant.

Tweede Koeij

Kost 165 gld. seewant.

Ick, Ondergeschreven Jeurie Probasco, bekenne ontfangen te hebben
uijt de handen van de E: Kerckenraedt van Breuckelen voor de Armen ter selfde Plaetse, seecker koeijbeest; ten eersten op de

[continued on p. 206]

Translation

COWS

OF THE DEACONRY

The first [cow]

Costs 150 guilders in sewan.

I, the undersigned Mr. Carel d'Beauvois, schoolmaster and precentor of the congregation of Breuckelen, acknowledge to have received from the hands of the consistory, for the benefit of the poor in the aforesaid place: a certain cow, free from butter-lease, but for the rest on the usual conditions of half-the-offspring[1] and the promise [on my part] to cover half of the loss if the beast comes to die. Done in the church meeting in the afore-mentioned place, May 14, 1662.

(signed)

Carel de Beauvois

The aforesaid cow produced on February 4, 1663: a bull-calf, which died on ......[2]

Mr. Carel d'Beauvois, who experienced a great deal of adversity and inconvenience with the aforesaid cow during the long winter, asked to be released [from the contract] after the expiration of the [first] year; this was granted and permitted. For this reason, it was resolved to fatten the aforesaid [cow].
The aforesaid cow was sold to Hendrick Jansen van de Vin for the sum of 145 guilders in sewan.

Second cow

Costs 165 guilders in sewan.

I, the undersigned Jeurie Probasco, acknowledge to have received from the hands of the Hon. Consistory of Breuckelen, for the benefit of the poor in the same place: a certain cow,

[continued on p. 207]

Original

[124^V]

Halve aenteelinge, ten tweeden op Boterpacht van tien pondt deses
lopende jaers ende van sestien pont met de navolgende jaren, 't
welcke belove met seewant in plaets van Boter op te brengen ten
beste van de voorn Armen; ende ten laesten met beloften, om de
Schade ten halven, oft 't Beest quam te sterven, te vergoeden.
Actum, Breuckelen, den 14 Maij, 1662.

(Onderteeckent)

Georgi Probasco

Waervan gekoomen is,
24 Jun. 1662, Seecker wonderlyck misdracht,
       1663, Een Veers-kalf,
25 Jun. 1664, Een Veers-kalf.

Dese Koe is van selfs gestorven.

Derde Koeij

Kost 140 gl. 19 st seewant.

Ick, Ondergeschrevene Pieter Prae, ledemaet van de Gemeente van
Breuckelen, bekenne mitsdesen ontfangen te hebben van de Diaconie der voorschr gemeente, een seecker koeij, achtervolgens de
gewoonelijcke Conditie van halve aentelinge in twalef pont boter, 't welcke belove 's jaerelijcks optebrengen ten profijten
van de Bovengemelte Diaconie, met eene om de Schade daerenboven
ten halven, oft 't Beest quam te sterven, te vergoeden. Actum
Breuckelen, den 20 dec. 1662.

(Onderteeckent)

Pieter Prae

En met syn versterf onderteeckent van syn Vrouw.   Actum Breuckelen, den 23 Jul. 1664.   't merck van

Catharina ᙠᙢ Lethie

Van de welcke gekomen is,
1663, Een Bulkalf,
1664, Een Veerskalf.

Dese koe is verkocht Aen Asper Levij voor 168 g

Joost Casperse Heeft Aengnoomen van de Diaconij van de Dorpe
Breuckelen Int Jaer Ao 1667 Den 29 Meij n Stijl een veers van

[continued on p. 208]

Translation

[on the following conditions:] first, half-the-offspring[1];
second, butter-lease of ten pounds during the present year and
sixteen pounds in the following years, which [I] promise to pay
in sewan instead of in butter for the benefit of the aforesaid
poor; and finally, with the promise to cover half of the loss if
the beast comes to die. Done in Breuckelen, May 14, 1662.

(signed)

Georgi Probasco

This cow produced
on June 24, 1662: a certain strangely deformed calf;
        in 1663: a heifer-calf;
on June 25, 1664: a heifer-calf.

This cow died of itself.

Third cow

Costs 140 guilders 19 stuivers in sewan.

I, the undersigned Pieter Prae, member of the congregation of
Breuckelen, acknowledge hereby to have received from the deaconry
of the aforesaid congregation: a certain cow, on the usual condition of half-the-offspring[1] and twelve pounds of butter, which
[I] promise to pay annually for the benefit of the afore-mentioned
deaconry; at the same time, [I promise] to cover, in addition to
that, half of the loss if the beast comes to die. Done in Breuckelen, December 20, 1662.

(signed)

Pieter Prae

And upon his death signed by his wife. Done in Breuckelen,
July 23, 1664.   The mark of

Catharina ⟨mark⟩ Lethie

This cow produced
in 1663: a bull-calf;
in 1664: a bull-calf.

This cow was sold to Asper Levij for 168 guilders.

In the year 1667, May 29, new style, Joost Casperse received
from the deaconry of the village of Breuckelen a 2-year-old

[continued on p. 209]

Original

2 Jaer, waer van hy belooft te betalen behoorlycke pacht ende
halfe aentelinge en half risico. Actum op den 6 April 1669.
Dit is het K merck van Joost Kaspersen met hant gestelt.

Vierdekoeij

Kost 177-10.

Ick, Ondergeschreeven Jan Jacobsen, woonende tot Breuckelen,
bekenne ontfangen te hebben uyt de handen van de E: kerckenraedt
van de Gemeijnte tot Breuckelen voor de Armen ter selfder Plaetse,
seecker koeij-beest; Voor eerst op de halve Aenteelinge, ten
tweeden op Boterpacht van 10 lb boter deses loopende jaers ende
van sestien Ponden met de navolgende Jaren, ten ware dat 't
Veers was 't Voorschr. Beest, om dat jaer dan te geeven na de
gewoonelycke manier Half so veel, 't Welcke beloove met Seewant
in plaetse van Boter op te brengen ten beste van de Voornoemde
Armen: Ende ten laesten met beloften om de Schade, So 't Beest
quam te sterven, ten halve of met de Eerste aenteelinge te vergoeden. Actum, Breuckelen, den 1. Maij. 1664.

'' 't Merck van $Ⓟ$ Jan Jacobsen van Rheenen

En daer van gekoomen is,
    8 Jun. 1664, Een Bulkalf,
 Int Jaer 1665, de koe veer,
In t Jaer 1666, een bul kalf,
In t Jaer 1667, een veers kalf,
In t Jaer 1668, een veers kalf.

Anno 1668 den 23 april so heeft de Diakenij de aentelinge gedeelt
met Jan Jacopsen, so is den Armen tot deel gevallen de aentelinge
van het Jaer 1666 en vant Jaer 1667 ende van het Jaer 1668.

Translation

heifer, for which he promises to pay proper lease and half the
offspring and half the risk.[3] Done April 6, 1669.

This is the ⟨K⟩ mark of Joost Kaspersen, signed with his own hand.

Fourth cow

Costs [Gld.] 177-10.

I, the undersigned Jan Jacobsen, living in Breuckelen,
acknowledge to have received from the hands of the Hon. Consistory of the congregation of Breuckelen, for the benefit of the
poor in the same place: a certain cow, [on the following conditions:] first, half-the-offspring[1]; second, butter-lease of 10 lbs.
of butter during the present year and sixteen pounds in the
following years - unless the aforesaid beast turns out to be a
heifer, in which case [I will] give half as much this year which
is customary - which [I] promise to pay in sewan instead of in
butter for the benefit of the aforesaid poor; and finally, with
the promise to cover half of the loss or to give the first offspring if the beast comes to die. Done in Breuckelen, May 1,
1664.

The mark of ⟨Q⟩ Jan Jacobsen van Rheenen
                      [= of Rhenen]

This cow produced
on June 8, 1664: a bull-calf;
in the year 1665: the heifer;
in the year 1666: a bull-calf;
in the year 1667: a heifer-calf;
in the year 1668: a heifer-calf.

On April 23, 1668, the deaconry divided the offspring with
Jan Jacopsen. The offspring of the year 1666, the year 1667,
and the year 1668, became the share of the poor.

[129^r: "254"]

MARRIAGE REGISTER

of

BREUCKELEN IN NEW NETHERLAND

[* Brackets [] followed or preceded by an asterisk * mark
passages which are illegible because of damage to the
original manuscript.]

1660, October 31:

  - Sigismund Lucasz,
    to Getruijd Buldering,
        with certificate "from the Manhatans".

1661, February 6:

  - Willem Janszen Traphagel,
    to Joosje Willems,
        with certificate "from the Manhatans".

1661, July 17:

  - Jan Clercq, "from Brasiel" (died November 15, 1661),
    to Annetie Hans, "from N[ieuw] Nederl[ant]";
        witnesses: Teunis Gijsbertsen, stepfather of the
        bride, Jan Jorissen, uncle of the bride.

1661, September 26:

  - Lambert Barentsz,
    to Leentie Dircks,
        with certificate "from the Manhatans".
  - Francois du Puis,
    to Grietie Willems,
        with certificate "from the Manhatans".

Translation

[130^V: "257"]

1661, October 30:

- Gerrit Dirckzen Crousen,
  to Neeltie Jans, "from N[ieuw] Nederl[an]t";
      witnesses: Jan Pietersz, father of the bride, Jeurie
      Janszen, on the side of the bridegroom.

1661, December 4:

- Wijnant Pieterszen, "from Eck in the Betuwe",
  to Anneken Auckens, "from Amsterd[am]";
      witnesses: Aucke Jans, father of the bride, Jan
      Jacobszen van Rheenen [= of Rhenen].

1662, March:[1]

- Jan de Wit,
  to Getruijd van Wyngaerden,
      with certificate "from the Manhatans".

1662, July 25:

- by Domine Megapolensis:
  Henricus Selijns, "from Amsterd[am]",
  to Mechtelina Specht, "from Uijtrecht",
      with certificate "from Uytrecht", and after three
      proclamations of banns "in N[ieuw] Amsterd[am] and
      Breuckelen".
- Huijbert Clomp,
  to Jannetie Willems.

1662, August 13:

- "married on the [Director-]General's Bowery [= farm]":
  Jan Ginom, "from Leijden",
  to Grietie Snedinx, "from Amst[erdam]";
      witnesses: Marcus Suson, Jan Duurkop.
- Jan Hendrickzen Bommel,
  to Annetie Abrahams,
      with certificate "from the Manhatans".

1662, September 17:[2]

- Arie Corneliszen, "from N[ieuw] Nederl[an]t",
  to Rebecca Idens, "from Nordingen";
      witnesses: Cornelis Aertsen, father of the bridegroom,
      Teunis Teunissen.

Translation

[131^r: "258"]

1662, October 8:

- Dirck Jansze Hooglant, "from Maerseveen",
  to Annetie Hans, widow of Jan Clerq,
      after three proclamations [of banns], and [with]
      certificate "from Middelwout".

1662, November 19:

- Marten Janszen Meijer,
  to Hendrickie Harmens,
      with certificate "from the Manhatans".

1662, December 3:

- Arie Willemse, "from N[ieuw] Nederl[an]t",
  to Annetie Jans;
      witnesses: Mr. Paulus van Diepenbeeck, stepfather of
      the bridegroom, Jan Thomasze, father of the bride.

1662, December 24:

- Paulus Heijmans,
  to Claesie Philips,
      with certificate "from the Manhatans".
- Thomas Martyn, "from Baston",
  to Hanna Gennes, "from Hertfort";
      witness: Miches Gennes.

1662, December 26:

- Claes Teuniszen, "from Appeldoorn",
  to Metie Bastiaens, "from Werckhoven";
      witness: Bastiaen Edens, "from Werckhoven".

1663, January 1:

- Lambert Janszen Bosch, "from Ootmarsum",
  to Sara de Plancken, widow of Pieter Monfoort.

1663, January 14:

- Jan Braun,
  to Marie Hendricks,
      with certificate "from the Manhatans".

1663, April 22:

- Marten Hermanszen Hoffman,
  to Lijsbeth Hermans.

213

Translation

[131^V: "259"]

1663, May 14:

- Marten Reijerszen, "from Amsterd[am]",
  to Annetie Joris, "from N[ieuw] Nederl[an]t";
      witness: Catarina Jeronijmus.

1663, May 27:

- Arie Huijbertszen,
  to Thijsie Gerrits,
      with certificate "from the Manhatans".

1663, June 10:

- Joost Casparszen, "from Groeningen",
  to Catharina Lethie, widow of Pieter Prae.
- Jan Montagne, "schout of N[ieuw] Haerlem",
  to Maria Farnelie,
      with certificate "from the Manhatans".
- Jan ter Bosch,
  to Rachel Farnelie,
      with certificate "as above" [= "from the Manhatans"].

1663, June 24:

- Mones Pieterszen, "from Arbou",
  to Magdaleentie van Tellingkhuijsen.

1663, August 24:

- "married in Middelwout":
  Jan Corneliszen Buys, widower of Ybe Lubberts,
  to Femmetie Jans, widow of Teunis Nysse,
      with certificate "from Breuckelen".

1663, September 16:

- Pieter Lambertsen de Heest, "from Amsterd[am]",
  to Fijtie Dircks, widow of Jan Martijn;
      witnesses: Mr. Jeurie Probasko, Heijltie Aertsen, both
      on the side of the bridegroom.
- Jacques Cresson,
  to Maria Peijnart,
      with certificate "from the Manhatans".

1663, October 14:

- Symon Hansen, "from Amsterd[am]",
  to Maria Fredrickx, widow of Jan Joriszen,
          with certificate from notary Block; witness: Hans
          Hanssen, father of the bridegroom.

Translation

[132^V: "261"]

1663, December 2:

- Guiliam d'Honneur,
  to Christina Steentiens,
      with certificate "from the Manhatans".

1663, December 23:

- Jan de Neger [= the Negro],
  to Annetie Abrahams,
      with certificate "from the Manhatans".

1664, February 10:

- Jan Pieterszen, "y[oung] m[an] from Amsterd[am]",
  to Stijntie Jans, "from Oetmarsum";
      witnesses: Annetie Pieters, grandmother of the
      bridegroom, Johannes Marcus, stepfather of the bride,
      Esje Hendricks, mother of the bride.

1664, May 4:

- Willem Teller, widower of Maggariet,
  to Maria Verleth, widow of Paulus Schrick,
      with certificates "from the Manhatans and Fort Orangien".

1664, June 2:

- Meijnard Jorneij, "y[oung] m[an] from Mardyck near Duynckercke",
  to Lijsbeth du Mon, "m[aiden] from Middelborg",
      with certificate "from the Manhatans".

1664, July 6:

- Ditmaer Janssen,
  to Gepien Pieters,
      with certificates "from the Manhatans".

1677, May 13:

- Poulus van der Beeck, "young man from Gowanis",
  to Sara Schouten, "maiden from Nieu Casteel".

1677, May 27:

- Jakop Jorissen, "young man [from] Amersvoort",
  to Elisabet Tommissen, "maiden from Nieuw Jorck";
      witnesses: Joris Jakopsen, father of the bridegroom,
      Tomis Lambersen, father of the bride.

Translation

[133^r: "262"]

1677, July 8:

- Jakop Hansen, "y[oung] m[an] from the Walebocht",
  to Elsjen Fredericks van der Kreeft, "maiden from the
      Manatas"; witnesses: Teunis Ghijsbertsen Bo[...]*,
      father of the bridegroom, Frederick Lu[...]*, f[ather]*
      of the bride.

1677, August 25:

- Jan Jakopsen Tolier, "y[oung] m[an] from Kernier in Walslant",
  to Mathaleen Louwerens, "m[aiden] from the Suijtrevier";
      witness: Jan Jakopsen, stepfather of the bride.

1677, November 11:

- Jan Mastingh, "y[oung] m[an]",
  to Geertje Franse, "m[aiden] from Amsterdam".

1680, September 5:

- Thomas Coeck, "y[oung] m[an] from N[ieuw] Jorck",
  to Harmtjen Dircks, "m[aiden] from Breukelen [and] living
      there".

1685, May 17:

- Pieter Jansen, "y[oung] m[an] from Bergen",
  to Elisabeth Sijmens van Uijthuijsen, "*[maid]en from
      Breukelen [and] living there"; witnesses: Jan Lubbersen,
      father *[of the bridegr]oom, *[.....]ansen Woertman,
      *[.....]ijt, guardians of the bride.

1685, May 26:

- Joris Kinbaer, "young man, born in Daffinsier in Weijmots in
      Engelant",
  to Maria Fentin, widow of Joseph Fentin, "born in Londen in
      Engelant".

1685, October 21:

- Jan Pietersen Mackelick, widower of Stijnje Jans, "born in
      Amsterdam",
  to Mrs. Hendrika Strockels, widow of Monsieur Michiel Hamel,
      "born in Deventer".

Translation

[134^r: "264"]

1685, November 22:

- Cornelis Rutsen van Brunt, "young man, born in Nieuw
  Uijttrecht [and] living there",
  to Trijntjen Adriaensen Bennet, "maiden, born in Nieuw
  Uijttrecht, living i[n]* Gowanes"; witness: Arie
  [.....]*, father of the bride.

1686, May 2:

- Corelis Pietersen, "y[oung] m[an] from Amerfoort",
  to Sara Katrijna Neesjes, "m[aiden] from Nieuw Jorck, living
  in Breuken"; witnesses: Jannitje Jans, stepmother of
  the bridegroom, Ariaenje Potters, mother of the bride,
  Jan Aertsen, stepfather of the bride.

1690, June 12:

- Jan Willem Bennit, widower of Aeltje Hendricksen,
  to Aeltje Wijnans, "maiden, born in the Walebocht, both
  living in Breukelen".

1690, November 22:

- Jakop Jansen Buijs, "young man from Vlackebos",
  and Merritje Jores, "maiden from the ferry", had their banns
  proclaimed; witness: Joris Jakopsen, her father, and
  also with consent of Jan Cornelissen Buijs, father of
  the bridegroom.

1691, January 3:

- Cornelis van Duijn, "young man, born in Nieu Amersvoort",
  and Machtelje Huyken, "maiden, also born in Nieuw Amersvoort",
  had their banns proclaimed, with consent of their
  parents: *[G]errit Cornelissen van Duijn, father of the
  bridegroom, *[...]ijntje van Duijn, his mother, Annije
  Huijke, mother of the bride.

1691, January 17:[3]

- Jan Dircksen Woertman, "young man, born under the jurisdiction
  of Breukelen",
  and Anna Marrija Andries, "also born under the jurisdiction of
  Breukelen", had their banns proclaimed, with consent, as
  far as I know, of Dirck Jansen Woertman, his father, and
  with consent of the stepfather of the bride and of
  Annitje Prara, her own mother.

Translation

[135^r: "266"]

1691, February 28:

- Samuel Berrij, "young man, born in Vlissingen",
  and Catalynje Martens, "maiden, born in Breuken",
        had their banns proclaimed, with consent, as far as
        I know, of Annitje Rappalje, mother of the bride.

1694, December 29:

- Teunis Dircksen Woertman, "young man, born near the ferry",
  and Katrijna Sprong, "maiden, born in Vlissingen",
        had their banns proclaimed, with consent of Dirck
        Jansen Woertman, father of the bridegroom.

1695, January 5:

- Jan Cornelissen van der Veer, "b[orn]* in Nieuw Amersvoort",
  and Femmitje [.....]* Bergen, "born in Betvoort", "young
        m[an and]* maiden, the bridegroom [.....]* and the
        bride in Breukelen", [had their banns]* proclaimed,
        with [consent .....]* and mother and br[.....]*.

1695, January 26:[4]

- Harmen Joorissen Joerissen[5], "young man, born near the ferry",
  and Neeltje Pietersen Staets, "maiden, born in Gowanes",
        had their banns proclaimed "in Breuhelen"; witness:
        Pieter Jansen Staets, father of the bride, and with
        consent of Joris Jakopsen, father of the bridegroom.

1695, July 27:[6]

- Joris Jeronimusen Rappaljee, "young man, born in the Wale-
        bocht",
  and Neeltje Janse Couwenoven, "born near the ferry",
        had their banns proclaimed, with consent of Jeronimus
        Rappalje, father of the bridegroom, and Jan Gerritse
        Couwenoven, father of the bride.

1695, August 2:

- Abram Pietersen Lot, "young man, born in the Flackebos",
  and Geertje Jans Dorlant, "maiden, born in Betvoort",
        had their banns proclaimed, with consent of the parents
        of the bridegroom and the bride.

1695, September 28:

- Jakop Cassou, "young man, born in Nieuw Jorck",
  and Anna Marij Johannes, "maiden, born in the Creupelbos",
        had their banns proclaimed.

Translation

[135^V: "267"]

1695, September 28 (continued):

  - Cornelis Jorissen, "young man, born near the ferry",
    and Annitje Staets, "maiden, *[b]orn in Gowanes",
        *[h]ad their *[ba]nns proclaimed, with consent
        [.....]* and Pieter Jansen, father of the bride,
        [.....]* Jakopsen.

[128^r: "252"]

1695, October 19:

  - Fijnsan Belli, "young man, born in Vrackrijck",
    and Macdeleentjen Jans, widow of the late Joost Kasperse,
        had their banns proclaimed; witnesses: Hendrick Jansen,
        her brother, and Michiel Palmentier.

1695, October 29:

  - Samuel Flipsen, "young man, born in Nieuw Engelant",
    and Aeltje Jans Damen, "maiden, born in Breukelen",
        had their banns proclaimed, with consent of the bride's
        father.

1695, November 9:

  - Willem Tornel, widower of Mijrija Davits, "born in Out
        Engelant",
    and Elisabeth Tijssen, widow of Anthoni Salm,
        had their banns proclaimed; witnesses: "I, Hendrick
        Slecht, and Elsje Barens".

1696, April 11:

  - Cornelis Slecht, "young man, born in the Vlackebos",
    and Johanna van de Water, "maiden, born in Nieuw Jorck, both
        living in Breukelen", had their banns proclaimed, with
        consent of the father and mother of each.

1696, June 6:

  - Jan Ariense Bennit, "young man, born in Niew Uijtrecht,
        living in Gowanes",
    and Femmitje de Rappalje, "maiden, born near the ferry,
        living in the Walebocht", had their banns proclaimed,
        with consent of Arien Bennit and Jeronimus de Rappalje,
        their parents.

REGISTER OF MEMBERS

of the

CONGREGATION OF BREUCKELEN

[* Brackets [] followed or preceded by an asterisk * mark
   passages which are illegible because of damage to the
   original manuscript.]

First List[1]

1663, March 25:

   1. Marten Reijerszen, "from Amsterdam", with an attestation
        "from Middelwout".
   2. Anneken Duurcoop, wife of Michael Zijperus, with an attest-
        ation "from the Manhatans".

1663, September 23:

   3. Pierre Parmentier, and
   4. Thonnet Terrin, [from] "Manheim au Palentinat Electoral",
        with an attestation "de la ville de Courtraij".
   5. Roelof Willemszen, [and]
   6. Willemken Tijssen, with an attestation "from Beverwijck".

1663, December 23:

   7. Cornelis van Bossum; witnesses: Jan Hijbon, Dirck Janszen.

   8. Geertie Gijsbert; witness: Grietie Jans.

   9. Jean Messural, [and]
  10. Jenne Carton, with an attestation "from Manheim".

1664, April 9:

   1. Meijnart Jorneij, with an attestation "from Manheim".

   2. Jacob Leendertssen, [and]
   3. Rebecca Fredricks, with an attestation "from Middelwout".

Translation

[138^r]

1664, April 9 (continued):

4. Albert Coninck, [and]
5. Tryntie Jans, with an attestation "from Middelwout".
6. Aert Teunissen Middag, "from Heijkoop"; witnesses: Teunis
   Gijsbertsen Boogaert, Jannet[ie]* Joris.
7. Janneken Jans, "from Almeloo"; witnesses: Paulus Dirckzen,
   Geertie Gijsberts.
8. Judith Joris, "from N[ieuw] Nederl[an]t"; witnesses: Catharina Joris, Theunis Gijsbertsen.
9. Janneken Montfoort, "from N[ieuw] Nederl[an]t"; witnesses:
   Sara de Plancke, Fijtie Dircks.
10. Anneken Rems, "from N[ieuw] Nederl[an]t"; witnesses: Janne-
    ken Joris, Catharina Jeronimus.
11. Neeltie Jans, "from N[ieuw] Nederl[an]t"; witnesses: Gerrit
    Crousen, Willem Gerritsen van Couwenhoven.

We, the undersigned, acknowledge that the afore-mentioned
people have been confirmed [as]* members of the congregation of
Breuckelen, both on the basis of attestations [and]* upon
confessions of the true and Reformed Faith. Done in the aforesaid place in our church meeting, July 23, 1664.

Henricus Selyns, Minister
in Breuckelen

Tunis Gijsbertsen Bogaert,
elder

Teunis Janssen

Translation

[139^r]

Second List of Members^2

[1677] March 12:

During the meeting of Domine Nieuwenhuijse with the consistory - Willem Willemsen and Tomis Lammersen, elders, and Merten Reijersen and Pieter Jansen, deacons - the following people were confirmed as members:

1. Jan Teunissen

2. Gerrit Klaessen

3. Hendrickje Jans, wife of Willem Joorissen

4. Stijnjen Gerrits

5. Lijsjen Jans

1677, June 11:

During the meeting of Domine Wilhelmus van Nieuwenhuijsen, minister, [with] the consistory of Breuckelen - Willem Willemsen and Tomis Lambertsen, elders, and Merten Reijersen and Pieter Jansen, deacons - the following persons were confirmed as members of the congregation of Breuckelen:

1. Hendrick Corssen

2. Aeltjen Jans, wife of Jan Frederiksen

3. Lijsbet Pietersen, wife of Willem Brouwer

4. Denijs Teunissen, young man

5. Hendrick Claessen, young man

1677, December 19:

During the meeti[ng]* of Domine Casparus van Suren with *[the con]sistory of Midwout, the following person was confirmed as a member:

1. Maria Willems Bennet

16[78]*, September 9:

In the presence of Domine van Suren and Teunis Ghijsbersen Bogaert, elder, the following persons were conf[irmed as * mem]bers:

1. Jakobus Beavois

2. Katrijn Beavois

3. Kornelia Beavois

Translation

[139^v]

1678, December 30:

In the presence of Domine van Suren and Teunis Ghijsbersen and Tomis Lammersen, elders, the following person was confirmed as a member:

1. Maria Joosten, wife of Jakobus Beauvois

1695, October 19:

In the presence of Domine Bertholf and the consistory of "Bruekelen", the following persons were confirmed as members:

1. Jakop van Doorn
2. Gerrit Middach
3. Jannitje van Nest
4.- Elisabeth Damen

1696, March 27:

In the presence of Domine Galiaem Bertholf and the consistory of Breuckelen, the following persons were confirmed as members:

1. Jan Woerman
2. Willem Bennit
3. Machtelt van Duijn
4. Neeltje Rappalje
5. Cornelis Slecht
6. Annitje Staets
7. Aeltje Bennit
8. Jakop Bennit
9. Joris Rappalje
10. Jeremijas Remse
11. IJsaack Remsen

1702, June:

In the presence of Daniel Rapalie [and]* Jores Hansen, Domine Deboois confirmed the following persons as members:

1. Jilles Provoost
2. Aeltie Roos

APPENDIX A

Two letters written by Domine Henricus Selijns

during his ministry in Breuckelen, 1660-1664

See the editor's introductory remarks on Selijns' letters, at
the beginning of this volume.

Original

First letter, dated October 4, 1660

Eerwaerdige, Wijse en Godtsalige Leeraren,

[Wij]* kunnen nochte ons selfs vergeeten, nochte oock aflat[en]*
*[on]se gemeente en kerckendienst UE: te communiceeren. Op zee
en wierde geen godtsdienst versuijmt: maer sochten dagh op dagh
door het gebedt, so 's morgens als 's savonts, godts geleijde en
bewaringe, en eijndigde eendrachtelijck met Psalmen de gebeeden.
Op sondagen en feestdagen geschiede bij beurten de verkondinge des
H. Euangeliums. Geen Sacramenten en sijn op het Schip bedient.
Geen siecken en sijn daer gevonden. Niet anders, als Godts genade
convoijeerde 't gantsche volck. Als wij in N. Nederlant arriveer-
de, sijn wij gehoort met den eersten op de Manhatans: maer de
Vredehandeling op de Esopus, daer wij oock waeren, en 't gemeene
Lants-beste stelde met reden onse bevordering dus lange uijt. Wij
preeckte onderwijls, so hier als op de Esopus en 't Fort Orangien,
en wierde in dese afwachtinge versorgt van Tafel en Logement.
Esopus ontbrack meer volcks: maer Breuckelen meer gelts; waer door
ick oock des Sondags, maer 's avonts, de Generaels Bouwerije op
kosten des E H d^r Generael bediene. Door de Achtb. H.H. Nicasius
de Sille, Fiscael, en Marten Kregiers, Burgerm., met oopen commissie des E H. d^r Generaels, geschiede de bevestinge in Breuckelen.
Op 't welcke ick wierde van Magistraet en Kerckenraet omhelst na
behooren; en d^o Polemius met den eersten oock soo bedanckt. Wij
preecken in geen kerck, maer korenschuur, en sullen te Winter door
Godts-Genade en gemeene hantreijckinge een kerck oprechten.
't Gehoor is tamentlijck. Uijt Middelwout, Nieuw Amersfort, en
dickwils 's Gravesande vermeert oock dit *[g]ehoor: maer 't meeste
van de Manhatans. Bij Breuckelen behoort oock het Veer, de Walebocht en Gujanes. Omtrent 2000 treeden is het Veer van Breuckelen,
maer 4000 *[v]oeten de Revier, ofte de Manhatans van 't Breu[cke-
*lensc]he Veer. 'k Vonde op Breuckelen 1 ouderling, 2 diaconen,
24 ledematen, 31 Huijsgesins, en 134 persoonen. De kerckenraet
sal bij provisie blijven alsse is. Men krijgt oock met ter tijdt
meer stoffe en kent oock de gemeente wat beter. Geen Catechisatien en kunnen voor de Winter geschieden, maer sullen ofte op
Werckdagen, ofte als men niet en preeckt op de Bouwerije, dit instellen. Het sal op kersdagen, paeschdagen, Pinxterdagen, en in
Septemb. 't bequaemste oock wesen het Avontmael des Heeren te houden, so heeft men op dese feestdagen 's daegs d'er aen de Danck-
predicatien. 'k Hadde op de Manhatans door de nabijgeleegentheijt
kunnen huijsvesten, maer mijn huijslieden bereijden gelijckerhant
een woonsteede. Van haer gewillicheyt en affectie en valt in geen
deele te klagen. Men preeckt dan 's morgens op Breuckelen, maer
na 't eijnde des Catechismi Predicatien van N. Amsterdam, op de
Bouwerije, dewelck een uytspanninge en 't vermaeck van de Manhatans is, Alwaer se uyt de Stadt om't Avontgebedt oock koomen.
Behalven de Huijslieden sijnder 40 Negers, wiens lants streecke de
Negers cust is. Hier is noch geen kerckenraet, maer de diaconen
van N. Amsterdam ontfangen bij provisie de aelmisse, en men sal

---

[* Brackets [] followed or preceded by an asterisk * mark
     passages which are illegible because of damage to the
     original manuscript.]

Translation

First letter, dated October 4, 1660

Reverend, Wise, and Godly Teachers,

[We]* can neither be forgetful, nor omit to inform you about our
congregation and church services. While at sea, the divine worship
was not neglected, but day after day, both in the morning and in
the evening, [we] sought God's guidance and protection through
prayer, and [we] concluded the prayers harmoniously with psalms. On
Sundays and feast-days, the preaching of the Holy Gospel was done
by turns.[1] No Sacraments were administered on board the ship. No
sick people were found there. Nothing but God's grace convoyed all
the people. Upon our arrival in New Netherland, we were immediately
received in Manhattan. However, the peace negotiations at the
Esopus, where we also were, and the general interest of the country
were good reasons for postponing our installation for a long time.
In the meantime, we preached, both here and at the Esopus and Fort
Orange, and during this time of waiting, we were provided with board
and lodging.[2] Esopus was lacking in people, Breuckelen, however,
in money; for this reason, I also serve the General's Bowery
[= farm] on Sundays (in the evening, that is), at the Hon. Lord
Director-General's expense. The installation in Breuckelen was
done by the Hon. Gentlemen Nicasius de Sille, Fiscal, and Marten
Kregiers, Burgomaster, with an open commission from the Hon. Lord
Director-General. Thereupon, I was duly embraced by the magistrates
and consistory; and Domine Polemius was equally duly thanked on the
first opportunity. We do not preach in a church but in a grain-
barn, and this winter we will erect a church through God's grace
and with the assistance of all people. The audience is fairly
large. Their number is increased by people from Midwout, New Amersfoort, and often Gravesend, but mostly by people from Manhattan.
The Ferry, the Wallabout, and Gowanus also belong to Breuckelen.
The Ferry is about 2000 paces from Breuckelen, but the river is
4000 feet [wide], which is the distance between Manhattan and the
Breuckelen Ferry. In Breuckelen I found 1 elder, 2 deacons,
24 members, 31 families, and 134 persons. The consistory will
remain as it is for the time being. As time goes on, we will have
more subjects for conversation[3] and we will know the congregation
somewhat better. It will not be possible to hold confirmation
classes before the winter, but [we] will institute them either on
working-days or when we will not be preaching at the Bowery. It
will be most suitable to administer the Lord's Supper on Christmas,
Easter, Whitsuntide, and in September, and on the day following
[each of] these feast-days we will preach a sermon of thanksgiving.
I could have taken up my residence in Manhattan in view of its prox-
imity, but my villagers are joining hands in preparing a dwelling
for me. I cannot complain by any means of their willingness and
affection. In the morning, I preach in Breuckelen, but after the
conclusion of the sermon on the catechism, in New Amsterdam at the
Bowery, which is the place for recreation and pleasure in Manhattan
where people from the town come for evening prayers as well.

[* Brackets [] followed or preceded by an asterisk * mark
passages which are illegible because of damage to the
original manuscript.]

Original

daer, so geen ouderling, immers diaken verkiesen. So syn dan
nevens mij in N. Neederlant D.D. Joannes Megapolensis en Samuel
Drisius in N. Amsterdam, D. Gideon Schaets op 't Fort Orangien,
D. Joannes Polemius te Middelwout en N. Amerfort, en D. Hermannus
Blom op de Esopus. Vorders niet anders, als ware danckbaerheijt
en schuldige erkentenis. UE: Eerwaerdigen, wijsen, en godtzaligen
leeraren in godts protectie en bescherminge onderwyls van herten
beveelende,

                                    Uwe Onderdanige
Uijt Amsterd. op de Manhatans
den 4 Octob. 1660.   Henricus Selijns, bedienaer
                                      des H. Euangeliums te
                                      Breuckelen.

Second letter, dated June 9, 1664

Seer Eerwaerdige, Godtsalige, en Hooggeleerde Broeders in Christo
Jesu,

Naer Christelijcke toewenschinge van Genade en Vrede dient den
Tegenwoordige, dat wij met behoorlijcke Subjectie de Vrijmoedig-
heyt sullen neemen om 't Aldereerwaerdighste Classis bekent te
maecken, so de Staet en welstant van de Kercke J. Christi, tot den
welcken Haer Eerw:^{e} mij beroepen hebben, als mijn Versoeck en
vriendelijckste bede tot favorabele ontslaginge.
Mij belangende, hadden Haer Eerw^e gesonden tot de Gemeijnte van
Breuckelen, om 't Euangelium daer te verkondigen en Sacramenten
te bedienen, 't geen wij gedaen hebben naer ons cleijn vermogen,
ende naer proportie van de Plaetse, met tamelijcke Winste van
Ledematen: want die seer weijnig waren met den beginne, sijn
omtrent geworden door Godts hulpe en genade Viermael so veel.
Maer vertrouwende, dat 't Haer Eerw:^{e} niet onaengenaem en Christi
Kercke seer profijtabel soude wesen, heeft 't ons licht gevallen,
dat seer moeijelijck was, om boven de bovengemelte Gemeijnte oock
waerteneemen de Gemeijnte van 's Generaels-Bouwerije; Welcke
Plaetsen van malkanderen door de tusschen-loopende Rivier gescheij-
den worden.
Dat wij Sochtens in de Durpe Breuckelen, en Savonts op de voorn.
Bouwerije preedicken, continueert, als wij te voren geschreeven
hebben: uijtgenoomen met de Bedieninge van 't Avontmael des Heeren,
want gelijckerwijs 's avonts 't Hooggemelte Avontmael te houden
bij Haer Eerw:^{e} niet gebruyckelyck is, dacht ons, naer Communicatie en rype Deliberatie van onse seer waerde Medebroeders van de
Gemeijnte tot Nieuw-Amsterdam, 't beste en Stichtelijckste te
wesen, om Sochtens daer te preecken voor die tydt, en 't Avontmael
na de Christelijcke gewoonte van ons Vaderlt te houden.

Translation

Besides the villagers, there are 40 negroes whose country of origin
is the Negro-Coast. There is no consistory here as yet, but the
deacons of New Amsterdam are receiving the alms for the time being,
and we will elect, if not an elder, at least a deacon. Besides
myself, there are in New Netherland the Domines Joannes Megapolensis
and Samuel Drisius in New Amsterdam, Domine Gideon Schaets at Fort
Orange, Domine Joannes Polemius in Midwout and New Amersfoort, and
Domine Hermannus Blom at the Esopus. [I have] nothing further [to
write] except [expressing my] sincere gratitude and respectful
acknowledgements. I heartily commend you, Reverend, wise, and godly
teachers, to God's protection and shelter, [and remain]

Yours obediently,

From Amsterdam in Manhattan,
October 4, 1660.
Henricus Selijns, Minister
of the Holy Gospel in
Breuckelen.

Second letter, dated June 9, 1664

Very Reverend, Godly, and Learned Brethren in Christ Jesus,

With Christian salutations of grace and peace, this [letter]
serves [to let you know] that with proper submission we will take
the liberty to inform the Most Reverend Classis of the condition and
well-being of the Church of Jesus Christ, to which Your Reverences
have called me, as well as of my request and very friendly petition
for an honorable dismissal.
As for me, Your Reverences had sent me to the congregation of
Breuckelen to preach the Gospel there and administer the Sacraments,
which we have done to the best of our limited ability and, in
proportion to the place, with a fair increase of members: whereas in
the beginning, their number was very small, it has [by now] increased, through God's help and grace, to about four times as many.
Trusting that it would not be displeasing to Your Reverences, and
very profitable to the Church of Christ, we found it easy - when it
was [in fact] very difficult - to serve, besides the afore-mentioned
congregation, the congregation of the General's Bowery as well.
These places are separated from one another by the river flowing
between them.
The situation whereby in the morning we preach in the village of
Breuckelen and in the evening at the aforesaid Bowery, is still
continuing as we described it to you before; with the exception of
the Lord's Supper, because as it is not customary among Your Reverences to administer the afore-mentioned Lord's Supper in the evening,
we deemed it best and most edifying, after consultations and careful deliberations with our very dear colleagues of the congregation
in New Amsterdam, to preach there in the morning before that time
and [then] to administer the Lord's Supper, in accordance with the
Christian custom of our fatherland.

Original

Ten aensien van den H. Doop wiert somtyts versocht bij de Negers,
dat wij haer kinders doopen souden, maer hebben 't ten deele ge-
weijgert door gebreck van kennisse en geloove, en ten deele door
't lichaemelijck en verkeert oogmerck van den Voorgemelte Negers,
die niet meerder gesocht hebben, als daer mede haer kinders te verlossen van lichaemelijcke Slavernije, Sonder te trachten na Godtsalicheyt en Christelijcke Deugden. Niettemin, 't welck betamelijck was, hebben naer ons vermogen veel moeijtens gedaen door Private en Publijcke Catechisatien, dat weijnig Vrucht bij de Oude,
die van geen begrijp syn, meer hoope gegeeven heeft van de Jonge,
welcke redelijckerwijse toegenoomen hebben. Ende dat sij niet toegelaten worden met den Voorn. reedenen tot den H. Doop, is oock
't gebruijck van den Voorn. Medebroederen.
Dit is 't Voornaemste, dat de Vader der Genade en Godt des Vredes
seer geseegent heeft na de rijckdom sijner Genade onser beijde Gemeente met ruste en Vrede, ende dat wij ten dien regarde geen
Stoffe gehadt hebben, om 't Aldereerwaerdigste Classis, die sulcks
ten goede neeme, met Gravamina te belasten, oft 't geen wij voorge-
noomen hadden, moeijelijck te vallen.
Middelerwijle, Seer verminderende onse Verbantjaren die wij aen de
E: Westindische Compagnie verbonden sijn, en Verbant altoos due-
rende die wij schuldig waren den geene die ons voortgebracht hebben, ende 't welcke natuurlyck is, gaerne sagen door de Hooge
Ouderdom, dat wij t'Huijs mochte coomen, dacht ons in de Vrese des
Heeren niet vreemt te wesen van kinderlijcke Subjectie, alles te
stellen buijten my, Gode te beveelen, ende volkomentlyck te laten
aen mijn Seer verlangende Ouders, om te blyven oft t'Huys te coomen naer Expiratie van verbintenisse.
Maer gelijck wij verstaen hebben, dat sij (neffens ons meest tot
mijn Wederkomst inclineerende) van de H.H. Bewinthebbers dimissie
ontfangen, en sulcks den E: Gedeputeerde ad Causas Indicas bekent
gemaeckt hebben, 't welck ons aengenaem was, Sullen niet minder
van Haer Eerw:^{e} vertrouwen, ende na Haer E: gewoonelijcke discretie
hoopen, als oock van Haer Eerw:^{e} te bekomen favorabel consent en
bewillinge.
Dat wij gedacht soude hebben, Haer Eerw:^{e} verbij te gaen ende
't alderminste misnoegen te geeven, zij verre: want hebbe door de
moeijelijckste dienst tot stichtinge van de Gemeijnte J. Christi
gesocht 't faveur van 't Aldereerwaerdigste Classis, en sijn oock
t'allentijden bereijt om haer Eerw^e ten dienste te wesen. Maer
ter contrarie, so wij t'huysquamen met expiratie van den voorgem.
Verbantjaren dien wy voldaen hebben, dachte aen Haer Eerw:^{e} mond-
eling Rapport te doen van onse dienst en Kercke, 't geen wij
Schuldig sijn en sullen doen; ende dat verseeckert sijn Haer Eerw:^{e},
't geen vergeeten is, door onweetentheijt geschiet te wesen.
D^O Samuel Megapolensis is behouden overgekoomen, maer D^O Warnerus
Hadson, die Haer Eerw:^{e} voor Predicant gesonden hadden na de
Suijdtrivier, is gestorven onderwegen. 't Soude nootsaeckelijck
wesen, zijn Plaetse te versien, ten deelen om de kinderen die
ongedoopt sijn sedert den doot van d^o Welij Sal^r, en ten deelen
door 't verfoeijende gevoelen van verscheijden Persoonen, die seer
smadelijck spreecken van de H. Schrifture.
Daerenboven, isser bij de Sweeden seecker Luthersche Predicant,
die geen Christelijck leeven leyt; mitsgaders seecker Persoon, die
den Lutherschen Preeckstoel voor 't Schoolmeesterschap verkoosen

Translation

As for the Holy Baptism, we were sometimes asked by the negroes to baptize their children, but we refused, partly because of their lack of knowledge and faith, and partly because of the material and wrong aim on the part of the afore-mentioned negroes who sought nothing else by it than the freeing of their children from material slavery, without pursuing piety and Christian virtues. Nevertheless, [we] have taken great trouble to the best of our ability, which was proper, through private and public catechizing, which bore little fruit among the old people, who do not understand, but gave more hope with regard to the young, who have improved reasonably well. And not admitting them to the Holy Baptism for the aforesaid reasons, is also the custom among our aforesaid colleagues.

The most important thing is, that the Father of Grace and God of the Peace has very much blessed both our congregations with calm and peace, in accordance with the richness of His grace, and that in that respect we have had no reason to burden the Most Reverend Classis - which should take this in good part - with serious problems, or to bother you with what we had in mind.

Meanwhile, since the years of our commitment to the Hon. West-India Company are quickly drawing to an end, and [since the other] commitment is continuing all the time, [namely] the one that we owe to those who brought us into this world and who in view of their old age would like us to come home, which is natural, [we] reflected upon these things in the fear of the Lord [realizing that] we were not lacking in feelings of filial obligation, [and I decided] to take the matter completely out of my own hands, to commend it to God, and to leave it entirely to my longing parents whether I should stay [here] or come home after the expiration of my contract.

But as we understand that they (who, like us, prefer my return) received [our] dismissal from the Lords Directors and informed the Hon. Deputies for Indian Affairs[4] thereof, which pleased us, [we] rely no less upon Your Reverences and hope to receive favorable consent and compliance also from Your Reverences, in accordance with your usual discretion.

That we might have intended to pass by Your Reverences and cause you even the slightest displeasure - far be it from us!; because through the very difficult service for the edification of the Church of Jesus Christ, [we] tried to win the favor of the Most Reverend Classis, and [we] are willing to serve Your Reverences at all times. On the contrary, upon my arrival at home after the expiration of the afore-mentioned years of the contract, which we have fulfilled, [we] intend to give Your Reverences a verbal account of our service and Church, which we owe you and which we will do. And you can be assured, Your Reverences, that whatever was forgotten, was done so through ignorance.

Domine Samuel Megapolensis arrived safely, but Domine Warnerus Hadson, whom Your Reverences had sent as a minister to the South River, died on the way. It is imperative to fill his place, partly in view of the children who have not been baptized since the death of the late Domine Welij, and partly because of the detestable sentiments of several persons who speak in a very insulting way of the Holy Scriptures.

In addition, there is among the Swedes a certain Lutheran minister, who is not leading a Christian life; as well as a certain person who has preferred the Lutheran pulpit to the office of

Original

heeft. Welcke buyten twijffel groote schade soude gedaen hebben
onder de Schapen, die dus lange sonder Herder Gedwaelt hebben,
ten ware den Voorgemelte Farheer niet en ware so onchristelijck
van leeven. Ende dat den Tweede, Christi kercke, tot geen af-
breuck sij, wil Godt verhoeden, ende Haer Eerw:^{e} met een geseegent
Instrument te voren koomen.
Met den bedroefde Staet van N. Nederlant, so ten aensien van de
Wilden, die sommige gedoot, sommige gequest, en sommige van de
onse gevangen, ja verscheijden Huysen verbrant hebben in de Esopus;
als voornamentlijck van de Engelsche, welcke verclaert hadden ons
Dorp met 't gantsche Lange Eylant voor den koning met 't Vliegende
Vaendel, heeft men van Julio laestleden den eerste Woensdag van de
Maent gehouden tot een Vast en Bededag, ten eynde om den Almachtigen seer ernstelijck te bewegen tot Vaderlycke ontferminge en mede-
dogentheijt. Maer alles heeft de goede Godt, die gepreesen zij,
gebracht ten besten met dit laeste Arrivement der Scheepen; de
Engelsche tot Stilte en Wilden tot Vrede: onse Weeclagen tot lof-
sangen, ende Maendelycke Vastdagen tot een dag van danckseginge,
die verleeden Woensdag tot besluijt der Voorgem Beêdagen gehouden
is. Godt zij danck, die de Oorloogen doet ophouden tot aen het
eijnde der Aerde, den Boge verbreeckt en spiese in tween slaet.
Ende Hiermede, Seer Eerwaerdige, Godtsalige en Hooggeleerde Broeders in Christo Jesu, zijt den Selfde Godt bevolen tot de Vol-
maeckinge der Heyligen ende opbouwinge des lichaem J. Christi.
Vale. Actum Breuckelen in N. Nederlt den 9 Jun. 1664.

Uwer Eerwaerdig.

Onderdanigste Broeder in Christo Jesu,

Henricus Selijns.

Translation

schoolmaster. This undoubtedly would have done great damage among
the sheep, who have wandered about for such a long time without a
shepherd, if the afore-mentioned [former] minister[5] had not been
leading such an un-Christian life![6] God forbid that the second
[minister] will do any damage to Christ's Church, and may Your
Reverences come forward with a blessed instrument.
    In view of the distressing condition of New Netherland - both
with regard to the savages who killed some people, wounded others,
took some of our people prisoner, and even burned down several
houses at the Esopus; and especially on account of the English who
with flying banners had claimed our village with all of Long Island
for the King - the first Wednesday of every month since last July
has been observed as a day of fasting and prayers in order to induce
the Almighty very urgently to [show] paternal pity and compassion.
However, the good God - praised be the Lord! - turned everything for
the best through the recent arrival of the ships: [He turned] the
English to silence, the savages to peace, our lamenting into hymns
of praise, and the monthly day of fasting into a day of thanksgiving,
which was held last Wednesday and which concluded the afore-
mentioned days of prayers. May God be thanked, who makes wars cease
to the end of the earth, breaks the bow, and smashes the spear in
two. And herewith, Very Reverend, Godly, and Learned Brethren in
Christ Jesus, be commended to the same God so that you will perfect
the saints and edify the body of Jesus Christ. Farewell. Done in
Breuckelen in New Netherland, June 9, 1664.

        Your Reverences'

                most obedient brother in Christ Jesus,

                    Henricus Selijns.

APPENDIX B

Explanatory List of Geographical Names

Mentioned in the Breuckelen Church Records

See the editor's introductory remarks on the List of Geographical
Names, at the beginning of this volume.

"Almeloo"
    = Almelo, The Netherlands (Prov. of Overijssel)

"Amerfoort" / "Amersvoort"
    = either: "Nieuw-Amersfoort"; or: Amersfoort, The Netherlands
      (Prov. of Utrecht)

"Amersvoort in Nieuw-Nederlant"
    = see "Nieuw-Amersfoort"

"Amstelredam"
    = see "Amsterdam"

"Amsterdam" / "Amsterd." / "Amst."
    = usually: Amsterdam, The Netherlands; in some cases: "Nieuw-
      Amsterdam"

"Amsterdam in Nieuw-Nederlant"
    = see "Nieuw-Amsterdam"

"Appeldoorn"
    = Apeldoorn, The Netherlands (Prov. of Gelderland)

"Arbou"
    = Åbo/Turku, Finland

"Arme Bouwerije" [Poor Bowery]
    = a farm run for the benefit of the poor, possibly not far
      from the "Creupelbos" (now in Brooklyn, N.Y.), in the
      direction of "Middelburg" (Newtown)

235

"Auspurg"
= Augsburg, Bavaria, West Germany

"Baston"
= Boston, Massachusetts

"Bergen"
= Bergen/Jersey City, New Jersey

"Betuwe"
= the southwestern part of the Province of Gelderland in the
Netherlands, the area between the Rhine and Waal Rivers

"Betvoort"
= Bedford on Long Island - now in Brooklyn, N.Y.

"Beverwijck" / "Beverwyck"
= Albany, N.Y.

"Blommendael"
= either: Bloemendaal, The Netherlands (Prov. of North
Holland, c. 12 miles west of Amsterdam); or: "Bloemendael",
an area west of Wallabout Bay (as shown in several
versions of Nicolaes Visscher's map of New Netherland,
e.g. the one of 1655) - now in Brooklyn, N.Y.

"Bocht" / "Bogt"
= see "Walebocht"

"Boschwijck" / "Boschwyck"
= see "Boswijck"

"Boswijck" / "Boswyck"
= Bushwick, Brooklyn, N.Y.

"Bowery"
= see "Generaels-Bouwerije"

"Brasiel" / "Brasilien" / "Braziel"
= Brazil

"Breuckelen" / "Breuckellen" / "Breuhelen" / "Breukelen" /
"Breuken" / "Brueckelen" [Brooklyn]
= the settlement in the northwest part of present-day
Brooklyn, N.Y., in the same area where now the Borough's
administrative and judicial centers are located

"Bunninck"
= Bunnik, The Netherlands (Prov. of Utrecht, c. 5 miles east
of the City of Utrecht)

"Campen"
= Kampen, The Netherlands (Prov. of Overijssel)

"Coppenhagen"
= Copenhagen, Denmark

"Courtraij"
= Kortrijk/Courtrai in Flanders, Belgium

"Couverden"
= Coevorden, The Netherlands (Prov. of Drenthe, c. 10 miles
southwest of Emmen)

"Creupelbos" / "Creupelbosch" / "Creupelb."
= The Dutch word "creupelbos" or "kreupelbos" (corrupted
into "cripplebush" in English) indicated thick or dense
growth by brushwood, shrubs, bushes, and/or small trees,
in short a thicket. The "Creupelbos" mentioned in the

Breuckelen Church Records was a thicket area with nearby
hamlet, southeast of Wallabout Bay - now in Brooklyn,
N.Y. - near the spot where Wallabout Creek crossed the
road to "Middelburg" (Newtown).

"Cujanes"
    = see "Gowanes"

"Culemborg" / "Culenborg" / "Culenburg"
    = Culemborg, The Netherlands (Prov. of Gelderland, c. 10
    miles southeast of the City of Utrecht)

"Daffinsier in Weijmots in Engelant"
    = literally: "Devonshire in Weymouth in England", which is
    rather puzzling as Devonshire is the county and Weymouth
    the town. "Weymouth in Devonshire" would have made only
    slightly more sense, however, since Weymouth is not located
    in Devonshire but in the adjacent County of Dorset.

"de Bocht" / "de Bogt"
    = see "Walebocht"

"de Nes"
    = see "Nes"

"den Haag" / "den Haeg"
    = 's-Gravenhage/The Hague, The Netherlands

"Deventer"
    = Deventer, The Netherlands (Prov. of Overijssel)

"Diemen"
    = Diemen, now part of Amsterdam, The Netherlands

"Diepe"
    = Dieppe, France

"Dordrecht" / "Dordregt"
    = Dordrecht, The Netherlands (Prov. of South Holland)

"Eck"
    = Eck, now part of the municipality of Eck en Wiel, The
    Netherlands (Prov. of Gelderland, c. 18 miles east-southeast
    of the City of Utrecht)

"Esopus" (river)
    = Esopus River, N.Y.

"Esopus" (settlement)
    = Kingston, N.Y.

"Ferry"
    = see "Veer"

"Flackebos"
    = see "Vlackebos"

"Fort Amsterdam" / "Fort Amsterdᵐ" / "Fort Amsterd."
    = the fort of "Nieuw-Amsterdam", at the southern tip of
    Manhattan

"Fort Orangien" [Fort Orange]
    = Albany, N.Y.

"Gardelupe" / "Gardulypen"
    = Guadeloupe in the Caribbean

"Generaels-Bouwerije" [the General's Bowery]
    = Director-General Petrus Stuijvesant's farm - now the
    Bowery, Manhattan, N.Y.

237

"Gowanes" / "Gowanis"
  = Gowanus, the hamlet around Gowanus Bay - now in Brooklyn,
    N.Y.

"Gravesande" / "Gravesant"
  = Gravesend, Brooklyn, N.Y.

"Groeningen"
  = Groningen, The Netherlands

"Gujanus"
  = see "Gowanes"

"Hamburg"
  = Hamburg, West Germany

"Heijkoop"
  = Heicop, now part of the municipality of Hei- en Boeicop,
    The Netherlands (Prov. of South Holland, c. 10 miles south
    of the City of Utrecht)

"Hertfort"
  = Hartford, Connecticut

"het Veer"
  = see "Veer"

"Holland" / "Hollant"
  = the 17th-century Province of Holland and West Friesland,
    roughly covering the area of the present-day Provinces
    of North Holland and South Holland

"Jamaïca" / "Jamaica"
  = Jamaica in the Caribbean. There was also a settlement
    called Jamaica on western Long Island, of course (now in
    Queens, N.Y.). However, the only occasion on which
    "Jamaica" occurs in the Breuckelen Church Records (pp. 79-
    81), the Caribbean island is meant. Cf. "Simmeko".

"Kernier in Walslant"
  = probably: Caernarvon in Wales, Great-Britain

"Kings Contij" / "Kings Conty"
  = Kings County, N.Y.

"Lange Eijlant" / "Lange Eylant"
  = Long Island, N.Y.

"Leijden"
  = Leiden/Leyden, The Netherlands (Prov. of South Holland)

"Londen"
  = London, England

"Maerseveen"
  = Maarsseveen, The Netherlands (Prov. of Utrecht, c. 4 miles
    north-northwest of the City of Utrecht)

"Manatas" / "Manhatans"
  = Manhattan, N.Y.

"Manheim"
  = Mannheim, West Germany

"Mardyck bij Duynckercke" [Mardyck near Dunkerque/Dunkirk]
  = The editor was not able to pinpoint "Mardyck". Obviously,
    it was located near Dunkirk in the northernmost part of
    France.

"Marrelbeeck"
    = Merelbeke in Flanders, Belgium, c. 5 miles south of
    Gent/Ghent

"Meulen" [mill]
    = The only mill known to have operated on the westernmost
    part of Long Island as early as the 1660's, was located
    near Gowanus Bay - now in Brooklyn, N.Y. According to
    Henry R. Stiles [History of the County of Kings and the
    City of Brooklyn, N.Y., from 1683 to 1884, 2 vols. (New
    York, 1884), I, 87], the mill was occupied jointly by
    Adam Brouwer and Isaac De Forrest.

"Middelborg"
    = either: "Middelburg" on Long Island - now Newtown, part
    of Queens, N.Y.; or: Middelburg, The Netherlands (Prov.
    of Zeeland)

"Middelwout" / "Midwout"
    = see "Vlackebos"

"mill"
    = see "Meulen"

"Mispadt"
    = Mespath, now part of Queens, N.Y.

"N. Amerfort" / "N: Amersvoort"
    = see "Nieuw-Amersfoort"

"N. Amsterdam" / "N. Amsterd."
    = see "Nieuw-Amsterdam"

"Negers cost" [Negro-Coast]
    = the Slave Coast on the Gulf of Guinea, West Africa

"Nes"
    = either: Nes on the Amstel River, The Netherlands (Prov.
    of North Holland, c. 7 miles south of Amsterdam); or: Nes,
    The Netherlands (Prov. of Friesland, c. 17 miles northeast
    of Leeuwarden); or: Nes, The Netherlands (Prov. of Fries-
    land, c. 10 miles south of Leeuwarden); or: Nes on the
    Island of Ameland, The Netherlands (Prov. of Friesland,
    c. 17 miles north of Leeuwarden)

"Neuten Eijlant" [Nut Island/Nuts Island]
    = Governor's Island, Upper Bay, New York City

"New ..."
    = All names beginning with "New ...": see "Nieuw-...".

"N. Haerlem"
    = see "Nieuw-Haerlem"

"Niekerck"
    = either: Niekerk, The Netherlands (Prov. of Groningen,
    c. 10 miles west of the City of Groningen); or: Niekerk,
    The Netherlands (Prov. of Groningen, c. 15 miles northwest
    of the City of Groningen)

"Nieu Amersvoort"
    = see "Nieuw-Amersfoort"

"Nieu Casteel"
    = Newcastle, Delaware

"Nieuw-Amersfoort" / "Nieuw Amersfort" / "Nieuw Amersvoort"
    [New Amersfoort]
    = Flatlands, Brooklyn, N.Y.

"Nieuw-Amsterdam" [New Amsterdam]
    = New York City (southern part of Manhattan)

"Nieuw Engelant" [New England]
    = the northeastern part of the United States

"Nieuw-Haerlem" [New Haarlem]
    = Harlem, New York City

"Nieuw-Jorck"
    = New York City (Manhattan)

"Nieuw-Nederlant" / "Nieuw-Nederl^t"
    = New Netherland

"Nieuw-Uijtrecht" / "Nieuw Uytrecht" / "Nieuw Wtrecht" /
    "Niew Uijtrecht"
    = New Utrecht, Brooklyn, N.Y.

"N. Jorck" / "N. Jorcke" / "N. Jork"
    = see "Nieuw-Jorck"

"N. Nederlant" / "N. Nederl^t" / "N. Nederl."
    = see "Nieuw-Nederlant"

"Nordingen"
    = probably: Nordlingen in Bavaria, West Germany

"Nut Island" / "Nuts Island"
    = see "Neuten Eijlant"

"N. Uytrecht" / "N. Uytregt"
    = see "Nieuw-Uijtrecht"

"Oetmarsum"
    = see "Ootmarsum"

"Oostvrieslant"
    = East Friesland, West Germany (the area around the North
    Sea port of Emden)

"Ootmarsum"
    = Ootmarsum, The Netherlands (Prov. of Overijssel, c. 10
    miles east-northeast of Almelo)

"Osch"
    = Oss, The Netherlands (Prov. of North Brabant)

"Out Engelant" [Old England]
    = England, Great-Britain

"Palentinat Electoral"
    = the Electoral Palatinate, also called Rhine Palatinate,
    Palatinate, or Pfalz, West Germany

"Poor Bowery"
    = see "Arme Bouwerije"

"Rheenen"
    = Rhenen, The Netherlands (Prov. of Utrecht, c. 15 miles
    west of Arnhem)

"'s Generaels-Bouwerije"
    = see "Generaels-Bouwerije"

"'s Gravesande"
    = see "Gravesande"

"S Hertoogenbosch"
   = 's-Hertogenbosch/Bois le Duc, The Netherlands (Prov. of
     North Brabant)

"Simmeko"
   = possibly: Jamaica, Queens, N.Y.

"South River"
   = see "Suijdtrivier"

"Staten Eijlandt" / "Staten Eijlant"
   = Staten Island, N.Y.

"Straicfort"
   = Stratford, Connecticut

"Suijdtrivier" / "Suijtrevier" [South River]
   = Delaware River

"'t Veer" / "tveer"
   = see "Veer"

"t Vlackebos" / "'t Vlackebosch"
   = see "Vlackebos"

"Uijtrecht" / "Utregt" / "Uytrecht" / "Uytregt"
   = either: "Nieuw-Uijtrecht"; or: Utrecht, The Netherlands

"Uijtrecht in Nieuw-Nederlant"
   = see "Nieuw-Uijtrecht"

"Veer" / "het Veer" / "'t Veer" [the Ferry]
   = the hamlet grouped around the landing of the ferry which
     linked New Amsterdam with Breuckelen and the other
     settlements on Long Island. The landing was located at
     the foot of present-day Fulton Street, Brooklyn, N.Y.

"Vlackebos" (also called "Midwout") / "Vlackebosch" /
   "Vlacke-bosch" / "Vlacke Bosch" / "Vlakbos"
   = Flatbush, Brooklyn, N.Y.

"Vlissingen" / "Vlissinge"
   = either: Vlissingen/Flushing, The Netherlands (Prov. of
     Zeeland); or: "Vlissingen" on Long Island - now Flushing,
     part of Queens, N.Y.

"Vrackrijck"
   = France

"Walebocht" / "Walebogt"
   = Wallabout, the hamlet around Wallabout Bay, now in
     Brooklyn, N.Y.

"Werckhoven"
   = Werkhoven, The Netherlands (Prov. of Utrecht, c. 8 miles
     southeast of the City of Utrecht)

"Wijnschoot" / "Wijnschoten" / "Wynschooten" / "Wynschoten"
   = Winschoten, The Netherlands (Prov. of Groningen, c. 20
     miles east of the City of Groningen)

NOTES

Notes to Dr. Hageman's Introduction

This brief presentation of Domine Henricus Selijns' Brooklyn days has drawn heavily from three sources:
- A. Eekhof, De Hervormde Kerk in Noord-Amerika (1624-1664), 2 vols. ('s-Gravenhage/The Hague, 1913), I, 186-222 - henceforth: Hervormde Kerk.
- Henry R. Stiles, A History of the City of Brooklyn, 3 vols. (Brooklyn, 1867-1870), I, 127-151 - henceforth: History of Brooklyn.
- History of the First Reformed Protestant Dutch Church of Breuckelen, 1654 to 1896, compiled by order of the Consistory [by Henry Whittemore] (Brooklyn, 1896), 9-16. For a recent outline of the early history of the Reformed Church in all the Dutch communities on western Long Island, see
- Gerald F. De Jong, 'The Founding of the Dutch Reformed Church on Long Island', in: De Halve Maen, Quarterly Magazine of The Dutch Colonial Period in America (published by The Holland Society of New York), vol. LIV, no. 2 (New York, Summer 1979), 1-3, 12-13, 17.

1. Stiles, History of Brooklyn, I, 129

2. ibid., I, 131-132

3. Eekhof, Hervormde Kerk, I, 205-206

4. ibid., I, 211

5. cf. this volume, pp. 3 and 227

6. ibid., 3-13

7. ibid., 227

8. ibid., 212

9. ibid., 91-93

10. Letter from the Church of New York City to the Classis of Amsterdam, February 25, 1681, in: Rev. Edward T. Corwin, editor, and Hugh Hastings, supervisor, Ecclesiastical Records, State of New York, 7 vols. (Albany, 1901-1916), II, 761.

Notes to the Protocol, pages 1-107

See also the editor's introductory remarks on the Protocol, at the beginning of this volume, and the List of Geographical Names in Appendix B, pp. 235-241.

1. "Lords Directors": the Directors of the Amsterdam Chamber of the Dutch West India Company, who were the immediate superiors

NOTES TO PAGES 5-13

of Director-General Petrus Stuijvesant.

2. cf. Corwin's translation of this passage in vol. I, 479-481 of: Rev. Edward T. Corwin, editor, and Hugh Hastings, supervisor, Ecclesiastical Records, State of New York, 7 vols. (Albany, 1901-1916) - henceforth: Ecclesiastical Records.

3. "there": Selijns' destination, i.e. Breuckelen

4. "ordinary": nonclerical

5. "p.t." = "pro tempore", which means "for the time being".

6. "Deputies for Indian Affairs": The "Deputati ad Causas Indicas" were a kind of permanent executive committee delegated by the Amsterdam Classis of the Dutch Reformed Church. Since 1636, there were four "Deputati". They took care of all Church-related affairs in the many colonies settled around the world under the supervision of the Dutch East India and West India Companies. The "Deputati" corresponded with the ministers overseas, held meetings, and acted in close cooperation with the Executive Boards of Directors of the commercial Companies. They were also known as "Deputati ad Res Externas" (Deputies for Foreign Affairs) or "Deputati ad Res Maritimas" (Deputies for Maritime Affairs). [cf. vol. I, 8-9, of: A. Eekhof, De Hervormde Kerk in Noord-Amerika (1624-1664), 2 vols. ('s-Gravenhage/The Hague, 1913) - henceforth: Hervormde Kerk. See also Ecclesiastical Records, I, 19-20.]

7. "here": in Amsterdam

8. The Dutch text of Selijns' call was also published by Eekhof [Hervormde Kerk, I, 208-210], who transcribed the original letter in the New York State Library in Albany [New York Colonial Manuscripts, vol. XIII, 69ff.]. In the Protocol of the Breuckelen Church Records, Selijns wrote a copy of his letter-of-call - verbatim, but in his own spelling; he skipped a handful of unimportant words. The translation published by Corwin in Ecclesiastical Records, I, 466-468, was probably made from the letter preserved in Albany.

9. cf. Ecclesiastical Records, I, 468

10. cf. Corwin's translation of this passage in Ecclesiastical Records, I, 472

11. "grace": This is one of four words that are only partially legible in this portion of the original text, owing to damage to the paper (see the passages marked by an asterisk on p. 10). Three of the four gaps can easily be filled in; the fourth one, "grace", is based upon the translator's assumption that Selijns wrote "genaede" (only the "g" is legible). Unfortunately, Corwin [Ecclesiastical Records, I, 481] made some basic errors in his translation of this sentence, as a consequence of which his interpretation of the mutilated part cannot be ascertained.

12. cf. Corwin's translation of this passage in Ecclesiastical Records, I, 481-482

13. "so that Moses and Aaron would stand together" (in Selijns' words: "opdat Moses en Aäron mochten t'samen gaen"): a somewhat cryptic remark which is explained, however, in the very next sentence. The congregation assumed that cooperation between clerical and nonclerical authorities would advance the construction of a house for the new minister.

14. In the original volume, this passage is followed by a small slip of paper attached to the bottom of the page with a pin. It records the purchase of tobacco by "Frederijck Flijpsen" (Frederick Philipsen) in May, 1663. The editor has included the transaction in the Financial Records, p. 191.

15. cf. Corwin's translation of this passage in Ecclesiastical Records, I, 482. This is not the first instance where Corwin and/or his transcribers seem to have had some trouble reading names in the original documents (see also the passages referred to in notes 8, 9, 10, and 12). In this case, however, the errors are so grave - virtually every name on the list was misread - that as for the September 12, 1660, entry at least, Corwin must have relied on someone else's transcriptions. Corwin was a much too experienced and careful scholar to commit inaccuracies of this magnitude himself (cf. also his translation of the introductory sentences of this entry!).

16. "unruly": Selijns wrote "ongerelge", a slip of the pen; he probably meant "ongereegelde" (cf. p. 94, 9th and 10th lines).

17. "Gld. 101-0": Obviously, this should be "Gld. 201-0" (cf. the Accounts, p. 167).

18. "Claertie de Mof": In the Dutch language, "mof" is a disparaging term for a German. The derogatory meaning of the word dates from as early as the 16th century. For a moment, the translator was tempted to write "Claertie the Kraut", but, needless to say, that would have been very anachronistic.

19. "Michiel Tades": This makes no sense. Obviously, Selijns committed an error here; he should have written "Evert Duijcking". (See also the first episode of this story, recorded in the August 7, 1661, entry, p. 25.)

20. "ex officio": a somewhat ambiguous term. Usually, "ex officio" means "officially" or "by virtue of office" (e.g. on p. 39), in some cases, however, "unofficially", "off the record", etc. From the context it appears that in this passage, "ex officio" has the latter meaning.

21. "the town": New Amsterdam

22. "handball and other ball games": Stuijvesant wrote "kaetsen, Balslaen". We do not know which specific ball games are indicated here. Sometimes, "balslaen" is translated as "tennis", but that seems far-fetched and anachronistic to the editor.

23. cf. Corwin's translation of this passage in Ecclesiastical Records, I, 516-518

24. "he": Selijns

25. "we": Selijns (with Wilhelmus Bredebend)

26. "him": Gerrit Croesen (also spelled "Crousen" by Selijns). Apparently, Croesen became so enraged when Selijns and Bredebend discreetly questioned him about the rumors in Breuckelen, that he held the minister responsible for the accusations and filed a libel suit against him. Selijns' indignation at having been cited in a secular court is evident from the fact that the Croesen affair covers no less than ten full pages in the original Protocol (18^V through 23^r, "Pag. 35" through "Pag. 44" = pp. 36 through 47 of this volume).

27. "ex officio": "officially", "by virtue of our office" (cf. note 20)

28. "he": Selijns

29. "we": Selijns (with Bredenbend)

30. "him": Gerrit Crousen; cf. note 26

31. "at half the offspring" (orig. ms.: "op Halve aanteelinge"): The half-the-offspring clause of a cow-lease implied that if the cow produced two or more calves during the term of the contract, the offspring would be divided among the lessor and the lessee (in this case, the Breuckelen consistory and Carel d'Beauvois respectively).

32. "schepels": A "schepel" was an old Dutch unit of dry measure; 1 schepel = approximately ¾ bushel.

33. "previous marriages": As is evident from several entries in this volume (e.g. pp. 81, 195, and 197), Teuntie Straetsmans was married four times: to Jan Meijring, Georg Haff, Tieneman Jacobsen, and Gabriel Corbesij.

34. "els": An "el" was an old Dutch measure of length; 1 el = 0.69 meter. (The Dutch "el" was considerably shorter than the old English "ell" which measured 45 inches = 1.14 meter.)

35. "vims": A "vim" was an old Dutch grain measure; 1 vim = 100 to 104 sheaves of grain.

36. "morgens": A "morgen" was an old Dutch land measure; 1 morgen = 2.116 acres.

37. Selijns omitted to fill in the purchase price.

38. "at half the offspring": see note 31

39. "Instead of that": Selijns wrote "Contra". Under this heading, he indicated that there was a discrepancy between the expected surplus (as calculated by subtracting the expenditures from the receipts) and the actual contents of the treasury, which turned out to be higher.

40. "nominally": As it appears from this entry, the actual value of silver money was almost 2½ times as high as the denominations printed upon the coins.

41. "And in case some people take a pride in this": Stuijvesant wrote "en of eenige haer des mochten beroemen". What he meant by this, is evident from the rest of the sentence: apparently, there were people who took unwarranted pride in the fact that so far, they had remained immune from the contagious smallpox, and who expected their privileged position to continue.

42. "at half the offspring": see note 31

43. "els": see note 34

44. "osnaburg" (orig. ms.: "osenbrugs"): "Osenbrug" is a corruption of "Osnaburg" or "Osnabrück", the name not only of a German town but also of a durable fabric developed there; the plainly woven osnaburg was originally made of flax, later of cotton.

45. Selijns omitted to fill in the value of the blue linen.

46. Here, too, the value of the blue linen is not recorded (cf. the preceding note).

47. "Total: Gld. 350-5-8": This total is incorrect; it should be Gld. 350-15-8.

48. Selijns did not register the value of the hog.

49. "schepels": see note 32

50. "there": at the Cowanus

51. cf. Berthold Fernow's translation of this passage in vol. XIII, 383-384, of: Documents Relative to the Colonial History of the State of New York, 15 vols. (Albany, 1856-1887) - henceforth: NYCD. Corwin [Ecclesiastical Records, I, 547] copied Fernow's translation.

52. "they": the deacons, on behalf of the orphans

53. "Lords Directors": see note 1

54. "Lords Directors": ibid.

55. "M.D.": Actually, Selijns wrote "Medinæ doct^r", which should have been "Medicinæ doct^r".

56. cf. Fernow's translation of this passage in NYCD, XIV, 550-551. Corwin [Ecclesiastical Records, I, 551] copied Fernow verbatim, but corrected the spelling of the name of the first minister mentioned in Selijns' letter, Triglandius (Fernow read "Tuglandius").

57. "Lords Directors": see note 1

58. "Bowery": Director-General Petrus Stuijvesant's farm

59. "Lords Directors": see note 1

60. "Postil": A "postil" is a book of sermons on the Gospel or Epistle for every day of the year, to be read in the church service.

61. "the following Register of Members": Unfortunately, no other names of members confirmed in the years 1665-1675 have been preserved. The First List of Members published in this volume (pp. 221-222) ends in 1664; the earliest entry in the Second List (pp. 223-224) dates from 1676.

62. "our Christian congregations": Breuckelen, Midwout, and New Amersfoort, left without a minister since Domine Polhemius' death on June 8, 1676 (cf. p. 156). See also Domine Van Nieuwen-huijsen's letter to the Classis of Amsterdam, dated July 27, 1676 (second, identical copy: August 29, 1676), published by Corwin in Ecclesiastical Records, I, 688-689.

63. In the original manuscript, some space was left open to fill in Domine Nieuwenhuijse's first name (Wilhelmus); this was never done, however.

64. For an excellent discussion of the origin of the Coetus and the first lamentable years of its existence (1747-1771), see pp. 104-121 of: Rev. Edward T. Corwin, A Manual of the Reformed Church in America, 1628-1902, fourth edition (New York, 1902) - henceforth: Manual.

65. The entries written in the years 1750-1752, probably by Domine Ulpianus van Sinderen, are extremely hard to read. Although the editor managed to "decipher" almost all of the text, some words remained illegible. As for this passage, the missing word looks like "gewightige" = "important", but that would hardly

make sense within the context of the entry. On the contrary,
"unimportant" or "invalid" would fit much better: "The assembly
decided that there were no valid reasons to do so [viz. raising
objections against the newly elected elder and deacon], and that
this elder ... and deacon ... would be confirmed ... .

66. "Wednesday, September 5, 1751": a slip of the pen; the
date should be either "Thursday, September 5, 1751" or "Wednesday,
September 4, 1751".

67. "Arundeus' meddling": cf. Corwin's Manual, 299. On September 27, 1748, the Van Sinderen faction in the five villages of
Kings County submitted an official complaint to the Coetus, listing
numerous charges against Arundeus [Ecclesiastical Records, IV,
3029-3031]. Vols. IV and V of the Ecclesiastical Records include
a large number of documents from the period 1748-1754 illustrating
the endless bickering between the Coetus, Van Sinderen, and
Arundeus. Henry R. Stiles deals briefly with the Arundeus affair
in: A History of the City of Brooklyn, 3 vols. (Brooklyn, 1867-
1870), I, 184. See also notes 68, 71, and 72.

68. The Acts of the Coetus, held in New York, October 16-23,
1751, as well as other documents relating thereto, were published
by Corwin in Ecclesiastical Records, V, 3186-3196.

69. This line, scribbled at the bottom of the page, is virtually
illegible; only the first two words, "dog de" (however, the), are
clearly written. Possibly, the sentence runs as follows: "dog de
... tydt heeft geleert dat het niet geschiet is", which means:
"However, ... time has shown that it has not happened" - in other
words, the delegates eventually failed to settle the differences.

70. "they": the delegates

71. The Acts of the Coetus, held in New York, April 14-16, 1752,
were published by Corwin in Ecclesiastical Records, V, 3234-3236.

72. The judgement against Domine Arundeus, rendered by the
Classis of Amsterdam on January 12, 1751, was published by Corwin
in Ecclesiastical Records, V, 3149-3150.

Notes to the Baptismal Register, pages 109-164

1. See the editor's introductory remarks on the four Lists
of Baptisms, at the beginning of this volume, and the List of
Geographical Names in Appendix B, pp. 235-241.

2. "1678, June 31": Obviously, this should either be "July 1"
or "June 30".

3. In the original manuscript, both couples attending Rem's
christening are registered as "ouders" (parents). The editor
assumes that the second couple, Jan Aertsen van de Bilt and
Jannitje Remsen, were in fact witnesses.

4. For inexplicable reasons, this baptism was registered twice.
Notice the slightly different spelling of the mother's name in the
second entry.

5. In the original manuscript, both couples attending Neeltje's
christening are registered as "ouders" (parents). The editor

NOTES TO PAGES 134-164

assumes that the second couple, Folkert Hendricksen and Annitje
Para, were in fact witnesses.

6. Apparently, this baptism concerns an adopted or foster
child. The name "Jan Evertse Bout" implies that Jan's father was
called Evert, of the Bout family. Jan Woertman, therefore, cannot
have been the child's natural father. Jan Woertman and Anna Marij
married January 17, 1690 (cf. p. 217) and had two sons (Andries
and Dirck - cf. pp. 130 and 133) before adopting Jan.

7. In the original manuscript, Hendrikus Frees and Marijtj
Frees were initially listed as "ouders" (parents), but in the same
handwriting this was changed to "getuijge" (witnesses).

8. In the original manuscript, both couples attending Annitje's
christening are registered as "ouders" (parents). The editor
assumes that the second couple, Jeronumus and Annitje Rappalje,
were in fact witnesses.

9. In the original manuscript, the three baptisms on October 18,
1696, are followed by one on "15 november 1697", three on "13 desember 1697", and three on "27 desember 1697". Then follow the baptisms on February 21, 1697, March 19, 1697, etc. Obviously, the
November and December entries mentioned above should be dated 1696.

10. In the original manuscript, this entry ("den 9. Maart")
actually follows the one dated April 5 and precedes the baptism on
May 24. The possibility of a slip of the pen here should not be
excluded: the baptism dated March 9, 1708, may very well have taken
place on May 9. A mere imperfection in the chronology of the
Baptismal Register is not enough to be suspicious of the date of
an entry. The chronology of the baptisms registered in the first
half of 1709, for instance, is a complete mess (see pp. 69^V and
70^r [= "135" and "136"] of the original volume). In that case,
however, there is no doubt as to the accuracy of the dates since
the registrar created some order in the chaos by means of insertion
marks, brackets, and parentheses. Such marks are lacking in the
1708 entries, written by the same registrar.

11. see note 1

12. see note 1

13. "W. Lupardus": Domine Wilhelmus Lupardus. See the editor's
list of ministers mentioned in the Breuckelen Church Records, at
the beginning of this volume.

14. see note 1

15. "1719, May 18": In the original volume, the Fourth List
of Baptisms is dated "17019", which the editor interprets as 1719.

Notes to the Financial Records, pages 165-191

Please note that, in order to keep the number of notes limited,
unusual words occurring more than once were given the same note-
number throughout the Financial Records. See also the editor's
introductory remarks on the Accounts of the Deaconry and other
financial records, at the beginning of this volume, and the List
of Geographical Names in Appendix B, pp. 235-241.

NOTES TO PAGES 166-176

See the editor's remark at the bottom of p. 249.

1. In the original manuscript, part of the left margin of this page (105^v) is torn off, as a consequence of which four dates are missing.

2. "in the Creupelbosch" (orig. ms.: "in't Creupelbosch"): cf. Appendix B.

3. In the original manuscript, the next four lines in the left column of the page as well as the three lines juxtaposed in the right column, were crossed out, probably by Selijns himself.

4. "piece of eight" (orig. ms.: "Stuck van Achten"): A "stuck van achten", also called "reael van achten" (real of eight), was an old Spanish silver coin, more universally known as "peso"; the value of a "peso" equalled 8 "reals".

5. "els": An "el" was an old Dutch measure of length; 1 el = 0.69 meter. (The Dutch "el" was considerably shorter than the old English "ell" which measured 45 inches = 1.14 meter.)

6. "dozen-cloth" (orig. ms.: "dosijnties laecken"): "Dosijnties laecken" was a kind of coarse kersey (see note 19), woven in England in pieces of approximately 12 yards.

7. "schepel": A "schepel" was an old Dutch unit of dry measure; 1 schepel = approximately ¼ bushel.

8. "Mr.": "Mr." or "Meester" was a title indicating a schoolmaster or someone with a university degree, e.g. in Law or Medicine (cf. p. 181: "Mr. Harmen, surgeon").

9. "half-ducatoon" (orig. ms.: "Halve ducaton"): A "ducaton" or "dukaton" was a silver coin. At the time of this entry (1662), two kinds of "ducatons" were circulating in the Dutch Republic and its colonies: those minted in the Spanish Netherlands and the "ducatons" made in Holland since 1659. The former were worth 60 stuivers (= Gld. 3), the latter 63 stuivers (= Gld. 3-3). The nominal value of a "halve ducaton", therefore, was 30 or 31½ stuivers. Apparently, its actual value in New Netherland (Gld. 4 = 80 stuivers) was more than 2½ times as high. (See also note 16.)

10. "serge": Selijns wrote "chargie"; in the Orphan Records, he spelled the word "sargie" and "sarge" (see p. 200). In spite of its relatively high price, "sarge" or "serge", a woolen fabric still manufactured today, was popular with the poorer classes because of its excellent durability. As it appears from the Orphan Records (p. 201), the serge purchased for Laurens Haf was used to make several articles of clothing.

11. "Gld. 782-17-8": Selijns made an error here; the total should be Gld. 782-14-8.

12. "money for driving": Selijns wrote "Ryggelt", which probably means: the cost of having grain transported in carts.

13. "a half[-year of] service": Selijns wrote "een ½ dienst", which literally means "half a service"; cf. pp. 171 and 181, however.

14. "Instead of that": Selijns wrote "Contra". Under this heading, he indicated that there was a discrepancy between the expected surplus (as calculated by subtracting the expenditures from the receipts) and the actual contents of the treasury, which turned out to be higher.

15. "sewan" (orig. ms.: "seewant"): "Sewan", "seewant" or "zeewant" - also called "wampum" or "wampun" - were tube-shaped beads manufactured by Indians from shells that were found along the coast of Long Island. Strands of sewan were a popular medium of exchange, not only among the Indians and in their trade with the colonists, but also among the colonists themselves owing to a shortage in the conventional currencies. The Dutch soon took control of the highly important sewan industry. It is likely that they ran their own sewan factory on Long Island, employing Indian workers. Gradually, the Long Island shell beads were replaced by glass beads, imported in large quantities from Europe. The oldest glass beads were purchased in Venice; since the beginning of the 17th century, they were manufactured in Amsterdam. [The editor was one of the fortunate people attending the recent symposium "New Netherland Studies", held in Amsterdam on February 7 and 8, 1983. He is very grateful to the scholars Jan Baart, Charles F. Wray, and Karlis Karklins, on whose lectures part of this footnote is based.]

16. "nominally": As it appears from this entry, the actual value of silver money was almost 2½ times as high as the denominations printed upon the coins. (See also note 9.)

17. "small beer" (orig. ms.: "kleijn bier"): "Kleijn bier" or "cleijn bier", as distinct from "goet bier" (good beer), was an inferior, weak kind of beer, cheaper than the other brands.

18. "2¾ els": Judging from the purchase price (Gld. 17-5) and the price per el (Gld. 6), the quantity of kersey bought should actually have been 2 7/8 els. Selijns seems to have had some doubts himself when he recorded the purchase. Originally, he probably wrote "2 5/8 ellen", which he changed into "2¾ ellen". See also note 5.

19. "kersey" (orig. ms.: "Carzaij"): "Carzaij", "carsay" or "carsey" = kersey, a kind of coarse narrow cloth, woven from long wool and usually ribbed.

20. "duffel": a kind of thick, coarse woolen cloth, named after Duffel near Antwerp where it was first developed.

21. "osnaburg" (orig. ms.: "osenburgs"): "Osenburg" is a corruption of "Osnaburg" or "Osnabrück", the name not only of a German town but also of a durable fabric developed there; the plainly woven osnaburg was originally made of flax, later of cotton.

22. "misfortune": Selijns wrote "ongeluck", which means either "accident" or "misfortune". The editor prefers the latter, less specific term since we do not know what actually happened to Jan Martijn, except that whatever it was, it must have occurred shortly before this entry, dated May 12, 1663: on April 18, nothing seems to have been wrong when Jan adopted Annetie Prae (see pp. 69 and 197-199 of this volume). On September 16 of the same year, his widow Fijtie Dircks married Pieter Lambertsen de Heest (see p. 214). Their first child, Sara, baptized February 17, 1664 (see p. 114), must have been conceived at about the time of this entry.

23. Selijns omitted to fill in the value of the osnaburg linen given to Hendrick Martense van Coppenhagen.

24. Selijns wrote "5 1/8 osenbrugs linnen"; obviously, he meant "5 1/8 ellen osenbrugs linnen". See also note 5.

25. Again, Selijns failed to record the value of the linen (cf. note 23).

26. This entry, recording the sale of tobacco to Fredrick Philipsen in May 1663, was registered on the wrong page in the original volume. Selijns wrote it down at the bottom of 112^r, a page reserved for expenditures. He probably did so because on the opposite, correct page, 111^v, there was not enough space to insert the tobacco transaction. It appears from p. 112^v (p. 180 of this volume), that the deaconry did not get its money from Philipsen until November 1, 1663. See also p. 191.

27. "at half the offspring" (orig. ms.: "op halve aanteelinge"): The half-the-offspring clause of a cow-lease implied that if the cow produced two or more calves during the term of the contract, the offspring would be divided among the lessor and the lessee (in this case, the Breuckelen consistory and Carel d'Beauvois respectively).

28. "deuvekater", more commonly spelled "duivekater": a kind of pastry traditionally eaten in the Christmas season and around New Year. During these holidays, it was customary to give "duivekaters" to servants, housemaids, etc. The origin of the name - literally: "devil's cat" - is quite interesting. It seems that the earliest function of "duivekaters" was to replace sacrificial animals. This explains their rather unconventional shapes: they were baked in such a way that they resembled a joint, shank, or other part of an animal's anatomy, sometimes even an entire animal. Since cats had often been used for offerings, the name "duivekaters" reminded people of the origin of the pastry. The first part of the word, "duivel" (devil), added an element of sorcery to its meaning.

29. "surgeon" (orig. ms.: "chirurgyn"): A "chirurgyn" or "chirurgijn" was a physician whose license to practice medicine restricted him to certain activities. Many "chirurgijns" served on ships or in rural areas. The qualifications of a "chirurgijn" were considerably lower than those of a "medicinae doctor".

30. "Teunis": In the original manuscript, Selijns left open some space to fill in the family name, which he never did. He probably referred to Teunis Janssen Coevors.

31. "paid Nov. 1, 1665" (orig. ms.: "betaelt den 1 novem 1665"): These words were added to Selijns' notes in a different handwriting.

32. "[Gld.] 183-1": Selijns made an error here; the total should be Gld. 188.

33. "Gld. 176-12": This total, too, is incorrect; it should be Gld. 183-12.

34. "Received": Originally, Selijns wrote "Biddag, ontfangen" (Day of prayer, received), but he scratched out "Biddag".

35. In the original manuscript, the next three lines in the left column of the page as well as the four lines juxtaposed in the right column, were crossed out, probably by Selijns himself.

36. In the original manuscript, this entry, signed by Teunis Janssen, was crossed out.

37. "misfortune": Selijns, who drew up this statement by Pieter Lambertsen de Heest, wrote "ongeluck"; see note 22.

NOTES TO PAGES 187-191

38. There is no signature under this entry.

39. See the editor's introductory remarks on Henrick Jansen van de Vin's account, at the beginning of this volume.

40. "plets": a corruption of the English word "plaid" or "plaids". "Plets" was a coarse woolen fabric, originally woven in Scotland, later also in the Dutch Republic.

41. "2 one-vaen jugs": The "vaen" was an old Dutch unit of capacity; 1 vaen = approximately 4 liters, somewhat more than an American gallon.

42. "oxhooft": The "oxhooft" or "oxhoofd" was an old Dutch unit of capacity; 1 oxhooft = approximately 220 liters, somewhat more than 58 American gallons. (The English "hoxhead" was a bigger liquid measure than the Dutch "oxhooft"; it equalled 52.5 imperial gallons = 238.5 liters.)

43. Van de Vin omitted to fill in the prices of yellow and white peas respectively. Please note that this is the final entry on the Credit-side of the account; the Debit-side (pp. 188, 190) is twice as long.

44. In this entry, too, Van de Vin failed to fill in the prices of white and yellow peas respectively (cf. p. 189). See also his closing remark at the bottom of the account (p. 190).

45. The text is mutilated here due to the fact that along this line the account fell apart in two pieces. The two missing entries could partly be reconstructed.

46. Van de Vin did not fill in the final total.

47. The last digit of the year is missing. However, Van de Vin must have filed his detailed account after Teuntie Straetsmans' death on October 19, 1662 (see p. 51), and before the final settlement of all his claims on August 6, 1663 (see p. 73). Since the account is dated October 23, the only possible year is 1662.

48. See the editor's introductory remarks on Frederick Philipsen's transaction, at the beginning of this volume.

49. "[1663]": As it appears from an entry in the Protocol dated September 23, 1663 (see p. 75), the tobacco was sold to Frederick Philipsen after Teuntie Straetsmans' death on October 19, 1662 (see p. 51). Since the small slip of paper recording the transaction mentions May as the month in which it took place (in two stages), the only possible year is 1663. The editor is of opinion that Philipsen's note itself was not written at the time of the transaction but on November 1, 1663. That was the day when Philipsen finally paid the deaconry what he owed them for the tobacco (see Accounts, p. 180), mention of which he made in the final line of his note: "Paid in sewan: 218-10".

50. This is the only relevant fragment of text on an almost empty, very damaged page. The final amount of money mentioned in the fragment, "Gld. 53", may be missing some stuivers. See also the editor's introductory remarks on this final entry in the financial records, at the beginning of this volume.

51. "church": viz. the one in Midwout; see the editor's introductory remarks referred to in note 50.

Notes to the Orphan Records, pages 193-201

See also the editor's introductory remarks on the Orphan
Records, at the beginning of this volume, and the List of
Geographical Names in Appendix B, pp. 235-241.

1. Selijns omitted to fill in the orphan's age.

2. Selijns left open enough space to register the names of
the orphan's parents, which he never did.

3. "him": Selijns

4. "serge": Selijns wrote "Sarge" and "Sargie", on one
occasion "chargie" (see p. 175). In spite of its relatively
high price, "sarge" or "serge", a woolen fabric still manufactured today, was popular with the poorer classes because of its
excellent durability.

5. "innocent" (orig. ms.: "Jnnocent"): An "innocent" was
a loosefitting dressing gown, both for men and women. It derived
its name from the youthful appearance it gave to anyone wearing
such a garment.

6. "carsay" (orig. ms.: "Carzaij"): "Carzaij", "carsay" or
"carsey" = kersey, a kind of coarse narrow cloth, woven from long
wool and usually ribbed.

7. "barracan" (orig. ms.: "Bercaense"): a coarse woolen cloth
known for being water-proof and very durable. Originally, "barracan" referred to some costly eastern fabric; imitations were later
manufactured in Europe. In the 16th and 17th centuries, barracan
was usually made of the hair of the angora goat.

8. Selijns wrote: "Paer Sy-jette kousen". The editor has not
been able to identify the word "Sy-jette"; possibly, it refers to
some kind of silk.

Notes to the Cow Records, pages 203-209

Please note that, in order to keep the number of notes limited,
unusual terms occurring more than once were given the same note-
number throughout the Cow Records. See also the editor's introductory remarks on the Cow Records, at the beginning of this
volume, and the List of Geographical Names in Appendix B,
pp. 235-241.

1. "half-the-offspring" (orig. ms.: "Halve Aentelinge"): The
half-the-offspring clause of a cow-lease implied that if the cow
produced two or more calves during the term of the contract, the
offspring would be divided among the lessor and the lessee (in
this case, the Breuckelen consistory and Carel d'Beauvois
respectively).

2. In the original manuscript, Selijns left open some space
to fill in the date of the calf's death, which he never did.

3. "half the risk" (orig. ms.: "half risico"): The half-the-
risk clause of a cow-lease implied that if the cow came to die
during the term of the contract, lessor and lessee would each

NOTES TO PAGES 212-227

cover half of the loss (cf. the contract for the fourth cow, also on p. 209).

Notes to the Marriage Register, pages 211-219

See also the editor's introductory remarks on the Marriage Register, at the beginning of this volume, and the List of Geographical Names in Appendix B, pp. 235-241.

1. This entry is somewhat irregular in that it was written in the left margin of the page. Selijns did not mention the exact day of the wedding.

2. "1662, September 17": Originally, Selijns wrote "Den 16 Septemb.", but he changed it into "17".

3. In the original manuscript, this entry is dated "A° 1690 den 17 Januarius"; it is obvious from the chronology in the register that the year should be "1691".

4. In the original manuscript, this entry is dated "A° 1694 den 26 Januwarius"; it is obvious from the chronology in the register that the year should be "1695".

5. "Harmen Joorissen Joerissen": a slip of the pen; the registrar probably meant to write "Harmen Joorissen".

6. In the original manuscript, this entry is dated "A° 1694 den 27 Julij"; it is obvious from the chronology in the register that the year should be "1695".

Notes to the Register of Members, pages 221-224

1. See the editor's introductory remarks on the two Lists of Members, at the beginning of this volume, and the List of Geographical Names in Appendix B, pp. 235-241.

2. see note 1

Notes to Appendix A, pages 225-233

See also the editor's introductory remarks on Domine Henricus Selijns' letters, at the beginning of this volume, and the List of Geographical Names in Appendix B, pp. 235-241.

1. "by turns" (orig. ms.: "bij beurten"): Selijns referred here to the fact that he was not the only minister on board the ship: the passengers of De Vergulde Bever (The Golden Beaver) included his colleague Domine Hermanus Blom who had been called to be minister in Esopus (Kingston). [cf. vols. XIII, 155 and 158, and XIV, 461-462, edited by Berthold Fernow, of: Documents Relative to the Colonial History of the State of New York,

15 vols. (Albany, 1856-1887) - henceforth: NYCD; copied in
vol. I, 473 and 474, of: Rev. Edward T. Corwin, editor, and Hugh
Hastings, supervisor, Ecclesiastical Records, State of New York,
7 vols. (Albany, 1901-1916) - henceforth: Ecclesiastical Records.]
In his translation of this passage in Selijns' letter, Corwin
misread or misinterpreted "bij beurten" and translated it as "when
possible" [Ecclesiastical Records, I, 487].

2. "board and lodging" (orig. ms.: "Tafel en Logement"): On
September 2, 1660, almost three months after their arrival in New
Amsterdam on June 11, the Domines Blom and Selijns petitioned
Director-General Stuijvesant and the Councillors of New Netherland
for an allowance to cover the expenses of board and lodgings
during their stay in Manhattan. As Selijns noted in his letter to
the Classis of Amsterdam, their installation in Esopus and Breuckelen respectively was postponed for "good reasons": "the peace
negotiations at the Esopus [between Stuijvesant and the Indians
- ed.] ... and the general interest of the country". [cf. NYCD,
XIII, 155 and 186-187; copied by Corwin in Ecclesiastical
Records, I, 473 and 479]

3. "more subjects for conversation" (orig. ms.: "meer stoffe"):
The word "stoffe" has several meanings, the most common of which is
"fabrics" or, less specific, "material". However, "stoffe" can
also indicate "material" in the sense of "things that people talk
or write about", e.g. "subjects for conversation". Within the
context of Selijns' sentence, the latter meaning of the word makes
much more sense than the former. Moreover, in the letter he wrote
in 1664, Selijns again used "stoffe" and he clearly meant:
"subjects to write about", "noteworthy things" or "reasons to
write" (see p. 230/231, second paragraph). Both Corwin and Eekhof
misinterpreted "stoffe" in the 1660 letter. [Corwin, Ecclesiastical Records, I, 488: "material (to choose from)"; A. Eekhof,
De Hervormde Kerk in Noord-Amerika (1624-1664), 2 vols. ('s-Graven-
hage/The Hague, 1913), I, 216 - henceforth: Hervormde Kerk]

4. "the Hon. Deputies for Indian Affairs" (orig. ms.: "den
E: Gedeputeerde ad Causas Indicas"): The "Deputati ad Causas
Indicas" were a kind of permanent executive committee delegated by
the Amsterdam Classis of the Dutch Reformed Church. Since 1636,
there were four "Deputati". They took care of all Church-related
affairs in the many colonies settled around the world under the
supervision of the Dutch East India and West India Companies. The
"Deputati" corresponded with the ministers overseas, held meetings,
and acted in close cooperation with the Executive Boards of Directors of the commercial Companies. They were also known as "Deputati
ad Res Externas" (Deputies for Foreign Affairs) or "Deputati ad Res
Maritimas" (Deputies for Maritime Affairs). [cf. Eekhof, Hervormde
Kerk, I, 8-9; Corwin, Ecclesiastical Records, I, 19-20]

5. "the afore-mentioned [former] minister": Selijns probably
referred here to the Rev. Lars Carlson Lokenius, whose conduct was
labeled "un-Christian" in view of the fact that, nine months after
his wife had abandoned him and his children, he had married for the
second time before Stuijvesant had annulled the first marriage.
The Swedish minister was then temporarily removed from the pulpit.
[cf. Israel Acrelius, A History of New Sweden (Philadelphia, 1874),
101 - henceforth: New Sweden]

6. What Selijns meant to say in this sentence is the following:
Normally, a schoolmaster acting as minister would be very harmful
to a congregation. In this case, however, it was better to have

NOTES TO PAGE 233

this unordained schoolmaster in the pulpit than the "un-Christian"
Rev. Lokenius. Corwin's translation of this paragraph [Ecclesiast-
ical Records, I, 550] contains several serious errors. He misinterpreted Selijns' words "mitsgaders seecker Persoon, die den
Lutherschen Preeckstoel voor 't Schoolmeesterschap verkoosen
heeft", which implies that some schoolteacher decided to act as
minister - not the other way around (Corwin: "who has exchanged
the Lutheran pulpit for a schoolmaster's place"); this mistake
automatically led to other interpretational errors in Corwin's
version of this paragraph. Frederick J. Zwierlein [Religion in
New Netherland (Rochester, N.Y., 1910), 133-134] quoted from
Corwin. The "schoolmaster in the pulpit" was probably Abelius
Selskoorn [cf. Acrelius, New Sweden, 101].

The preparation of an index to a book with 17th and 18th-century Dutch records requires more than the alphabetization of names. Numerous cross references need to be included in order to compensate for the lack of consistency in the way people spelled three hundred years ago. Especially in the case of names, spelling seems to have been basically a matter of phonetics. To write a certain name, any combination of vowels and consonants could be used as long as the pronunciation of that combination resembled the sound of the spoken name. "Claes" and "Klaas" were pronounced the same way by a 17th-century Dutchman, as were "Cytie" and "Sijtje". The indexer's work is further complicated by the fact that many people used two or more variants of their first name. "Betje", "Elisabeth", and "Lijsbet" can all refer to the same woman, and so can "Maddaleentje" and "Lena". Another complicating factor was the inclination on the part of many registrars to simplify long and/or non-Dutch family names. "Van Couwenhoven", for instance, was also spelled "Kouehove"; "Bevois" was a simplification of "De Beauvois". All names appearing on the pages of this book were transcribed from the original manuscripts with the greatest possible care, and as a consequence, the reader may find as many as fifteen variations in the spelling of one individual's name. Not all of these spelling variations could be included in the index, of course. For the sake of space, some systematizing and standardizing was inevitable. However, in order to assist the reader, extremely distorted versions of a name were included in the index, with a reference to the more common spelling.

The historian or genealogist looking for a specific person may find him or her under several names in this index. To illustrate this, we will use the hypothetical examples of Jan Dircksen van Dam and Annetje Gerrits Verplanck. Ideally, the former would be listed in three different places in the index:

(a) under his family name: "VAN DAM, Jan Dircksen".
Many people did not bear a family name, however, and even if they did, it was not always mentioned in the records. For this reason, the researcher should not only check under the family name, but also,

(b) under the patronymic - in the case of our example, under "DIRCKSEN, Jan".
In addition, the baptism of the person whom the researcher is looking for, may also be registered in this volume. The index includes the first names of all children recorded in the four lists of the Baptismal Register of Breuckelen. Since every child's second name was determined by his or her father's first name, children bearing the same first name have been listed in such a way that the first names of the fathers follow in alphabetical order. To return to our example, Jan Dircksen's father's first name must have been Dirck. If we assume for a moment that Jan's paternal grandfather's first name was Pieter, then Jan's father's full name was Dirck Pietersen van Dam. In the index, Jan's baptism would have been listed,

(c) under "JAN, s.o. [= son of] Dirck Pietersen van Dam", immediately below "JAN, s.o. Cymen" and above "JAN, s.o. Dirck Poulussen".

The case of Annetje Gerrits Verplanck is more complicated. She may be listed,

(a) under her family name: "VERPLANCK, Annetje Gerrits";

(b) under her patronymic: "GERRITS, Annetje"; and

(c) under "ANNETJE, d.o. [= daughter of] Gerrit Martensen Verplanck" (if, for example, her paternal grandfather's first name was Marten). So far, Annetje's case is no different from Jan Dircksen van Dam's. Suppose, however, that Annetje marries Jan. She may keep her own family name, but she may also drop it and adopt "van Dam". Furthermore, she may keep her patronymic, "Gerrits", but she may also name herself after her husband: "Annetje Jans". Another problem with early Dutch records is that in many instances, along with the husband's full name, only the wife's first name is given: "Jan Dircksen van Dam and Annetje, his wife". In other words, a married woman may be listed in as many as six different places in this index: the possibilities #a through #c mentioned above, plus

(d) under a new family name, adopted from her husband: "VAN DAM, Annetje";

(e) under her husband's first name, replacing her original patronymic: "JANS, Annetje"; and

(f) under her own first name, with reference to her husband: "ANNETJE, w.o. [= wife of] Jan Dircksen van Dam".
Needless to say, if Annetje were widowed and married again, three more possibilities would be added to the six listed above.

In several sections of this book, a transcription of the original Dutch text has been printed along with an English translation. For the sake of space, the index entries do not refer to the names mentioned on the (even-numbered) "Dutch" pages in those sections, since all of these names also appear in the English translation on the opposite (odd-numbered) pages which were indexed. Finally, the index includes all names mentioned in the introductions by Dr. Howard G. Hageman and the editor. For technical reasons, however, those names could not be referred to with specific page numbers. Instead, symbols had to be used which are explained in the following list of abbreviations.

List of abbreviations used in the index

b.   = born

c.   = circa, around

d.   = died

d.o. = daughter of

Ed. = Editor's Introduction, passim

Ed.a = id., first part

Ed.b = id., remarks on earlier publications

Ed.c = id., remarks on unpublished translations

Ed.d = id., section headed "The Breuckelen Church Records - some general remarks"

Ed.e = id., remarks on the Protocol

Ed.f = id., remarks on the Baptismal Register

Ed.g = Editor's Introduction, remarks on the Financial Records
Ed.h = id., remarks on the Orphan Records
Ed.j = id., remarks on the Marriage Register
Ed.k = id., remarks on the Register of Members
Ed.l = id., remarks on Appendix A
fl. = flourished
h.o. = husband of
Int. = Introduction by the Rev. Dr. Howard G. Hageman
s.o. = son of
w.o. = wife of

AAFJE: see Aefje
AALTJE: see Aeltje
AART/AARTS/AARTSEN: see Aert/
　　Aerts/Aertsen
ABEEL/ABIELS
-, Elisabeth: 160
-, Magdalena/Machdaleentje: 123,
　　160
-, Marrijtje/Maria: 123
ABIGAEL/ABIGEL
-, w.o. Denten: 118
-, w.o. Leffert Pietersen: 148
-, d.o. Willem Appelbeij: 121
ABRAHAM/ABRAM
-, s.o. Abram Bennet: 151
-, s.o. Abraham Brouwer: 150
-, s.o. Abram van Duyn: 142
-, s.o. Dirk van Zutphen: 162
-, s.o. Gerrit Snedecker: 157
-, s.o. Hendrick van [...]: 164
-, s.o. Jan Fredericksen: 121
-, s.o. Jeurien Blanck: 134
-, s.o. Joris Abramsen: 135
-, s.o. Joris Rapalje: 149
-, s.o. Leendert van der Grift:
　　130
-, s.o. Leffert Pietersen: 131
-, s.o. Mathijs Cornelissen: 140
-, s.o. Pieter Pra: 111
-, s.o. Theodorus Polhemius: 137
-, s.o. Tomas Schilman: 147
ABRAHAMS/ABRAMS
-, Annetje: 212,215
-, Catrina: 111
-, IJda/Ida: 135
-, Lammitje: 136, 138
-, Trijntje: 130
ABRAHAMSEN/ABRAMSEN
-, Cornelis: 57
-, Dirk: 151
-, Frans: 135
-, Frans: 152
-, Frans: 154

ABRAHAMSEN/ABRAMSEN (continued)
-, Jan: 147, 151
-, Joris: 124, 132, 133, 135,
　　136, 137, 141, 147, 150
ACKERMAN: see Akkerman
ACRELIUS, Rev. Israel (1714-1800):
　　256, 257
ADAM
-, s.o. Adam Brouwer: 112
-, s.o. Jakop Brouwer: 136
-, s.o. Nicklaes Brouwer: 133
-, s.o. Pieter Pra: 109
ADAMS, Fijtje: 117
ADOLFUS, s.o. Willem Brouwer: 123
ADRIAAN/ADRIAEN: see also Arie
ADRIAAN/ADRIAEN
-, s.o. Abram Bennet: 147
-, s.o. Hendrick Hogelandt: 147
-, s.o. Hendrick Hogelandt: 149
-, s.o. Joseph Hegeman: 119
ADRIAANS/ADRIAENS
-, Annetje: 152
-, Jannetje: 159 (2x)
-, Marija/Maria: 125
-, Trijntje: see Bennet,
　　Trijntje Adriaens
ADRIAANSEN/ADRIAENSEN: see also
　　Ariensen
ADRIAANSEN/ADRIAENSEN, Gosen: 152
ADRIAENTJE, d.o. Jan Hansen
　　Bergen: 120
AEFJE/AAFJE
-, d.o. Jan Aertsen: 156
-, d.o. Joris Jacobsen: 110
AELTJE/AALTJE: see also Alida and
　　Ida
AELTJE/AALTJE
-, w.o. Abram Jorissen: 144
-, d.o. Adriaen Laforge: 124
-, w.o. Benjamin Oldis: 150
-, w.o. Cornelis Sybrich: 142
-, w.o. Dirk Abramsen: 151

ANDRIESSEN (continued)
-, Juriaen: 139, 144, 154
-, Lambert: 148, 152
ANENIETJE: see Angenietje
ANGENIETJE/AGNIETJE/ANENIETJE
-, w.o. Adriaan/Arje Bennet:
139, 143, 147
-, d.o. Arien Willemsen Bennet:
121
-, w.o. Casparus Blank: 148
-, d.o. Cornelis van Brunt: 160
-, d.o. Jacob Bennet: 143
-, d.o. Jacob van Dooren: 148
-, d.o. Jan Jansen: 125
-, w.o. Johannes Folkertsen: 153
-, w.o. Joris Danielsen Rapalje:
141, 147, 149
-, w.o. Willem Brouwer: 140
ANNA/ANNATJE/ANNEKE/ANNETJE/
ANNITJE/ANTJE
-, 110
-, d.o. Aart Aartsen: 145
-, w.o. Abram Remsen: 152
-, w.o. Adriaan Reyersen: 147,
149
-, d.o. Andries Emans: 163
-, d.o. Anthoni de Eijcke: 125
-, d.o. Antoni de Mot: 154
-, d.o. Arent Andriessen: 147
-, d.o. Carel Fonteyn: 112
-, w.o. Cornelis Barentsen: 148
-, d.o. Cornelis Barensen: 121
-, w.o. Cornelis Jorissen: 148
-, d.o. Cornelis Jorissen: 140
-, d.o. Cornelis Paulussen: 138
-, d.o. Cornelis van Duin: 161
-, d.o. Davidt Sprong: 136
-, d.o. Dirck Jansen Woertman:
123
-, w.o. Dirck Tyssen: 141
-, d.o. Gabriel Sprong: 135
-, d.o. Gerrit Dorlandt: 148
-, d.o. Gerrit Kroes: 116
-, d.o. Gerrit Schenk: 161
-, w.o. Gerridt Sprongh: 140,
141, 145
-, d.o. Gosen Adriaansen: 152
-, d.o. Hendrick Jansen: 132
-, d.o. Hendrick Jansen: 139
-, d.o. Hendrik Jansen: 159
-, d.o. Hieronymus/Jeronimus
Rapalje: 148
-, w.o. Jacobus Boubyn: 140
-, d.o. Jacob Casjouw: 141
-, d.o. Jacob Casjou: 152
-, d.o. Jakop Jansen: 125
-, d.o. Jacob Martensen: 146
-, w.o. Jacques Fonteijn: 139
-, w.o. Jan Barensen: 155
-, w.o. Jan Dorlant: 146
-, w.o. Johannes Pietersen: 142,
147

ANNA/ANNATJE/ANNEKE/ANNETJE/
ANNITJE/ANTJE (continued)
-, d.o. Johannes Pietersen: 146
-, w.o. Joris Abramsen: 141, 147,
150
-, w.o. Joris Brinkerhof: 154
-, d.o. Joris Hansen: 129
-, d.o. Joris Rappaljee: 137,
249
-, d.o. Joris Remsen: 145
-, d.o. Klaas/Claes Folkertsen:
147
-, d.o. Lukas Stevensen: 125
-, w.o. Mourus Koevers: 139
-, d.o. Niclaes Stilwil: 158
-, w.o. Philippus/Flip Nagel:
148, 151
-, d.o. Pieter Loijs: 126
-, d.o. Pieter Wijnantsen: 146
-, d.o. Roelof Verkerck: 123
-, d.o. Roelof Jansen Verkerck:
121
-, d.o. Stoffel Jansen: 121
-, d.o. Teunis Jansen: 110
-, w.o. Thomas Schilman: 144,
147
-, d.o. Willem Willemsen: 162
ANNA ELISABETH, d.o. Jacob
Brouwer: 161
ANNA MARIA/ANNEMARI
-, 119
-, w.o. Abraham Lefoij: 150
-, d.o. Frederick van Leeuwen:
125
-, d.o. Hendrik Jansen: 162
-, w.o. Jacob Casjouw: 141, 152
-, w.o. Jan Dircksen Woerman:
130, 133, 139, 249
-, d.o. Matthijs Boon: 110
-, w.o. Pieter Wijnansen: 134,
135, 136, 146
ANNEKE/ANNETJE/ANNITJE: see Anna
ANTHONETTA, d.o. Joost Duiere:
120
ANTHONISSEN, Aert: see Middag,
Aert Anthonissen
ANTJE: see Anna
ANTONIDES, Rev. Vincentius (1670-
1744): Ed.d
APPELBEIJ, Willem: 121, 122
APPELDOORN, Claes Teunissen: 89;
see also under Teunissen,
Claes
ARCHONIA HILLEGONDE, w.o. Lourens
de Sille: 117
ARENT/ARENTJE/ARENTS/ARENTSEN:
see Aert/Aertje/Aerts/Aertsen
ARIAENS
-, Jannetje: 135
-, Marritje: 134
ARIAENSEN
-, Jan: 121

ARIAENSEN (continued)
-, Jan: 145, 147
-, Elbert: 135
ARIAENTJE
-, d.o. Aart Aartsen: 142
-, d.o. Anthoni van Pelt: 129
-, d.o. Hans Teunissen Coevors:
  129
-, d.o. Matheus Aertsen: 148
-, w.o. Willem Bennet: 139
-, d.o. Willem Bennet: 162
ARIE/ARIEN/ARJEN: see also
  Adriaen
ARIE/ARIEN/ARJEN
-, 217
-, s.o. Dirck Cornelissen Hoog-
  lant: 115
-, s.o. Hendrick Jansen: 129
-, s.o. Isaeck Bennet: 139
-, s.o. Jan Bennit: 138
ARIENSEN/ARISEN/ARJENSEN
-, Jan: 146; see also Bennit,
  Jan Ariensen
-, Klaas/Claes: 143
ARNOUDSEN/ARNOUTSEN: see
  Aernoutsen
ARUNDEUS, Rev. Johannes
  (fl. 1741-1772): Ed.d, 105,
  107, 248
ATEN/AETE
-, Jan: 145, 147
-, Marytje/Maria: 147
-, Tomas: 145, 147
AUCKES/AUKES
-, Abigael/Abigel: 123, 131
-, Anneken/Annetje: 111, 113,
  125, 212
-, Femmitje: 123, 125, 161
-, Geertje: 123
-, Jannetje: 160
AUCKESSEN/AUKESSEN
-, Jakobus: 123
-, Jan: 125, 135, 149, 157;
  cf. Oucus, Jan
-, Jan: 152

BAART, Jan: 251
BACKER: see also De Backer
BACKER, Jacobus: 110
BADDIA, Maria: 101
BAHNHAM, John: 143
BALDE/BALDEE, Barent: 19, 63, 85,
  166, 168, 176, 177, 183
BARBARA/BERBARA/BERBERTJE
-, d.o. Achijas Jansen: 122
-, w.o. Arje Bennet: 143
-, d.o. Frans Abramsen: 154
-, d.o. Gerrit Spronk: 128
-, w.o. Jacob Bennet: 143
-, w.o. Johannes Coerten: 149
-, w.o. Lucas Coevers: 141
-, d.o. Willem Pos: 128

BARCULO: see Van Barculo
BARENT, s.o. Jan Hendricksen: 114
BARENT, Lange [= Tall]: 33, 49
BARENTJE, w.o. Benjamin Hegeman:
  146
BARENTS/BARENS
-, Albertje: 127
-, Anenietje/Angenietje: 127,
  129
-, Anneken: 21
-, Annetje: 127, 142, 161
-, Elbertje: 130
-, Elsje/Elisabeth: 117, 132,
  157, 219
-, Femmetje: 161
-, Fijtje: 159
-, Getruijt: 13, 21, 110
-, Grietje: 114
-, Ida: 163
-, Margriet: 133
-, Marritje/Maria: 128
BARENTSEN/BARENSEN
-, Claes/Klaes: 129; see also
  Blom, Claes Barensen
-, Cornelis: 119
-, Cornelis: 121, 126, 148; see
  also Van der Wijck, Cornelis
  Barentsen
-, Jan: 155
-, Jan: 162
-, Lambert: 211
BARTELS, Geertruijt: 120, 122
BARWA, Katrijna/Catarina: 135
BAS
-, Annetje: 145
-, Roelof: 144
BASTIAENS, Metje: 213
BEAUVOIS/BEAVOIJS/BEAVOIS: see
  De Beauvois
BEDUEW, Steven: 146
BEEKMAN, A.J.: Ed.b
BEEKMAN/BEECKMAN
-, Gerardus: 123, 125, 141, 160
-, Johannes: 160
-, Machdeleentje/Magdalena: 125
-, Metje: 130
-, Neeltje: 130
-, Wilhelmus/Willem: 123
BEEN, Hendrick Jansen: 112
BELLI, Fijnsan: 219
BENJAMIN, s.o. Willem Britte: 158
BENNET/BENNIT
-, Abram: 147, 149, 151, 153
-, Adriaan: 147
-, Aeltje: 136, 224
-, Angenietje: 138, 147
-, Arie/Arien/Arje: 143
-, Arie/Arien/Arje Willemsen:
  121, 125, 138, 139, 143, 147,
  219; see also Willemsen,
  Arie
-, Femmitje: 138, 148

BENNET/BENNIT (continued)
-, Isaeck: 139, 143, 147,
148 (2x), 150
-, Jacob: 143, 224
-, Jan: 136, 146
-, Jan: 160
-, Jan Ariensen: 138, 142, 219
-, Jan Willemsen: 217
-, Maria Willems: 126, 223
-, Trijntje Adriaens: 160, 161,
217
-, Willem: 139, 160, 162, 224
-, Willem Willemsen: 99; see
also Willemsen, Willem (1st)
BENNETJE, w.o. Hendrick
Hendricksen: 147
BERBER/BERBARA/BERBERTJE: see
Barbara
BERGEN
-, Femmitje: 218
-, Frerick/Frederick: 164
-, Hans: 153
-, Jacob Hansen: 153; see also
Hansen, Jacob
-, Jan Hansen: 120, 138, 145;
see also Hansen, Jan (1st)
-, Jannetje: 138
-, Joris Hansen: 137, 144, 147;
see also Hansen, Joris
-, Michiel Hansen: 137; see also
Hansen, Michiel
-, Sara: 138
BERGEN, Teunis G.: Ed.b, Ed.c,
Ed.f
BERJAN: see Berrien
BERRIEN/BERJAN/BERRIJ
-, Catelijntje/Kathalijntje:
130, 139
-, Claas/Klaas: 143, 151
-, Cornelis Jan: 120, 158; see
also Jansen, Cornelis (3rd)
-, Jakobus: 130
-, Jan: 139, 143, 149 (2x), 150
-, Pieter: 139, 151
-, Samuel: 130, 135, 139, 218
-, Trijntje: 162
BERRIJ: see Berrien
BERTHOLF, Rev. Giliam (1656-
c.1726): Ed.d, 224
BETJE: see Elisabeth
BETTIJ, d.o. Jeseijas Drets: 140
BEULINGS, Besje: 53, 77
BEVOIS: see De Beauvois
BIBOU/BIBOUT
-, Jan: 130
-, Metje: 140, 152
BIOSIE/BIJOSE, Lowijs/Lovys: 110,
114
BLAAUW
-, Abram: 152
-, Dina: 154
-, Frederick: 152

BLAAUW (continued)
-, Grietje: 147
-, Jan: 147, 154
-, Magdaleentje: 150
BLANCK/BLANK
-, Casparus: 148
-, Hester: 134
-, Jeurien: 118, 122, 134
-, Klaesje/Claesje: 118
-, Nicklaes: 118
BLOCK, notary: 214
BLOETGOET, Frans: see Van der
Goude, Frans Bloetgoet
BLOM
-, Claes Barensen: 133, 140, 141
-, Cymen/Sijmen: 149
-, Rev. Hermanus (b. 1628): Int.,
229, 255, 256
-, Lijsbet/Elisabeth: 149
BOCQUE/BOCKQUI/BOKEE
-, Abram: 135
-, Anna/Anthe: 122, 125
-, Janneken: 135
-, Jannetje Reronimus: 117
BOEKHOUTE, Aeltje: 142
BOERMARK, Arje: 148
BOFI, Mathijs: 135
BOGAERT
-, Aert Teunissen: 132
-, Annetje: 133
-, Catalijn: 123
-, Gijsbert: 129 (2x), 133, 135,
137, 146 (2x)
-, Jan Cornelissen: 116
-, Jan Laurenssen: 113, 201
-, Jannetje: 129, 133
-, Teunis Gijsbertsen: 61, 63,
83, 85, 89, 111, 113, 117,
177, 199, 216, 222, 223; see
also Gijsbertsen, Teunis
-, Wijntje: 161
BOGARDUS/BOGARDES
-, Annetje: 124, 126, 129, 161
-, Cornelia: 129
-, Rev. Everardus (1607-1647):
37
-, Katrijna/Catarina: 128, 136
-, Saartje: 163
-, Willem: 126
BOKA, Jannetje: 129
BOKEE: see Bocque
BOMMEL, Jan Hendricksen: 212
BOOCH, Elisabeth: 133
BOOM/BOON, Matthijs: 110
BOOMS/BOONS
-, Anneke: 113
-, Janneke: 113, 121
BORCULO: see Van Barculo
BORDAN, Lijsbet: 144
BOSCH: see also Ter Bosch
BOSCH, Lambert Jansen: 89, 213

BOSLEIJDINGH: see Van Bosleij-
dingh
BOUBYN, Jacobus: 140
BOUDI
-, Marrij/Maria: 138
-, Thomas: 138
BOUMAN, Tomas: 152
BOURDET, Susanna: 150
BOUT, Jan Evertsen: 134, 249; see
also Evertsen, Jan
BRACHUNEE/BRACKUNEE, Aeltje: 13,
21, 113
BRAGON, s.o. Hans Coevors: 136
BRAUN, Jan: 213
BRECHJE
-, d.o. Abram Remsen: 152
-, d.o. Gerrit Middach: 131
BREDENBENT/BREDEBEND, Willem: 11,
13, 15, 17, 19, 21, 41, 43,
45, 47, 55, 57, 59, 61, 81,
83, 85, 89, 95, 97, 113 (2x),
167, 176, 184, 186, 195, 199,
245, 246
BREES, Sara: 147
BRIES
-, Cornelis: 143
-, Folckert Hendricksen: 140,
143, 145; see also
Hendricksen, Folckert
BRIJEL, Louseijn: 110
BRINKERHOF
-, Antje: 149
-, Dirck: 154
-, Jan: 149
-, Joris: 154
BRITTE/BRITTEN
-, Nathaniel: 158
-, Willem: 158 (2x)
BRODHEAD, John Romeyn: Ed.1
BROEKAAR/BROKAER: see Broucar
BRONTIJN, Marij/Maria: 110
BROUCAR/BROEKAAR/BROKAER
-, Bergon/Borgenson/Bourgon:
116, 117, 120
-, Catalijntje: 144
-, Isaack: 136, 144 (2x), 146
BROUWER
-, Abram: 107
-, Abram: 129, 133, 137, 140,
150, 164
-, Adam: 13, 109 (2x), 111,
112 (2x), 239
-, Adam, Jr.: 127, 131, 134,
137, 140
-, Adoleves/Adolphus: 164
-, Aeltje: 117, 118, 123, 124,
127
-, Antje: 127, 136, 154, 155
-, Betje: see id., Elisabeth
-, Cornelia: 137
-, Elisabeth/Betje: 118, 123,
127

BROUWER (continued)
-, Fijtje: 124, 129, 134
-, Hendericus/Hendrick: 159
-, Jacob/Jakop: 124, 126, 129,
136, 161
-, Jacob: 155
-, Jannetje: 133, 137, 152
-, Jannetje: 159
-, Johannes: 160
-, Maddaleentje/Magdalena: 133
-, Magtelt: 159
-, Marritje/Maria: 121, 124
-, Marritje/Maria: 134, 137
-, Marta: 148
-, Mathijs: 121, 124, 132
-, Nicklaes: 132, 133, 137, 140,
141, 144 (2x), 151
-, Pieter: 121, 131, 161
-, Rachel: 132, 137
-, Sara: 129
-, Sijbrandt: 155
-, Willem: 118, 123, 127, 223
-, Willem: 140
-, Willem: 146, 150, 154
BUDET, Steven: 150, 153
BUIJL/BUYL, Thijs: 144, 145
BUIJS/BUYS
-, Cornelis: 118
-, Jacob: 137, 139, 147
-, Jacob Jansen: 130, 133, 217
-, Jan: 114, 117, 118 (2x), 121,
125, 130, 131, 143, 156
-, Jan Cornelissen: 89, 117,
214, 217
-, Jan Jansen: 122
-, Machtel: 117
-, Marretje/Maria: 139
-, Thijs: 143, 147
BUIJTENHUIJSEN, Jan: 114
BULDERING, Gertruijd: 211
BUYL: see Buijl
BUYS: see Buijs
BUYTENHUYSEN: see Buijtenhuijsen

CALJER/CALJERS
-, Cornelis: 140, 141
-, Doorethee/Dorothea: 124
-, Geertruijt: 137, 141
-, Jeuriaen: 137
-, Jochom: 137
-, Marritje/Maria: 137, 153
CARBOSIE: see Corbesij
CARDELJOUW/CARELJOUW/CORDELJOUW/
CORSIOU/KARTELJOU/KARTIOU/
KERTELJOU
-, Cornelis: 159
-, Helena: 131, 160, 163 (2x)
-, Jacques: 112, 114
-, Jacques: 159, 160, 163
-, Maria: 135, 160, 161 (2x),
162
-, Neeltje: 116

CARDELJOUW/CARELJOUW/CORDELJOUW/
  CORSIOU/KARTELJOU/KARTIOU/
  KERTELJOU (continued)
-, Pieter: 161
CAREL/KAREL, s.o. Johannes
  Fontein: 160
CARELS/KARELS, Maria: 129
CAROS, Antje: 152
CARTON, Jenne: 79, 91, 221
CARVOIJ
-, Jan: 109
-, Stephen, Sr.: 109
CASE, Jurie: 144
CASJOUW/CASSOU, Jacob: 134, 141,
  145, 152, 218
CASPER/CASPARIS, s.o. Jesaias
  Draake: 144
CASPERS, Jannetje: 135
CASPERSEN
-, Johannes: 119, 123
-, Joost: 89, 119, 123, 207,
  209, 214, 219; see also Van
  Groeningen, Joost Caspersen
-, Melchert/Melckgert: 120, 122,
  157
CASSOU: see Casjouw
CATALINA: see also Lijntje
CATALINA/CATELIJN/KATHALINA
-, d.o. Aart van Pelt: 162
-, w.o. Dirck Middagh: 139
-, d.o. Jakobus de Beavoijs: 132
-, d.o. Jeronimus de Rappalee:
  124
-, d.o. Marten Schenk: 148
CATARINA: see also Trijntje
CATARINA/CATRIJNTJE/KATHARINA/
  KATRIJNA
-, d.o. Abraham de Toiet: 117
-, w.o. Bourgon Broucar: 117
-, d.o. Chaerlis/Charles
  Fonteijn: 136
-, d.o. Dirck Jansen: 156
-, d.o. Gerardus Beekman: 160
-, w.o. Giliam Lerue: 149
-, d.o. Hendrick Corsen: 129
-, w.o. Jan Abramsen: 151
-, w.o. Jan Brinkerhof: 149
-, d.o. Jan Dorlant: 149
-, d.o. Jan Quitans: 153
-, d.o. Jan van ter Veer: 136
-, w.o. Jochom Verscheure: 146
-, d.o. Johannes Jansen: 133
-, d.o. Joost Caspersen: 119
-, d.o. Joost Caspersen: 123
-, d.o. Joost de Baane: 162
-, d.o. Joris Cimmer: 135
-, d.o. Leendert Huijgen de
  Klijn: 140
-, d.o. Melchert Caspersen: 157
-, w.o. Michiel de Gree: 146
-, d.o. Niclaes Stilwil: 158

CATARINA/CATRIJNTJE/KATHARINA/
  KATRIJNA (continued)
-, d.o. Paulus van den Enden:
  150
-, w.o. Pieter Cornel: 144
-, d.o. Pieter Tijssen: 134
-, d.o. Pieter Wijnansen: 134
-, d.o. Steven Budet: 150
-, w.o. Steven Jansen: Ed.f,
  153, 155
-, d.o. Stijntje Hans: Ed.b,
  117
-, w.o. Theunus Woertman: 142,
  148
-, d.o. Theunus Woertman: 148
-, d.o. Thomas Boudi: 138
CEBERING/CEBERINGH: see
  Sebering
CHELLWER, Jan: 148
CHRISTIAEN/CHRISTIAAN/CRISTIAEN
-, s.o. Jacob van Dooren: 142
-, s.o. Pieter du Joo: 120
CHRISTIAANSEN, Jacob: 161
CHRISTINA/CRISTIJNA/CRISTINA
-, d.o. Barent Slecht: 132
-, d.o. David Sprong: 151
-, d.o. Joost de Bane: 135
-, w.o. Michiel van der Voort:
  141
-, d.o. Pieter Para: 139
-, w.o. Roelof Sibering: 147
CHRISTOFFEL, Johannes: 117
CIJMONSE: see Sijmensen
CIJTIE/CIJTJE: see Sijtje
CIMMER
-, Joris: 135
-, Marij: 135
CLAES/KLAES/KLAAS
-, s.o. Gerrit Klaessen: 134
-, s.o. Jochom Verscheure: 146
-, s.o. Sijmon Claessen: 110
CLAES/KLAES/KLAAS
-, Aeltje: 111
-, Geertje: 109, 110
-, Janneken: 31
-, Jannetje: see Van Leender-
  sloot, Jannitje Klaes
-, Lummitje: 134
-, Marritje/Maria: 115, 121, 130;
  see also Van Huijse, Marietje
  Claes
-, Neeltje: 163
-, Pieterje/Pietertje: 120
-, Trijntje: 110 (2x), 114, 116,
  130, 136
CLAESSEN/KLAESSEN/KLAASSEN
-, Ariaen/Arien: 121, 137
-, Bartel: 53
-, Capt.: 195
-, Cornelis: 126
-, Gerbrandt: 121, 130, 141-2

CLAESSEN/KLAESSEN/KLAASSEN
(continued)
-, Gerrit: 134, 223
-, Gerrit: see Vechten, Gerrit
   Claessen
-, Hendrick: 134, 136, 159, 223;
   see also Vechten, Hendrick
   Claessen
-, Jan: see Van Huijsse, Jan
   Claessen
-, Pieter: 113, 118
-, Simon: 109 (2x), 110, 114,
   115, 116
CLEEFT: see Van Cleef
CLEINE: see also De Klijn
CLEINE, Pieternelle: 161
CLEMENT, Jan: 156
CLERCK/CLERQ, Jan: 29, 55, 211,
   213
CLOMP, Huijbert: 212
COBA: see Jacoba
COBUS: see Jacob
COECK: see also Koeck
COECK, Thomas: 216
COERT, s.o. Steven Coerten: 161
COERTEN/COURTEN
-, Aaltje: 161, 162
-, Albert: 162
-, Gerrit: 161, 162
-, Johannes: 149
-, Meindert: 160, 163
-, Neeltje: 161
-, Steven: 156, 161
COESJEE, Jan: 119
COEVORS/COVORS/KOEVERS/KOVORS
-, Aeltje: 128
-, Barbara/Berbara: 128, 137,
   145
-, Hans Teunissen: 129, 136,
   140; see also Teunissen,
   Hans
-, Jannetje: 136
-, Lucas/Luijkas: 129, 141
-, Marritje/Maria: 136
-, Mourus/Maurits: 139
-, Sara: 128
-, Teunis Jansen: Ed.g, 17, 59,
   61, 83, 113, 119, 129, 131,
   181, 183, 187, 252; see
   also Jansen, Teunis (1st)
COLEUERT, Louwerens/Laurens: 115
COLFS
-, Geertje: 118, 120, 124, 130
-, Geertje: 129
-, Saertje: 118
COLIES, Jannetje/Jennetje: 148
COLJOUW/CULJOUW
-, Isaack: 156
-, Pieter: 158
COLVE, Sara: 154
COMMENS, Joris: 158

CONINCK/CONINGK, Albert: 85, 222
COOL, Barent: 153
COOP A GROEN, Rev. Samuel
   (fl. 1660): 7
CORBESIJ/CARBOSIE, Gabriel: 51,
   53, 75, 77, 81, 169, 171, 179,
   180, 186, 187, 188, 189, 195,
   197, 246
CORDELJOUW: see Cardeljouw
CORNEL
-, Jannetje: 155
-, Johannes: 144
-, Lammetje: 147
-, Pieter: 144
CORNELIA/KORNELIA
-, 137
-, w.o. Abram Brouwer: 140, 150
-, d.o. Cornelis Seberingh: 135
-, d.o. Cornelis van Duyn: 153
-, d.o. Cornelis Corsen Vroom:
   120
-, w.o. Engelbart Lot: 145
-, w.o. Gerridt Middagh: 151
-, d.o. Hendrick Jansen: 124
-, d.o. Pieter Brouwer: 131
-, d.o. Pieter Usile: 132
-, w.o. Pieter Uziele: 145
CORNELIS/KORNELIS
-, s.o. Abram Slegt: 152
-, s.o. Anthoni Salm: 131
-, s.o. Arje Bennet: 143
-, s.o. Barent Follemon: 136
-, s.o. Coert Stevensen: 158
-, s.o. Cornelis Jansen Seeuw:
   130
-, s.o. Cornelis van Duin: 148
-, s.o. Cornelis Verhoeve: 140
-, s.o. Dionijs Theunissen: 163
-, s.o. Dirck Middagh: 139
-, s.o. Gerrit Dorlant: 136
-, s.o. Jan Berrien: 139
-, s.o. Jan Buijs: 156
-, s.o. Jan Damen: 113
-, s.o. Jan Laurensen: 163
-, s.o. Jan Lowise: 148
-, s.o. Joris Rapalje: 147
-, s.o. Matheus Aertsen: 151
-, s.o. Mathijs Cornelissen: 134
-, s.o. Philip/Flip Nagel: 151
-, s.o. Pieter Berjan: 151
-, s.o. Pieter Galjamsen: 120
-, s.o. Theodorus van der Wijck:
   134
CORNELIS/KORNELIS
-, Aeltje: 111
-, Claesje/Klaesje: 109, 124
-, Fijtje: 143
-, Grietje: 113
-, Lijsbet/Elisabeth: 160
-, Maijke: 161
-, Marritje/Maria: 121

DE BALIE, Catharina: 112, 114
DE BEAUVOIS/D'BEAUVOIS/
DE BEAUTOIS/BEAVOIJS/BEVOIS
-, Mr. Carel: 23, 47, 49, 53,
   63, 69, 77, 95, 97, 112,
   171, 173, 175, 177, 179,
   181, 183, 185, 205, 246,
   252, 254
-, Carel: 150, 154
-, Carel/Karel: 103
-, Catharina/Katrijna: 55, 129,
   135, 223
-, Getruijd: 55
-, Jacob/Jakobus: 129, 132, 138,
   150, 223, 224
-, Kornelia/Cornelia: 223
-, Marijtje/Maria: 138
DE BON, Jan: 110
DEBOOIS: see Du Bois
DEBORA
-, d.o. Samuel Berrij: 130
-, d.o. Teunus Wilze: 153
DE CLEIN: see De Klijn
DE CONSELJE, Jan: 128
DE EIJCKE/DE IJCK, Anthoni: 122,
   125
DE FOREEST/DE FORREST
-, Isaac: 114, 239
-, Jan: 116
DE GRAUW
-, Harmen: 137
-, IJbitje: 137
DE GREE, Michiel: 146
DE HART
-, Claasje: 162
-, Elias: 162
DE HEEST, Pieter Lambertsen: 187,
   214, 251, 252; see also
   Lambertsen, Pieter
DE HONNEUR: see D'Honneur
DE IJCK: see De Eijcke
DE JONG, Gerald F.: 243
DE KLIJN: see also Cleine
DE KLIJN, Leendert Huijgen: 140
DE LA FORSE/LAFORGE, Adriaen:
   124, 128
DE LEEVER, Salomon: 159
DELEFEEBRE: see Lefebvre
DE MAREE, Mathijs: 138
DE MAT, Mathijs: 147
DE MOF, Claertje: 25, 245
DE MOT, Antoni: 154
DE MOURCOURT, Rev. Johannes
   (fl. 1660): 9
DE NEGER [= the Negro], Jan: 215
DE NIJCK
-, Elisabeth/Lijsbet: 134, 139
-, Thobijas: 134, 139
DENIJS, s.o. Dirck Jansen: 117
DE NOORMAN, Rachel Dircks: 115
DENTEN: 118

DE PLANCKE, Sara: 13, 19, 27, 85,
   112, 213, 222
DE POTTER: see also Potter
DE POTTER, David: 57
DE RAPPALJE/D'RAPPALIE/RAPPALJE
-, Angenietje: 149, 150
-, Annetje: Ed.f, 130, 137, 218,
   249
-, Catalijntje/Catalina: 146
-, Catalina/Kathalijntje Jeronim-
   us: 117
-, Catarina: 112
-, Catharina Joris: 59, 111; see
   also Joris, Catharina
-, Daniel: 101, 130, 139, 146,
   224
-, Elisabeth: see id., Lijsbeth
-, Femmitje: 219
-, Hieronymus: see id., Jeronimus
-, Jan Jorissen: 111 (2x), 195
-, Jannetje: 122
-, Jeronimus/Hieronymus: Ed.f,
   115, 117 (2x), 124, 127, 128,
   130, 133, 137, 148, 163, 218,
   219, 249
-, Jeronimus/Hieronymus: 148, 150
-, Joris: see id., Joris Dan-
   ielsen
-, Joris: see id., Joris Jansen
-, Joris: see id., Joris Jeronim-
   ussen
-, Joris Danielsen: 141, 147,
   149 (2x)
-, Joris Jansen: 59, 61, 111
-, Joris Jeronimussen: Ed.f, 137,
   218
-, Kathalijntje: see id., Catal-
   ina
-, Lijsbeth Joris: 115
-, Neeltje: Ed.f, 137, 138, 224
-, Sara: see id., Sara Joris
-, Sara Joris: 19, 113, 157; see
   also Joris, Sara
-, Theunus: 142, 145-6, 146
DE RONDE, Lambertus: 105, 107
DE SEEUW: see De Zeeuw
DE SILLE/DE ZILLA
-, Gardijntje/Gedijne/Gerdijna:
   111, 117, 132
-, Lourens: 117
-, Mr. Nicasius: Int., 3, 11,
   227
DE SUSON: see Suson
DE VOS/D'VOS, Matheus: 188
DE WIT
-, Dieuwertje: 161
-, Jan: 212
DEYOO: see Du Joo and Andogo
DE ZEEUW/DE SEEUW/SEEUW
-, Cornelis Jansen: 118, 120,
   130

DE ZEEUW/DE SEEUW/SEEUW (contin.)
-, Jan Cornelissen: 21; see also
Cornelissen, Jan (1st)
-, Pieter Jansen: 118
DE ZILLA: see De Sille
D'HONNEUR, Guillaume: 215
DIEUWERTJE/DIVERTJE
-, w.o. Cobus Evertsen: 143
-, d.o. Cobus Evertsen: 143
-, w.o. Teunus Wilze: 153
DINA
-, d.o. Frederick van Leeuwen:
134
-, d.o. Gerrit Middach: 138
-, d.o. Jan Fredericksen: 126
DIRCK/DIRK
-, s.o. Abram Jorissen: 156
-, s.o. Dirck Poulussen: 125
-, s.o. Gerrit Croesen: 112
-, s.o. Goris Storm: 135
-, s.o. Jacob van der Bilt: 163
-, s.o. Jan Woertman: 133, 249
-, s.o. Stoffel Langestraat: 163
-, s.o. Teunus Rapalje: 146
-, s.o. Willem Aertsen: 134
DIRCKS/DIRKS
-, Fijtje: 19, 85, 111, 112,
114, 179, 183, 187, 214,
222, 251
-, Geertje/Geertruijt/Grietje:
113, 114, 135
-, Harmtje/Harmje: 125, 130, 216
-, Jannetje: 123
-, Leentje: 211
-, Rachel/Raguel: 118; see also
De Noormán, Rachel Dircks
DIRCKSEN/DIRKSEN
-, Folckert/Volckert: 113, 118,
120, 123, 125
-, Gerrit: see Croesen, Gerrit
Dircksen
-, Hendrick: 167
-, Jan: 131; see also Woertman,
Jan Dircksen
-, Jan: see Van der Vliet, Jan
Dircksen
-, Joris: 11, 13, 17, 19
-, Paulus: 59, 83, 85, 125, 222
-, Paulus: 143
-, Teunis/Tuenis: 115
-, Teunis: see Woertman, Teunis
Dircksen
-, Volckert: see id., Folckert
DITMARSEN: see also Van Ditmarsen
DITMARSEN, Louwerens: 103
DIVERTJE/DIWERTJE: see Dieuwertje
DOLSTEIN, Margriet: 146
DONLUS, Helena: 135
DORITHEA: see Dorothea
DORLAND/DORLANDT/DORLANT
-, Annetje: 145, 149

DORLAND/DORLANDT/DORLANT
(continued)
-, Bennetje: 162
-, Cornelia: see id., Kornelia
-, Geertje Jans: 218
-, Gerrit: 136
-, Gerrit: 148, 162
-, Gerrit Jansen: 136
-, Jan: 144, 145, 148
-, Jan: 145, 149
-, Jan Gerritsen: 116, 131, 133,
146; see also Gerritsen, Jan
-, Kornelia/Cornelia: 136
-, Lammert/Lambert: 157
-, Lambert Jansen: 115
-, Lena: 148
-, Marijtje/Maria: 147, 162
-, Rem: 162
DOROTHEA/DORITHEA
-, w.o. Cornelis van de Water:
154
-, w.o. Wouter Ghijsbersen: 120
DOUSCON, Lena: 151
DOYAUX/DOYO: see Du Joo and Andogo
DRAAKE: see Drake
DRABBE, Elisabeth: 161, 162
DRAKE/DRAAKE/DRAECK/DREAFS/DREETS/
DRETS
-, Jesaias/Jesaijs: 123, 124,
127, 140, 144
-, Sara: 147
D'RAPPALIE: see De Rappalje
DREAFS: see Drake
DREETS/DRETS: see Drake
DRISIUS, Rev. Samuel (1600-1673):
79, 81, 93, 95, 229
D'SUSON: see Suson
DUBBELS, Susanna: 13, 109, 113,
156
DU BOIS/DEBOOIS
-, Abraham: 119
-, Rev. Gualtherus (1671-1751):
Ed.d, 224
DUERJE/DUIERE/DULJE
-, Antenette: 148
-, Joost, Sr.: 148
-, Joost: 120, 125, 133, 146,
148
-, Madleen/Magdalena: 120
DUIJCKING/DUYCKING, Mr. Evert:
25, 245
DU JOO [= possibly Doyo or Deyoo;
cf. Andogo]
-, Cristiaen/Christiaen: 120
-, Pieter: 120
DULJE/DULJEE: see Duerje
DU MON, Lijsbeth/Elisabeth: 215
DU PUIS, Francois: 211
DU TOIET, Abraham: 117
DUURKOOP/DUURKOP
-, Anneken/Annetje: 63, 112, 221

DUURKOOP/DUURKOP (continued)
-, Jan: 212
-, Jannetje: 112
DUYCKING: see Duijcking
D'VOS: see De Vos

ECHJE: see Eeghtje
EDENS, Bastiaen: 213
EEGHT, s.o. Jan Thijssen: 121
EEGHTJE/ECHJE
-, d.o. Gabriel Sprong: 137
-, d.o. Gerrit Sprong: 145
EEKHOF, Prof. Albert: Int., Ed.b,
    Ed.l, 243, 244, 256
EGBERTJE: 157
EIJTJE, d.o. Jeurien Hendricksen:
    127
ELBERT, s.o. Benjamin van de
    Water: 152
ELBERTS
-, Aeltje: 156
-, Heijltje: 156, 158
ELBERTSEN
-, Capt. Elbert: see Stoothoff,
    Capt. Elbert Elbertsen
-, Elbert: 156
-, Johannes: 150
ELDRETS, William: 146
ELISABETH/ELSJE/BETJE: see also
    Lijsbeth
ELISABETH/ELSJE/BETJE
-, 131
-, d.o. Abraham Slegt: 148
-, d.o. Albert Coerten: 162
-, w.o. Antoni de Mot: 154
-, d.o. Cornelis Gerritsen: 160
-, d.o. Cornelis Sybrich: 142
-, d.o. Ferdinandus van
    Sichelen: 148
-, w.o. Frans Abramsen: 154
-, d.o. Hendrick Hendriksen: 147
-, w.o. Jacobus Cranheidt: 153
-, w.o. Jacob Hansen Bergen:
    153 (2x), 164
-, w.o. Jacob Salomonsen: 154
-, w.o. Jacobus van de Water:
    152
-, d.o. Jan Fredericksen: 128
-, d.o. Jan Fredericksen: 137
-, w.o. Jan Quitans: 153
-, d.o. Jan Roelofsen Seubering:
    126
-, d.o. Jan van der Vliet: 146
-, w.o. Jan Verkerk: 146, 148
-, d.o. Joris Cimmer: 135
-, d.o. Lammert Dorlant: 157
-, w.o. Nicasius van Couwen-
    hoven: 149, 152
-, d.o. Paulus van der Voort:
    149
-, w.o. Pieter Berjan: 151

ELISABETH/ELSJE/BETJE (continued)
-, d.o. Pieter Jansen: 111
-, d.o. Pieter Schamp: 123
-, d.o. Randolf Evens: 123
-, d.o. Steven Budet: 153
-, d.o. Theodorus Polhemius: 133
-, w.o. Tomas Aete: 145, 147
-, d.o. Thomis Killeman: 133
-, w.o. William Eldrets: 146
-, d.o. Willem Heuijken: 125
-, d.o. Willem Jorissen: 116
-, d.o. Willem Jorissen: 128
ELSEN, Jan: 158
EMANS
-, Andries: 103, 163
-, Sara: 162
ENGELTJE
-, w.o. Benjamin van de Water:
    143, 152
-, d.o. Benjamin van de Water:
    143
-, d.o. Cornelis Slegt: 142
-, d.o. Cornelis van de Water:
    154
-, w.o. Jacobus van de Water:
    142
ETCEL/ESSEL, Jannetje: 139, 149
EVA: 152
EVENS
-, Margriet: 123, 124
-, Randolf: 123, 124
EVERARDES, s.o. Jakop Brouwer:
    129
EVERT: 115
EVERTJE, w.o. Jan Auckes: 149
EVERTS, Cornelia: 113
EVERTSEN
-, Cobus/Jacobus: 143
-, Jan: 13; see also Bout, Jan
    Evertsen

FALENTIJN: see Valentijn
FARDON: see Verdon
FARNELIE
-, Maria: 214
-, Rachel: 214
FEMMETJE/FEMMITJE
-, 136
-, d.o. Aucke Jansen: 111
-, d.o. Barent Gerritsen van
    Swol: 109
-, w.o. Dirk Andriessen: 142,
    145
-, d.o. Dirck Jansen: 114
-, w.o. Gosen Adrieaansen: 152
-, w.o. Henricus Fereest: 143
-, d.o. Jacob Buijs: 139
-, w.o. Jan Bennet: 142
-, d.o. Jan Theunissen: 119
-, d.o. Johannis Willemsen: 162
-, w.o. Joris Remsen: 145

FEMMETJE/FEMMITJE (continued)
-, w.o. Michiel Hansen: 139
-, d.o. Rem Jorissen: 153
FENTIN
-, Joseph: 216
-, Maria: 216
FERDINANDUS, s.o. Samuel
  Gerritsen: 163
FEREEST: see Frees
FERNOW, Berthold: Ed.1, 247, 255
FERRIS, Morris Patterson: Ed.c
FIELE, Cornelis: 136
FIJN
-, Anna: 141
-, Hester: 141
-, Jacob: 141
-, Johannes: 141
FIJTJE/FYTJE
-, d.o. Cobus Evertsen: 143
-, w.o. Mathijs Cornelissen: 140
FILKIN, Henrie/Henry: 143
FLIP/FLIPSEN: see Philip/
  Philipsen
FOCHIE, Amadoor: 114
FOLCKERT/FOLKERT/VOLCKERT
-, s.o. Abram Bennet: 149
-, s.o. Johannes Folkertsen: 153
-, s.o. Jurien Naghel: 139
FOLCKERTS/FOLKERTS/VOLCKERTS
-, Grietje: 139
-, Machtelt: 147
-, Rachel: 147
-, Sara: 154
FOLCKERTSEN/FOLKERTSEN/
VOLCKERTSEN
-, Claes/Klaas: 147, 154
-, Dirk: 161
-, Hendrick: 109, 110
-, Johannes: 153
-, Philippus: 154
FOLLEMON
-, Barent: 136
-, Trijntje: 136
FONTEIJN/FONTEYN
-, Anna: 125, 140
-, Carel/Karel: 112, 114
-, Charles/Chaerlis/Charel: 136,
  142
-, Jacques/Jaques: 124 (2x),
  136, 139
-, Johannes: 135-6, 160
-, Lea/Leentje/Leja: 120, 124,
  125, 136
FOREEST: see De Foreest
FRANCISCUS, Pieter: 161
FRANS, s.o. Dirck Croes: 128
FRANS
-, Geertje: 122, 216
-, Jacomijntje: 110
FRANSIJNA/FRANSIJNTJE
-, 135
-, d.o. Arent Pral: 156

FRANSIJNA/FRANSIJNTJE (continued)
-, w.o. Claas van Dijk: 152
FREDERICK/FREDRICK
-, s.o. Fredrick Sijmonsen: 140
-, s.o. Jan Jorissen de Rappalje:
  111
FREDERICKS/FREDRICKS/VREDERICKS
-, Aeltje: 129, 131, 132
-, Elsje: 123, 126; see also Van
  der Kreeft, Elsje Fredericks
-, Maria: 15, 110, 111 (2x), 214
-, Marij/Maria: 120, 160, 161
-, Rebecca: 85, 221
FREDERICKSEN/FREDRICKSEN/
VREDERICKSEN
-, Arent: 119, 128, 135
-, Jan: 116, 118, 121, 124, 126,
  128, 134, 137, 223
FREEMAN, Rev. Bernardus (d. 1743):
  Ed.d
FREES/FEREEST
-, Hendrikus: 136, 143, 249
-, Marijtje/Maria: 136, 249
FRIELINHUYSEN, Rev. Johannis/Jan
  (1727-1754): 105, 107
FYTJE: see Fijtje

GABRIEL, the cowherd: 173
GABRIJ/GABRY, Timotheus: 91
GALJAMSEN: see also Guillaume
GALJAMSEN, Pieter: 120, 125
GANCEL, Jan: 139
GEERTJE: see also Geertruijd and
  Gerardina
GEERTJE
-, w.o. Abraham Lot: 145
-, w.o. Abram van Duyn: 142
-, w.o. Albert Ammerman: 148
-, d.o. Cornelis Jansen Schers:
  129
-, w.o. Cornelis Lowize/Lowyse:
  139, 143
-, w.o. Cornelis Wijkhof: 145
-, d.o. Dirk van Zutphen: 159
-, w.o. Ferdinandus van Sichelen:
  148
-, d.o. Hendrick Jansen: 143
-, d.o. Jacob Martensen: 151
-, d.o. Jacques Cardeljouw: 159
-, d.o. Jan Gerritsen Dorlant:
  116
-, w.o. Jan van der Vliet: 146
-, d.o. Jan Vliet: 123
-, w.o. Sijmen/Cymen Blom: 149
GEERTRUIJD: see also Geertje and
  Gerardina
GEERTRUIJD
-, w.o. Abraham Hegeman: 155
-, d.o. Barent Joosten: 114
-, w.o. Gabriel Sprongh: 140,
  143, 145, 149
-, w.o. Jacob Remsen: 145

HAINEL/HAINELLE/HAMEL (continued)
-, Michiel: 116, 118, 156, 216
HAMEL: see Hainel
HANS
-, s.o. Gerrit Hansen: 126
-, s.o. Jacob Hansen: 157
HANS
-, Anneken/Annetje: 49, 55, 211,
    213
-, Brechtje: 37, 49, 112
-, Cathalijntje/Kathalijntje:
    125, 126
-, Marie: 57
-, Stijntje: 117
HANSEN
-, Gerrit: 126, 134
-, Hans: 214
-, Jakop: 123, 124, 127, 134,
    153, 157, 164, 216; see also
    Bergen, Jacob Hansen
-, Jan: 112, 124, 161; see also
    Bergen, Jan Hansen
-, Jan: 147
-, Joris: 57, 101, 123, 127,
    129, 134, 153, 224; see also
    Bergen, Joris Hansen
-, Michiel: 117 (2x), 123, 130,
    131, 139, 139-40, 140; see
    also Bergen, Michiel Hansen
-, Sijmon/Symon: 89, 113, 120,
    160, 214
HARDERS: see Hadders
HARMEN
-, 175
-, s.o. Joris Jacobsen: 114
-, the soldier: 47, 173
-, Mr., the surgeon: 181, 250
HARMENS: see also Hermans
HARMENS
-, Hendrickje: 213
-, Lijsbeth/Elisabeth: 113
HARMTJE/HAREMTJE
-, w.o. Abram Metzelaar: 147,
    148
-, d.o. Dirck Jansen: 109
-, d.o. Gerrit Dorland: 162
HARPERT, s.o. Pieter Gerbrandt-
    sen: 149
HARTENBROCK, Johannes: 164
HARTMAN, Johannes: 128
HARTMANS, Annetje: 128
HASTINGS, Hugh: Ed.b, Ed.f, 243,
    244, 256
HAVENS, Janna/Johanna: 163
HEBBELEM, Jan: 138
HEDLOCK, Elisabeth: 131
HEGEMAN/HEGEMANS
-, Abraham: 155
-, Adriaen: 45, 175
-, Adriaan: 155
-, Ariaentje: 134
-, Benjamin: 134, 136, 146

HEGEMAN/HEGEMANS (continued)
-, Catrijna: 119
-, Elisabeth: 125
-, Geertruijt: 136
-, Henderikes/Hendrikus: 119, 134
-, Jakobus/Cobus: 135, 139
-, Jannetje: 134
-, Joseph: 119, 126, 162
-, Joseph, Jr.: 155
-, Loeckreesje/Lucretia: 139
-, Neijus/Neyus: 146-7
HEIJ, Marike/Marrijtje/Maria: 128,
    133
HEIJLTJE/HEYLTJE
-, w.o. Albartus van de Water:
    139
-, w.o. David Aertsen: 146
-, d.o. Gijsbert Jansen: 157
-, w.o. Jeremias Remsen: 153
HEIJMANS/HEYMANS, Paulus: 89, 213
HELENA
-, d.o. Adam Brouwer: 109
-, d.o. Antonij van Pelt: 162
-, d.o. Jaques Cardeljouw: 163
-, d.o. Pieter Usiel: 135
-, d.o. Willem Davidsen: 157
HENDRICK/HENDRIK/HENDRIKUS/HENRICUS
-, 164
-, s.o. Adam Brouwer: 140
-, s.o. Albartus van de Water:
    139
-, s.o. Aucke Reiniersen: 143
-, s.o. Barent Slecht: 136
-, s.o. Claas van Dijk: 152
-, s.o. Cornelis Barensen: 119
-, s.o. Cornelis Bries: 143
-, s.o. Cornelis Slegt: 146
-, s.o. Daniel Polemus: 143
-, s.o. Gerrit Hendricksen: 112
-, s.o. Hendrick Corsen: 122
-, s.o. Hermen Hendricksen: 118
-, s.o. Jakop Hendricksen: 136
-, s.o. Jan Aerisen: 146
-, s.o. Jan Fredericksen: 134
-, s.o. Jan Hansen: 147
-, s.o. Jeronimus/Hieronymus
    Rapalje: 150
-, s.o. Joris Brinkerhof: 154
-, s.o. Marten Hendricksen Wils:
    132
-, s.o. Rijk Hendricksen: 144
HENDRICKJE/HENDRIKJE
-, 113
-, w.o. Benjamin van Cleef: 149
-, w.o. Isaak Remsen: 150, 152, 155
HENDRICKS/HENDRIKS
-, Aeltje: 217
-, Cornelia/Karnelia: 119
-, Eijtje/Eytje: 144, 146
-, Elsje/Elisabeth: 13, 215
-, Francijntje: 161, 163
-, Geurtje: 116

HENDRICKS/HENDRIKS (continued)
-, Gijsje: 114
-, Grietje: 118
-, Hillegont: 131
-, IJda/Ida: 136
-, Jannetje: 154
-, Lummitje: 126
-, Mardaleen: 116
-, Marie/Maria: 213
-, Marritje/Maria: 121
-, Maritje/Maria: 159 (2x), 163
-, Marritje/Maria: 131
-, Rijntje: 131
-, Stijntje: 118
-, Trijntje: 59
-, Willempje: 122
HENDRICKSEN/HENDRIKSEN
-, Adriaen: 157
-, Albert: 124
-, Barent: 140
-, Daniel: 141
-, Evert: 117, 124, 129
-, Folckert/Folkert: 101, 127,
    130, 131, 137, 249; see also
    Bries, Folckert Hendricksen
-, Frederick: 121
-, Gerrit: 112
-, Hendrick: 147
-, Hendrick: 149
-, Hermen: 118
-, Jakop: 129, 135, 136, 146
-, Jan: 114
-, Jan: 125
-, Jan: 150
-, Jeurien: 127, 129
-, Marten: see Wils, Marten
    Hendricksen
-, Rijck: 136, 144, 147
-, Willem: 149, 161
HERCKZE, Jacobus: 147
HERMANS: see also Harmens
HERMANS
-, Geurtje: 159
-, Lijsbeth/Elisabeth: 213
HERMANSEN, Marten: see Hoffman,
    Marten Hermansen
HESTER
-, 110
-, w.o. Hendrick Jansen: 143
HEUIJKEN: see Huijken
HEYLTJE: see Heijltje
HEYMANS: see Heijmans
HIBON, Jan: 13, 29, 31, 79, 221
HICKAM, Thomis: 130
HIERONYMUS: see also Jeronimus
HIERONYMUS: s.o. Jan Bennet: 142
HIJIJER/HUIJER, Sara: 164
HILLEGONT/HILLEGONDA, d.o. Adam
    Brouwer: 137
HILLETJE
-, w.o. Hieronymus/Jeronimus
    Rapalje: 148, 150

HILLETJE (continued)
-, w.o. Isaak Broekaar: 144, 146
-, w.o. Jan Snedeker: 147, 148
HILTIN, Willem: 140
HOECK, Gerrit: 148
HOF, Theunus: 149
HOFFMAN, Marten Hermansen: 213
HOGEBOOM/HOOGEBOOM, Marie/
    Marijtje: 59, 113
HOGELANDT: see Hooglandt
HOIJER, Cornelis: 129
HOLLA, Gerrit: 159
HOOGEBOOM: see Hogeboom
HOOGLANDT/HOGELANDT
-, Dirck Cornelissen: 115
-, Dirck Jansen: 55, 89, 213
-, Helena/Lena: 145, 146
-, Hendrick: 147, 149
-, Jakoba: 136
-, Jan: 136
-, Joris: 134
HOPKIMS, David: 79, 81
HORA, Joris: 151
HUIJBERTSEN/HUYBERTSEN, Arie: 89,
    214
HUIJER: see Hijijer
HUIJGEN
-, Gerrit: 116
-, Leendert: see De Klijn,
    Leendert Huijgen
HUIJKEN/HUIKEN
-, Annetje: 122, 127, 161, 217
-, Machteltje: 161, 217
-, Marritje/Maria: 134
-, Willem: 122, 125, 127
HUNTINGTON, Edna: Ed.c
HUYBERTSEN: see Huijbertsen

IDA/YDA: see also Aeltje and Alida
IDA/YDA
-, w.o. Aucke Reiniersen: 142,
    143
-, w.o. Jan Aerisen: 146
IDENS, Rebecca: 212
IJACOB: see Jacob
IJANNETJE: see Jannetje
IJANSEN: see Jansen
IJOHAN: see Johan
IJSAACK: see Isaack
INSIEL: see Usiel
ISAACK/ISAECK/IJSAECK/YSAAK
-, s.o. Abram Bokee: 135
-, s.o. Borgenson Brokaerd: 116
-, s.o. Cornelis Sebering: 132
-, s.o. Isaak Bennet: 143
-, s.o. Ysaak Remsen: 155
-, s.o. Jan Aukessen: 135
-, s.o. Jan Auckessen: 152
-, s.o. Jan Haesbroeck: 119
-, s.o. Joris Abramsen: 141
-, s.o. Salomon de Leever: 159

ISAACK/ISAECK/IJSAECK/YSAACK
(continued)
-, s.o. Thomis Jansen van Dijck:
   120
ISAACKSEN, Arent: 116
ISABELLE/YSABELLE
-, w.o. Frans Abrahamsen: 152
-, d.o. Frans Abrahamsen: 152

JACOB/JACOBUS/JAKOP/COBUS
-, s.o. Antoni Couzaar: 146
-, s.o. Bartel Jakopsen: 135
-, s.o. Carel Bevois: 154
-, s.o. Cornelis Berrien: 158
-, s.o. Cornelis Sueberingh: 138
-, s.o. Dirck Zutvin: 123
-, s.o. Evert Hendricksen: 117
-, s.o. Frederick Bergen: 164
-, s.o. Hans Bergen: 153
-, s.o. Hendrick Jorissen: 124
-, s.o. Heyndrick Rijcke: 115
-, s.o. Isaak Bennet: 150
-, s.o. Jakop Brouwer: 124
-, s.o. Jacob Brouwer: 155
-, s.o. Jakop Hansen: 123
-, s.o. Jakop Jorissen: 122
-, s.o. Jacob van Doorn: 147
-, s.o. Jan Jacobsen: 112
-, s.o. Jan Pietersen: 113
-, s.o. Jan Snedeker: 147
-, s.o. Jan Stevensen: 136
-, s.o. Jan Woutersen: 157
-, s.o. Joost Dulje: 125
-, s.o. Lourens Haf: 128
-, s.o. Marten Reijersen: 117
-, s.o. Pieter Brouwer: 161
-, s.o. Pieter Strijcker: 127
-, s.o. Rem Jansen: 111
-, s.o. Stoffel Parabaski: 121
-, s.o. Willem Verdon: 164
JACOBA/JAKOBA/COBA
-, d.o. Cornelis Jansen: 125
-, w.o. Jan Couwenhoven: 149
-, d.o. Thomas Luwes: 138
JACOBS/JAKOPS
-, Annetje: see Van der Grift,
   Annetje Jakops
-, Catrijna: 136
-, Eijtje/Itje/Jtje: 115, 122
-, Grietje: 125
-, Hendrickje: 134, 163
-, Itje/Jtje: see id., Eijtje
-, Magdalena/Magdaleentje: 13,
   109, 112
-, Marritje/Maria: see Vroom,
   Marritje Jakops
-, Sijtje: 136
JACOBSEN/JAKOPSEN
-, 219
-, Bartel: 135
-, Christiaen: see Wolf,
   Christiaen Jakopsen

JACOBSEN/JAKOPSEN (continued)
-, Gerrit: see Strijker, Gerrit
   Jakopsen
-, Jan: 85, 112, 181, 183, 209,
   216; see also Van Rheenen,
   Jan Jacobsen
-, Jan: see Tolier, Jan Jakopsen
-, Joris: 110, 114, 115, 123,
   215, 217, 218
-, Tieleman/Tieneman: 51, 79,
   117, 197, 246
JACOMIJNTJE/JAKEMIJNTJE
-, d.o. Cornelis van Duyn: 142
-, d.o. Gerridt Couwenhoven: 140
-, d.o. Gerrit Couwenhoven: 144
-, w.o. Klaas/Claes Arisen: 143
JACQUES: see also Siaeck
JACQUES, s.o. Lovys Biosie: 114
JAMES: see Jeems
JAMESON, J. Franklin: Ed.1
JAMISEROL: see also Messural and
   Miserol
JAMISEROL, Jannetje: 118
JAN
-, 117
-, s.o. Abraham Leek: 163
-, s.o. Aert Anthonissen Middag:
   112
-, s.o. Aart Laanen van Pelt: 159
-, s.o. Andries Jansen: 135
-, s.o. Aris Jansen van de Bilt:
   158
-, s.o. Barent Slecht: 140
-, s.o. Cornelis Jansen Seeuw:
   118
-, s.o. Cymen: see id., s.o.
   Sijmen
-, s.o. Dirck Poulussen: 131
-, s.o. Gabriel Sprongh: 140
-, s.o. Gerrit Middach: 132
-, s.o. Gerrit Sprong: 131
-, s.o. Giliam Lerve: 149
-, s.o. Hendrick Jansen Been: 112
-, s.o. Isaak Goedink: 161
-, s.o. Jakop Jansen Buijs: 130
-, s.o. Jacobus Lowyssen: 144
-, s.o. Jacob Martensen: 154
-, s.o. James: see id., s.o.
   Jeems
-, s.o. Jan Bennit: 136
-, s.o. Jan Cornelissen Buijs:
   117
-, s.o. Jan Dorlandt: 145
-, s.o. Jan Fredericksen: 116
-, s.o. Jan Hebbelem: 138
-, s.o. Jan Jansen: 123
-, s.o. Jan Remsen: 126
-, s.o. Jan Stevensen: 125
-, s.o. Jan Woutersen: 157
-, s.o. Jeems/James: 141
-, s.o. Jesaijas Dreets: 127
-, s.o. Jeurien Blanck: 118

JANS (continued)
-, Hilletje: 132, 136
-, Jannetje/Janneken: 85, 217, 222
-, Jannetje: 124
-, Lijsbeth: see id., Elisabeth
-, Lijsje: 223
-, Magdalena/Magdaleentje/ Maddalena: 119, 123, 219
-, Magdalena/Maddalena: 136, 155
-, Margrietje: 160
-, Marritje/Maria: 119, 124, 127, 129, 161 (2x)
-, Martha: 122, 126, 135 (2x)
-, Mincke: 131
-, Neeltje: 126, 130; see also Damen, Neeltje Jans
-, Neeltje: 87, 112 (2x), 116, 212, 222
-, Stijntje/Stintje: 99, 115, 116, 215, 216
-, Swaentje: 15; see also Potters, Swaentje
-, Trijntje: 85, 111, 122, 222
-, Wolfje: 132
JANSEN
-, Abraham: 161
-, Achijas: 122, 126
-, Aggias: see Van Dijck, Aggias Jansen
-, Albert: see Steenwijck, Albert Jansen
-, Andries: 135
-, Andries: 163
-, Arien: 124
-, Aris: see Van de Bilt, Aris Jansen
-, Aucke: 15, 49, 53, 55, 111, 113, 123, 175, 212
-, Barent: 127, 134; see also Verkerck, Barent Jansen
-, Carel: see Van Dijck, Carel Jansen
-, Casper: 120, 123, 135
-, Claes/Klaes: 117; see also Romijn, Claes Jansen
-, Claes: see Van Hasijmes, Claes Jansen
-, Cornelis: 109
-, Cornelis: 57
-, Cornelis: 121; see also Berrien, Cornelis Jansen
-, Cornelis: 125; see also Sebering, Cornelis Jansen
-, Cornelis: see De Zeeuw, Cornelis Jansen
-, Cornelis: see Schers, Cornelis Jansen
-, Cors/Kors: 53, 77

JANSEN (continued)
-, Dirck: 19, 21, 79, 83, 109 (2x), 110, 114, 117, 174, 221; see also Woertman, Dirck Jansen
-, Dirck: 122, 125, 156
-, Dirk: 160
-, Dirck: see Hooglant, Dirck Jansen
-, Dirk: see Van der Vliet, Dirk Jansen
-, Ditmaer: 215
-, Elbert: 152
-, Evert: 142
-, Gerrit: 189; see also Van Aernhem, Gerrit Jansen
-, Gerrit: see Dorlan, Gerrit Jansen
-, Gijsbert: 157
-, Hendrick: 57
-, Hendrick: 116
-, Hendrick: 121, 124, 127, 129, 139, 161
-, Hendrick: 122, 135, 219
-, Hendrick: 132, 143, 159, 162
-, Hendrik: 136
-, Hendrick: 143
-, Hendrick: see Been, Hendrick Jansen
-, Hendrick: see Van de Vin, Hendrick Jansen
-, Hermen: 188
-, Isaack: 164
-, Jakop: 125
-, Jakop: see Buijs, Jakop Jansen
-, Jacob: see Van de Bilt, Jacob Jansen
-, Jan: 111
-, Jan: 123, 126 (2x), 131
-, Jan: 125; see also Van Dijck, Jan Jansen
-, Jan: 125
-, Jan: 130
-, Jan: 155
-, Jan: see Buijs, Jan Jansen
-, Jeurie/Jeurien: 118, 212
-, Johannes: 130
-, Johannes: 133
-, Joris: see De Rappalje, Joris Jansen
-, Kasper: see id., Casper
-, Klaes: see id., Claes
-, Lambert: 159
-, Lambert: see Bosch, Lambert Jansen
-, Lambert: see Dorlant, Lambert Jansen
-, Laurens: 156
-, Lourens: 132, 163
-, Marten: see Meijer, Marten Jansen

JANSEN (continued)
-, Minicus: 151
-, Pieter: 15, 111, 113, 120,
   123, 128 (2x), 156, 223
-, Pieter: 216
-, Pieter: see De Zeeuw, Pieter
   Jansen
-, Pieter: see Staats, Pieter
   Jansen
-, Quirijn: 163 (2x)
-, Rem: 37, 61, 83, 110, 111,
   116
-, Roelof: 111
-, Roelof: see Verkerck, Roelof
   Jansen
-, Sijmen: 110, 120, 133
-, Steven: 153, 155
-, Stoffel: 121, 157
-, Teunis: 13, 17, 19, 25, 27,
   29, 51, 55, 81, 85, 91, 95,
   97, 110, 114, 176, 177, 184,
   186, 187, 195, 222, 252; see
   also Coevors, Teunis Jansen
-, Theunis: 159
-, Thomas: 19, 25, 27
-, Thomis: see Van Dijck, Thomis
   Jansen
-, Willem: 115
-, Willem: see Traphagel, Willem
   Jansen
-, Wolfert: 158
-, Wouter: 131
JEEMS [James?]: 141
JEETS/JITEE, Sara: 125, 127, 131
JEREMIAS/JEREMIJAS
-, s.o. Aris Jansen van de Bilt:
   135
-, s.o. Jeremias Remsen: 153
JERONIMUS: see also Hieronymus
JERONIMUS
-, Catalina/Kathalijntje: see De
   Rappalje, Catalina Jeronimus
-, Catharina: 59, 85, 115, 214,
   222
JERONIMUSSEN, Joris: see De Rap-
   palje, Joris Jeronimussen
JEURIAEN
-, s.o. Hendrick Volckersen: 109
-, s.o. Hendrick Volckersen: 110
-, s.o. Jakobus van de Water:
   124
-, s.o. Jochom Caljer: 137
-, s.o. Melchert Caspersen: 120
JEURIAENS/JURIAENS
-, Annetje, Anneken: 110, 114
-, Dirkje: 160
-, Engeltje: 124, 127
-, Jannetje: 121, 127
-, Teuntje: 120, 123
JEURIAENSEN/JURIAENSEN
-, Barent: 163

JEURIAENSEN/JURIAENSEN (continued)
-, Laurens: 156
JEURIE: see also Jurrie
JEURIE, Mr.: 77; see also
   Probasco, Mr. Jeurie
JILLIS/JILLISSEN: see Gillis/
   Gillissen
JITEE: see Jeets
JOCHEMSEN, David: 114
JOHAN: see Johannes
JOHANNA
-, w.o. Cornelis Slegt: 142, 146
-, d.o. Jakobus de Beavoijs: 129
-, w.o. Minicus Jansen: 151
-, d.o. Pieter Couwenhoven: 135
-, d.o. Pieter Schamp: 119
JOHANNES/IJOHANNES/JOHAN
-, 164
-, s.o. Abraham Lefoij: 150
-, s.o. Albert Hendricksen: 124
-, s.o. Anthoni Salm: 128
-, s.o. Barent Gerritsen: 113
-, s.o. Barent Gerritsen: 114
-, s.o. Cornelis Neefjes: 123
-, s.o. Dirck Poulussen: 119
-, s.o. Divertje Tijssen: Ed.b,
   136
-, s.o. Engelbart Lot: 145
-, s.o. Jacob Casjouw: 145
-, s.o. Johannes Sybrink: 143
-, s.o. Laurens Jansen: 156
-, s.o. Pieter Cornel: 144
-, s.o. Roelof Sibering: 147
-, s.o. Theodorus Polhemius: 124
-, s.o. Willem Brouwer: 127
-, s.o. Willem Hendriksen: 149
-, s.o. Wouter Teunissen van
   Pelt: 126
JOHANNES/JOHANNIS
-, Anna: 112
-, Anna Marij: 218
-, Hendrickje: 116, 122
-, Marrij/Maria: 117, 132
-, Metje: 133
JOHANNESSEN, Alexander: 126
JOHNSON, General Jeremiah: Ed.b
JONATHAN, s.o. Jonathan Marel: 138
JOOSJE/JOOSTJE
-, d.o. Barent Joosten: 111
-, d.o. John Bahnham: 143
JOOST
-, 175
-, s.o. Barent Joosten: 113
-, s.o. Michiel van der Koek: 147
JOOSTEN
-, Barent: 111, 113, 114
-, Catharyn: 57
-, Kasper/Casper: 128
-, Maddalena/Magdaleentje: 129,
   162
-, Marritje/Maria: 57, 132, 224

JOOSTEN (continued)
-, Sijmon: 21, 57
JOOSTJE: see Joosje
JORIS
-, s.o. Gerret Hansen: 134
-, s.o. Jakop Jansen Buijs: 133
-, s.o. Jan Brinkerhof: 149
JORIS
-, Aeltje: 13, 57, 111
-, Annetje: 117, 121, 214
-, Annetje: 135
-, Catalina: see id.,
    Kathelijntje
-, Catharina: 85, 179, 180, 222;
    see also De Rappalje,
    Catharina Joris
-, Eechtje/Eegtje: 121, 123
-, Elisabeth: see id., Lijsbeth
-, Femmitje: 134
-, Hillegont: 114
-, Janneken/Jannetje: 85, 111,
    222; see also Van Couverden,
    Janneken Joris
-, Judith: 85, 222
-, Kathelijntje/Catalina: 121
-, Lijsbeth/Elisabeth: see De
    Rappalje, Lijsbeth
-, Marritje/Maria: 121
-, Marritje/Maria: 128,
    130 (2x), 133, 217
-, Sara: 21, 110, 117, 119; see
    also De Rappalje, Sara Joris
JORISSEN
-, Abram: 135, 144, 156
-, Cornelis: 136, 140, 148, 219
-, Daniel: 57
-, Harmen/Hermen: 128, 130, 140,
    218, 255
-, Harmen Jorissen: see id.,
    Harmen
-, Hendrick: 109, 111, 124
-, Jacob/Jakop: 57, 122, 215
-, Jan: 13, 15, 19, 29, 33, 37,
    49, 53, 55, 57, 59, 211,
    214; see also De Rappalje,
    Jan Jorissen
-, Joris: 17
-, Rem: 153
-, Willem: 57, 116 (2x), 128,
    133, 223
JORNEIJ, Meijnart/Meijnard: 85,
    215, 221
JOSEPH
-, s.o. Adriaan Hegeman: 155
-, s.o. Joseph Hegemans: 126
-, s.o. Willem Britte: 158
JOSIJNTJE, d.o. Gerrit
    Stoffelsen: 160
JUDITH/JUDICK
-, w.o. Jan Gancel: 139
-, d.o. Jan Woutersen: 157

JURIAENS/JURIAENSEN: see
    Jeuriaens/Jeuriaensen
JURJE
-, d.o. Fredrick Blaauw: 152
-, d.o. Niclaas Brouwer: 144
JURRIE: see also Jeurie
JURRIE
-, s.o. Casparus Blank: 148
-, s.o. Philippus Nagel: 148

KADT, Catrijna: 138
KAER, Johanna: 140
KAREL/KARELS: see Carel/Carels
KARKLINS, Karlis: 251
KARTELJOU/KARTIOU: see Cardeljouw
KASJAERT, Ledia: 120
KASPER/KASPERSEN: see Casper/
    Caspersen
KATHALIJN/KATHALINA: see Catalina
KATHARINA/KATRIJNA: see Catarina
KEERSEN, Jan: 116, 136
KEIJSERRIJK, Annetje: 163
KERTELJOU: see Cardeljouw
KHATARINA/KHATRIJNA: see Catarina
KILLEMAN/KILLEMANS
-, Annetje: 133
-, Elsje/Elisabeth: 133
-, Thomis: 133
KINBAER, Joris: 216
KIP, Hendrikus: 136
KIPS, Catharijna: 138
KLAES/KLAESSEN: see Claes/Claessen
KLEEFT: see Van Cleef
KLEIN/KLEINE: see Cleine and
    De Klijn
KLOCK, Sara: 130, 138
KLOMP: see Clomp
KLOPPERS, Heijltje: 158
KOCKUIJT/KOEKUIT
-, Elisabeth: 123
-, Joost: 114
KOECK: see also Coeck
KOECK, Lourens: 133, 146
KOEVERS: see Coevors
KORNELIA/KORNELIS/KORNELISSEN:
    see Cornelia/Cornelis/
    Cornelissen
KORSEN: see Corssen
KOUWENHOVEN: see Van Couwenhoven
KOVORS: see Coevors
KREGIER/CREGIERS
-, Elisabeth: 130
-, Mr. Marten: Int., 3, 11, 227
KRIJNTJE, d.o. Cornelis Barensen:
    119
KROES/KROESEN: see Croes/Croesen
KUME, Arien Pietersen: 125

LAANEN/LANE
-, Aart: see Van Pelt, Aart
    Laanen
-, Maijke: 163

LIJSBET/LIJSBETH (continued)
-, w.o. Gerridt Couwenhoven:
140, 144
-, w.o. Jacobus Lowyssen: 144
-, d.o. Jan Masten: 122
-, w.o. Jan Remsen: 150
-, w.o. Marten Schenk: 146
-, d.o. Matheus Aertsen: 145
-, w.o. Matijs Smarck: 148
-, d.o. Melbert Caspersen: 122
-, d.o. Michiel Parmentier: 141
-, d.o. Michiel van der Voort:
141
-, d.o. Niclaas Brouwer: 141
-, d.o. Pieter Lowijsen: 139
-, d.o. Pieter Uziele: 145
-, d.o. Simon Claessen: 114
-, d.o. Theunus Woertman: 142
-, w.o. Thijs Buys: 143, 147
-, w.o. Willem Verdon: 164
-, d.o. Wouter van Pelt: 150
LIKUJE: see also Lequieer
LIKUJE, Giljam/Guillaume: 134
LOCH, Kuyertje: 146
LODOWIJCKS
-, Anneke/Annetje: 109, 110,
114 (2x), 115, 116
-, Elisabeth: 125
LOIJE/LOIJIS/LOIJISSEN/LOIJS:
see Lowijs/Lowijssen
LOKENIUS, Rev. Lars Carlson
(fl. 1664): 256, 257
LOKERMANS/LOOKERMANS, Jakop: 138
LORIJN, Maria: 119
LORK, Margrietje: 142
LOT/LOTH
-, Abraham: 103, 105
-, Abram Pietersen: 145, 218
-, Engelbart/Engelbaert: 122,
145
-, Geertje: 151
-, Jan/Johannis: 103, 107
LOUIS: see Lowijs
LOURENS/LOURENSSEN: see Laurens/
Laurenssen
LOVIES: see Lowijs
LOWIJS/LOVIES
-, s.o. Lowijs Bijose: 110
-, s.o. Rithsart/Richard
Machielsen: 158
LOWIJS/LOWISE/LOIJS
-, Geertje: 148
-, Jannetje: 128
-, Sara: 126, 128, 135
LOWIJSSEN/LOWIZE/LOIJISSEN
-, Cornelis: 139, 143, 144
-, Jacobus: 144
-, Jan: 148
-, Pieter: 126, 135, 139
LUBBERTS, Trijntje: 141, 143

LUBBERTSEN/LUBBERSEN
-, Frederick: 59, 83, 112, 216
-, Gerrit: 125
-, Ibe/Ybe: 214
-, Jan: 216
-, Thijs: 122
LUCAS/LUIJCAS
-, s.o. Eldert Luijcassen: 157
-, s.o. Gabriel Sprong: 145
-, s.o. Lucas Coevers: 141
LUCAS/LUIJCAS
-, Annetje: 148
-, Barber/Barbara: 13, 110, 113,
129
-, Marriken/Maria: 119
LUCASSEN/LUIJCASSEN
-, Eldert: 157
-, Jan: 149
-, Sigismund: 211
LUMMITJE, w.o. Hendrick Klaessen
Vechten: 132
LUPARDUS, Rev. Wilhelmus
(d. 1702): Ed.d, Ed.f, 137,
163, 249
LUWES/LUWISS/LUWWES [= Lewis?]
-, Fransijntje: 138
-, Geesje: 138
-, Sara: 148
-, Thomas: 138

MACHDALENA: see Magdalena
MACHIEL/MACHIELSEN: see Michiel/
Michielsen
MACHTEL, w.o. Cornelis van Duyn:
142 (2x), 148, 153
MACKELIJCK, Jan Pietersen: 99,
115, 216; see also Pietersen,
Jan (6th)
MADALEENTJE/MADELEETJE: see
Magdalena
MAERGRIETA: see Margriet
MAGDALENA/MADALEENTJE/MACHDALENA
-, 129
-, d.o. Abram Brouwer: 137
-, d.o. Adam Brouwer: 131
-, w.o. Gerardus Beekman: 141
-, w.o. Isaak Bennet: 150
-, w.o. Jan van der Voort: 147
-, w.o. Joost Duerje: 146
-, d.o. Joost Duerje: 148
-, w.o. Leendert Huijgen de
Klijn: 140
-, d.o. Willem Brouwer: 118
MAGGARIET/MAGRIET: see Margriet
MAHITEBEL, d.o. Jan Elsen: 158
MAIJKE/MAEIKE
-, d.o. Hendrick Tijssen: 132
-, w.o. Jan Luikassen: 149
-, d.o. Joost de Baane: 161
MAKKELIJK: see Mackelijck
MAN, Eduard: 7

MARCUS, Johannes: 13, 59, 116,
    215
MAREL
-, Jonathan: 138
-, Judith: 138
MARGARIETJE: see Margriet
MARGEN
-, Jan: 158
-, Thomas: 158
MARGRIET/MARGRIETJE/MAGGARIET/
MARIGRIET
-, d.o. Abram Marlet: 157
-, d.o. Arent Andriessen: 144
-, w.o. Carel de Beautois: 150,
    154
-, d.o. Cornelis Buijs: 118
-, w.o. Cornelis Couwenhoven:
    143, 149
-, d.o. Daniel Polhemus: 148
-, d.o. Dirck Andriessen: 142
-, d.o. Jan Barensen: 162
-, d.o. Jan Fredericksen: 118
-, d.o. Jan Pietersen: 116
-, w.o. Lourens Koek: 146
-, d.o. Sijmon Claessen: 116
-, w.o. Theodorus van Wijk: 150
-, d.o. Tobijas de Nijck: 139
-, d.o. Thomas Margen: 158
-, d.o. Willem Huijken: 127
-, w.o. Willem Teller: 215
MARIA/MARIJ/MARRITJE/MERRITJE/
MARICA
-, 129
-, d.o. Abram Brouwer: 140
-, w.o. Adam Brouwer: 140
-, d.o. Adam Brouwer: 134
-, w.o. Adriaan Hegeman: 155
-, d.o. Adriaen Hendricksen: 157
-, d.o. Adriaan Laforge: 124
-, d.o. Carel de Beautois: 150
-, d.o. Clement Salomonsen: 118
-, w.o. Coert Stevensen: 161
-, d.o. Cornelis Pietersen: 120
-, d.o. Cornelis van Brund: 161
-, d.o. Cornelis Wijkhof: 145
-, d.o. Daniel Polemus: 140
-, w.o. Dirck Jansen: 117
-, d.o. Dirck Jansen Woertman:
    125
-, d.o. Gabriel Sprong: 149
-, w.o. Gerbrandt Claassen:
    141-2
-, w.o. Gerrit Dorlandt: 148
-, d.o. Gijsbert Bogaert: 146
-, d.o. Gijsbert Thijssen: 159
-, d.o. Hendrikus Frees: 136
-, w.o. Hendrick Jansen: 139
-, d.o. Hendrick Jansen: 127
-, w.o. Hendrick Wijkhof: 145
-, d.o. Isaak Remsen: 144
-, w.o. Jacob Buys: 147

MARIA/MARIJ/MARRITJE/MERRITJE/
MARICA (continued)
-, w.o. Jacob Casjouw: 145
-, w.o. Jacobus de Beautois: 150
-, d.o. Jakop Larsiljeer: 120
-, w.o. Jacob van Dooren/
    van Doorn: 142, 147, 148
-, d.o. Jan Ariansen: 145
-, d.o. Jan Bibou: 130
-, w.o. Jan Blaauw: 147
-, d.o. Jan de Bon: 110
-, w.o. Jan Dorlandt: 145, 149
-, d.o. Jan Gancel: 139
-, d.o. Jan Hansen: 124
-, w.o. Jan Lowisen: 148
-, w.o. Jan Miserol, Jr.: 139,
    146, 154
-, d.o. Jan Staats: 159
-, w.o. Joost Springhstien: 154
-, d.o. Joris Cimmer: 135
-, d.o. Joris Remsen: 145
-, w.o. Joris van Neste: 141,
    143
-, d.o. Joris van Neste: 141
-, d.o. Joris Wolseij: 117
-, d.o. Lambert Andriessen: 152
-, d.o. Lambert Jansen Dorlant:
    115
-, d.o. Lourens Koeck: 133
-, w.o. Matheus Aertsen: 145,
    148, 151
-, w.o. Meindert Courten: 160
-, d.o. Michiel de Gree: 146
-, w.o. Minicus van der Veer: 148
-, d.o. Pieter Galjamsen: 125
-, d.o. Pieter Pra: 128
-, w.o. Rem Remsen: 145
-, w.o. Steven Beduew: 146
-, w.o. Steven Budet: 150, 153
-, w.o. Steven Richard: 144
-, d.o. Teunis Woertman: 137
-, d.o. Tijs Pietersen: 136
-, d.o. Thomis Hickam: Ed.b, 130
-, w.o. Willem Britte: 158
-, w.o. Willem Brouwer: 154
-, d.o. Willem Thijssen: 148
-, w.o. Wouter van Pelt: 150
MARLET, Abram: 157
MARTA: see Martha
MARTENS/MERTENS
-, Annetje: 125
-, Catalijntje: 218
-, Fijtje: 47, 110, 113, 115,
    116, 119, 128; see also
    Damen, Fijtje Martens
-, Sophia: 119
MARTENSEN/MERTENSEN
-, Cornelis: 147, 151
-, Hendrick: 75, 77; see also
    Van Coppenhagen, Hendrick
    Martensen

NEEFJENS/NEEFJES (continued)
-, Sara: 136
NEELTJE
-, w.o. Claas/Klaas Folkertsen: 147, 154
-, d.o. Claas Folkertsen: 154
-, d.o. Cornelis van Couwenhoven: 149
-, d.o. Cornelis Verweij: 117
-, w.o. Daniel Polemus: 140, 143, 148, 151
-, d.o. Dionijs Theunissen: 160
-, d.o. Dirck Kroesen: 130, 248
-, d.o. Folckert Hendricksen Bries: 140
-, w.o. Gerrit Schenk: 149
-, d.o. Jakobus van de Water: 127
-, d.o. Jan Jansen: 126
-, d.o. Joris Abramsen: 150
-, w.o. Michiel Parmentier: 141
-, d.o. Michel Parmentier: 160
-, w.o. Paulus van der Voort: 149
-, d.o. Pieter Cardeljouw: 161
NEESJES, Sara Katrijna: 217
   [= possibly Neefjes]
NEIJT/NEYT, Sara: 144
NEVIUS
-, Pieter: 146, 151
-, Sara: 151
NICKEE, Angeniet: 120
NICOLAAS, s.o. Niclaas Brouwer: 151
NICOLARUS, s.o. Hendrik Vechten: 148
NIESTJE, d.o. Tuenis Dircksen: 115
NIEUWENHUIJSEN, Rev. Wilhelmus: see Van Nieuwenhuijsen, Rev. Wilhelmus
NIGT, Thomas: 147
NIJSSEN/NYSSEN, Teunis: 13, 19, 21, 41, 57, 59, 109, 214
NIJSSENS/NYSSENS, Femmetje: 41, 43

OBEE, Hendrick: 57, 110
O'CALLAGHAN, Edmund B.: Ed.b, Ed.l
OLDIS, Benjamin: 150
OUCUS, Jan: 158 [= possibly Auckessen, Jan (1st)]

PALMENTIER: see Parmentier
PARA: see Prae
PARABAKO/PARABASKI: see Probasco
PARMENTIER/PALMENTIER/PERMENTIER
-, Michiel: 116, 119, 128 (2x), 129, 130, 132, 133 (2x), 141, 160, 219

PARMENTIER/PALMENTIER/PERMENTIER (continued)
-, Neeltje: 133
-, Pierre/Pieter: 73, 83, 119, 221
PAUELSEN/PAULISSEN: see Paulussen
PAULUS, Mr.: see Van der Beeck, Mr. Paulus
PAULUS/POULUS
-, s.o. Jeurien Blanck: 122
-, s.o. Poulus van der Beeck: 120
PAULUS/POULUS
-, Elisabeth/Lijsbeth: 125, 129, 133
-, Elisabeth: 137
-, Geertje: 127
-, Jannetje: 140, 141, 142
-, Lijsbeth: see id., Elisabeth
-, Marrytje/Maria: 145
PAULUSSEN/POULUSSEN
-, Cornelis: 138, 141, 144
-, Dirck: 119
-, Dirck: 124, 125, 127, 129, 131
-, Johannes: 141, 145
PEIJNART, Maria: 214
PERDON, Jacob: 156
PERMENTIER: see Parmentier
PESSEN, Jan: 164
PETERS: see Pieters
PETRANELLE: see Pieternelle
PETRUS: see also Pieter
PETRUS, s.o. Jan Martijn: 111
PHILIPS/FLIPSEN
-, Annetje: 115, 118, 120
-, Catrina: 150
-, Claesje: 213
PHILIPSEN/FLIPSEN
-, Frederick: Ed.d, Ed.g, 75, 180, 181, 191, 245, 252, 253
-, Samuel: 145, 219
PIETER: see also Petrus
PIETER
-, s.o. Adriaen de la Forse: 128
-, s.o. Cornelis Jorissen: 148
-, s.o. Cornelis Pietersen: 118
-, s.o. Gerrit Coerten: 161
-, s.o. Jan de Conselje: 128
-, s.o. Jan Woertman: 139
-, s.o. Jochem Gulik: 160
-, s.o. Johannes Pietersen: 142
-, s.o. Joris van Neste: 143
-, s.o. Laurens Juriaensen: 156
-, s.o. Lourens Koek: 146
-, s.o. Marten Pietersen: 162
-, s.o. Michiel Palmetier: 119
-, s.o. Pieter Franciscus: 161
-, s.o. Pieter Jansen: 113
-, s.o. Pieter Staats: 160
-, s.o. Pieter Strijker: 137
-, s.o. Thomis Killeman: 133
-, s.o. Wijnant Pietersen: 113

QUITANS, Jan: 153

RACHEL/RAGEL
-, w.o. David Sprong: 143, 151
-, d.o. Jan Leurst: 118
-, w.o. Paulus Dirksen: 143
-, d.o. Thomas Nigt: 147
RAPALIE/RAPALJE/RAPPALJE/
 RAPPALLEE: see De Rappalje
REBECCA
-, d.o. Niclaes Stilwil: 158
-, d.o. Willem Traphagel: 111
REIJDER/REYDER, Bernardus: 105,
 107
REIJER, s.o. Adriaen Reijersen:
 157
REIJERSEN/REYERSEN
-, Adriaen/Arien: 125, 147, 149,
 157
-, Marten: 57, 63, 83, 89, 117,
 121, 214, 221, 223
REIJNIER/REINIER
-, s.o. Charel Fontein: 142
-, s.o. Hendrick Vechten: 144
REIJNIERS/REYNIERS/RIJNIERS
-, Gerritje: 121, 126, 136
-, Jannetje: 136
-, Marijtje/Maria: 136
-, Trijntje: 129, 160
REIJNIERSEN/REYNIERSEN
-, Aucke: 131, 142, 143, 160
-, Hendrik: 143
-, Wiggert: 15, 53, 77
REM
-, s.o. Ares Jansen van de Bilt:
 125, 248
-, s.o. Isaak/Yzaak Remsen: 141
-, s.o. Jan Remsen: 122
-, s.o. Jan Remsen: 150
REMS/REMSEN/REMZEN
-, Anna/Anneken/Annetje/Antje:
 57, 85, 116, 126, 131, 133,
 150, 157, 222
-, Cathalijntje/Catalina: 135
-, Femmitje: 119, 126, 139-40,
 153, 162
-, Hilletje/Hille: 116, 119,
 125, 126, 132, 135
-, Jannetje: 125, 126, 134, 141,
 150, 158, 248
-, Sara: 132
-, Trijntje: 143
REMSEN/REMZEN
-, Abram: 138, 152
-, Daniel: 149
-, Dirk: 107
-, Hieronymus: 147, 149, 150,
 151, 153, 154, 155, 162
-, Isaac/Yzaak: 141, 144, 145,
 150, 152, 155, 224
-, Jacob/Jakop: 132, 135, 145,
 152

REMSEN/REMZEN (continued)
-, Jan: 119, 122, 126 (2x)
-, Jan: 150
-, Jeremias: 135, 150, 153, 224
-, Jeronimus: see id., Hieronymus
-, Joris: 134, 142, 144, 145
-, Joris: 145 (2x)
-, Rem: 126, 145, 150
RENSJE, d.o. Albert Minnes: 131
RERONIMUS, Jannetje: see Bockqui,
 Jannetje Reronimus
REYDER: see Reijder
REYERSEN: see Reijersen
REYNIERS/REYNIERSEN: see
 Reijniers/Reijniersen
RICHARD/RITHSART
-, s.o. Jan Berjan: 149
-, s.o. Jan Berjan: 150
-, s.o. Willem Britte: 158
RICHARD, Steven: 144
RICHOU
-, Cathalijntje: 136
-, Johannes: 135, 163
-, Poulus: 136
RIJCK, s.o. Hendrick Rijcken: 115
RIJCKEN
-, Hendrick/Heyndrick: 115, 122
-, Jacob: 149
RIJNIERS/RIJNIERSEN: see
 Reijniers/Reijniersen
RIKER, James: Ed.c
RITHSART: see Richard
RITSEMA, Johannes: 105, 107
RITSERS, Susanne: 161
ROELOF, s.o. Arent Isaacksen: 116
ROELOFS
-, Machtel: 125
-, Willempje: 156
ROELOFSEN
-, Cornelis: 119
-, Jan: see Sebering, Jan
 Roelofsen
-, Marten: 132
ROEMERS, Jannetje: 116
ROMIJN, Klaes Jansen: 125; see
 also Jansen, Claes (1st)
ROOS, Aeltje: 224
ROSEKRANS, Maddaleen: 134
ROSENDAL, Annetje: 126
ROSSILLON, Lijsbeth/Elisabeth:
 19, 47
RUBEL, Rev. Johannes Casparus
 (1719-1797): Ed.d
RULICIUS, Rev. Johannes
 (fl. 1660): 9
RUTGERS/RUTHGERS
-, Antoni: 152
-, Mentje: 115
-, Trijntje: 156
RUTH/RUTJE, w.o. Jan Berrien:
 139, 143, 149, 150

RUTSEN, Cornelis: see Van Brundt,
    Cornelis Rutsen

SAARTJE/SAERTJE: see Sara
SACHARIASSEN, Lambert: 161
SALAMONS/SALAMONSEN: see
    Salomons/Salomonsen
SALM
 -, Anthoni: 128, 129, 131, 219
 -, Marten: 148
 -, Trijntje: 148
SALOMONS/SALAMONS
 -, Johanna: 118
 -, Susanna: 152
SALOMONSEN/SALAMONSEN
 -, Clement: 118
 -, Jacob: 154
SAMUEL
 -, s.o. Clement Salomonsen: 118
 -, s.o. Jan Berry: 143
 -, s.o. Samuel Berrij: 139
 -, s.o. Willem Brouwer: 150
SARA/SAARTJE/SAERTJE/SARAI/ZARA
 -, w.o. Arje Boermark: 148
 -, w.o. Cornelis Bries: 143
 -, d.o. Cornelis Claessen/
    Klaessen: 126
 -, d.o. Cornelis Martensen: 147
 -, w.o. Daniel Rapalje: 139, 146
 -, w.o. Dirck Poulussen: 129
 -, d.o. Dirck Poulussen: 127
 -, d.o. Evert Hendricksen: 129
 -, d.o. Folkert Dircksen: 118
 -, d.o. Ghijsbert Bogaert: 129
 -, w.o. Hans Bergen: 153
 -, w.o. Hendrick Hogelandt: 147,
    149
 -, d.o. Isaack Jansen: 164
 -, w.o. Isaak Remsen: 141, 144
 -, w.o. Jan Ammerman: 148
 -, d.o. Jan Ammerman: 148
 -, d.o. Jan Chellwer: 148
 -, d.o. Jan Monfoor: 136
 -, d.o. Jan Pietersen: 112
 -, w.o. Jan Schenk: 149
 -, d.o. Jan Teunissen: 124
 -, d.o. Jan van der Vliet: 161
 -, d.o. Jeronimus Rappalje: 127
 -, d.o. Jesaijas Draeck: 123
 -, w.o. Joris Hansen Bergen:
    144, 147
 -, d.o. Marten Pietersen: 160
 -, d.o. Michiel Hansen: 117
 -, w.o. Michiel van der Koek:
    143, 147
 -, d.o. Mourus Koevers: 139
 -, d.o. Pieter Lambertsen: 114,
    251
 -, w.o. Pieter Lowijsen: 139
 -, d.o. Poulus van der Beeck:
    117
 -, d.o. Sijmen Hansen: 120

SARA/SAARTJE/SAERTJE/SARAI/ZARA
  (continued)
 -, w.o. Theunus Rapalje: 142,
    145-6, 146
 -, w.o. Thomas Nigt: 147
 -, d.o. Walter: 135
SAR DEE, Susan: 161
SCHAARS, Marijtje/Maria: 160
SCHAETS/SCHAATS, Rev. Gideon
    (1607-1694): Ed.d, Ed.f, 37,
    156, 229
SCHAMP
 -, Jannetje: 129
 -, Pieter: 119, 123, 129
SCHAR, Stoffel: 149
SCHECARLA, Debora: 145
SCHENCK/SCHENK
 -, Elisabeth: 136
 -, Gerrit: 149, 161
 -, Jan: 149
 -, Jannetje: 148
 -, Maddaleentje: 135
 -, Marten: 136, 146, 148 (2x),
    161
 -, Marten: 107
 -, Roelof Mertensen: 121
 -, Steven: 103
SCHERS, Cornelis Jansen: 129
SCHILMAN
 -, Joost: 103
 -, Lijsbet: 145
 -, Thomas: 144, 147 (2x)
SCHOUTEN
 -, Sara: 117, 120
 -, Sara: 117, 120, 215
SCHRICK, Paulus: 215
SCHULTETUS, Mr. Abraham: 95
SCHUTS, Fijtje: 128
SEBERING/CEBERINGH/SEUBERINGH/
  SIBERING/SUEBERINGH/SYBRICH/
  SYBRINK
 -, Aeltje: Ed.f, 135, 138
 -, Ariaentje: 137
 -, Catarina: see id., Katrijn
 -, Cornelis Jansen: Ed.f, 121,
    123, 131, 132, 135, 138, 140,
    142, 147; see also Jansen,
    Cornelis (4th)
 -, Cristina: 151
 -, Ida/IJda: 123
 -, Jacob: 103
 -, Jan Roelofsen: 126
 -, Johannes: 143, 162
 -, Katrijn/Catarina: Ed.f, 135
 -, Roelof: Ed.f, 135, 143, 147
SEEUW: see De Zeeuw
SEGERTSEN, Gerrit: 185

SELIJNS/SELYNS, Rev. Henricus
    (1636-1701): Int., Ed., 3, 5,
    7, 9, 11, 13, 19, 21, 29, 31,
    33, 39, 41, 43, 45, 47, 51,
    53, 55, 59, 73, 81, 89, 91,
    93, 95, 97, 99, 167, 176,
    184, 186, 195, 197, 199, 201,
    212, 222, 229, 233, 243, 244,
    245, 246, 247, 250, 251, 252,
    254, 255, 256, 257
SELSKOORN, Abelius (fl. 1664):
    257
SEUBERINGH: see Sebering
SEVENHOVE, Maria: 149
SIAECK: see also Jacques
SIAECK, Pieter: 133
SIBERING: see Sebering
SIERICKS, Tijte: 114
SIJBREGH, s.o. Roelof Verkerck:
    134
SIJMEN/SIMON
-, s.o. Ghijsbert Bogaert: 133
-, s.o. Joost Duljee: 133
-, s.o. Klaes Sijmensen: 131
SIJMENS/SIJMONS/SIMENS/ZIJMENS
-, Annetje: 134
-, Catharina/Catrijn: 121, 123,
    159
-, Elisabeth: see Van Uijt-
    huijsen, Elisabeth Sijmens
-, Geertje: 118, 120
-, Grietje: 131
-, Hilletje: 143
-, Trijntje: 13, 132
SIJMENSEN/SIJMONSEN/CIJMONSEN
-, Frederick: 133, 139, 140
-, Joost: 57
-, Klaes: 131
-, Remmerich: 160
SIJTJE/SIJDTJE/CIJTIE
-, w.o. Jacob Rijken: 149
-, d.o. Jan Hoochlant: 136
-, d.o. Jan Verkerk: 148
-, d.o. Pieter Strijker: 161
SIMMER: see Cimmer
SIMON/SIMONS/SIMONSEN: see
    Sijmen/Sijmens/Sijmensen
SIMSON, Jeems: 141
SINKAM
-, Debora: 122
-, Pieter: 122
SJAECK: see Siaeck
SJEROL, Jan: 129
SLECHT/SLEGT
-, Abraham: 148, 152
-, Anna Catrina: 146
-, Barent: 101, 132, 136, 140,
    141
-, Cornelis: 132, 142, 146, 148,
    219, 224

SLECHT/SLEGT (continued)
-, Hendrick: Ed.d, Ed.e, Ed.f,
    Ed.j, Ed.k, 101, 116, 136,
    219
-, Hilletje: 140, 141
-, Johannes: 146
SMAL, Mathijs: 163
SMARCK, Matijs: 148
SMIT
-, Barnardus: 139
-, Gerritje: 124
SNEDECKER/SNEDEKER/SNEDIKER
-, Elsje/Elisabeth: 163
-, Gerrit: 157 (2x)
-, Jan: 147, 148
-, Sara: 147
SNEDINX, Grietje: 212
SODDER, Mergriet/Margriet: 118
SOISSON: see Suson
SOPHIA/SOPHIJA
-, d.o. Jakobus de Beavoijs: 138
-, d.o. Jan Cornelissen Damen:
    116
-, d.o. Jan Cornelissen Damen:
    119
-, d.o. Pieter Usielle: 130
SPECHT, Mechtelina: Int., Ed.d,
    49, 212
SPIEGELAERS, Gerritje: 131, 163
SPRINGHSTIEN, Joost: 154
SPRONG/SPRONGH/SPRONK
-, Annetje: 128, 137
-, Barber/Barbara: 131
-, Catarina: see id., Katrijn
-, David: 136, 143, 151
-, Gabriel: 134, 135, 137, 140,
    143 (2x), 145, 149
-, Geertruij/Geertruijt: 135, 137
-, Gerrit: 128, 131, 134, 137,
    140, 141, 145
-, Katrijn/Katrijna: 136, 218
-, Maritje/Maria: 134
-, Ragel/Rachel: 136
STAATS/STAETS
-, Annetje/Antje: 137, 140, 152,
    161, 219, 224
-, Elsje/Elisabeth: 147
-, Jan: 145, 149 (2x), 159
-, Jan Pietersen: 138
-, Neeltje Pieters: 218
-, Pieter: 152, 159, 160, 161
-, Pieter Jansen: 130, 136, 137,
    160, 218, 219
STEENTIENS, Christina: 215
STEENWIJCK
-, Albert Jansen: 135
-, Cornelis: 120
STEENWIJCKS, Grietje: 120
STEPHEN/STEVEN
-, s.o. Jan Carvoij: 109
-, s.o. Luijcas Stevensen: 157

STEPHENS/STEVENS
-, Aaltje: 163
-, Hendrickje: 116
-, Jannetje: 125
STEPHENSEN/STEVENSEN
-, Coert: 158, 161
-, Jacob: 175
-, Jan: 125, 136
-, Lukas: 125, 131, 148, 157,
   161
-, Sir Olof: 75, 77, 177, 179,
   183
STIJCKER/STIJKER: see Strijcker
STIJNTJE/STINTJE
-, w.o. Eldert Luijcassen: 157
-, w.o. Jacob Martensen: 146,
   151, 154
-, d.o. Jacob Wijkhof: 151
-, d.o. Jan Mackelyck: 115
-, w.o. Michiel van der Voort:
   147
-, w.o. Pieter Gerbrandtsen:
   141, 148, 149
STILES, Henry R.: Ed.b, Ed.l,
   239, 243, 248
STILLEWIL/STILWIL
-, Annetje: 158
-, Catharina: 158
-, Daniel: 158 (2x)
-, Dirck: 113
-, Marij/Maria: 158
-, Martha: 156, 158
-, Niclaes: 158
-, Richard/Rithsart: 158
-, Thomas: 158
STILLWELL, William Henry: Ed.c
STINTJE: see Stijntje
STOFFELS, Annetje: 132, 134
STOFFELSEN, Gerrit: 134, 160
STOOTHOFF, Capt. Elbert Elbert-
   sen: 156
STORM
-, Dirck: 99, 115, 119, 158
-, Goris: 135
STRACKEN, Josius: 118
STRAETSMANS/STRAETSMAN
-, Barentje: 51, 75, 77, 179,
   180, 186
-, Teuntje: Ed.g, 51, 57, 73,
   75, 79, 81, 175, 177, 179,
   180, 181, 182, 183, 186,
   188, 189, 190, 195, 197,
   199, 246, 253
STRIJCKER/STRIJKERS/STIJKER
-, Aeltje: 132, 151
-, Angenietje: 116, 137
-, Annetje: Ed.f, 123, 129, 137
-, Eijtje: 121, 126, 127
-, Gerrit: Ed.f, 129, 151, 161
-, Gerrit Jakopsen: 126
-, Hendrick: Ed.f, 123

STRIJCKER/STRIJKERS/STIJKER
(continued)
-, Ida: 161
-, Jakop: 121
-, Jan: Ed.f, 123, 127
-, Jannetje: 120
-, Pieter: Ed.f, 116, 123, 127,
   129, 137, 156, 158, 161
-, Sara/Sarai: 116, 123,
   127 (2x), 129, 134, 156
-, Swaentje: Ed.f, 123
-, Teuntje: 126
-, Weijntje/Wijntje: 129
STROCKELS, Hendricka: 116, 136,
   216
STRYKER-RODDA, Mrs. Harriet Mott:
   Ed.c
STUIJVESANT, Gov. Petrus: Int., 3,
   13, 19, 31, 35, 67, 73, 81,
   197, 244, 245, 246, 247, 256
SUEBERINGH: see Sebering
SUIJDAM/SUYDAM, Jan: 107
SUSANNA
-, d.o. Hendrick Jansen: 121
-, d.o. Hendrick Jorissen: 109
-, d.o. Joris Abramsen: 132
SUSON/DE SUSON/SOISSON/SUSOIJ,
   Marcus: 19, 85, 91, 112, 171,
   173, 175, 177, 182, 183, 212
SUYDAM: see Suijdam
SWAAN, Jacob: 150
SWART, Johannes: 161
SYBRICH/SYBRINK: see Sebering
SYMEN/SYMENS/SYMENSEN: see Sijmen/
   Sijmens/Sijmensen
SYTJE: see Sijtje

TADES/TATENS, Michiel: 25, 27, 29,
   110, 245
TAMMES/TAMMESSEN: see Thomas/
   Thomassen
TAMZE, Gabriel: 146
TATENS: see Tades
TELLER, Willem: 215
TER BOSCH: see also Bosch
TER BOSCH, Jan: 214
TERRIN, Thonnet: 73, 221
TEUNIS/THEUNIS/THEUNUS
-, s.o. Gerrit Sprong: 134
-, s.o. Joris Abramsen: 137
-, s.o. Nijs Teunissen: 131
-, s.o. Reinier Aartsen: 160
-, s.o. Rijn Arens: 136
-, s.o. Wouter van Pelt: 160
TEUNIS/TEYNIS/THEUNIS/TONIS/TUENIS
-, Aecht: 57
-, Aeltje: see Gijsbertsen,
   Aeltje Teunis
-, Aeltje: see Jansen, Aeltje
   Teunis
-, Aertje: 124 (2x), 126, 129

TRIJNTJE (continued)
-, w.o. Cornelis van Brunt: 150,
    151
-, w.o. Daniel Hendriksen: 141
-, w.o. Elbert Jansen: 152
-, w.o. Hendrick Hendriksen: 149
-, w.o. Hieronymus Remsen: 147,
    151, 153, 155
-, d.o. Minicus Jansen: 151
-, w.o. Roelof Martensen: 161
-, d.o. Tijte Siericks: 114
-, d.o. Willem Willemsen: 114
TYS/TYSSEN: see Thijs/Thijssen

UIJTHUIJSEN: see Van Uijthuijsen
ULDRICKS, Pieternelle: 131
USIEL/USIELLE/USILE/UZIELE/INSIEL
-, Kornelia: 135
-, Pieter: 128, 130, 132, 135,
    145, 160

VALENTIJN/FALENTIJN
-, Margrieta Willems: 154
-, Tijme: 141
VAN AERNHEM/VAN ARNHEM, Gerrit
    Jansen: 189; see also Jansen,
    Gerrit (1st)
VAN BAERLE, David: 7
VAN BARCULO, Willem: 157
VAN BOSLEIJDINGH, Joseph: 119
VAN BOSSUM
-, Cornelis: 79, 83, 172, 221
-, Hermanus: 109, 110
VAN BRUNDT/VAN BRUNT
-, Cornelis Rutsen: 150, 151,
    160, 161, 217
-, Joost: 149, 160, 161, 162
VAN CAMPEN, Jan Martijn: 69, 197;
    see also Martijn, Jan (1st)
VAN CENT: see Van Sent
VAN CLEEF/CLEEFT/KLEEFT
-, Annetje: 135-6
-, Benjamin: 149
-, Cornelis: 163
-, Engeltje: 163
-, Jan: 25, 27, 49
-, Neeltje: 163
-, Rebecca: 163
VAN COPPENHAGEN, Hendrick Marten-
    sen: 75, 77, 81, 179, 186,
    187, 251; see also Martensen,
    Hendrick
VAN COUVERDEN, Janneke Joris: 37;
    see also Joris, Janneke, and
    Prins, Janneke
VAN COUWENHOVEN/COUWENHOVEN/
    KOUWENHOVEN
-, Cornelis: 143, 149
-, Gerardina: 149
-, Gerrit: 140, 144, 147, 151
-, Jan: 149

VAN COUWENHOVEN/COUWENHOVEN/
    KOUWENHOVEN (continued)
-, Jan Gerritsen: 117, 132, 140,
    218; see also Gerritsen, Jan
-, Jannetje: 135
-, Neeltje Jans: 218; see also
    Jans, Neeltje (2nd)
-, Nicasius: 149, 152
-, Pieter: 135
-, Willem: 135, 143
-, Willem: 103, 105, 107
-, Willem Gerritsen: 13, 17, 27,
    57, 59, 61, 63, 83, 87, 89,
    97, 156, 183, 185, 199, 222
VAN DER BEECK/VERBEECK
-, Aeltje: 122, 125
-, Coerades: 120
-, Hester: 118, 122
-, Khatarina/Catarina: 117
-, Maritje/Marij/Maria: 122, 132
-, Mr. Paulus: 49, 53, 114, 117
-, Poulus: 117, 120, 156, 215
VAN DE BILT/VAN DER BILT/
    VANDERBILT
-, Ares Jansen: 119, 125, 126,
    132, 135, 152, 158
-, Jacob: 163
-, Jacob Jansen: 158
-, Jan: 103
-, Jan Aertsen: 125, 248
VAN DEN BURGH, Antje: 154
VAN DEN ENDEN, Paulus: 150
VAN DER GOUDE, Frans Bloetgoet: 15
VAN DER GRIFT
-, Annetje Jakops: 120
-, Jacob Leendertsen: 27; see
    also Leendertsen, Jacob
-, Johannes: 130
-, Leendert: 130
-, Maritje/Maria: 159
-, Stijntje: 130
-, Stijntje: 130
VAN DER HOEVE/VERHOEVE
-, Cornelis: 140, 144, 152 (2x)
-, Elsje/Elisabeth: 144, 148
-, Susanna: 152
VAN DER KOEK, Michiel: 143, 147
VAN DER KREEFT, Elsje Fredericks:
    216; see also Fredericks,
    Elsje
VAN DER VEER/VAN TER VEER
-, Catrina: 153
-, Cornelis: 136
-, Femmitje: 136
-, Hendrickje: 143
-, Jan Cornelissen: 136, 149, 218
-, Maria: 140
-, Minicus: 148
-, Neeltje: 162
-, Trijntje: 136, 145

VAN DE VIN/VAN DER VEN, Hendrick
Jansen: Ed.d, Ed.g, 51, 73,
75, 77, 85, 179, 181, 182,
183, 184, 188, 190, 205, 253
VAN DER VLIET/VLIET
-, Dirck Jansen: 158, 163
-, Hendrick: 123
-, Jan Dircksen: 123 (2x), 146,
161
-, Marijtje/Maria: 163
VAN DER VOORT
-, Jan: 147
-, Michiel: 141, 147
-, Paulus: 149
-, Pieter: 103, 107
VAN DE WATER
-, Albartus: 139
-, Ariaantje: 160, 162
-, Benjamin: 143, 144, 148, 152
-, Cobus: see id., Jacobus
-, Cornelis: 154
-, Elisabeth: see id., Lijsbeth
-, Engeltje: 133, 135, 148
-, Grietje: 160
-, Hendrick: 103, 107
-, Jacobus/Jakobus: 122, 123,
124, 127, 142, 143, 152, 153
-, Johanna: 219
-, Johannes: 162
-, Lijsbeth/Elisabeth: 143, 150
-, Marijtje/Maria: 162
VAN DER WERF, Cornelis: 135, 162
VANDER WEYDE, Dr. P.H.: Ed.b
VAN DER WIJCK/VAN WIJK
-, Abram: 156
-, Anna/Annetje: 144, 148
-, Anthonie: 156
-, Cornelis: 151
-, Cornelis Barensen: 134; see
also Barentsen, Cornelis
(2nd)
-, Margrietje/Mergrietje: 134
-, Marrij/Maria: 132
-, Theodorus: 132, 134, 150
VAN DEVENTER
-, Adriaentje: 158
-, Femmetje: 163
-, Maayke: 142
VAN DIEPE, Pieter Prae: 67; see
also Prae, Pieter
VAN DIEPENBEECK, Paulus: 213
VAN DIJCK/VAN DIJK
-, Achias: 163
-, Aggias Jansen: 157
-, Agnietje: 160 (2x)
-, Annetje Jans: 123; see also
Jans, Annetje (1st)
-, Carel Jansen: 127
-, Claas: 149, 152, 161
-, Claes Thomassen/Tomissen:
129, 134
-, Hendrick: 149

VAN DIJCK/VAN DIJK (continued)
-, Jan Jansen: 122, 127, 163; see
also Jansen, Jan (3rd)
-, Jannetje: 149
-, Magdaleentje: 143
-, Maijke: 163
-, Marritje/Maria: 129
-, Pieter: 142
-, Theuntje: 163
-, Thomis Jansen: 120
-, Trijntje: 149
VAN DIJCKHUIJS/VAN DYCKHUIJS, Jan
Theunissen: 156
VAN DITMARSEN: see also Ditmarsen
VAN DITMARSEN
-, Ariaentje: 134
-, Jan: 134
VAN DOESBORGH
-, Hendrick: 157
-, Maritje/Maria: 157
VAN DONCK, Daniel: 171
VAN DOORN/VAN DOOREN, Jacob: 142,
147, 148, 224
VAN DUIJN/VAN DUYN
-, Abram: 134, 142 (2x)
-, Aeltje: 142
-, Cornelis: 137 (2x), 142, 148,
153 (2x), 161, 217
-, Denijs/Dionijs: 134
-, Gerrit Cornelissen: 217
-, Machtel/Machtelt: 137, 224
-, [...]ijntje: 217
VAN DYCKHUIJS: see Van Dijckhuijs
VAN EEKELEN/VAN EKELEN
-, Johannes: 128, 130
-, Trijntje: 128, 130
VAN ELSLANT, Claes, Sr.: 112
VAN GHIJSEN/VAN GIJSEN
-, Machdaleen: 119
-, Rinier: 119
VAN GROENINGEN, Joost Casparsen:
67; see also Caspersen, Joost
VAN HAAGEN, Josijntje: 160
VAN HASIJMES, Claes Jansen: 126
VAN HEKEL, Geesje: 149
VAN HERT, Lijsbeth Aertsen: 127
VAN HOVE, Mearcy: 144
VAN HUIJSE/VAN HUIJSSE
-, Jan Claessen: 116
-, Marietje Claes: 116; see also
Claes, Maritje/Maria
VAN LANGENDIJCK, Magdaleen
Pieters: 49; see also Pieters,
Magdaleen
VAN LEENDERSLOOT, Jannetje Klaes:
119
VAN LEEUWEN/VAN LEEUW
-, Frederick: 125, 134
-, Katrijn/Catarina: 125
VAN MULLEM, Getruijd: 31, 113
VAN NEST/VAN NESTE
-, Jannetje: 224

VAN NEST/VAN NESTE (continued)
-, Joris: 141, 143
-, Marretje/Maria: 139
-, Pieter, Jr.: 122, 129
VAN NIEKERCK, Gerrit Cornelissen: 59, 79, 197; see also Cornelissen, Gerrit (1st)
VAN NIEUWENHUIJSEN, Rev. Wilhelmus (d. 1681): Ed.d, Ed.f, 99, 156, 223, 247
VAN NOORT, Rev. Lucas (fl. 1660): 7
VAN NUYS, Willem: 103, 107
VAN OOSTRANT, Johannes: 149
VAN PELT
-, Aart Laanen: 159 (2x), 162
-, Anthoni: 129, 162
-, Hendrik: 163
-, Marij: 126
-, Pieter: 163
-, Wouter Teunissen: 126, 132, 150, 160
VAN RHEENEN, Jan Jacobsen: 91, 187, 209, 212; see also Jacobsen, Jan (1st)
VAN ROSSUM, Jan: 191
VAN RUIJVEN/VAN RUYVEN, Cornelis: 35, 67, 79, 87, 93
VAN SENT/VAN CENT
-, Annetje: 137
-, Jan: 116
VAN SEVENTER, C.: 91
VAN SICHELEN/VAN SICKLEN
-, Ferdinandus: 118, 148
-, Johannes: 162
-, Marytje/Maria: 146-7
VAN SINDEREN, Rev. Ulpianus (1708-1796): Ed.d, Ed.e, 103, 105, 247, 248
VAN SUEREN/VAN SUREN: see Van Zuuren
VAN SUTPHEN: see Van Zutphen
VAN SWOL, Barent Gerritsen: 109; see also Gerritsen, Barent
VAN TELLINGKHUIJSEN, Magdaleentje: 214
VAN TILBURG, Barent: 154
VAN TUIL/VAN THUIL, Neeltje: 159 (2x), 162
VAN UIJTHUIJSEN/UIJTHUIJSEN
-, Elisabeth Sijmens: 216
-, Hilletje: 137
VAN VECHTEN, Lummitje: 118
VAN WIJCK/VAN WIJK: see Van der Wijck
VAN WIJNGAERDEN, Gertruijd: 212
VAN WIJNSCHOOTEN/VAN WIJNSCHOTEN, Gerrit Dircksen Croesen: 37, 39; see also Croesen, Gerrit Dircksen
VAN ZUTPHEN/VAN SUTPHEN/ZUTVIN
-, Dirk: 123, 159, 162

VAN ZUTPHEN/VAN SUTPHEN/ZUTVIN (continued)
-, Jacob: 149
VAN ZUUREN/VAN SUEREN/VAN SUREN
-, Rev. Casparus (1648-c.1704): Ed.d, Ed.f, 157, 223, 224
-, Mrs.: 117
VARICK, Rev. Rudolphus (d. 1694): Ed.d
VECHTEN
-, Gerret Klaessen: 132, 133
-, Gerritje: 133
-, Hendrick Klaessen: 126, 132, 133, 138, 144, 148, 150; see also Claessen, Hendrick
-, Machdalena/Maddaleentje: 132, 133
VERBEECK: see Van der Beeck
VERBRUGGE
-, Catrijntje/Catarina: 110
-, Helena: 126
VERDON/FARDON
-, Femmitje/Femmije: 121, 162
-, Jakop: 121, 122, 161, 162
-, Johannes: 164
-, Thomas: 31, 83, 121
-, Willem/Vijllem: 164
VERHOEVE: see Van der Hoeve
VERKERCK/VERKERKE
-, Antje: 148
-, Barent Jansen: 121; see also Jansen, Barent
-, Barentje: 123
-, Geertje: 121, 123 (2x), 161 (2x)
-, Jan: 146, 148, 161
-, Katrijna/Catarina: 134
-, Roelof Jansen: 121, 123, 134, 159
VERLEDT/VERLETH
-, Maria: 215
-, Susanna: 116
VERNIER, Sara: 113
VERPLANCK, Hendrickje: 122
VERSCHUER/VERSCHEUR
-, Dorothea: 161
-, Jochom Woutersen: 127, 129, 146
-, Johannes: 145
-, Lena: 139
-, Margrietje: 120, 125
VERSTEEG, Dingman: Ed.b, Ed.c
VERVEELEN, Sir Johannes: 25
VERWEIJ, Cornelis: 117, 118
VIJNAN[...]: 164
VINCENT
-, Adriaen: 114
-, Annetje: 112
-, Hester: 114
VISSCHER, Nicolaes: 236
VLIET: see Van der Vliet
VOLCKERSSEN: see Folckertsen

WILLEMSEN (continued)
 -, Willem: 31, 83, 85, 89, 95,
     97, 113, 114, 185, 186, 223;
     see also Bennit, Willem
     Willemsen
 -, Willem: 134
 -, Willem: 162 (2x)
WILLET, Thomas: 158
WILS, Martin Hendricksen: 132
WILZE, Teunus: 153
WITTE, Elisabeth: 134
WOERTMAN/WOERMAN
 -, Anna/Annetje/Antje: 135, 145
 -, Anna Marij: 134
 -, Catharijna: 137
 -, Dirck Jansen: 123, 125, 133,
     137, 216, 217, 218; see also
     Jansen, Dirck (1st)
 -, Elisabeth: see id., Lijsbeth
 -, Jan: 224
 -, Jan Dircksen: 130, 133, 134,
     139, 217, 249; see also
     Dircksen, Jan
 -, Lijsbeth: 142
 -, Pieter: 134
 -, Teunis Dircksen: 136, 137,
     142, 145, 148, 218
WOLF, Christiaen Jakopsen: 117
WOLFJE, w.o. John Bahnham: 143
WOLPHERTSEN, Pieter: 110
WOLSEIJ
 -, Joris: 117
 -, Rebecka: 117
WOUTER, s.o. Hendrik Jansen: 161
WOUTERSEN
 -, Jan: 131, 157
 -, Jochom: see Verschuer, Jochom
     Woutersen
WRAY, Charles F.: 251

YDA: see Ida
YSAAK: see Isaack
YSABELLE: see Isabelle

ZARA: see Sara
ZEVENHOVE: see Sevenhove
ZIJMENS: see Sijmens
ZIJPERUS/ZYPERUS, Michiel: 63,
     221
ZUTVIN: see Van Zutphen
ZWIERLEIN, Frederick J.: 257